WILDLIFE CONSERVATION

Principles and Practices

Edited by:
Richard D. Teague
Eugene Decker

The Wildlife Society
Washington, D.C.
1979

Cover and book design: Charlotte Wolf
Production coordination: Betty Jo McKinney
Printing: Colorado State University Printing Service

Library of Congress Cataloging in Publication Data
Main entry under title:

Wildlife conservation.

    Earlier ed. published in 1971 under title: A manual
of wildlife conservation.
    Includes index.
    1. Wildlife management. 2. Fishery management.
3. Wildlife conservation. I. Teague, Richard D.
II. Decker, Eugene.
SK353.M35 1979   639'.9   79-2960
ISBN 0-933564-06-6

International Standard Book Number 0-933564-06-6
Library of Congress Catalog Card Number 79-2960

First edition 1979.
Printed in the United States of America.

For information, or to order, address: The Wildlife Society,
7101 Wisconsin Avenue N.W., Suite 611, Washington, DC 20014

ii

B Kerh

TABLE
OF
CONTENTS

iii

FOREWORD

Two of The Wildlife Society's major objectives are to encourage the proper management of wildlife and other natural resources along sound biological lines and to publish information to help accomplish this goal.

Efforts to meet these objectives have been carried out through publication of *The Journal of Wildlife Management* for more than 40 years, more than sixty special *Wildlife Monographs*, and several books: *Wildlife Management Techniques, The Wild Turkey and Its Management, Readings in Wildlife Conservation, Natural Resources and Public Relations, Ways of Wildlife,* and *A Manual of Wildlife Conservation.* Each of these books serves both the scientific community and the general public.

Weak communications among resource professionals, decision makers and citizens have been a long standing concern of The Wildlife Society. The Society was pleased when Colorado State University established a Short Course in Game and Fish Management in 1965 to help strengthen communications. The Short Course has been conducted annually and has reached hundreds of elected and appointed wildlife commissioners, staff members of numerous federal, state and provincial agencies, and citizen leaders.

A Manual of Wildlife Conservation was designed and published in 1971 to encourage similar workshops across North America and to assist busy wildlife professionals in conducting such educational sessions. In the nine years since the Manual was first released, it has been utilized primarily as a college text. This new fully revised edition, renamed *Wildlife Conservation—Principles and Practices,* has emerged to meet these several purposes.

This new edition brings together the latest thinking on diverse wildlife conservation subjects by a variety of highly-skilled professionals. The trying aspect of assembling this volume involved difficult choices in deciding what material to include and to exclude. Many facets of wildlife conservation are covered in the nearly 50 chapters. This information will be especially helpful to those interested in wildlife conservation, be they staff personnel of conservation agencies and organizations, commissioners and board members, students, or dedicated citizen conservationists.

Finally, we dedicate this publication to the memory of one of the contributing authors, Dr. Roger M. Latham, who was killed in May 1979 by a fall in the Swiss Alps while on a wildlife photographic assignment. Roger was a biologist, naturalist, photographer, outdoorsman, and in his position as outdoor editor of the Pittsburgh Press, was one of our nation's foremost conservation communicators. His efforts were recognized by the many awards he received from a variety of conservation organizations. It has been a special privilege to work with such dedicated men as Roger Latham in preparing this publication on wildlife conservation.

Laurence R. Jahn, President
The Wildlife Society

ACKNOWLEDGMENTS

Natural resources authorities from all parts of North America have given their time and talents to make this publication possible. Without their expertise, enthusiastic support, review, and tolerance of editorial adjustments, there would be no publication.

Institutional and professional support from Colorado State University and the University of California were substantial.

Thanks are due The Wildlife Society Council, Publications Committee, and professional staff for financial support and guidance.

Special gratitude is extended to Lynn Marino, graduate student in ecology at the University of California, Davis, who spent hundreds of hours reviewing manuscripts, contacting authors and artists, providing editorial suggestions, and doing the indexing.

For the many typings and re-typings, the correspondence with authors, and the execution of the numerous miscellaneous operations necessary to complete a publication such as this one, a personal note of thanks is due Mrs. Edna Watson and Mrs. Barbara Monroe at the University of California, Davis. We also appreciate the valuable services of Paul Gorenzel, Staff Research Associate with Cooperative Extension, University of California, Davis, in researching materials for the chapter "Wildlife Enterprises on Private Land."

Our acknowledgments would be sorely incomplete without noting the generosity of the contributing wildlife artists. The Canada goose drawing by the late Francis L. Jaques is used by permission of Gustav A. Swanson, owner. The generosity of Charles W. Schwartz, well-known artist from Jefferson City, Missouri, is especially appreciated. Both Charles Schwartz and Ralph Oberg, free lance artist from Denver, Colorado, were contributors to the original *Manual of Wildlife Conservation*.

Our gratitude is given to three new contributing artists: Mrs. Penny Edwards, accomplished western wildlife artist of Oakland, California; Daniel Delany, Wildlife Management biologist, Bureau of Land Management, Carson City, Nevada; and Mrs. Karen Daniels (nee Barth), young artist now living in Palo Alto, California.

The Editors
Richard D. Teague, University of California, Davis
Eugene Decker, Colorado State University, Fort Collins

WILDLIFE
AND
MAN

HISTORICAL HIGHLIGHTS IN AMERICAN WILDLIFE CONSERVATION

Gustav A. Swanson

The American wildlife conservation program may well be the strongest, most comprehensive, and most effective in any of the overdeveloped countries. The term conservation as employed here is in the sense proposed by Gifford Pinchot and Theodore Roosevelt, including use and management as well as preservation. Hundreds of foreigners visit the U.S. each year to study what has been accomplished in wildlife conservation so that they may adapt it to their own needs. As developed in the United States, wildlife conservation is deservedly world famous, but we tend in this country to take it for granted, and to be unduly critical, impatient, unappreciative, and even bitter about our progress.

This is not meant to imply that room exists for complacency, because there is still much to be done, and the need for improvement is urgent. Nor does it mean that we excel in all respects, because there are many instances where other countries have done better than the United States. One example is Great Britain, which began its effective control of the widespread use of the hard pesticides of the chlorinated hydrocarbon group earlier than we did. Another is Western Europe in general, in its policy toward ownership of wildlife so that the landowner benefits much more definitely from the presence on his land of game animals than is usual in this country.

But on balance, considering the entire program, the political and legislative aspects, the scientific and professional developments, and the specific accomplishments in developing public awareness, in developing and preserving habitat, and in bringing back to high population levels many species of wildlife that were once rare, Americans have much of which to be proud, and American sportsmen have played the major role in these accomplishments.

In reviewing the history of American wildlife developments from Colonial times to the present, I have identified over 100 significant events that I consider important enough to be called milestones. Naturally some are far more important than others, and just as naturally some people would have different choices.

From this comprehensive list I have selected the "top ten" time periods and their associated events, with the reasons for their selection briefly mentioned:

1900—The *Lacey Act*, passed by Congress, brought the federal government into the business of wildlife law enforcement. Its most important feature was that it made it a federal offense to transport across state lines game taken or possessed in violation of state laws. This Act effectively con-

Swanson, Gustav A.   Emeritus Chairman and Professor of Wildlife Biology, Colorado State University, Fort Collins

trolled market hunting. Other features were that it prohibited further unregulated importation of wildlife that might become pests, as the house sparrow and starling had, and that it required a federal permit to import *any* exotic wildlife.

1901-1909—During the administration of President *Theodore Roosevelt*, more than 148 million acres were added to the national forests, and the first 28 national wildlife refuges were established, among many other important conservation accomplishments.

1911—Several important wildlife conservation events were recorded in this year. The *American Game Protection and Propagation Association* was formed. This was the predecessor of the American Game Association, which initiated the annual game conferences that were succeeded in 1936 by the annual North American Wildlife Conferences. Also, the *Fur Seal Treaty* was ratified with Russia, Japan, and Canada. The program under this treaty saved the Alaska fur seals from extinction and is one of the most dramatic success stories of wildlife management in the world. Finally, on the state level, the precedent-setting *Bayne Law* was enacted in New York state to prohibit the sale of all game birds, domestic or foreign, which belonged in the same family as species protected in New York state.

1916—The *Migratory Bird Treaty* with Canada was ratified, followed in 1918 by congressional passage of the Migratory Bird Treaty Act to implement the treaty, which in part provides protection of songbirds, prohibits traffic in all wild migratory birds, and establishes management of migratory game birds. These events set the stage for similar treaties later with Mexico, Japan, and the U.S.S.R.

1925-1948—During this period *Aldo Leopold* made the monumental contributions to American wildlife conservation for which he is properly called the "Father of American wildlife management." Among his many contributions the following are outstanding:

1928-1931: He conducted game surveys supported by the Sporting Arms and Ammunition Institute (SAAMI), which resulted in publication of his "Game Survey of the North Central States";

1929-1930: He persuaded the SAAMI to establish the first doctoral fellowships in the wildlife field; recipients were R. T. King, Minnesota; Paul Errington, Wisconsin; and Ralph Yeatter, Michigan;

1929: By invitation of the University of Wisconsin he gave an important lecture series on game management;

1930: He presented the American Game Policy to the American Game Conference;

1933: At the University of Wisconsin he became the first professor of wildlife management in the United States, and his text, *Game Management*, was published. His text is still in print, still widely used, a monument to his critical and advanced thinking;

1948: Aldo Leopold died, and the next year his classic *Sand County Almanac* was published; chiefly an anthology of some of his earlier brief publications, it contained new material as well.

1929—The *Migratory Bird Conservation Act* (Norbeck-Andresen Act) authorized a national system of waterfowl refuges and a Migratory Bird Commission to implement it, and within this excellent framework the refuge system has developed. Unfortunately, with the economic depression beginning that same year, Congress appropriated very little of the money that had been authorized, so the funds had to come later and by other means.

1934-1935—Jan N. "Ding" Darling was appointed Chief of the Bureau of Biological Survey by President Franklin D. Roosevelt. In the 20 months he was Chief, his accomplishments were monumental:

a) Established the waterfowl refuge system by securing 20.7 million dollars in emergency funds with which to purchase one and one-half million acres plus three million that were set aside by Executive Order;
b) Established the Cooperative Wildlife Research Unit program in land grant universities to assure the availability of professionally trained men for wildlife management work;
c) Initiated in 1934 the first nationwide effort to census wintering waterfowl;
d) Persuaded President Roosevelt to sponsor the "First North American Wildlife Conference," which was held in February 1936. This has continued since then under the sponsorship of the Wildlife Management Institute;
e) Organized, at the conference, the National Wildlife Federation, of which he was the first president and which has become the largest citizen conservation group in the world;
f) Reorganized and revitalized the Bureau of Biological Survey into an effective agency and selected as his successor Dr. I. N. Gabrielson who served with distinction as its Chief, and then Director of the Fish and Wildlife Service, until 1946;
g) Persuaded businessmen to form the American Wildlife Institute (later Wildlife Management Institute), which has sponsored and provided financial support to many wildlife conservation activities including the Cooperative Wildlife Research Units and the North American Wildlife Conferences;
h) Helped get through Congress a number of important acts including the Duck Stamp Act and the Fish and Wildlife Coordination Act in 1934. The former provided money for acquiring waterfowl habitat from the sale of mandatory duck stamps to hunters, and the latter required that federal, state, and other agencies cooperate in increasing wildlife populations.

1937—The *Pittman-Robertson Act* (Federal Aid to Wildlife Restoration Act) passed, providing a new source of funds for wildlife work from a tax on firearms and ammunition. Even more important, through the standards and regulations under which the act was administered by the Fish and Wildlife Service, a nationwide upgrading of employment and professionalism in the wildlife field resulted.

1961—The one hundred five million dollar *Wetlands Loan Act* for the preservation of wetlands for waterfowl was passed by Congress, the funds to come from future duck stamp sales. I place this in my "top ten" not only because of the large amount of money involved, but because the Congress and the Fish and Wildlife Service recognized the urgent need for slowing down the destruction of the thousands of small wetland areas, too small to be administered as National Wildlife Refuges. Before passage of this act, both the federal and state governments had concentrated their attention primarily upon large areas, but acre for acre the small wetlands, often called "potholes," are even more productive than large marshlands, and these were being destroyed at a rapid rate by drainage for agriculture, sometimes subsidized by the federal government. The authorization ceiling was raised to $200 million in 1976.

1973—The *Endangered Species Act,* passed late in the year, gave the federal government far greater authority, responsibility, and scope than its predecessor act of 1966. The new act mandated close cooperation with the states and authorized federal financial aid to the states for endangered species programs.

The thoughtful reader will have noted that much of the important conservation legislation was passed in response to a crisis. The Lacey Act, the

Fur Seal Treaty, and the Wetlands Loan Act are examples. If only we had displayed the foresight to make those moves even a few years earlier, they would have been more effective and easier to implement. To give credit where it is due, however, we must express gratification for the wisdom of such conservation statesmen as Theodore Roosevelt, Aldo Leopold, and J. N. Darling, who dealt not only with the crises of their day, but built enduring foundations for the nation's future.

The wildlife conservation movement in America is a dynamic one and must remain so to meet the new challenges that develop constantly. The list of current social and economic forces that will affect our wildlife habitats and wildlife populations is an endless one. A few examples will suffice. The growing population here and abroad, increasing affluence, the greater mobility of our population, increasing leisure time, more intensive agriculture to boost production, growing energy needs, the development of larger and still larger earth-moving equipment, the craze for off-the-road recreational vehicles—all of these and many more are modern developments that have serious implications for fish and wildlife habitat. They underline the importance of a continuing strong and aggressive wildlife conservation movement if future generations are to enjoy some of the advantages that nature and wildlife contribute to the quality of our lives.

HUNTING AND FISHING VALUES AND CONCEPTS

C. H. D. Clarke

Hunting and angling are interactions between man and nature. They take many forms, and quality is one of those things that is easier to recognize than to define. When we talk about them, we think of the pursuit of animals with lethal weapons. However, viewed as interactions between man and nature, hunting, fishing and indeed all the original food-gathering activities of our ancestors fit into one piece. We seek out game, fish, clams, mushrooms, fruit, or whatever it may be; we reduce it to possession, and we consume it.

Each of these three stages requires its own special skills, and brings its own rewards. Satisfaction depends, with notable exceptions, on the realization of all three. The emphasis may vary. Identifying ducks may not be the key to the finding process for a hunter, though the day for ignorance is passing. But, the gatherer of wild mushrooms must know. What is more, his wife and his friends must trust his knowledge. After that, knowing where to go, when to gather, and how to cook take their place.

When we talk of quality hunting and angling, we are thinking largely of the opportunity both to attain and to exercise knowledge and skill in finding and capturing game and fish, whose possession and consumption are valued in the society in which we live. Different kinds of hunting and angling also vary in the characteristics that determine quality.

Many years ago, as a teenager, I met an American fishing for trout on a big northern Ontario river. It was, and still is, a good trout stream; but logs had been driven that spring and fishing was slow. I offered to take him through the bush several miles to a lake where the fishing was easy. He replied that he was getting trout, liked the river, and appreciated the challenge to his skill. I think it was then that I learned that quality in angling lay in the role of the person involved.

In many highly touted hunts, the so-called hunter is merely an executioner whose function, so far as quality is concerned, has been to subsidize the skills of others. Of course, many sporting activities require such help, but down through the years the vitality of the whole system has depended on the sponsor, whether old-world prince or American dude, having a complete understanding and appreciation of what was going on.

In the medieval hunt, quality was the responsibility of the host. When the hunt was over, he was judged by whether or not the guests considered that the conduct of the hunt had been a tribute or an insult to the game.

Curiously enough, it is in America where one finds respect for the game carried to the ultimate degree. This is seen in Kantor's *The Voice of Bugle*

Clarke, C. H. D. Retired. Former Chief, Fish and Wildlife Branch, Ontario Department of Lands and Forests, Toronto

Ann. The fox hunters of Missouri, and many other areas, never kill their fox. They just sit in a convenient place, supposedly with a jug of corn whiskey, and listen to the chase. Quality lies in the performance of the hounds. The reduction of game to possession, and its consumption, was not involved.

There are moral and ethical considerations to all field sports. The advertisement that appeared some time ago in European sporting magazines— "Polar bears will soon be protected. Get yours now, before it is too late"— was an appeal to which one would think any hunter would be ashamed to respond. There was not much quality to the hunt either, potting the bear at close range from the deck of a vessel cruising in floe ice in a baited area. The fact that the same authority permitted commercial hunting of polar bears with set guns is hardly an extenuating circumstance.

Quality sport has first of all to be morally and ethically sound. The sportsman never condones lawbreaking even if he disagrees with the law. He will, however, work to change a law that he thinks is not justified. His own personal standards should be higher than the law, which can never be the custodian of morals except at the lowest level. His knowledge should be enough that he knows when to be ashamed, and he should never do something that he is ashamed of, even though the law allows it. Not all animals that should be protected are everywhere protected, and to take advantage of this is, in the literal sense of the word, dishonest. Dishonor and quality are incompatible. It generally is not illegal to shoot where wounding is more probable than a kill or where game cannot be retrieved. Clean kills demand both skill and knowledge. They are not always possible, and skill and certainty in retrieving wounded animals add a quality that should be highly satisfying.

The retrieving of game is commonly done with the aid of dogs. Dogs also are used in finding, marking, and driving. The possession, training, and handling of a working dog adds a very high level of quality. It is a rewarding experience to know what the dog should be doing, and be able to judge its performance.

To what degree is the certainty of getting fish and game an element in quality? It is possible to run a put-and-take shoot in which the certainty is 100 percent, or literally to furnish fish in a barrel, but this is not quality. What little skills are required are those of execution. It is also part of quality that the productive capacity of the land and water should be realized—or, in other words, that there should be good management. As there cannot be good management, or quality field sports, in a deteriorating environment, it follows that the sportsman, by being interested in environmental quality, can improve his own opportunities. Knowledge concerning environmental limitation is part of his essential equipment, and there should be an intelligent interest in maintaining and improving it. There may be more pride in using the opportunities, even limited, of a well-managed area than in helping destroy a wilderness, or luxuriating in a put-and-take barnyard.

One should also ask whether quality hunting and angling should be private and exclusive. For many, this is the ideal, a private preserve fully stocked with game and fish that are easy to take. This is not a new idea. In Goethe's *Faust*, the fool who could have had anything he wanted in the world, and chose a country house with a deer forest and a trout stream, was counted a wise man. It is not quite so simple. I have seen disgusting exhibitions of greed and selfishness, with men quarreling over game when there was more than enough for all. Conversely, I have known occasions when game was scarce, yet hunters were both unselfish and generous. Quality means a reasonable opportunity to exercise knowledge and skill, and certainly not an unlimited scope for greed. Displays of greed are incompatible with quality.

The quality of hunting and angling is determined by two things. One is what the participant brings with him to the field, and the other is what he finds there. These two sources of quality are not totally unrelated and sometimes have to be examined side by side.

The most obvious thing the participant brings to the field is himself. In a democratic society, virtually every man is eligible to apply for a license. Quite generally, a hunter is now required to prove that he is capable of conforming to reasonable standards of safety. Increasingly, he is being required to know more and more about the laws, about the wildlife itself, and about his own responsibilities. Possible extension of this principle to angling has been suggested.

The fact remains that we still find ourselves, in the words of the Scripture, casting pearls before swine, and unless the swinish people are deprived of their privileges we are stuck with them. There are sensitive and responsible persons in all levels of society, and they will make quality hunters and anglers. At the same time, we realize that sensitivity and responsibility must be related to sport through experience, and can be learned by association and experience.

There is an ancient motto, "Use enough gun!", which certainly applies. It goes for angling, too. A thirty-pound muskellunge, dead or rotting on shore or in the weeds, wound in 100 feet of monofilament, is not a pretty sight. It is a matter of responsibility toward the quarry and, if you wish, toward nature. The hunter or angler also brings his skill, which is simply a capacity to use his equipment in accordance with standards that must be self-imposed. The most important of all ingredients is knowledge and understanding, which is, so far as responsibility goes, something that the man has equipped himself with. It is the true source of his enjoyment.

What a hunter or angler finds in the field is determined in part by his use of money and leisure, helped by a travel service for those who really go far afield. His own knowledge must guide him to a wise choice, but there is a real satisfaction, and therefore quality, in knowing enough to hunt and fish

For many big game hunters, quality means remote, wide-open country. (courtesy of R. Teague)

successfully near home, and in producing or helping to produce good sport by sound management. Let us repeat, intelligent support of a public management agency brings its own rewards, as does active participation in the fight for environmental quality.

Confronted with momentous causes such as environmental quality, it is easy to gloss over the question of what is done with game and fish when reduced to possession. To do so would be a total betrayal of our medieval predecessors. To them, both meat and trophies had to be treated with respect. The sultan, El Jallal, gave alms for all creatures killed that were not needed for subsistence. Indians paid homage to the spirit of the dead quarry. It must never be sordid. It is an essential part of the sportsman's skill to dress and prepare his kill and trophies. If this is not done well, he incurs disgrace for misuse. The angler who brings home a fish that has lain all day half in the sun and half in the bilge water has thrown away quality, and by his lack of appreciation for the fish has diminished the good in his appreciation of the fishing.

To no small degree this is ritual. We people do indeed have our ritualized responses to each other and to nature. The more ancient the human activity the more likely it is to be ritualized, and the greater the emotional satisfaction, and quality, inherent in the performance. Field sports are very old; and, if they are done right, they take their place with those ancient gratifications now embodied in the fine arts. To the degree that they fall short, they are frustrating. The hunter and angler keep alive an ancient response to nature in something like an early form, and the search for quality is instinctive.

In the world of nature, the responses of individual animals to others, both of their own and other species, are ritualized. The effect of this is to keep them out of trouble. Not surprisingly, the ritual that aids survival becomes a fundamental part of the species makeup. Such disastrous behavior as human war is now interpreted not as ancient ritual, but as a result of the breakdown of the responses that once kept man, and still keeps apes, from hurting each other. The hunter's ancient rituals were to keep harmony between man and nature, and nothing is more incompatible with quality than disharmony.

Thus, we see that the hunter and angler develop and display skills in the oldest association of man and nature, and learn to know and respect nature in the process. The state, on which now devolves active management, makes its contribution to the extent that it provides the opportunity to do all of these things. The end product will be quality, in forms that can be described and defined.

KAREN
BARTH

QUALITY IN WILDLIFE MANAGEMENT

J. V. K. Wagar

Quantity of fish and game, without regard to quality, satisfies many fishermen, hunters, and wildlife managers. The full creel! The bag limit! Quantity is how much, how big, how heavy, how many.

Quality is also how good, how excellent. "Good for what?" we may ask.

QUANTITY CAN BE QUALITY – SOMETIMES!

The Boone and Crockett Club records make comparisons of "how big," but size alone is not a measure of quality. The fact that recent records stack up rather well with those of decades ago shows that wildlife management—combined with forestry, range management, etc.—is doing a good job. That's quality.

Then, too, the larger animals got that way because they probably were smarter than younger ones shot in previous years. Outwitting a big, smart old buck or bull is a credit to the hunter; and big, old animals aren't as common as younger ones. Uncommonness always rates as quality because it is a rarity. We easily recognize rarity among man-made things, such as rare coins, rare stamps, rare first-edition books, "classic" cars, and rare paintings by old masters. In the West, some ranchers hunt for big heads the first week, then shoot their meat and go home. Although a "trophy" was wanted, a more common critter would fill the license and was acceptable as a last resort. Big fish also represent quality. They are probably smarter and more challenging to catch than smaller fish which are easier to hook.

Quantity can mean quality when the sportsman plans to harvest all of the different species of fish or game. The fisherman may plan to catch all of the kinds of trout, bass, or pike. The hunter may hope to kill each of the varieties of North American big game animals, or all of the species of bighorn sheep (the "grand slam"). Psychologists call this desire to harvest or collect all of any kind of thing "the completion complex," of which there are many interesting examples. A Michigan hunter traveled to Colorado to kill a mule deer buck, a species with different antlers and habits than his deer at home. Failing to identify it as such, he shot one of Colorado's few white-tailed bucks. Then he asked, "Why leave Michigan if I just wanted another white tail?" A Pennsylvania fisherman who caught a brook trout in Rocky Mountain National Park was similarly disappointed when he learned it was not a native species.

The same kind of thinking makes it an honor to have climbed all (more than 50) of Colorado's 14,000-foot peaks. Here again, things we can count—

Wagar, J. V. K.   Emeritus Head, Department of Forest Recreation and Wildlife Conservation, Colorado State University, Fort Collins

numbers and heights—mean quality. Such an accomplishment is good for personal satisfaction and public recognition.

Wildlife managers try to improve wildlife resources through good management. Their reports of how many deer, pheasants, and rabbits were harvested is an indication of quality of management.

How can such examples of quantity actually mean quality? Because of the challenges and the contests involved. Other factors are leaving home and spending time, money, and effort! Still others are risking hardship or even danger, or making good on a promise or boast to one's self or others.

THE CHALLENGE AS QUALITY

General George Custer, in a letter to his wife from Bear Butte Creek, Dakota Territory, wrote: "I have reached the highest round of fame. I have killed my grizzly." The grizzly bear rates high in quality because he's rare, big, and often dangerous. However, his value for meat is low. His hide and hair are poorer than many other kinds for leather and furs. Even grizzly rugs rate poorly except as a kind of badge to give credit to the hunter.

Fishermen, hunters, and wildlife managers generally agree on the comparative quality of various wildlife. Such quality comparisons usually suggest the challenge, or contest, involved in harvesting them. The "action," or danger, also counts. Trout usually rate higher in quality than carp, moose higher than deer, and grouse higher than cottontails.

Many harvesters set their own standards of quality. Fly fishermen with light tackle rate their quality above that of the bait fisherman with heavy bamboo pole. The archer believes he is more sporting than the man with the latest automatic rifle. The rifleman who handicaps himself with a single-shot, frontier-type rifle rates himself right along with the bow hunter.

Different animals pose different kinds of challenges or contests. During the hunting season, bighorn sheep usually are found in high, rough mountains. Shots tend to be long—and few. Sheep range often is steep and dangerous. Bighorns are not found in every state, nor are they numerous where found. These facts, plus the desire for massive horns on a big head, contribute to most hunters' opinions that the bighorn is one of our highest quality trophies.

Pronghorn antelope introduce another kind of contest. They range in open country and can be seen for miles. The result is that irresponsible hunters shoot wildly as long as animals are in sight or the cartridges last. Hunter success on antelope is high, but so are wounding losses. However, the skillful hunter who knows how to judge distances, how to handle his rifle, and how to hunt antelope can harvest a handsome buck with a single shot at 100 yards or less. Wyoming's famous One-Shot Antelope Hunt accents the

The possession, training, and handling of a working dog add a high level of quality to the hunting experience. (courtesy of Conservation Department, Winchester-Western)

skill and quality of clean kills under the handicap of one cartridge per hunter on each state team.

Fishing can be a fine contest. Henry Van Dyke wrote in *Fisherman's Luck*: "There is nothing that attracts human nature more powerfully than the sport of tempting the unknown with a fishing line." The effort to catch a huge fish which "breaks water" is a contest. It also is a challenge to figure out whether fish are feeding on the surface or near the bottom and to choose lures and more skillful casts that prove successful.

ANCIENT MEN—AND MODERN

We can guess that cave men were more interested in quantity of wildlife than quality, or at least had a concept of quality different from ours. Easily hunted and fat animals were preferred. Trophies meant something different. Taxidermy didn't exist as it does now, therefore trophies were things like bear-claw necklaces, eagle-feather headdresses, and human scalps. Trophies were worn, not hung on the wall.

Our pioneer ancestors valued qualities similar to those sought by cavemen. "Rabbit starvation" meant eating plenty of lean rabbits, squirrels, and deer in the winter when fatter meat was needed. Lewis and Clark, exploring the Missouri and Columbia rivers in 1804-1805, noted that they enjoyed the fat animals killed more than the big ones. However, the fact that Lewis and Clark brought back to President Jefferson the antlers of a large Rocky Mountain elk and a large moose indicates an interest in this type of quality, too.

CHEATING, PERVERSIONS, AND PRETENSE

A hunter shot a nice two-point mule deer (two antler points on each side) at a Rocky Mountain ranch. He was very happy with it until one of the ranch hands harvested a big four-pointer. Then the hunter traded his deer, some cartridges, and money for the larger deer to take home and to show his family, neighbors, and friends. We ponder if he ever wondered how his own deer tasted?

An out-of-state hunter came through a Colorado check station with a spike bull elk that didn't look just right. The carcass seemed small, the separated antlers were very dry, and moth work was found in some of the remaining hair. Questioning proved that the hunter had been unsuccessful and had paid a cowpoke $50 for a cow elk carcass and a pair of old spike bull antlers from the bunkhouse!

Recent magazine articles tell of guaranteed mountain lion hunts in which captive lions were released for the paying hunter. Guaranteed black bear hunts in which caged bears were shot for trophies are equally revolting.

Furthermore, how does the modern, wealthy, polar bear hunter stack up? He hires the ability and adaptability of a skillful guide and "bush pilot." He uses a rifle, cartridges, and 'scope. He has possession and position that enable him to enjoy this polar bear hunt. The pelt and the hunter's stories will impress many, but is there real quality here? How good are this hunter and his bear hide?

STANDARDS FOR QUALITY

As implied previously, quality is a relative term. The conditions which constitute a quality hunting or fishing trip may vary from one sportsman to another. Fishermen in one part of the country may consider dough-balling for channel catfish the epitome of fishing experience and eating anticipation. In some parts of the country, dry fly fishing for native trout is considered the finest.

Quality of a hunting or fishing experience may also include the environment of the experience, the difficulty of the chase or access to the fishing water, the method used, and the number of other sportsmen in the area.

LEVELS OF ENJOYMENT

Great thinkers from Buddha (563?-483? B.C.) on have discovered different levels of enjoyment. In simplified form, I offer these as four levels of enjoyment in reference to wildlife and the outdoors:

1. *Sensation* — the observation in a pine forest of a strange, small, short-legged, long-tailed brown animal with quick movements

2. *Perception* — recognition that it is a pine marten

3. *Intellection* — it is one of the *Mustelidae*, which includes weasels, mink, otter, wolverines, and others (they are fierce carnivores, have acrid scent glands, and their furs are valuable).

4. *Husbandry* — to perpetuate marten populations, squirrel and mouse numbers must be maintained, suitable habitats must be protected, and harvest systems (trapping) must be regulated.

Leopold (1949) mentions five components of enjoyment. Briefly stated, they are:

1. The pursuit of things by outdoorsmen (lowest level), such as game animals with their associated symbols of achievement (the hide or trophy)

2. The feeling of being close to nature

3. The simple pleasure of breathing fresh air and viewing a change of scenery

4. The perception of what makes nature tick and the application of the principles of ecology to this understanding

5. The sense of husbandry — actually doing something constructive through application of the art of management of resources (this is the highest level).

Teddy Roosevelt probably experienced each of these levels of enjoyment during his lifetime. He pursued many game species with the rifle, but he also authored several influential books, started bringing the bison back from extinction, and was the moving force behind numerous valued resource programs.

Aldo Leopold (1933), who authored our first good book on game management, wrote: "The enjoyment of wildlife is inverse to its artificiality." In other words, "the enjoyment (or recreational value) of wildlife is in proportion to its naturalness."

In America's fishing classic, *The Tent Dwellers*, Albert B. Paine values most highly "the full-grown, wild fish, in his native waters." He implies quality in the unstocked big fish, "born free" in wild rivers or other natural bodies of water.

MANAGING FOR QUALITY

Man, with his small teeth and weak hands but potentially able mind, has developed tackle, tools, or weapons to harvest his crops, to shape his habitat, and when faced with sheer survival, to fish or hunt. But when fishing or hunting for sport, he limits these artificial aids (or managers limit them for him). Examples include archery seasons and areas, "fly fishing only" seasons and waters, and flintlock and caplock muzzle-loading rifle seasons.

To fashion one's own duck call and decoys is an art and a satisfaction. Likewise, to use one's own elk, moose, or turkey call can become a challenge and a contest. In contrast, a battery-operated electronic imitator of wild creature sounds as a lure is forbidden. The sportsman can personalize his skill and contest in other ways; i.e., tying his own flies, whittling his own wooden minnows, loading his own cartridges and shells, or making his own bows and arrows.

Limiting the kill to the most admirable and challenging creatures heightens the contest and may be a useful management tool. Some examples are establishing seasons for bucks or rams only, keeping only fish above a certain size, or returning all fish to the water. Such action may require the sportsman to learn something of interest or importance such as what kinds of fishes were present, how often and how soon they will return to be caught again, or how they may strike at a given time and place. Calvin Rustrum, in his *Way of the Wilderness*, wrote: "To catch fish merely to see them struggle seems very low in . . . intellectual soundness. It is one of those things intelligent people outgrow."

How about exotics? Ring-necked pheasants in cornlands, which have wiped out original sagegrouse and prairie chicken habitat, serve an acceptable substitute in providing adventure and meat. Barren waters may be stocked with exotics more productive than native species. We may desire to introduce endangered African game animals in order to safeguard their future. Envious game managers can introduce and manage Rocky Mountain goats in states lacking them. But the greatest contests and rewards are always reaped in the lands and waters that evolved these creatures through countless centuries.

Shall we permit big game hunting with modern magnum pistols? Not until we can test and certify that such pistol shooters are experienced, steady, big game hunters who can judge effective distances. Modern magnum pistols can wound badly far beyond their effective range.

CERTIFICATION OF HUNTERS AND FISHERMEN

Nature once certified outdoorsmen. As long as nature dominated vast areas, she did a splendid jób of it. Men who were weak, foolish, or improvident often paid for their mistakes by failing to return from wildernesses they had entered. But today hunter safety programs are required, and more are needed. Fishermen and hunters should be examined for their ability to identify fish, waterfowl, and other wildlife species. They should be examined on basic habitat ecology and wildlife management principles. Hunters should be required to demonstrate their firearm handling abilities. Such tests would both add to pleasure of the chase and be an effective management tool for perpetuation of the sport and the species.

SELECTED REFERENCES

Kozicky, E. L. 1977. Tomorrow's Hunters—Gadgetteers or Sportsmen. Wildl. Soc. Bull. 5(4):175-178.

Leopold, A. 1949. A Sand County Almanac. Oxford Univ. Press, New York. 226 pp.

Leopold, A. 1933. Game Management. Charles Scribner's Sons, New York. 481 pp.

Wagar, J. V. K. 1940. Certified Outdoorsmen, American Forests, November. Am. Forestry Assoc., Washington, D.C.

Wagar, J. V. K. 1954. Quality Standards for Forest Recreation and Wildlife Production and Harvest. Proceedings, Soc. of Am. Foresters Annual Meeting.

LANDOWNERS AND SPORTSMEN

James S. Lindzey and Robert G. Wingard

Hunting and fishing, which must be considered specialized recreational uses of the land, have caused conflicts because they are frequently incompatible with the traditional economic uses of land.

Planning for future wildlife recreational opportunities is a major challenge during this period of increasing awareness of the values of the natural environment. There is a need to develop philosophies, systems, formulas, and management methods that will permit the maximum utilization of wildlife resources for recreational hunting and fishing on both private and public land. The ability of the natural resources administrator and manager to find ways of making game and fish production compatible with other uses of both private and public lands will eventually determine the extent of public use of lands for hunting and fishing. Because recreation occurs as a state of mind in the individual, the conditions surrounding hunting and fishing determine its recreational values, and these conditions must be an important concern of management.

The landowner's right to control his land on which wildlife may be present is unquestioned. However, the ownership of wildlife is legally vested with the state. Because wildlife is a public resource, sportsmen and many landowners readily accept the idea of public hunting and fishing on private as well as public land. Public ownership of wildlife, however, does not grant the right or privilege to trespass. A license does not guarantee a place to hunt or fish on private property, and individuals who pursue wildlife must understand their responsibility to respect private landowner rights. When this responsibility is ignored, the result is "posted land"—a symptom of the sportsmen-landowner problem.

THE PROBLEM

Access to land and water is a central issue in wildlife recreation. Without access there is no opportunity for wildlife recreation.

Environmental quality influences the fate of wildlife species as well as people, and also influences strongly the level of enjoyment of the out-of-doors experience. Orderly and pleasant access arrangements also influence individual satisfaction with recreation and must be of major concern in the management program.

Lindzey, James S.   Leader, Cooperative Wildlife Research Unit and Adjunct Professor, Pennsylvania State University, University Park

Wingard, Robert G.   Professor, Wildlife Management Extension, Pennsylvania State University, University Park

In the early years of development in North America, land was plentiful, sportsmen were few, and land-use conflicts were less of a problem. Those days are gone, and today there is strong competition for land for intensive agriculture, industry, homes, highways, and other recreation. Rapid changes in the environment and the society make it clear that present access arrangements are not adequate for maintaining the hunting and fishing opportunities required by present and future generations.

PUBLIC WILDLIFE

Wildlife is unique among natural resources. The public owns it, government administers it, private landowners help produce it, business benefits from it, recreation-minded people use it, and many misunderstand its place, uses, and values.

State and federal laws, as well as the courts, have upheld the public ownership of fish and wildlife resources. The state holds resident fish and wildlife resources in trust for all people. Federal laws, treaties, and regulations provide protection to migratory birds. Simultaneously, laws and the courts have clearly defined private property rights, including the right to post land against public trespass. In this situation, sportsmen are faced with a legal paradox. The need is urgent to bridge the gap between public ownership of wildlife and the landowners' right to control access and, thereby, use of the wildlife. This need is made more urgent by the problems that arise where animals like deer cannot be harvested and animal damage problems occur due to overpopulations.

PRIVATE LAND

Legitimate access by sportsmen to private land is conditioned not only by appropriate licenses and hunting and fishing regulations, but also by the attitudes and desires of the individual landowner. Landowners have a legal right to determine who shall hunt or fish on their land and the terms under which users will be admitted.

Our concept of free public hunting evolved from a relatively recent agrarian society. Historically, everyone made a living on the land or was closely associated with those who did. The institution of open and free hunting and fishing has grown into a tradition that both sportsmen and some private landowners hold high in their personal values.

Today's sportsmen are a generation or two removed from the land, and many have lost rapport with landowners. Simultaneously, new ownership objectives have developed for rural lands and are forcing change in the traditions of keeping land open to sportsmen. This change is especially evident near urban centers where recreational pressures are high.

CHANGING LAND USES

New technology and mounting population pressures are accelerating changes in the use and ownership of land. Many new developments and changes in land use are excessively wasteful of land and disruptive of ecological processes. The extent to which these changes continue, in the absence of ecological planning, will determine the environmental aspects of wildlife's future. When ecological thought is included in land-use planning, environmental losses will be reduced or minimized. The National Environmental Policy Act, approved in 1970, with its requirements for environmental impact statements, is an attempt to guide development projects and minimize disturbance of wildlife habitats. While the requirements and review of impact statements may protect certain habitats, it is clear that much wildlife habitat is still subject to exploitation. Preservation of critical wildlife habitat is one feature of the Endangered Species Conservation Act of 1969 that is a new approach in species management.

Despite past losses, a vast amount of productive wildlife habitat on private lands remains potentially available for wildlife recreation. But as recreation pressure increases on private lands, a hodgepodge of counteractions and land posting is appearing.

SIGNS OF THE TIMES

The variety of posted signs is eloquent proof of landowners' resistance to uncontrolled public use of their lands. All the signs are directed at more orderly access and use of land for wildlife recreation according to the terms of the individual landowner.

Some landowners eliminate all public access with the ultimate message, "Positively No Trespassing." Access status is restricted when land is posted "No Gunning or Fishing Permitted." Some want to control the kind of hunting—"No Deer Hunting" or "No Groundhog Shooting" on some areas. Other signs restrict the kind of equipment used by sportsmen—"No Bow Hunting" and "Fly Fishing Only." Many seek to control the sex of the game pursued by posting "No Doe Hunting" signs. These signs are not used entirely by disgruntled landowners. Many sportsmen groups also control access to their land by posting. Regardless of the sign, it is clear that resource owners and resource users are searching for a satisfactory and acceptable land use arrangement that will insure more orderly access for wildlife recreation.

However, many landowners find trespass or posting restrictions difficult to enforce. They find less satisfaction with posting than they anticipated because of their personal responsibility in enforcement. While posting may restrict sportsmen, it may increase the problem of damage caused by wildlife. Inadequate big game harvest contributes to deer-automobile collisions on the nation's highways, problems of damage to agriculture, and impoverished animals on overstocked ranges.

Further education is required, and should be intensified to the point where sportsmen participate in mandatory educational programs as part of the license procedure. Overriding the need for education of sportsmen, however, are the needs for public policies and programs that come to grips with the issue of public use of private land. Here is an opportunity for research, education, and administration to guide the type of access arrangements wanted and needed by sportsmen and landowners.

PUBLIC LANDS

National wildlife refuges, national forests, Bureau of Land Management lands, state forests, parks, and game lands are examples of public lands dedicated to public use, including most forms of wildlife recreation. However, owners of private lands adjacent to public lands may block public access when the private owners control the roads.

The federal government owns over 770 million acres, and the states over 78 million acres of the 2,271 million acres in the United States. Over 37 percent of the land in the U.S. is in public ownership, and new public acquisitions are made daily. This raises the question of where public acquisition will end, if it ends at all? Should all wildlife recreation be provided by or limited to public areas? Can we afford to have enough public land to satisfy an almost unlimited demand? How can the costs be allocated equitably among those who benefit from wildlife recreation? And, of great importance, how can proper management of a resource requiring animal harvest be maintained if private lands are not adequately managed in their own right and in recognition of uses of adjoining lands? Many authorities feel that public lands alone cannot supply our future recreation needs. These unresolved issues are at the heart of the sportsmen-landowner problem.

PRIVATE LANDS OPEN BY PUBLIC PROGRAMS

Some state fish and game agencies have been successful in leasing hunting rights from landowners. Basically, the public agency serves as the negotiator to obtain access to private lands for sportsmen who are often unable to gain access individually.

Pennsylvania's Farm Game Cooperative program and Safety Zone program keep open over 4 million acres of land, owned by some 27,000 landowners, for many of the 1.1 million hunters of the state. Washington and Utah pioneered the "Triangle" Hunting by Permission programs. Lands under these programs are posted with distinctive signs depicting the three groups—landowners, sportsmen, game department—which are essential to orderly access and harmonious relations between landowners and sportsmen. New York's Fish and Game Management Act provides for agency participation to provide sportsmen access to private lands. Nebraska and other Great Plains states have enlisted landowner participation in "Acres for Wildlife" programs that enhance wildlife habitat and provide hunting opportunities for sportsmen. Other states have devised similar systems.

EASEMENTS

An easement is a legal transaction that conveys certain privileges or rights to use the lands of another. Easements offer an alternative to simple fee purchase when minimum rights, such as access to fish streams or lakes, are involved. Access to western public lands has frequently been difficult because private lands adjoining public lands prevent public access. Both state and federal agencies are actively engaged in seeking guaranteed access for the public.

PRIVATE CLUB ACQUISITION

Sportsmen's clubs already control extensive land by purchase or lease. Many sportsmen who are not affiliated with a landowning group may deplore club posting. And while sportsmen have strong opinions that land should be open for public use, they are often the first to close land for their exclusive use.

LANDOWNER LEASE OR FEES

More and more large landowners, especially those strategically located, are utilizing fish and wildlife resources by selling seasonal leases or charging daily fees. They are finding plenty of sportsmen willing to pursue their sport according to these access terms. The amount of the fee exchanged for access depends upon the species and relative abundance of wildlife and availability of open (public) lands that offer the sportsmen an alternative. Waterfowl areas are highly prized by sportsmen in many areas because of the good hunting opportunities. Landowners benefit from the high lease fees. Many forest and range lands lease for comparatively lower values. This system of leasing is also used by corporations and companies to pay for the administration and development of their lands and for the repair of damage to their lands from public use.

Another system involves selling individuals access for hunting or fishing where natural and/or introduced game or fish is available. Payment is usually made on the basis of actual game killed or fish caught.

LANDOWNER ASSOCIATIONS

Individual landowners who find it difficult to manage the access of sportsmen sometimes join with adjacent landowners to form associations. The larger, combined acreage and mutual interest of the owners may provide a method to control the access of sportsmen more easily than single ownerships.

Success with landowner associations varies with the degree of satisfaction of the owners. The traditional independence of some landowners also tends to discourage full participation because it may involve giving up some individual right in favor of the rules of the association.

THE CHALLENGE

An array of options are available to landowners and sportsmen in their quest for orderly access for wildlife recreation. Between the extremes of all public ownership and all private enterprise is the hodgepodge of poster signs that are causing concern for the future of wildlife recreation. Particularly on small holdings, the search for access arrangements has yielded less than satisfactory results for both owners and users.

If we do nothing, disenchantment of private landowners and sportsmen will continue. The challenge to concerned landowners, sportsmen, and wildlife administrators is to develop the kind of access programs that are satisfactory and acceptable to both groups. Equally important is the opportunity to enhance wildlife resources in the process. Sportsmen and some enthusiastic landowners are interested. Administrators must bring the groups together with programs that provide for the future welfare of wildlife and are acceptable to all concerned.

THE FUTURE

All trends point to more pressure and competition on a diminishing wildlife habitat base. While good relations between sportsmen and landowners will not correct all environmental ills, a high potential for wildlife recreation on private agricultural and forest lands does exist. The significance of the problem deserves the best of wildlife research, education, and administration to develop policies and programs now and for the future.

It has been pointed out that free public hunting and fishing are not really free—they have been cheap. Sportsmen spend a great deal of money in pursuit of fish and wildlife, but little of this goes toward a management-access system to enhance the recreational opportunity. Costs of producing and harvesting wildlife on private lands accrue to the landowner who may have little chance for, and sometimes little interest in, direct recovery of these costs. But the private landowner has a big voice in wildlife, especially for restraining the harvest. It seems safe to predict that sportsmen must face up to higher costs and more restrictions of where, when, and how wildlife recreation takes place, including programs for access to private lands.

The state game agency should lead in the development of access programs, but the roles of the sportsmen, the various agencies of the U.S. Department of Agriculture, and the U.S. Department of the Interior are critical, too, in working with private landowners. The general public must also be represented because of their broad concerns for community planning for the use of land and the development of public understanding.

These cooperative programs must spell out concisely the functions and responsibilities of all parties. Any restrictions in season of use, type of use, type or number of harvest or concentrations of use, and other related items should be delineated. Compensation to the landowners should also be clearly indicated.

Only an orderly system of management that provides for access to the wildlife resources on private lands will continue to make this resource available and solve present landowner-sportsmen problems.

SELECTED REFERENCES

Barclay, J. S. 1965. Significant factors influencing the availability of privately owned rural land to the hunter. Paper No. 116. Pennsylvania Cooperative Wildl. Research Unit, Pennsylvania State Univ., University Park. (mimeo) 20 pp.

Berryman, J. H. 1961. The responsibility of state agencies in managing hunting on private lands. Trans. N. Amer. Wildl. Conf., Washington, D. C. 26:285-292.

Hunting in the United States—its present and future role. 1962. Report 7, Outdoor Recreation Resources Review Commission. Govt. Printing Office, Washington, D. C. 180 pp.

McIntosh, K. D. 1967. Posting of land in West Virginia and landowner attitudes regarding posting, hunting fees, and the hunter. Bull. 542. Agr. Exp. Sta., West Virginia Univ., Morgantown. 40 pp.

Munger, J. A. 1968. Public access to public domain lands—two case studies of landowner-sportsmen conflict. Misc. Pub. No. 1122, USDA, Govt. Printing Office, Washington, D. C. 64 pp.

Wildlife Management Institute. 1974. Placing American wildlife management in perspective. Wildlife Management Institute, 1000 Vermont Avenue, N.W., 709 Wire Building, Washington, D. C. 20005. 27 pp. illus.

Wingard, R. G. 1968. Forest game cooperatives. Paper No. 138, Pennsylvania Cooperative Wildl. Research Unit, Pennsylvania State Univ., University Park. (mimeo) 15 pp.

LAW
ENFORCEMENT—
A TOOL
OF MANAGEMENT

William B. Morse

Law enforcement is not only a tool of wildlife management, it is a basic tool of management. Fish and wildlife management had its beginning in control of the harvest; control of the harvest always involves some form of law enforcement.

Aldo Leopold (1933) defined game management as "the art of making land produce sustained annual crops of wildlife for recreational use." To produce that sustained annual crop for recreational use involves protection, regulation, and thus, law enforcement. Without adequate law enforcement the finest research and management programs would have little meaning. Illegal kills would reduce or exterminate most wildlife; the nation's limited wildlife population at the turn of the century showed this.

Law enforcement has come far since the old days of the county game warden. The conservation officer is no longer a politically hired "woods cop." He is a well-trained generalist, charged with multiple duties and often holds a bachelor's degree in wildlife management. He spends 61 percent of his time on law enforcement; the rest of it is spent in some phase of management (Table 1).

TABLE 1. How the Conservation Officer Spends His Time (Morse 1976)*

Section of the Country	Percent of Time						
	Enforcement	Wildlife Mgt.	Fishery Mgt.	Hunter Safety	Youth Educ.	Public Relations	Misc.
West	67	8	4	1	1	7	11
Midwest	47	6	5	4	3	11	24
Northeast	60	3	2	4	2	11	17
Southeast	67	4	4	4	3	5	14
Nationwide	61	6	4	3	2	8	16

*Data based on estimates by the states.

Law enforcement affects all other management programs. Look at the chapter headings in this book. Law enforcement is and should be involved in nearly every one of them if they are to function well. After all, laws form the very foundation of resource management.

The modern conservation officer is uniformed, drives a marked car, and is responsible for most of the activities of the fish and wildlife department in his area. His basic task is to enforce all state laws and regulations affecting wildlife. In some states, he may be required to enforce other laws such as

Morse, William B.   Northwest Field Representative, Wildlife Management Institute, Portland, Oregon

those pertaining to water pollution, litter, forestry, parks, and boating. He is a peace officer in 24 states, authorized to enforce all state laws. There is no typical day for the conservation officer; it varies with the locality, the season, and particular wildlife problems.

POLICY AND ADMINISTRATION

Law enforcement personnel are vitally affected by policy and administration as they set the tone and scope of the enforcement effort, giving guidance and furnishing necessary funds. Nationwide, enforcement personnel comprise over 30 percent of fish and wildlife employees and use about 28 percent of the budget. Conservation officers are the main contact that many citizens have with the resource agency (Table 2). These daily efforts, small individually, serve to establish a valuable, acceptable image of the department statewide. The conservation officer's routine educational activities are a big factor in the general public's acceptance of laws, regulations, and management programs. The conservation officer is often the first to locate areas of significant wildlife value for acquisition or easement by his department. In some states, he functions as the initial negotiator on acquisition projects.

The main source of revenue for department support is derived from the sale of hunting and fishing licenses. In the early days of law enforcement, the greatest enforcement effort was devoted to checking licenses. This is still important. Without general enforcement of the licensing laws, funds for all fish and wildlife agencies would be seriously curtailed, and programs would be reduced. If there were only one overriding reason that enforcement is a tool of management, license enforcement could be that one.

Analysis of any state system of laws and regulations concerning wildlife will show that about one-half are not directly related to the conservation of wildlife. Rather, they are to allow each hunter and angler an equitable chance to share in the harvest. Such sociological regulation is necessary, but it adds obvious complications to the life and duties of the conservation officer. He is, in effect, a referee of the hunt and must adjust his attitudes and public contacts accordingly.

TABLE 2. Scope of Conservation Officer's Job (Morse 1976)

Item	West	Midwest	Northeast	Southeast	Nationwide
Arrests/C.O. (does not include supervisors)	54	61.5	46.5	54.7	54.6
Arrests/1000 hunters and anglers	6.4	5.6	7.3	10	7.4
Percent convictions	94.3	95.5	97	90.8	93.6
No. hunters and anglers per C.O.	8,030	10,904	6,344	5,428	7,326
No. C.O. with wildlife degree	371	99	26	100	596
No. states requiring a wildlife degree	8	2	2	1	13
No. states with no residence requirement for hiring C.O.	11	8	7	9	35
Average patrol district, sq. mi.	1,051	580	159	340	495
Female C.O.	8	2	1	1	12
Minority C.O.	27	15	1	53	96

WILDLIFE MANAGEMENT

Conservation officers obtain part of the basic population data necessary for management by doing assigned wildlife census work. They also furnish extra protection for newly introduced species and usually participate in a follow-up of the success or failure of these animals.

The conservation officer is usually responsible for managing special hunting seasons and operating checking stations to measure the harvest. He locates areas for wildlife habitat improvement; he sometimes helps with the physical work in improvement of habitat. He frequently gives the landowner advice on how to improve his own property for fish and wildlife. He protects songbirds and other nongame wildlife.

Some states give the conservation officer an active role in predator control. In others, it is only on his recommendation that predator control is undertaken.

Perhaps the most common wildlife management activity of the officer is handling wildlife damage problems. In most states, all but the largest chronic damage problems are routinely handled by the conservation officer. He may issue permits to the landowner to remove offending animals, trap them himself, or drive them away from areas where they are doing damage. He may furnish the landowner with repellents or panels to fence haystacks from big game animals. Such activities are conducted within the scope of state laws, policy, and procedure.

Most conflicts between enforcement officials and wildlife managers have been due to poor internal communications. For example, the manager may not have convinced the officer of the value and necessity for a new program before it was presented to the public. It is essential to do this if the conservation officer's participation in management is to be effective and result in maximum public relations value.

FISHERIES MANAGEMENT

Most activities by enforcement officers in fisheries management are related to measuring the catch and liberating hatchery-raised fish. A good share of creel census work, to find out how many fish are caught and thus determine fish numbers, is conducted by conservation officers. Exact methods are prescribed by the biologist and by the forms provided for reporting the information. The officer sometimes participates in stream improvement projects and often informs landowners about construction and management of farm ponds. He sometimes recommends allocations of hatchery-reared fish.

The conservation officer is a front-line fighter in the war against pollution. Reports of fish kills and water pollution are usually received or discovered by the enforcement officer before any of the technical staff hears of it. In states or areas where pollution is a large problem, he may receive special training and work with highly trained pollution control biologists. Enforcement in this area is the most difficult, yet can be some of the most effective work the officer does.

CONSERVATION EDUCATION

The conservation officer must be a jack-of-all-trades, particularly capable in conservation education. He is engaged in education every time he talks to somebody. Worth repeating is the fact that the conservation officer is the only member of the department that most hunters, fishermen, or members of the general public will ever see. As a result, the impressions he leaves and the information he gives are of vital importance to public acceptance of the department's long-range programs. In addition to the individual contacts, the conservation officer is expected to attend sportsmen's meetings in his district, to talk to school classes about wildlife, and to participate in summer camps for youth groups.

The conservation officer is the liaison officer between the landowner and the sportsman. Most cooperative small game hunting projects on private land are developed and patrolled by conservation officers. He usually teaches hunter safety classes and supervises volunteer hunter safety teachers.

As the officer becomes acquainted with business leaders, sportsmen, and others, he functions as an important citizen in his community. He belongs to, or at least attends meetings of, various civic organizations. Within two or three years, his advice will be sought in matters far afield from wildlife or conservation. Several conservation officers have assumed leadership in civic organizations; a number have been elected to such local offices as the school board. With such community trust and respect, the conservation officer can function at a high professional level as the conservation agency's local representative.

SUPERVISION AND TRAINING

The conservation officer is the man who makes enforcement a tool of management. We have discussed some of the things he does that are directly related to management. Remember, however, that law enforcement itself is management, because without enforcement there would be limited supplies of fish or wildlife to manage.

Law enforcement officers are usually well supervised, with from five to ten men reporting to a district supervisor. Effective enforcement efforts are closely related to this supervision and the attendant discipline. The best state programs usually have the best discipline—not an arrogant, authoritative discipline, but one where each man knows where he stands and what he can do.

The officer deals with three distinct kinds of violators:

1. The accidental violator who has no intention of violating the law and has made a human mistake;

2. The opportunist violator, who leaves home with no intention of violating a law—but the fishing is so good, or the birds are so abundant in the adjacent closed area that he is carried away and goes after them;

3. The criminal, who leaves home with the full intention of violating the law.

Each of these classes must be handled in a different manner. The officer must ask, "Will my handling of this case aid conservation and stimulate the interest of this individual and his respect for law and the department?"

Administrators and biologists sometimes disagree with the attitudes of conservation officers. They must remember that there are differences in how field problems can be solved. The biologist can make his study, go back to the office, search the literature, consult with experts and colleagues, and in a week or a month or more, reach a decision. The conservation officer, on the other hand, must make on-the-spot decisions, such as "Will I arrest or warn this man?" He then has to live with that decision. It may involve him in a suit for false arrest or may even be appealed to the Supreme Court. As Gilbert and Sullivan said, "A policeman's lot is not a happy one."

The conservation officer is in much the same position as a traffic enforcement officer. He usually deals with average citizens, not criminals. Most average citizens do not like to be told what to do or to be apprehended for what they consider minor infractions. Even though the conservation officer is respected in his community, he is often resented when performing his duty. Some of this may be due to the actions of old-time wardens with a "man-hunting" complex; some may stem from the present views of police by some young people. At any rate, perhaps the conservation officer, like the good policeman, has many acquaintances but few intimate friends.

The Idaho Fish and Game Commission has an official creed for its conservation officers that stresses the human relations of law enforcement:

"To assist the public in their compliance with regulations; to save unfortunate offenders from unnecessary humiliation, inconvenience, and distress; to have no compromise for crime and to resolutely seek the violator but with judgment charitable toward the minor offender; never to arrest if a citation will suffice; never to cite if a warning would be better; never to scold or reprimand but rather to respect and inform."

Long-range effectiveness of the enforcement staff is closely related to the selection of new officers, their initial training, and their continuing education. Careful selection is a must. Initial training should be a formal mixture of classroom and field experience covering enforcement and all other field activities of the department. The best states spend at least three months on this phase.

Most states have an inadequate continuing or in-service training program. The usual three- or four-day personnel meeting each year accomplishes little in the way of training. It is essential, as it gives employees in a lonely job a feeling of belonging, and it brings them up-to-date on new laws and policies. It is not a substitute for frequent, short, intensive training periods conducted by specialists at the district and regional level.

There is a discernible trend to broaden the basic laws enforced by conservation officers. If this trend continues at its present rate, the conservation officer may soon become a recreation policeman charged with enforcing all management and human conduct laws in an even smaller district. Enforcement programs must then have a broader financial base. Present funds will need to be supplemented by appropriations from general tax revenues and other agency appropriations.

Another trend is the adoption of a professional law enforcement image by the conservation officer. The amount of time spent on law enforcement is increasing; the amount of time on other activities is decreasing. In 1976, the law enforcement personnel in 20 states were unionized in police officer type unions. One of the stated goals is the creation of a general police officers' retirement system with an early retirement. This type of retirement system does not allow a conservation officer to move to a general retirement system, and thus precludes him from becoming a biologist or administrator.

If this trend persists, the conservation officer may be on the way out, replaced by a professional police officer. Such a move would involve a decrease or elimination of wildlife education requirements and a reduction of officer numbers. States have only limited funds and many tasks that must be accomplished. If law enforcement is done by officers doing only law enforcement, then other employees will have to pick up the management and educational duties now done by conservation officers. The budget allows only a finite number of man-years work, regardless of how they are spent.

Law enforcement is a tool of management—even more, law enforcement is a basis of management. Without a good, adequate enforcement program, other management tools are limited or nonexistent. It behooves administrator, biologist, educator, and sportsman alike to appreciate the values, contributions, and needs of law enforcement and the law enforcement staff.

LITERATURE CITED

Leopold, A. 1933. Game management. Charles Scribner's Sons, New York. 481 pp.

Morse, W. B. 1976. Wildlife law enforcement. 1976 Proc. Western Assn. State Fish and Game Comm. 56:127-145.

SELECTED REFERENCE

Sigler, W. F. 1956. Wildlife law enforcement. Wm. C. Brown Company, Dubuque, Iowa. 318 pp.

WILDLIFE LAWS AND THE LANDOWNER

Gustav A. Swanson

The private landowner in the United States occupies a key position as custodian of wildlife and purveyor of recreational opportunities for sportsmen. To a degree this has long been recognized, as for example in the American Game Policy (Leopold et al.,1930), from which the following excerpts are taken:

Compensation to the landowner in some form or other is the only workable system for producing game on expensive private farm land.

Only the landholder can practice management efficiently, because he is the only person who resides on the land and has complete authority over it. All others are absentees. Absentees can provide the essentials: protection, cover, water, and food, but only with the landholder's cooperation, and at a higher cost.

With rare exceptions, the landholder is not yet practicing management. There are three ways to induce him to do so: (1) buy him out, and become the landowner; (2) compensate him directly or indirectly for producing a game crop and for the privilege of harvesting it; (3) cede him the title to the game, so that he will own it and can buy and sell it just as he owns, buys, and sells his poultry.

The first way is feasible on cheap lands, but prohibitive elsewhere.

The second is feasible anywhere.

The third way is the English system and incompatible with American tradition and thought.

Recognize the landowner as the custodian in public game on all other land, protect him from the irresponsible shooter, and compensate him for putting his land in productive condition. Compensate him either publicly or privately, with either cash, service, or protection, for the use of his land and for his labor, on condition that he preserves the game seed and otherwise safeguards the public interest. In short, make game management a partnership enterprise to which the landholder, the sportsman, and the public each contributes appropriate services, and from which each derives appropriate rewards.

These excerpts from the American Game Policy are as true now as they were 50 years ago, and it is disappointing that so little has been done to implement this policy. Nevertheless, the states, through their legislatures or

Swanson, Gustav A.   Emeritus Chairman and Professor of Wildlife Biology, Colorado State University, Fort Collins

27

game and fish commissions, have enacted many laws and regulations designed to help the landowner with problems involving fish, wildlife, or sportsmen. The most common constraints are described here under appropriate categories. In general their purpose is to provide the landowner with protection or privileges that will encourage good landowner-sportsman relationships.

1. *Controlling Trespass.* Because trespass on private property occurs most often for hunting, the state laws regulating trespass are usually in the game and fish law. The provisions vary widely. In some western states entering private property for hunting or fishing is legal only with written permission of the landowner, and he has no legal responsibility to post the boundaries of his land. In other states, especially eastern ones, the landowner who wishes to prohibit or selectively control hunting on his land is required to post his boundaries in a legally prescribed manner, which may include size of sign and lettering, distance between signs, name and address of owner or lessee, and even the months when such signs must be placed or renewed.

A careful reading of posting or trespass laws for each state reveals some interesting quirks. For example, in New York an owner may not legally post his land or water against hunting, fishing, or trespass if it has been stocked by the state with fish or game since April 17, 1896! One may question the appropriateness or even constitutionality of such a provision, but there it is. In many states, streams or lakes are legally state property, so that a hunter or fisherman may travel a stream even though the owner of the adjoining land has prohibited trespass.

Many states have a "safety zone" provision that automatically prohibits shooting within a specified distance of occupied buildings without owner permission. A radius of 500 feet, a commonly selected distance, makes a circle enclosing over 18 acres.

2. *Owner Liability Protection.* When some landowners began to fear that sportsmen on their land or water might sue for damages if they suffered an accident, many states, with assistance from the Council of State Governments, countered by passing laws. The typical one provides the landowner freedom from liability claims by sportsmen who were using his land free of charge, whether or not they had been granted permission. According to some attorneys this type of law is of questionable constitutionality, but until tested in the courts and set aside it meets one type of landowner concern.

3. *Special Hunting Privileges for Landowners.* Some states do not require that a landowner purchase a hunting or fishing license to hunt or fish on his own property. Some provide that when a limited number of permits are issued for big game hunting involving private land, the landowners be given special consideration in the applications. In some cases, landowners' applications are considered before the drawing is opened to the general public. In some cases, a proportion of the permits have been reserved for landowners. The rationalization is that the landowner who has provided habitat for the game should have priority over the person who has provided nothing. Furthermore, a landowner who wished a permit and did not draw one could easily retaliate by closing his land to all hunting.

4. *Legal Limitations on Numbers of Hunters.* Many landowners are willing to welcome a few hunters on their land, but become concerned when there are "too many." A consequence in some states has been provision of a law or regulation to limit the number of hunters at any one time to an agreed level. This has been accomplished in several ways. At one time in New York it was required that the hunter present written permission from a landowner before he was eligible to purchase a permit for deer hunting in the area. Other regulations, administered under such state provisions as the Pennsylvania Farm Game Cooperative Program or the New York Fish and Wildlife Management Act, may limit the number of hunters on a property by requiring

them to park in areas limited to a particular number of autos. Many other arrangements have been tried, some throwing the entire responsibility on the landowner, and others providing state regulatory aid. In any event, the regulation of hunter numbers is a matter of great concern to landowners.

5. *Crop Damage Payments or Control.* Under certain conditions, otherwise valuable wildlife can do serious damage to crops or other property. A bear can ruin an apiary in a night. A flock of herring gulls can devastate several acres of blueberries in a morning. A herd of deer in an orchard or a herd of elk in haystacks can do thousands of dollars in damage in a few nights. A complete list would be long, but would include woodchucks in pastures or hayfields, ducks in grain crops, blackbirds in rice or sweet corn, and scores of others.

After thorough investigation, some states will pay the farmer for the loss he has suffered from protected game animals. Others will provide only preventive measures, such as fencing the apiary, orchard, or haystack, or live-trapping and transplanting an offending colony of beaver or other offending species. One common arrangement is to attempt to reduce the crop damage by reducing the population of wildlife causing the damage. Sometimes special hunting seasons have been employed. It is quite common to permit the landowner to destroy the wildlife if it is actually seen committing damage or to issue damage control permits for the killing of a specified number of offending animals; for example, deer.

For a number of years the province of Saskatchewan has operated a waterfowl crop damage insurance system to reimburse wheat farmers for the losses of grain from waterfowl depredations. The modest insurance premium paid by the farmers has been supplemented, when necessary, from hunting license income. This system has worked well enough to attract favorable attention in several countries where similar problems occur, but thus far it has not been tried in the United States (National Academy of Sciences 1970a,b).

6. *Encouraging Fish or Wildlife Management.* Some states have recognized that many fishing regulations designed for public waters are not suitable, or would be a definite hindrance, if applied to privately owned ponds or reservoirs. Therefore, they have issued farm pond licenses that allow the owner greater latitude in length of season, bag limits, methods of taking, etc., than permitted on public waters. The idea is that sound, intensive management should be fostered, not impeded, by the law.

Similar objectives are served in the terrestrial environment through provision for habitat improvements on private lands or for protection through establishment of refuges on private land or water. Most states also have laws encouraging private enterprise in such ventures as game farms, fish hatcheries, and fishing or shooting preserves through the issuance of licenses or permits.

7. *Income to the Landowner from His Fish or Wildlife.* Some states actively assist the landowner in realizing financial gain from the presence of fish and wildlife on his property. Two arrangements that have been widely used are described in other papers in this manual. The federal payment (with state participation) under the Crop Adjustment Program of the U.S. Department of Agriculture has been terminated, but it was temporarily used in 35 states during the first year, 1966 (Boyce 1967). In shooting preserves, which have a counterpart in fishing preserves or fee-fishing arrangements, the states usually regulate or control, rather than encourage or participate in, the ventures.

One arrangement is in Wyoming where pronghorn antelope hunting is allowed on a permit basis. The permit includes a coupon that the hunter surrenders to the landowner on whose land he is hunting. The landowner can then deliver the coupons he has collected to the State Game and Fish

Department for payment. In this way he is paid for his custodianship of the pronghorns and for permitting the hunters on his land.

Texas illustrates another case wherein the state facilitates the traditional landowner charge for deer hunting. The commercial deer hunting programs in that state are described by Teer and Forrest (1968) who estimate that probably two-thirds of the 239,000 deer taken in Texas in 1967 were taken under the hunter leasing arrangement that is so widespread in that state. The leases fall into four main categories: season leases, day-hunting, the hunting broker or outfitter, and the hunting of introduced exotic big game. The income to Texas landowners was estimated by Klussman (1966) as 13 million dollars on hunting leases for 22 million acres in 1965.

In Ontario, some counties adjacent to large urban populations have hunting pressure too high to be tolerated if unregulated. Here the law provides for a special county license, which both limits the number of hunters and provides a source of income.

DISCUSSION

These efforts and many others are among those with which the state fish and game agencies have tried to encourage better relationships between the sportsman and the landowner. Among the efforts not described, because not as directly important to the landowner, are educational programs to improve hunter behavior or gun safety, requirements that hunters must be identifiable in the field through the wearing of readily visible license tags, and special efforts to check law violators quickly and efficiently. It seems clear that despite all the efforts that are being made to win his favor, the landowner often is the unwilling and unappreciated partner in the fish and wildlife and recreation program. Much more needs to be done to persuade him that it is in his best interests, as well as those of the sportsman and the state game agency, to arrange an orderly harvest of game and fish from his property.

LITERATURE CITED

Boyce, A. P. 1967. Results of the Cropland Adjustment Program in Michigan. Trans. N. Amer. Wildl. Conf. 32:96-102.

Klussman, W. G. 1966. Deer and the commercialized hunting system in Texas. *In* Proceedings, The white-tailed deer: its problems and potentials. Texas A & M Univ. 110 pp.

Leopold, Aldo, et al. 1930. Report to the American Game Conference on an American Game Policy. Trans. Am. Game Conf. 17:284-309.

National Academy of Sciences. 1970a. Land use and wildlife resources. Washington, D. C. 262 pp.

National Academy of Sciences. 1970b. Principles of plant and animal pest control. Vol. 5. Vertebrate pests: problems and control. Washington, D. C. 153 pp.

Teer, J. T. and N. K. Forrest. 1968. Bioeconomic and ethical implications of commercial game harvest programs. Trans. N. Am. Wildl. Conf. 33:192-204.

STATE-FEDERAL RELATIONSHIPS IN WILDLIFE MANAGEMENT

J. David Almand and Michael D. Zagata

There are about 2.3 billion acres of land within the United States, most of which provide habitat for the nation's rich wildlife heritage. This highly diverse habitat ranges from the glaciated peaks of Alaska and the shimmering deserts of the Southwest to the deciduous forests of the East and the coastal flatlands and swamps of the southern coastline.

The wildlife, including fish, living in this habitat is important to our nation's health and well-being. First, certain fish and wildlife provide an important source of protein for mankind. Moreover, wildlife is increasingly recognized for its high intrinsic value (it feeds our souls!) and because it serves as an indicator of the health of our environment. We have learned that if wildlife populations are in poor shape, the environment in which we live is also often degraded. For example, the lower reproductive rates of bald eagles and peregrine falcons served as a warning to mankind that pollution of our environment by chemicals such as DDT could have an impact on man's health.

Some of our wildlife resources were once jeopardized by market hunting. Today, the major threat to wildlife is clearly the destruction of the habitat upon which it depends. Unlike most of our renewable natural resources, wildlife has no bill of sale nor currently recognized economic value in the market place; it has generally ranked low with regard to commodity oriented economic considerations.

The responsibility for protecting and enhancing our nation's wildlife resource is vested in both the state and federal governments. Because of the nature and distribution of our wildlife resource, it is essential that the various levels of government cooperate, not only among themselves, but with private interests as well, in exercising their stewardship over this public resource. In fact, only through a partnership arrangement can our nation's wildlife heritage be effectively maintained.

The discussion that follows treats state-federal jurisdictional matters relative to fisheries in a broad manner. Also, space does not allow us to address the complex subject of Indian or native subsistence rights or international treaties.

EARLY CONSERVATION EFFORTS

In 1639, Newport, Rhode Island, made conservation history as the first colony to establish a closed season for wildlife, intended to protect deer.

Almand, J. David. Assistant Chief, Division of Wildlife, Bureau of Land Management, Washington, D.C.

Zagata, Michael D. Director, Project Development Office, Board on Agriculture and Renewable Resources, National Academy of Science, Washington, D.C.

Other colonies followed, and by the time of the American Revolution, all had enacted laws for the protection of wildlife. In 1865, Massachusetts established the first State Fish and Wildlife Administration. By 1880, all the states had passed laws for the protection of fish and wildlife, and many had hired conservation officers to enforce the law.

In 1975, the state agencies responsible for fish and wildlife employed more than 25,000 people and operated on a combined budget of about one-half billion dollars per year. During the same period, the United States Fish and Wildlife Service, the Bureau of Land Management, the Forest Service, the National Park Service, the National Marine Fisheries Service, and the Soil Conservation Service employed nearly 4,030 people with combined budgets exceeding 679 million dollars in 1979 (Table 1).

TABLE 1. State and Federal Budgets and Personnel Devoted to Wildlife Programs

| | FY 75 | Federal Government (FY 79) | | | | | | |
	States	FWS[1]	FS[1]	BLM[1]	NPS[1]	NMFS[1]	SCS[1]	Total Federal
Budget ($ million)	500	517	28.9	12.1	*	118	3	679*
Personnel	25,000	2,700	350	257	69	548	106	4,030

*Budget figure not available from the NPS.
[1]FWS—Fish and Wildlife Service; FS—Forest Service; BLM—Bureau of Land Management; NPS—National Park Service; NMFS—National Marine Fisheries Service; SCS—Soil Conservation Service.

As greater recognition was given to our nation's fish and wildlife resources and as the complexity associated with managing these resources grew, the federal government began to assume a greater share of the responsibility for their management. Historically, the state fish and wildlife agencies have been responsible for the management of resident species of fish and wildlife, and the federal government has been charged with the responsibility of managing migratory species. However, many gray areas exist. The history of the responsibility for managing these species, recent litigation, and, in some cases, legislation have clouded even more the issue of who is responsible for what.

GROWING FEDERAL RESPONSIBILITY

The question of which governmental body, state or federal, had the ultimate authority for the regulation of wildlife was not cause for debate until wildlife management programs were established at both levels. Once established, however, competition arose between state and federal agencies with regard to the management of fish and wildlife resources.

Historically, the states tended to emphasize law enforcement, refuges, and fish propagation programs, while the federal government assumed the initiative for introducing fish and birds, conducting research, and establishing wildlife refuges, primarily for migratory waterfowl and wading birds. In 1916, the Migratory Bird Treaty established the basis for federal management of a wildlife resource. This legislation was supplemented in 1929 by the Migratory Bird Conservation Act, which gave the federal government the authority to acquire lands, with the consent of the affected states, for migratory bird refuges. Funding for these acquisitions was provided by the Migratory Bird Hunting Stamp Act of 1933.

The question of who retained authority for the management of resident species was clouded in 1915 when the Bureau of Biological Survey was given an appropriation for animal damage control (coyotes, prairie dogs, and other depredating animals). Generally, animal damage control programs were carried out by that federal agency in cooperation with the state agency representing farming and ranching interests. In essence, the states granted *de facto* jurisdiction over the taking of pests to the federal government.

It was an animal damage control program that caused the issue of state versus federal authority over fish and wildlife to be brought before the public and the Supreme Court of the United States. The historic Kaibab Case, *Hunt vs. United States* 278 U.S. 96 (1928), was the first in a series of tests of the authority of the federal government to manage resident species of wildlife. When the mule deer population of the Kaibab Forests in Arizona increased beyond the carrying capacity of the range, both the range and the condition of the deer deteriorated. Thus the Forest Service decided to permit public hunting to reduce the size of the deer herd. At that point, the state threatened hunters for violation of state law. This resulted in a suit by the federal government to prevent interference by state officials in a wildlife reduction program being conducted on public lands.

In summary, the courts decided that the federal government could protect its property by reducing the deer herd, but it must do so with its own personnel and not with licensed hunters. Following the Kaibab and a somewhat similar case in the Pisgah National Forest, the U.S. Forest Service issued regulation G-20-a (in 1934), which stated that when the secretary of agriculture deems it necessary "he shall designate such national forests or portions thereof, establishing hunting and fishing seasons therefore, fix bag and possession limits, specify sex of animals to be killed, [and] fix the fees to be paid. . . ."

This would have removed the responsibility for the setting of seasons and bag limits for resident species of wildlife from the states. Regulation G-20-a was never implemented. Regulation W-2, however, was implemented. It established the basis for cooperative wildlife activities between the states and the Forest Service. In essence, the Forest Service retains responsibility for habitat but works cooperatively with the states on wildlife problems, in accordance with the Forest Service's legislative mandate for multiple-use management of the national forests.

The federal government, simply because it administers so much land, significantly influences the nature and extent of wildlife habitat in this country. It does this in several ways, but each is modified by the land management policies and philosophies that the various administering agencies follow. To illustrate, the policies of a single-use agency, like the Fish and Wildlife Service, in administering land may be significantly different than those employed by multiple-use agencies like the Forest Service or the Bureau of Land Management. The reason stems from the fact that multiple-use agencies are directed by law to consider and provide for a variety of uses, whereas single-use agencies are usually required to manage for a more specific use. For example, management of national wildlife refuges by the Fish and Wildlife Service is primarily for waterfowl and other wildlife. On the other hand, national forests may be managed for a combination of uses, including timber, watershed values, wildlife, livestock grazing, and recreation.

As a result of the Kaibab and Pisgah court cases, the states became highly apprehensive about the erosion of their authority for the management of resident fish and wildlife. Attention shifted from the Forest Service to the Fish and Wildlife Service and the issue of taking resident fish and wildlife on lands in the national wildlife refuge system. The Fish and Wildlife Service was requested by a committee of the International Association of Fish and Wildlife Agencies to secure a legal opinion from the Department of the Interior on the question of the secretary's authority to regulate hunting and fishing in the national wildlife refuge system. The rendered opinion sustained the concept that the Department of the Interior, as a sovereign as well as a proprietor, could regulate the taking of wildlife on lands it administers (71 I.D. 469 1964). The states viewed this opinion as a disaster.

The Department of the Interior agreed to accept state regulations regarding the taking of fish and wildlife as long as those regulations were consistent with the objectives for which a refuge was established.

At about the same time, the National Park Service was recommending that a research project involving the examination of deer stomachs be conducted at Carlsbad National Park because of concern that the high deer population was overutilizing the vegetation of the park. The state of New Mexico agreed to the study and informed the National Park Service that legal state permits would be issued for the taking of deer for research purposes following proper application by the park service. At this point, the National Park Service assumed the posture that because the deer were federal property residing on federal land and eating federal vegetation, no state permit was required. As a result, the state of New Mexico brought suit against the secretary of the interior and the National Park Service to enjoin the taking of deer without state permits. The 10th Circuit Court upheld the park service's action.

At this point, the western states felt that their only alternative was to seek legislative relief. As a result, bills to place the regulation of federal lands' wildlife largely in state hands were introduced in both houses of Congress. Due to a lack of support in the House of Representatives, these efforts failed.

To summarize the situation, the positions of the federal agencies during the late 1960s were: (1) the Fish and Wildlife Service generally agreed that the federal government would adopt state regulations regarding the taking of fish and wildlife on national wildlife refuges if those regulations would not be detrimental to the primary purpose of the refuge; (2) the Forest Service was committed to the provisions of regulation W-2 which left the management of the wildlife itself to the state agencies and the management of its habitat to the Forest Service; (3) the Bureau of Land Management adhered to the provisions of the Taylor Grazing Act which mandated state regulation of all hunting and fishing on grazing districts; and (4) the National Park Service maintained the position that they would decide about the management of resident fish and wildlife on National Park Service administered lands.

Interior Secretary Hickel cleared the air by approving a policy statement for federal-state cooperation (43 C.F.R. Part 24) which stated that the federal government would abide by state law in managing resident wildlife on lands administered by the Department of the Interior. Thus, it was reaffirmed that the state fish and wildlife agencies are responsible for the management of resident fish and wildlife on lands within their state and that the federal government would manage the habitat associated with those lands (see Figure 1).

THE POT BOILS AGAIN

The issue of state versus federal authority over the management of resident fish and wildlife was raised again with the passage of the Wild and Free Roaming Horses and Burros Act of 1971. Stories of alleged cruel and inhumane treatment of horses and burros on public lands aroused the American public who then got the attention of Congress. As a result, the Wild and Free Roaming Horses and Burros Act was passed, making it a federal violation to harass or to take those animals on public lands.

In most cases, the state agriculture departments, rather than the fish and wildlife agencies, were responsible for wild and free roaming horses and burros. When unbranded burros strayed from the public domain in New Mexico, agents of the state's Livestock Board seized and sold them at public auction. The Bureau of Land Management, under the auspices of the Wild and Free Roaming Horses and Burros Act, demanded the return of the animals. New Mexico then brought suit against the Secretary of the Interior claiming that the Wild and Free Roaming Horses and Burros Act was unconstitutional. The Supreme Court, on appeal, rejected the state's contention and issued the opinion that Congress has "complete power" over the public lands including the power to regulate and protect the wildlife living there (*Kleppie* vs. *New Mexico*, 426 U.S. 529 [1976]). Because the Supreme Court dealt with wildlife in general, rather than specifically with wild and free roaming horses and burros, its decision may lead to further federal legislation giving broader responsibility for the management of resident wildlife on public lands to the federal government.

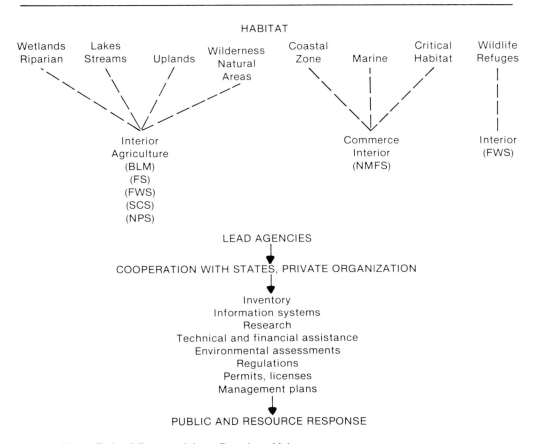

Fig. 1. Major Federal Responsibilities Based on Habitat

Further fuel was added to the fire in 1975 when the state of Alaska decided to control the wolf population on certain public lands in conjunction with their moose (and later, caribou) management programs. The Alaska Fish and Game Department felt it necessary to reduce the number of wolves in certain areas to protect moose calves (and later the declining caribou population). The Department of the Interior did not participate in the state's program, but federal aid money was to be used. Suit was brought against the federal government by the Defenders of Wildlife, and on February 14, 1977, the Federal District Court for the District of Columbia issued an order temporarily enjoining the Secretary of the Interior from permitting the aerial killing of wolves by agents or permittees of the state on certain public lands in Alaska. In compliance with the court's order, the Secretary closed the lands in question to such hunting until further notice. Subsequently, Alaska filed suit requesting the Federal District Court for Alaska to declare that the Department of the Interior had no authority to interfere with the state's wolf control program. On April 11, 1977, the Alaska court denied the requested relief. Certain aspects of the litigation are still pending.

MORE CONFUSION

Three recent, major pieces of federal legislation are viewed as reducing the autonomy of the states with regard to their control of resident wildlife, while a fourth tends to strengthen their autonomy. Those that are viewed as weakening the state's autonomy are the Marine Mammal Protection Act of 1972, the Endangered Species Act of 1973, and the Fishery Conservation and Management Act of 1976. The enhancing legislation is known as the Sikes Act of 1974.

The first of these acts, the Marine Mammal Protection Act of 1972 (Public Law 92-522 as amended), established total federal authority for the management of marine mammals and preempted state authority, even for animals within their jurisdiction. With the exception of Alaska, neither the states nor the federal government had undertaken the development of comprehensive management programs for marine mammals. The controversy that arose between commercial tuna fishermen and conservationists concerned with the protection of porpoises from death in the yellowfin tuna nets focused public attention on the need for legislation to provide protection for marine mammals in general and was a strong factor in passage of the act.

Even though the wording of the act was intended to ensure that state and local government employees retained authority for taking beached or stranded marine mammals, two basic problems existed in their exercising this authority. First, possession of dead animals or parts thereof had to be carefully documented to avoid violation of the law. Second, state officers, upon finding stranded or beached animals, had to ensure that the animals received competent care from a veterinarian and that they were placed in facilities (such as aquariums) where their survival could be reasonably assured. The considerable time and expense to the state brought about by these procedural requirements caused them to be reluctant to exercise their responsibilities for "taking marine mammals." This problem was resolved in 1974 when the National Marine Fisheries Service and the Fish and Wildlife Service issued regulations that made provision for cooperative enforcement programs with the states and provided for federal deputization of state enforcement officers. Thus, the states became more directly involved in implementing the act. Also, by becoming federal officers through the deputization process, much of the red tape and expense of handling both live and dead animals were significantly reduced.

Another complication arose with the subsistence hunting of walrus by Eskimos in Alaska. Historically, the state of Alaska had worked cooperatively with the Alaskan natives living along the coast to ensure that marine animals important to their cultural needs and used for food, clothing, art, and commercial purposes did not adversely impact the walrus population. Following the passage of the 1972 act the state could no longer work directly with the villagers because they were specifically exempt from this legislation, and the state's cooperative program with villagers disappeared. This was unfortunate because the U.S. Fish and Wildlife Service, due to severe limitations in funding and staffing, was not able to effectively monitor the walrus hunting, and thus uncertainty arose regarding the status of walrus populations. In 1976, after development of management plans for marine mammals, the Department of the Interior granted the state of Alaska the responsibility for managing the walrus which is viewed as a step toward more state control of those species.

A heightened public sentiment for the protection of wildlife in general was focused on the plight of endangered species such as the whooping crane. Conservation organizations like the National Audubon Society and the National Wildlife Federation devoted considerable effort to educating their membership regarding the plight of many species due to the adverse impact of man's actions on their habitats. They also mobilized their memberships to push for legislative relief for these species.

The federal government started in 1913, with passage of the Migratory Bird Treaty Act, an effort to save the plume bearing birds (like the egrets) from extinction. However, these and other efforts were not enough, and interest by the general public prompted Congress to pass the first Endangered Species Act in 1966. This act granted the secretary of the interior authority to fund research and acquire habitat for those species threatened with extinction, and it provided limited authority for protection of those species. Many people felt that this act was inadequate and pushed for stronger legislation which resulted in the 1973 Endangered Species Act. The 1973 act provides for the listing of species as either threatened or endangered by the secretaries of the Interior and Commerce and provides federal protection for species so designated. The states view this as a further erosion of their authority for the management of resident species because once listed, the species is effectively removed from state control.

Section 7 of the Endangered Species Act prohibits any federal agency from taking an action that will adversely impact the species or its critical habitat.

Many felt that by removing a species from state control, a problem similar to that which existed with the Marine Mammal Protection Act would arise, and the species would be left with virtually no protection. Concern was also expressed that emotionalism rather than biological facts may rule and that species would be listed simply for political reasons with little or no state input. These fears were somewhat realized when the grizzly bear in Montana, Idaho, and Wyoming, said by the states to have a stable population, was listed as a threatened species. The timber wolf in Minnesota was placed on the endangered list against the state's advice.

The states are concerned that the listing process may actually result in a negative backlash and thus further jeopardize the existence of the species.

The situation with the timber wolf in Minnesota seems to illustrate the need for their concern. Some citizens in Minnesota allegedly attempted to deliberately reduce the number of timber wolves, in spite of the fact that the animals were protected under the Endangered Species Act, because they felt that the wolves were in conflict with both cattle and deer production. As a result, the timber wolf was reclassified as threatened, and a procedure for removal of depredating wolves was established. A disagreement ensued between those interested in the total protection of the wolves and those at the other end of the spectrum. Such disagreements could contribute to either a weakening of the Endangered Species Act, so that less protection is afforded to those species requiring it, or it could place greater responsibility for control of resident wildlife in the hands of the federal government.

In addition to the backlash generated by those directly concerned with the status of a particular species, a considerable backlash can also be generated by development interests concerned with the impact that the presence of a threatened or endangered species or its habitat can have on a given development project. For example, the presence of the famed snail darter in the waters of the Little Tennessee River caused the Endangered Species Act to come to the forefront when the courts ruled that the Tellico Dam could not be completed because the project was in violation of the Endangered Species Act. Again, public sentiment was aroused, and Congress adopted amendments that would require interagency review of highly controversial projects in the future. Section 6 of the act, providing for federal-state cooperation, was strengthened by Congress in 1978.

Recent fisheries legislation has been passed establishing a mechanism that some may view as a preemption of the state authority over the jurisdiction of fisheries in the territorial water of those states. The Fishery Conservation and Management Act (P.L. 94-265), passed in 1976, establishes eight Regional Fishery Management Councils that have jurisdiction over the fisheries in the territorial waters of the states and out to the limits of the 200-mile fishery zone. These councils have the authority to set seasons, catch limits, gear limits, size limits, define areas, and control the amount of fishing effort.

Not all the legislation that has been passed can be viewed as eroding what the states have felt is their responsibility—management of resident wildlife. In 1974, the Sikes Act, P.L. 86-797, was amended by P.L. 93-452. The act originally authorized the Defense Department to expend money for wildlife on its lands. Public Law 93-452 amended the original act to cover lands administered by the Forest Service, the Bureau of Land Management, the Energy Research and Development Administration, and the National Aeronautics and Space Administration. It directed the secretaries of agriculture and the interior to develop, in consultation with the state agencies responsible for fish and wildlife, a comprehensive plan for conservation and rehabilitation programs on their lands. In 1978, the act was further amended to extend appropriations authorizations for the affected agencies.

The Sikes Act reinforces the authority of the states to manage resident wildlife on federal lands. It has gained broad acceptance by the states, especially in the West. On those lands that are part of the conservation rehabilitation program, the act provides that the fishing, hunting, and trapping of resident species shall be allowed in accordance with state law. At the same time, the act affords a cooperative mechanism through the development of comprehensive management plans for the state wildlife agencies to have an impact on decisions concerning fish and wildlife habitat on public lands. The federal agencies have been reluctant to request monies under the Sikes Act, but considerable work has been done by the states in the development and implementation of habitat management plans.

Conservationists became concerned with the status of the national wildlife refuge system, established primarily for the benefit of migratory waterfowl. They expressed dismay at the failure of the federal government to live up to its commitments to provide sound stewardship for the migratory component of our nation's wildlife resource. Thus, the debate continues as to who should have the greater responsibility of the management of resident wildlife—the state agencies, who are closer to the issues at hand and appear to have been more successful in devoting funds and manpower to wildlife needs, or the federal government that has a potentially unlimited source of revenue to devote to these programs if the constituency demands it.

The Federal Aid in Fish and Wildlife Program administered by the U.S. Fish and Wildlife Service has also demonstrated that the states and federal government can work together cooperatively for the benefit of the resource. In 1937, the Congress passed the Pittman-Robertson Wildlife Restoration Act (16 U.S.C. 669, 50 Stat. 430) which established an 11 percent excise tax on sporting arms and ammunition earmarked for the states for wildlife restoration. Through fiscal year 1977, this fund has totaled $762 million with an annual average of about $60 million. Similar legislation was passed for fisheries restoration by Congress in 1950. The act, known as the Dingell-Johnson Sport Fish Restoration Act of 1950 (16 U.S.C. 777, 64 Stat. 430-P.L. 81-681) provided a 10 percent excise tax on certain items of sport fishing equipment. A total of $267 million has been collected since its inception, and the fund has recently averaged about $26 million per year.

Because these programs are funded via an excise tax, they are not subject to the whims of Congress and thus tend to be relatively stable, to increase as inflation increases or as increased user demand occurs, and to develop a recognizable constituency. The state fish and wildlife agencies and federal government, via the Fish and Wildlife Service, have worked cooperatively in the administration of the federal aid programs. These programs have provided funding for research, direct management of fish and wildlife, and habitat acquisition that benefits game and nongame species alike. Because of the success of the Pittman-Robertson program, current efforts are underway to pass a similar program designed to benefit the nongame species.

STATE AND FEDERAL GOVERNMENT NEED TO WORK TOGETHER

It is today generally recognized that the real threat to our nation's fish and wildlife resource is not excessive hunting or the lack of it, but the continued loss of habitat essential for wildlife's survival. Thus, the state and federal agencies must work in harmony with the public in general in a major effort to identify and neutralize those forces that would intentionally or otherwise destroy that habitat.

It is essential that the state and federal agencies place the good of the resource first and their parochial interest second. Both need to educate the public in general about the problems facing our nation's fish and wildlife. And, both need to work together in harmony to develop federal and state legislation that will ensure the strongest possible safeguards for wildlife and wildlife habitat in a commodity oriented society. Without cooperation, we must readily admit that it will not be important who, the state or federal government, has the responsibility for the management of resident wildlife because the issue will be moot.

The federal government can assume a much greater role in providing legislative and financial support, enabling the states to broaden their existing programs to encompass all wildlife. It should immediately begin to develop laws and enabling regulations that will provide incentives encouraging the protection of fish and wildlife habitat rather than its destruction. Examples of this include tax incentives for landowners to retain fish and wildlife habitat, tax incentives rather than disincentives in our nation's agricultural subsidy program, and pollution reduction programs like the Section 208 program of the Water Pollution Control Act.

The federal government must continue to recognize that the states have a legitimate concern with regard to their real or perceived loss of jurisdiction over resident species of wildlife. One of the obvious reasons, at this time, is that the income sources for the states, especially in the West, are tied directly to hunting and fishing on public lands. If these activities were significantly reduced or eliminated, state fish and wildlife agencies in the West would be severely crippled or paralyzed.

In addition, state agencies feel they have the intimate knowledge and personnel capability to deal with problems associated with resident wildlife. They have seen the instability of federal programs in the face of shifting political whims. Last, the states echo an often expressed sentiment that when decisions are made by authorities closest to the people they govern, those decisions more closely adhere to the democratic philosophy upon which our nation was founded.

THE LEGISLATIVE PROCESS

Thomas L. Kimball

The legislative process, as practiced in the United States, was unique when first established by our Constitution. It is one of only three systems that provide a process of checks and balances against irrational actions. Therefore, the place of the legislature is to enact laws that the executive branch of the government administers under processes that are deemed to be legal by the judicial branch. The legislative process is often cumbersome and unwieldy; yet, when practiced properly, it provides for honest, sincere, and comprehensive review of laws, rules, and regulations with which the public will be saddled. It appears inevitable that more and more laws will be enacted as the result of stresses and strains developed by conflicts within an expanding human population.

The legislative process, which will be described later, is applicable in principle to most state legislatures, county and borough governments, and municipal bodies. As a consequence, this process will be described in relation to the U.S. Congress because of its broad application and influence on the entire nation.

The legislative process represents the finest opportunity for the American public to express its will, both in terms of the enactment of legislation and the administration of programs. Set out in the most basic terms, members of the Congress, as with the president and vice-president, will remain in office only so long as they generally express the will of the people they represent. As a consequence, most responsible legislators welcome and even solicit the viewpoints of their constituents. This situation allows interested individuals and groups to make significant contributions to the overall expression of the public will to their legislators. Persons interested in the proper management of natural resources have a responsibility and duty to express their viewpoints to their representatives in the Congress and other legislative bodies. (Certainly, many groups interested in selfish exploitation of natural resources will be expressing their viewpoints.) This situation is especially applicable to professionals in the various fields of resource management, because they are best equipped to know what improper laws and regulations can do to adversely affect the environment.

POINTS ON LEGISLATIVE PROCEDURES

Except in unusual cases, the process of enacting national legislation into laws is long and laborious. While this procedure is tedious, it does offer the opportunity for careful review—and time for expressions of opinions to be transmitted by the public to their members of the Congress.

Kimball, Thomas L.   Executive Vice President, National Wildlife Federation, Washington, D.C.

All bills, except those involving appropriations, follow the same general procedure. Upon introduction, a bill is referred to the committee that handles matters in this particular area of activity. The committee then usually assigns it to a subcommittee, which conducts hearings. In most cases, the federal department or departments concerned are asked to comment on a bill, and hearings often are delayed until these reports are submitted.

As an example, here is how a Senate bill establishing a new national park would be considered. When introduced, the bill would be referred to the Senate Energy and Natural Resources Committee and would be referred within that committee to the Subcommittee on Parks and Recreation, which would hold public hearings on the bill. The subcommittee would "mark up" the bill, that is, make whatever revisions in the original provisions it wishes to make, and, if a majority favored it, would report it to the full committee. The full committee also might mark up the subcommittee's version. If a majority of the full committee favors the bill, they will order it reported to the full Senate, where it is again subject to amendment. The bill passes the Senate if a majority of those senators present and voting vote for it.

KAREN
BARTH

Upon Senate passage, it is referred to the House of Representatives, where it would be referred to the Interior and Insular Affairs Subcommittee on National Parks and Insular Affairs. The process in the House is the same, except that a bill must go to the House Rules Committee before going to the House floor. The Rules Committee functions as a traffic control committee, setting the length of time permitted for debate, types of amendments permitted, and other procedural matters. A bill is usually dead if the Rules Committee votes against granting it a "rule" for floor consideration. Differences, if any, between House and Senate versions would be settled by a House-Senate conference committee. The compromise worked out by the committee must be approved by both House and Senate before the bill is sent to the president. Once signed by the president, the bill becomes law.

Variations do occur. Identical bills can be introduced in both houses as "companion" measures so that committee work is conducted simultaneously. On rare occasions, a committee in one body may accept information gathered in hearings by the other body to expedite reporting a bill without delay.

All money, or appropriations, bills originate in the House within the Committee on Appropriations and are not given numbers until the committee is ready to report them. The Senate Appropriations Committee conducts hearings simultaneously but does not act until it receives the House bill. The president's proposed budget is the basis for consideration. Both House and Senate, however, the budget committees that make independent assessments of budget priorities and set various target and budget ceiling levels for the authorizing and appropriating committees.

Public expressions on bills can be made at these points:

1. Before hearings, work is most effective on members of the subcommittee or full committee. Always send copies of correspondence to your own congressman and senators.

2. During hearings, concentrate on members of the subcommittee. This is the most critical point and where a major part of the work is accomplished.

3. Next, concentrate on the full committee. Prior work in providing background information is valuable.

4. The House Rules Committee directs legislative traffic and votes on allowing a bill to reach the House floor for debate. Permission for a specified amount of floor debate is called "granting a rule." Many bills have been halted entirely or hopelessly delayed by this committee.

5. Floor action approves, amends, or rejects, and the votes of all members count here.

6. During conference committee consideration, the conferees accept either the language in the House or Senate version of the bill or some compromise between the two.

7. Finally, the president signs or vetoes the bill. Action to override a veto requires two-thirds majorities in both the House and the Senate.

Individual, spontaneous responses often are more effective than campaigns obviously organized. Personal contacts are most effective. Telephone calls, letters, and telegrams are other effective media. Most members of Congress are well briefed, so know your subject!

Know what actions motivate your members of the Congress and to whom they are obligated or indebted. Working through an influential friend often is more effective than direct contact.

When referring to a bill, always mention both the number and subject. Bills that fail to pass are not held over into another Congress. If reintroduced, they get a new number. Never refer to an obsolete bill number.

It is much easier to block a bill than to enact it.

GLOSSARY

"Report"—A bill is ordered reported by a subcommittee only when the action is favorable. Unfavorable action results in no report.

"Conference Committee"—A bill that passes both the House and the Senate in differing versions is referred to a conference committee. Conferees are appointed by presiding officers, who usually name members of committees that originally handled the proposal. A conference committee can act only on points of difference. Provisions in only one version of a bill can be eliminated or compromised. Each body of the Congress must adopt or reject the conference committee report. It cannot be amended.

"Consent Calendar"—Bills (reported from a committee) that have no apparent calendar and can thus bypass the Rules Committee. If there is no objection, a bill is passed on the consent calendar without a recorded vote. However, if there is even a single objection voiced on the floor, it gets "passed over." Unless this objection is removed, the bill must go to the Rules Committee for a "rule."

"Suspension of Rules"—Bills that may have only minor opposition, after proper notice, can be brought to the House floor under suspension of the rules without going through the Rules Committee. A two-thirds majority is necessary to pass a bill under suspension of the rules.

"Sessions of Congress"—Senators are elected for six-year terms, representatives for only two-year terms. Thus, a Congress covers two years, the first and second sessions. Bills not acted upon the first session of a Congress are held over into the second session. However, bills cannot be held over from one Congress to the next. They may be reintroduced, in which case new numbers are assigned.

"Clean Bill"—When a proposal is amended extensively in committee, it is a common practice to introduce a "clean bill" that incorporates the changes. Since consideration is a formality, "clean" bills often move rapidly. This practice can lead to confusion, particularly when a letter-writing campaign has been developed on the basis of an obsolete number for a proposal.

"Legislative Record"—People often ask what type of a legislative record a member of the Congress has with respect to conservation. This frequently is difficult to determine unless the member is on a resources committee or deliberately seeks to build a record through introduction of bills, or by the presentation of speeches or testimony. Perhaps as many as 25,000 bills and resolutions may be introduced in the two sessions of a Congress, although some are duplicates. Probably not more than 2,000 or 3,000 of these will even get a hearing in either the House or the Senate, and not more than one-half of those gain committee approvals. Probably less than 1,000 public bills will be enacted into law by a Congress. A large majority of bills are passed under procedures requiring only a voice vote. All boiled down, there may be only three or four conservation bills brought to a vote where individual "yes" or "nay" votes are recorded. Thus, a conservation record may not be as easy to determine as many might think.

TIPS ABOUT WRITING CONGRESSMEN

1. In the address, say "Representative (or The Honorable) Charles Jones." It is appropriate to use "Mister" in the salutation in writing to a representative, but it should not be used in the inside address or when addressing a senator. If you know them well enough personally, it is quite acceptable to use first names. Following are the most commonly used ways of addressing congressmen: Note separate ZIP Codes for House (20515) and Senate (20510).

Senator Charles W. Jones
Senate Office Building
Washington, D.C. 20510
Dear Senator Jones:

Rep. (or The Honorable) Charles W. Jones
House Office Building
Washington, D.C. 20515
Dear Mr. (or Congressman) Jones:

2. Be respectful and dignified.

3. Use your business letterhead or personal stationery, and write in your style. Avoid stereotyped wording as it is an earmark of pressure campaigns. Be brief, but not terse. Be specific, positive—do not hedge.

4. Present the local viewpoint—how the issue in question would affect conservation, you, your business, your suppliers, your family, etc.

5. Be reasonable—do not ask the impossible. But request action and an answer.

6. In opposing legislation, do not "knock" it; build your case with a positive approach.

7. Express appreciation where it is due.

8. It is not necessary, but if you send the Washington office of private conservation organizations a "blind" informational copy of your outgoing letter and any meaningful replies you receive, this can often be helpful in making a representation for you more effective. The most continually useful action, however, is regular contact—written and face-to-face—with your representative and senators.

9. Although congressmen get more mail than most people, it still helps to write to them. A well-written, constructive, thoughtful letter—sent at the right time—can accomplish much. Politically-sensitive congressmen regularly check and ask "How's the mail running?" in an effort to determine how they might vote on a particular bill. Keeping in touch with your elected representatives is an essential part of our dynamic political process.

SELECTED REFERENCES

Conservation Report. Weekly digest of congressional action (journal). Nat. Wildl. Fed., 1412 Sixteenth St., N.W., Washington, D.C. 20036.

National Wildlife Federation. 1977. The citizen and environmental policy. Washington, D.C. 6 pp.

POLITICAL
CONSIDERATIONS

Henry P. Caulfield, Jr.

Environmental quality is now, and has been since the mid-1960s, a central domestic policy issue. Rachel Carson's lonely voice in *Silent Spring* and Stewart Udall's *Quiet Crisis*, both published in the early sixties, show that the current sense of popular urgency has not always existed. The Nixon and Ford administrations enhanced the general principles of the New Conservation developed in the sixties. Russell Train, the first chairman of the Council of Environmental Quality in 1970 and the administrator of the Environmental Protection Agency in the Ford administration, gave environmentalists great confidence that their interests were well represented in both of these administrations. President Carter's Environmental Message of 23 May 1977 gave assurance of his administration's adherence to the New Conservation.

The New Conservation differs from the traditional conservation movement in that it concerns itself with more than just providing fish and wildlife for hunting and fishing. It is broader in scope, dealing with the whole relationship of man in nature on a sustainable basis. Ecology, although poorly understood by many, is becoming man's scientific guide to relating himself to his environment. Increasingly, our society is arriving at these conclusions:

1. The maintenance of a high level of genetic diversity of both flora and fauna is essential to environmental stability.

2. Human population cannot increase forever in a finite world.

3. Economic growth cannot increase forever in a finite world.

4. Pollution of our total environment, unless checked, could end the existence of all life on earth.

5. Environmental planning, followed by public decisions and implementation, is needed. This is required if the nation is to maintain a viable mix of all resource uses so as to support a high level of economic goods and services and a high quality environment.

POLITICAL ENVIRONMENT OF THE PAST

Before looking at the present and future of fish and wildlife management within this New Conservation, let us consider past responses of fish and wildlife management to the political environment. As an outsider, but more than a casual observer, my perceptions are these:

1. Political support for fish and wildlife management has been based upon the demands of fishermen and hunters, and the desire that manufacturers of equipment and supplies have for expanding markets.

2. The primary concern of fish and wildlife management has been to maintain a sustained yield of fish and game while holding to the opinion that

Caulfield, Henry P., Jr., Professor of Political Science, Colorado State University, Fort Collins

45

economic development is the chief measure of human progress. This has often led to conflicts detrimental to wildlife populations.

3. State authority, established in the last century over resident fish and game, has provided the basic legal authority for fish and game management. States generally have developed strong fish and game organizations. Federal functions are relatively weak except with respect to migratory waterfowl, endangered species, and anadromous and commercial fisheries.

4. Financial support has come almost solely from state license fees paid by fishermen and hunters, and from the automatically allocated proceeds of federal taxes on guns, ammunition, and fishing tackle.

5. Autonomy for fish and game management within state executive structures has been sought and usually achieved. Financial support based upon legislatively authorized revenues has fostered this independence. The legislative branch, under the influence of fish and game clientele groups, has been the strongest and most reliable source of political support. Often, however, this support has been misguided, leading to lost revenues and wasted wildlife resources.

6. Traditional land uses (e.g., farming and grazing) are often in competition with those of fish and wildlife, and resource agencies have attempted to resolve the competition in favor of fishermen and hunters. Camera hunters and others who appreciate wildlife without killing have not been similarly aided. Nor has the competition between wildlife and settlement, recreational, and timber interests been adequately appreciated and dealt with.

7. Resource agencies fostered strong ties with clientele groups, particularly the National Wildlife Federation, Izaak Walton League, Trout Unlimited, Ducks Unlimited, Sport Fishing Institute, and Wildlife Management Institute.

8. There has been a continuing controversy between state and federal wildlife agencies over the authority to manage wildlife. The states feel they should have responsibility over wildlife within their boundaries and so seek to limit overriding federal controls.

9. Fish and wildlife interests, whether private, state, or federal, have generally reacted to the proposals of others instead of initiating their own proposals to meet changing times.

In short, state fish and wildlife agencies have held an embattled position and have developed a largely justified, defensive strategy to deal with hostile legislation.

THE PRESENT

The New Conservation in recent years has had an important impact on fish and wildlife management. Of most significance, in terms of implementing scientific ecology, is the Endangered Species Act of 1973 (Public Law 93-205) which is administered by the U.S. Fish and Wildlife Service in cooperation with state fish and game agencies. Another significant act is the Water Pollution Control Act of 1972 (P.L. 92-500) that has as its ultimate objective a total curtailment of pollution entering rivers, streams, and lakes and an interim standard of "fishable and swimable" by 1983. The Environmental Protection Agency, which administers this act, also has provided major financial support for the initiation and operation of the Office of Biological Services within the U.S. Fish and Wildlife Service. This innovative, highly trained, and intellectually broad-based staff is providing an impetus within the service to broaden and deepen its concern with the natural environment.

The New Conservation, at the more popular level of concern, in recent years has been fostering "nongame" programs. A nongame wildlife bill would (if enacted and funded) assist the states in developing and implementing comprehensive fish and wildlife resource management plans for nongame fish and wildlife. Some states, Colorado for example, have already established nongame programs. The Colorado program is partly financed by funds from persons indicating that part of their state income tax returns be used for non-game work. Many more people responded than had been expected.

Thus, a broadening of concern beyond sport and commercial fish and wildlife is occurring. This deepening concern for the natural environment has a long way to go, however.

THE FUTURE

The defensive strategy that served fish and wildlife interests well in the past is being supplemented by a positive, offensive strategy. But what of the future? Fish and wildlife people must develop this positive posture, as individual state leaders have recognized, while still maintaining defensive strength. More specifically, in my view, fish and wildlife management must:

1. Foster an ecological research and survey agency at the state level on as broad a basis as possible. This will require joining with or developing much closer operational relationships with environmental protection, forestry, park recreation, state comprehensive planning, and possibly other state agency functions.

2. Further develop the long-standing alliance with university teaching and research.

3. Broaden its clientele to include all who are interested in the survival of natural living things.

4. Support private multiple-use management plans for farms and ranches that will provide new rural income from all renewable resources including wildlife and related recreation. Much has been accomplished, but much more needs to be done in this area.

5. Participate in state air, water, and land-use planning by projecting long-term sustainable relations between man and other living things and by positively and aggressively representing its findings in overall state and federal-state decision making.

6. Participate in water and related land-use planning, generally, through the federal-state river basin commissions authorized by Title II of the Water Resources Planning Act of 1965 (P.L. 89-90). A greater recognition of environmental values is being reflected in the recommendations of federal-state comprehensive water and related land resource studies than is generally realized.

7. Participate area-wide (usually intrastate) in state waste treatment studies implementing Section 208 of the Water Pollution Control Act, as amended. Unless fish and wildlife interests are well represented in these studies so as to foster local appreciation of the broadly based benefits of cleaning up rivers, those participating in the studies who are most cost conscious will tend to prevail.

8. Develop jointly with the state and federal wildlife resource agencies, or under the aegis of a national study commission, a clear understanding of federal and state responsibilities. This is necessary to enable the U.S. Fish and Wildlife Service to undertake national leadership in its allocated sphere without fear of state repudiation and to allow the states to feel secure in their own realms. Agreement might be reached on a draft ecological survey and research act which, if enacted and funded, could help finance state ecological surveys and university ecological research. The Council on Environmental Quality, in its concern about overcoming deficiencies in ecological knowledge, could usefully encourage such an effort.

9. Seek appropriation of general state funds to support its new broadened responsibilities and to escape from its present financial trap of limited, legislatively dedicated revenues. Success will require a clear definition of goals and public support of programs in fish and wildlife management that are of general interest to the public.

SUMMARY

If the New Conservation is the wave of the future, then the political ecology of fish and wildlife management at all levels of government and in related education, research, and extension in universities needs to be studied and considered anew. In fact, the whole fraternity of fish and wildlife managers needs to reappraise its activities in the context of what the future holds in store rather than in terms of what has worked well in the past. Hopefully, what has been stated above will assist this reappraisal and lead to desirable change.

THE ROLE OF
POLICY MAKING
BOARDS AND COMMISSIONS

William E. Towell

Fish and game commissions are an outgrowth of chaos that results from state legislatures attempting to make everyday policy decisions and regulations relating to wildlife management. In some states they were born of public revolt against political greed, resource mismanagement, and even dangerously threatened wildlife populations. Few states today reserve all wildlife regulatory authority to their legislatures, because it has proved too slow and cumbersome for these deliberative bodies. Instead, most of the authority for wildlife decisions in the United States has been delegated entirely or partially to boards or commissions, or in a few cases to single commissioners serving in the executive branch of the state government.

Most commissioners are nonsalaried and nearly all are politically appointed. In a real sense, they are small legislatures responsible to the people for the well-being of public resources. A commissioner is a representative in our democratic process of government. His responsibility is the same as any other elected or appointed official whose job is to represent the people, but he has a specific responsibility for public resources as well. Sometimes his responsibility for natural resources must outweigh the will or desires of the people he represents, and herein lies the distinction between a good and a bad commissioner.

Resources are managed for people and, in the long run, the public must be satisfied with their management. No form of government is more stable than its acceptance by the people it represents, yet resource management decisions often must be made contrary to public opinion. When popularity and wise resource use are in conflict, the resource must come first. But the authority that goes with control also carries a responsibility to fully inform and convince the public who protests that decisions made are in its own best interests. It is not enough to be right unless a commission, over a reasonable period of time, can convince most of the people that it is right.

This role of representing the public and at the same time making policy decisions for a resource management agency is uniquely a commissioner's task. He is the vital link between need and action. He must represent public desire and acceptance and, at the same time, show primary concern and responsibility for resources. A commission or commissioner who cannot or will not do both cannot endure.

It has been said that the only basis for fish and game regulations should be welfare of the wildlife itself plus the equitable distribution of any available surplus for harvest. A third ingredient must be added. This is taxing the

Towell, William E. Executive Vice President, American Forestry Association, Washington, D.C., Former Director, Missouri Conservation Department.

acceptance and temperament of the public, or the willingness of nonprofessional but concerned individuals, to understand and accept restrictions or liberalizations for their benefit. Only a politically responsible elected or appointed official, or in this case a commissioner, can provide this. People must be brought into all wildlife decisions and their desires adequately interpreted. This is the commissioner's job. In addition, he must be the political buffer between a nonpartisan department staff and the executive and legislative branches of politically oriented state governments.

PRIMARY FUNCTION OF COMMISSIONERS

No better system than the commission form of fish and wildlife resource government has yet been devised, yet it has several inherent weaknesses. A discussion of some of these may help commissioners and administrators alike and, it is hoped, lead to better resource conservation. Here are a few observations on the performances of commissioners.

Delving into administrative affairs of the department is one of the most common failings of a commission or a commissioner. Usually it is the chairman who feels that he must exercise administrative functions that rightfully belong to a director. Sometimes it is the whole commission that gets into management details that should be left to their chief administrator. The commission's role is strictly one of policy determination, and it should leave implementation of that policy to its hired executive. If the director cannot or does not perform to its satisfaction, the answer is not to take over the job for him but to hire someone who can perform satisfactorily.

Unfortunately, too many commissioners tend to deal in personalities and minor administrative matters. It weakens the director's position and creates constant politicking and unrest within the department. No director can do a good job or have the confidence of his staff unless the commission leaves administrative details to his judgment. This does not mean that the director is always right or that his decisions should never be challenged. Everyone should have the right of appeal to higher authority and the commission should encourage such appeals, but the one fatal error to a proper relationship between the commission and the director is for the policy board members to begin making routine administrative decisions.

There is more than enough for a commission to do without invading the director's field of activity. The commission should, of course, approve all major policy changes. It should establish game and fish regulations, approve budgets, set permit fees, review all major program recommendations, approve land purchases, adopt salary scales, and set personnel qualifications. Most of these actions will be backed by intensive study and the recommendation of the director and his staff, but because of their importance to the whole program, they should be subject to commission approval or confirmation. The breakdown comes when the commission starts acting independently of administrative management or demands authority over routine executive matters.

PROVINCIALISM A PROBLEM

A second major weakness in commissioner performance is a tendency toward provincialism or regional representation by individual commissioners. This is fostered in some states by laws that designate political or geographic boundaries for commission representation. The problems come when any commissioner begins to think only in terms of the district he represents. Wildlife must be managed on the basis of habitat requirements and hunting and fishing pressures, not on the whims of a local commissioner or the constituents in his area. Some species must be managed on a statewide basis for biological or enforcement reasons, and regional regulations only tend to confuse department personnel and sportsmen alike.

Zones for wildlife harvest often are desirable or necessary for adequate protection and harvest distribution, but they should have a purpose. They should be well-defined and justified on the basis of management needs. Commissioners in some states have been known to set up their own district regulations, to be more restrictive than necessary, to demand longer or earlier seasons than are biologically justifiable, to vacillate back and forth on zone regulations due to local influences, or to be swayed unduly by pressure groups.

Commissioners should never forget their responsibilities for wildlife resources in the state as a whole. They should be just as concerned for other regions as for their own. Never should they demand or support regulations because of local sentiment or pressures that cannot be biologically justified or defended. Another problem is when a commissioner is appointed to represent a specific segment of the population or interest group, such as labor, agriculture, industry, recreation, or similar groups. He/she tends to "come alive" only when that interest group is involved, or he/she represents only that one point of view. It is better to have a commission made up of seven farmers or seven publishers who have *broad* interests and concerns than to have seven special or narrow interest commissioners who represent seven "areas" out of a potential countless number of interests. The best commissions are those serving under laws that do not provide regional or district representation but where all members serve the state at large. Even with such district handicaps, however, a good commissioner can rise above provincialism. To do so often is neither easy nor popular with the folks back home.

AN OPEN MIND IMPORTANT

Another major failing on the part of commissioners is the tendency for some to adhere to preconceived beliefs and refuse to listen to or accept facts that contradict their own notions. Hunters and fishermen are notorious for having all the answers on fish and wildlife management, and too frequently being an ardent sportsman is about the only qualification some have for appointment to a commission. A few carry their beliefs to commission meetings. They know all the answers and cannot be dissuaded. Instead of relying on research data and the recommendations of professionals, they tenaciously cling to their own misconceived notions. Good wildlife regulations, therefore, become difficult if not impossible.

Many state wildlife agencies are victims of their own past mistakes. Years of artificial stocking, wasted predator control efforts, unnecessarily restrictive bag or size limits, single sex deer season, bounty payments, and winter feeding programs come back to haunt wildlife managers through well-intentioned but misinformed commissioners. Some states are unable to terminate wasteful programs because their commissioners have been sold on their value many years previously. Every new commission appointment presents the possibility of such preconceived beliefs and a challenge to the department staff to "reeducate" each such official. Every state wildlife agency should have a program for educating new commissioners, and new commissioners should welcome such an educational opportunity.

The good commissioner will listen and learn; the poor commissioner never changes his beliefs, no matter how reliable the information given him. Nothing undermines the morale of a technical fish and game staff more than reinstituting programs that have already been tried and proved worthless. Some commissioners will argue that such an activity is desired by the public, that it is harmless to wildlife, so why not give the people what they want? The reason, of course, is obvious. It perpetuates a fallacy and only more firmly entrenches the erroneous belief in the public mind.

Sometimes, in the face of such demands from one or more commission members, needed program changes cannot be accomplished. Effort then must be directed toward education of commissioners and public alike, which means delay in implementing desirable new programs. Delay is not as serious, however, as going in the wrong direction. Commissions must guard against reversals in direction that destroy public confidence and department morale. There are times when a commissioner must defy public demands and stand up for what he knows is right. This is the mark of a good commissioner.

POLITICAL PRESSURES INTENSE

Every commissioner is the target of pressures and favor-seeking both from outside the department and within. Either can cause grave problems. A commission member who formerly was active in some organized sportsmen's group, for example, may find it difficult to assume his new role of state responsibility due to this allegiance and friendship in the former group. Some never rise above their previous affiliations and become a powerful tool of that particular organization. This can lead to unjustified emphasis on certain activities or imbalance of fund allocations.

Another very strong pressure that can lead to serious commission problems is that which comes from the political force that was instrumental in securing the appointment in the first place. This can be from a governor, a member of the legislature, or some political boss. Some commissioners are little more than hatchet men, appointed for the specific purpose of changing an organization or its personnel. Others never learn to think for themselves but place political considerations first in all their decisions. A good commissioner will defy even the governor who appointed him if he knows he is right and that his action is in the best interests of the resources and the people.

Politics is a fact of life, however, and any fish and game administrator soon learns, if he is to survive, that both he and his commission must get along with the governor and the state legislature. The best bridge between the department and politics is the commission. Members of the commission are political appointees, their party affiliations well known. They can help absorb some of the pressures and also temper their policies and regulations to make them both biologically correct and politically acceptable. This is a difficult road to follow but an important one to the success of any state conservation program.

Internal political pressures can be equally as troublesome as partisan politics. Sometimes it is difficult for a commissioner to show an equal interest and concern for all department programs and activities because he has been wooed and swayed by attention from one or more particular groups. Often it is the conservation officer or enforcement group that has won over a commission member, but it can be the biologists or the information and education staff. The result can be overemphasis on one or more divisions resulting in an imbalance in number of personnel, in salary scales, or in program budgets. Internal feuding between divisions or sections, low morale, and general program deterioration can result.

PERSONAL GAIN A TEMPTATION

Misuse of department funds, equipment, or personnel by commissioners has caused serious problems in many state fish and wildlife agencies. Nothing is worse for destroying public confidence in the wildlife program. Scandals involving commissioners are so commonplace that few states have escaped them, and legislative or constitutional reforms often are the result of their public disclosure.

It would be easy to cite specific examples, but there is little to be gained from it. The types of activity are well known, however, and range from use of department personnel as personal hunting and fishing guides or chauffeurs, to misappropriation of hatchery fish or animals for personal use, to use of department equipment and personnel for private construction, or actual misuse of department funds for personal gain.

Every commissioner is in the public eye and must be doubly careful not to tarnish his own reputation because it reflects on the department as well. This is particularly true with respect to abiding meticulously to all hunting and fishing regulations. Even a completely legal but overdisplay of activity with rod or gun can cast suspicion on the commissioners and the department. There are always those eager to believe that a commissioner is taking advantage of his official position or is being given opportunities or assistance not available to the general public.

COMMISSION SYSTEM STILL BEST

More could be said about the pitfalls, but there is a danger of appearing negative about the commission system. In spite of many weaknesses, it is the most effective and representative form of wildlife administration.

I have been concerned, personally, about the efforts of the Council of State Governments and others to push for individual appointed commissioners of natural resource agencies as replacements for multimember boards and commissions. It appears to be a maneuver on the part of political forces to regain legislative and executive authorities that have been lost by state legislatures and governors through the commission system.

There is merit to the proposals in many states and at the national level to combine all resource agencies into a single natural resources department for better coordination and more effective administration. But, here again, I am concerned both by the political implications and the fear that fish and wildlife agencies, forestry and park departments, and others will lose both their identity and their effectiveness. Natural resource management must be above partisan politics. Great progress has been made by these agencies that are identified so directly with conservation and environmental quality. We need to evaluate very closely any move to consolidate or reorganize a system that has been so effective.

Fish and wildlife commissions vary greatly in the states, from those with little or no power other than advisory to almost completely autonomous bodies. But, the system works. Much has been written about the ideal commission but, here again, the best has been known to fail and the poorest can function well. Ideally, a commission should be balanced to be politically bipartisan if possible, and it should be relatively small; four to seven members are usually recommended. Almost universally it is felt that all commissioners should serve their states at large and not represent political or geographical districts.

Qualifications for commissioners vary greatly among states also, but in most, the individuals appointed must possess only a demonstrated interest or knowledge in wildlife affairs. The most important qualifications are integrity, interest, and an open mind. Some of the best commissioners I have known were bankers and business or professional men with little or no previous knowledge of fish and wildlife management.

In the final analysis, it is the individual that makes or breaks the commission. Any reasonably intelligent, honest individual can make a good commissioner if he is interested and will listen. But he must listen two ways—to the professionals who work for him and to the public he represents. He is the bridge between them. After weighing all evidence he must make just one decision and that decision, in each case, must be what he feels is best in the long run for the wildlife resources entrusted to his care. Nothing less will do.

SELECTED REFERENCES

Sport Fishing Institute. 1968. Fish conservation highlights, 1963-1967. Pp. 20-24. Washington, D.C.

State of Arkansas. 1970. The Arkansas Game and Fish Comm.—A review and recommendations by an independent study team. 49 pp.

Wildlife Management Institute. 1968. Organization, authority and programs of state fish and wildlife agencies. Washington, D.C.

THE ROLE OF
SOCIAL SCIENCES IN
WILDLIFE MANAGEMENT

Richard D. Teague

Just what are the relationships between social sciences and wildlife management? How can each contribute to the well-being of man and wildlife? Cain (1960) is one of the many scientists who have pondered these questions:

> Man is more complex than deer or fish. It is more difficult to make the human behavioral sciences scientific and the results predictable than it is to examine the ethology of nonhumans, but strong effort in that direction should help wildlife managers and others to diagnose their problems and approach their solutions.

> We have quite properly studied the biology of wildlife species in many aspects: life cycle . . . ecology . . . population structure and dynamics, the role of the species in its ecosystem, prey-predator relationships, pathology . . . habitat management. There is a scattering of investigations of natural resource administration agencies, of resource law and its enforcement, conservation education, etc. Economic studies have been made, especially as to unit costs, such as how much does it cost to raise a legal-sized trout? Yet the solution to many of our management problems would seem in the end to depend on the habits, behavior, and views of the consuming public. . . .

Giles has defined wildlife management, in another section of this book, as "the science and art of making decisions and taking actions to change the structure, dynamics, and interactions of habitats, wild animal populations, and people to achieve specific human goals by means of the wildlife resource." The study of man as a social animal involves consideration of the structure, problems, and history of people living together in social groups. Obviously, man apart from the rest of the living world is a perilous delusion, and wildlife management without consideration of the many vagaries of man is folly.

Over one-quarter of a century ago Shea (1948) pointed out that wildlife management has been working on the edges of the human relations problem, recognizing that the human element is always more difficult to handle than the management of wild creatures. As a social scientist, Shea indicated that methods and tools were available, or being forged, to change certain types of human behavior and social patterns. During the past two decades, we have seen how these methods and tools have been used by psychologists and sociologists in the business world to promote sales of various products. Motivational research has been an effective tool in convincing persons that they needed all sorts of commodities—many originally not wanted, not needed, or

Teague, Richard D.   Assistant Director, Wildlife Specialist, Cooperative Extension, University of California, Davis

55

even not good for them (Packard 1957). Wildlife managers and administrators, however, have not availed themselves of the full potential of the methods of the social sciences to help achieve the goals of wildlife husbandry.

Aside from isolated studies such as those of Shea (1948) and Peterle (1961), the dearth of socio-wildlife research indicates that despite early recognition of the importance of people management, this aspect has been largely overlooked since wildlife management became recognized as a profession in the early 1930s. Winston Mair (1960), in his critique of the Twenty-fifth North American Wildlife Conference, had this to say: "I am disturbed, too, at the apparent complete lack of research into the social and cultural aspects of the wildlife conservation field. We are spending significant sums of money on wildlife now and plan to spend much more in the future. . . . But there has been at this Conference no mention of research into the mores of our people, their motivation and their real needs."

SOME FACTORS OF INFLUENCE

There is much interesting speculation regarding man's behavior toward wildlife resources as influenced by religion, culture and tradition, politics, economics, and the individual's sex, age, occupation, and education. This paper will consider examples of the many possible relationships and problems dealing with people and wildlife.

Religion

The hunter, said the ancients, is not the one who will be found wanting in due reverence to the gods. The Bible records hunting as an acceptable practice. The Mosaic Law provides some of the most practical advice on wildlife management and hygiene found anywhere in the literature. Some religions prohibit the killing or eating of certain, or all, species of wildlife.

This "reverence for all life" religion is more than casually embraced by many individuals in North America. Clarke (1958) cited the example of Albert Schweitzer in his discussion of this topic. Schweitzer apparently believed that man should tear no leaf from a tree, break no flower, and take care not to crush any insect as he walked. Death, as a fundamental part of life, was apparently not recognized. On the other hand, some religions consider wildlife as "God-given" for many to enjoy. Further, man has been charged to exercise scientific wildlife husbandry and the stewardship to leave the land more alive and fruitful than he found it. The true hunter, in the words of the old European hunter's pledge, "honours the Maker in His handiwork." Both of these religious viewpoints will, in some degree, be felt by those responsible for wildlife management programs.

Culture and Tradition

In most areas of our own culture and in most primitive cultures, the "chase" is an integral part of life where true harmony between man and nature exists (Clarke 1958). For examples, the rural landscape of England, with its hedges and copses (thickets) and beautiful, managed fields, is basically a sporting landscape. Without fox hunting, the hedges would come down; without pheasant shooting, the copses would disappear. The historical waterfowl wetlands of the Central Valley of California would probably be drained and plowed for rice and safflower if it were not for the private duck hunting clubs.

Some psychologists feel that hunting and fishing have their roots in man's old and harmonious relationship with nature, for wildlife is as truly his prey as it is that of any other predator. Furthermore, the role of all predators, including man, is still vital in the harmonious functioning of the natural community. The hunter and fisherman often become the alternate of disease and starvation.

Down through history, each nation, race, or culture has acquired certain values about wildlife. How these values were formed and what it would take to change them are questions yet to be answered. A case in point is the wholesale killing of songbirds in America, before and at the turn of the century, by immigrants from Southern Europe and "by the negroes and poor whites of the South" (Hornaday 1913).

Southern Europeans have trapped, netted, and shot song and insectivorous birds for centuries for use as food. Hornaday felt the way to discourage this practice was to "prohibit the use of firearms in hunting by any naturalized alien from Southern Europe until after a 10-years' residence in America." How he determined it would take 10 years to change a tradition that "killing songbirds for food is right" is not clear. It may be speculated that the killing of songbirds by "negroes and poor whites" in the South was a matter of survival of low income groups or possibly just a handy source of recreation.

Habitat destruction, not uncontrolled hunting, was the primary reason for reduction of wildlife populations 50 to 100 years ago. Hunting was a factor, however, and as a result public indignation mounted to the boiling point in opposition to some forms of hunting. Conservation organizations, schools, churches, and other groups began promoting "preservation" of wildlife in order to change the American tradition that her wildlife resources were inexhaustible. Leading conservation organizations adopted a drastic code of ethics. One such tenet was so well "sold" that it plagues wildlife managers yet today. It reads: "The killing of a female hoofed animal, save for special preservation, is to be regarded as incompatible with the highest sportsmanship; and it should everywhere be prohibited by stringent laws" (Hornaday 1913). This code has been so deeply inculcated in the minds of many people that it has been difficult to obtain adequate, and necessary, big game harvests in many areas of North America (Longhurst 1957).

Paul Tillett's book *Doe Day* (1963) is a case history of the antlerless deer controversy in New Jersey. Many interests and factions battled for the type of deer season that they "thought good for the deer." Most of the hunters fought against killing of doe deer because they thought "saving mothers" would improve deer hunting, while farmers closed their land to hunting as a rebuttal to those who refused to kill enough deer to reduce crop damage. The irony is that adequate harvest of surplus animals, both bucks and does, would have benefited both factions.

Why is it that people do not change their attitudes when confronted with sound scientific evidence? Psychologists tell us that people are "selective readers" and often pay little attention to material that conflicts with their preconceptions. When they do read something that they disagree with, they will not remember facts contrary to their opinion. This is called "selective retention."

Even semantics play an important part in prohibiting wise wildlife programs. A case in point is associated with the deer controversy in California. Somehow through the years, the term "deer management" has acquired the meaning to many people of killing female deer. When biologists try to sell "deer management," individuals with this limited mental image of the term will not listen to biological facts—although "deer management" may properly require any number of management techniques, from closed seasons to liberal killing of both sexes of deer. University of California scientists have found that where the term "deer husbandry" is substituted, most people will listen.

Understanding what makes hunters "tick" becomes more difficult when we probe deeper. Why is it that hunters will accept doe shooting as a routine game management tool in one state and reject the idea in an adjoining one?

Or, why do many hunters who will not shoot female deer prefer killing cow elk?

Still another hunting paradox exists in some areas. Many hunters enjoy hunting both sexes of quail, grouse, doves, ducks, and geese, but reject the killing of hen pheasants. Does color have something to do with this phenomenon, or is it all right to kill a female if you do not know it is one?

The problem of polarization in people's attitudes is a social one and, in the wildlife field, the hunter is at one end and the preservationist at the other, each with his rigid attitudes that often are based to a large extent on misunderstandings or ignorance.

The Yellowstone elk herd controversy is a good example of a situation where the biological facts were clear, yet the attitudes of people for a long time prevented the implementation of recommendations based on biological findings, simply because they were opposed to "slaughter" of the elk in the National Park. Other people were opposed to killing the elk at all and were completely unwilling to recognize the limitations of carrying capacity and that the habitat was being severely damaged.

While Wendell **Swank** was director of the Arizona Game and Fish Department, he expressed the opinion that most of the letters he received objecting to hunting seasons and killing of wild animals came from women (1966). He attributed this to the fact that women, historically, were the keepers of the home. Man, on the other hand, had developed through the centuries the desire to hunt.

Clarke (1958) is convinced that the interest in hunting is established before adolescence. It would appear that opportunity to hunt and fish in early years has a profound influence on an individual's activities and preferences in these sports. It is the opinion of many wildlife authorities that we are raising a new generation of urbanites and suburbanites who do not hunt and fish and do not understand the ecological necessity of wildlife harvests by man.

Political Aspects

Political expediency is often a greater influence than biological facts when dealing with wildlife. Wildlife management is inextricably involved in and influenced by local, state, and federal politics. Conservation agency administrators and biologists that ignore this fact cannot promulgate necessary programs. Education programs designed for only portions of interested segments of the public are not adequate.

Cain (1960) cites the Michigan deer herd problem as an example. As was true in so many areas of North America, deer herds in Michigan made fantastic recovery in the 1930s and 40s until starvation, disease, and depredations of roving dogs accounted for thousands of deaths each winter. Persistent educational programs in the 1950s were so successful that by 1960 nearly two-thirds of the hunters understood the necessity and agreed to hunting does and fawns in some parts of the state. In spite of the hunters' opinions, the state legislature had apparently not been exposed to similar information on deer management and called for a "moratorium on killing mothers and babies."

At the local community level, Shea (1948) identified two groups of leaders that need to be enlisted and convinced of the worthiness of a new program before the community as a whole will accept it. These two groups are "leaders of opinion" and "action leaders." Leaders of opinion are prominent persons with reputations made, usually middle-aged or older. These are the "gate-keepers" to community acceptance, but it takes the second group, "action leaders," to get action. People in the community have learned by experience that "action leaders" are usually right in their judgment and will carry things through to a successful conclusion.

Sociologists have found that people oppose any program or idea, real or imaginary, that threatens their security. Threat to security may be financial or a threat to a traditional community leadership role. An example would be the person who for many years has led the valiant battle to "bring the local deer herds back from near extinction." This man has established himself as the deer authority in the community because the deer herds have come back, although the change in deer habitat probably was a greater influence on increased deer populations than the restrictive hunting seasons advocated by him. It would be good public relations, psychology, game management, and politics to enlist the leadership of this man in any new deer management program. Remember, it is human nature to believe peers in preference to outsiders.

Although wildlife supplies considerable numbers of man-days of recreation, it contributes an increasingly smaller proportion of the nation's recreational activity. There could possibly come a time when management of wildlife, from a recreational viewpoint only, may invoke the question, "Why have wildlife for the enjoyment of so few?" It is not wise to wait and have to take the defensive on such issues but rather generate an offensive to prevent damaging confrontations. Ammunition for this type of action will not come entirely from biological research but also from a better understanding of society itself, which may ask the questions and which can permit wildlife resources to live or die.

CONCLUSION

Most wildlife management problems start out as biological problems but eventually become people problems. Despite much publicizing and bemoaning of this early recognized fact, we have continued to stockpile scientific evidence for better wildlife management, but have failed to apply human ecology to the behavior of human organisms as they are related to wildlife work.

The wildlife professional with the most difficult job of all, that of dealing directly with people, is the conservation officer. In addition to upgrading educational requirements, including training in the social sciences, state conservation agencies would do well to budget for special social science studies as an integral part of wildlife management investigations. Universities could be enlisted and contracted to handle the social aspects of wildlife research problems.

Because we are dealing with a social science problem, we should use concepts and procedures that have been developed in the social sciences: particularly human ecology, anthropology, sociology, economics, political science, history, and social psychology. These working tools of the social scientists are at hand but gathering dust in the wildlife management workshop.

LITERATURE CITED

Cain, S. A. 1960. Wildlife management and the customer. Trans. N. Amer. Wildl. Conf. 25:472-481.

Clarke, C. H. D. 1958. Autumn thoughts of a hunter. J. Wildl. Manage. 22(4):420-427.

Hornaday, W. T. 1913. Our vanishing wildlife. New York Zoological Society, New York. 411 pp.

Longhurst, W. M. 1957. The effectiveness of hunting in controlling big-game populations in North America. Trans. N. Amer. Wildl. Conf. 22:544-569.

Mair, W. W. 1960. Natural resources and American citizenship: a critique of the 25th North American Wildlife and Natural Resources Conference. Trans. N. Amer. Wildl. Conf. 25:487-496.

Packard, V. 1957. The hidden persuaders. Pocket Books, New York. 242 pp.

Peterle, T. J. 1961. The hunter—who is he? Trans. N. Amer. Wildl. Conf. 26:254-266.

Shea, J. P. 1948. A new approach to farmer-sportsmen cooperation. Trans. N. Amer. Wildl. Conf. 13:163-169.

Swank, W. G. 1966. Our hunting heritage. Part I. Wildlife Views, Ariz. Game and Fish Dept. 13(2):8-9.

Tillett, P. 1963. Doe day: the antlerless deer controversy in New Jersey. Rutgers Univ. Press, New Brunswick, New Jersey. 126 pp.

Penny Edwards

INTRODUCTION TO ECONOMICS OF GAME AND FISH RESOURCES

Kenneth C. Nobe

Public game and fish management agencies seldom employ economists. Within recent years, however, there have been increasing opportunities for economists to assist game and fish managers indirectly in various decision-making processes. For example, economists are often asked to participate in planning meetings and training sessions. Some economists are conducting research under contract to game, fish, and park agencies. It appears that economic input is moving rapidly from the role of "window dressing" to that of an integral part of policy formulation and administration of game and fish resources, particularly as they relate to the "people management" aspects.

THE ROLE OF ECONOMICS

How can economics be brought to bear on game and fish problems? Some definitions of economic elements are needed.

Economists have been formally described as "professional social scientists who study man's behavior in producing, exchanging, and consuming material goods and services." Such a description contrasts with the usual layman's concept of an economist—a glorified accountant who juggles figures with dollar signs attached. In practice, economists have broadened their interests and competence to include consideration of a large number of non-monetary elements, particularly those related to social goods and services. A case in point is our concern about the so-called intangibles associated with wildlife resources and the quality of the environment.

Initially, we should clarify what economists have done in the past so that their specific functions can be understood. Over time, they have developed a set of principles for arriving at decisions, providing guidelines for establishing laws and other institutions, and setting policies for dealing with social problems. They have identified an institutional state of mind—the market—where, through the price mechanism, the unlimited wants of consumers are put up against the relatively limited supply of things that producers offer for sale. Economists have pointed out that, in the final analysis, the value of inputs required to provide individual consumer goods is a function of the value consumers place on the final goods and services produced. For some material goods, such as a pair of shoes or a side of beef, these principles are clearcut and sufficient. For products dependent on other resources such as wildlife, the economist's explanation of man's behavior is far less satisfactory and certainly is still incomplete.

One more definition is needed: the meaning of the term "natural resources." In an economic context, a natural resource is more than merely a

Nobe, Kenneth C.   Chairman and Professor, Department of Economics, Colorado State University, Fort Collins physical object; its use must be people-oriented. An economic resource then can be defined, as Dr. Ciriacy-Wantrup (1969) has done, as implying "people needs and know-how." Dr. Marion Clawson has said, "A natural resource is some characteristic of nature that we know how to use economically toward an end (objective) that we know how to achieve at any point in time." With these added dimensions, it becomes apparent that the values of natural resources are continuously changing. Certainly, this has been true in the case of wildlife resources.

At any given point in time, the value of a particular resource is dependent upon its relative scarcity in relation to demand. For most resources, and for final consumer products, the marketplace functions to allocate possession or control to those people who are willing to pay the highest price. Also, as prices go up, private producers are usually given added incentive to increase the supply. But are these principles followed in the case of wildlife resources? Unfortunately, the answer is no.

For the most part, wildlife is utilized to produce a type of goods or services which economists refer to as being "extra-market" in character. This simply means that the market fails to provide an effective means of auctioning off the available supply. This observation also suggests that the market usually fails completely to provide sufficient incentives for private interests to expand the supply. This is why, for the most part, society has relegated to government the role of supplier of wildlife in the same manner that we depend upon public agencies for other non-market products such as police protection, highways, schools, and wilderness areas.

Society has decided, and sanctioned by law, that wildlife resources are owned by the public at large and are to be managed by an administrative agency of government. By and large, economists focus their efforts on carrying out the management function as efficiently as possible. Historically, during the period when the supply of wildlife resources was relatively abundant compared to demands upon it by consumers, efficiency in management was focused primarily on the biological aspects of production and the physical elements of habitat. In recent years, the increasing demands upon these relatively scarce wildlife resources have forced us to turn to a greater consideration of the "people-oriented" aspects of game and fish management. No longer can we be concerned only with what is good for fish and wildlife. We must also take into full account what people want to do with these resources.

Consumer demands on wildlife resources are not only accelerating rapidly, but major internal conflicts in the desired kinds of use are evident. Depending on whom you ask, these resources should be: held on wildlife preserves and completely protected against man and his technology, exterminated whenever they interfere with other economic processes like growing crops or using a lake for motorboating, put in areas where other economic uses are prohibited and where they will be provided "free" to the public, and so on.

Economists only recently have become concerned with wildlife problems, and available economic tools are still rather crude. Conversely, in such areas as irrigation, flood control, and hydroelectric power, we have had slowly evolving systems of economic analysis that required 50 years or more to reach their present levels. Similar concern with the economic aspects of wildlife resources, particularly when viewed as elements in multipurpose water and land development projects, was practically nonexistent before World War II.

In 1962, President Kennedy signed an executive order that made the economic evaluation standards contained in Senate Document 97 (1962) binding on those federal agencies responsible for multipurpose natural resource development projects; e.g., Agriculture, Interior, Defense, and Health, Education and Welfare. But this legal requirement alone did not insure that the economist's tools were sufficiently perfected to carry out this new function. Further refinement in both procedures and policies followed. The standards presently in use were specified in a directive prepared by the Water Resources Council, "Water and Related Land Resources: Establishment of Principles and Standards for Planning" (*Federal Register*, September 1973). These rules became binding on various natural resource oriented federal agencies on October 25, 1973. Thus, while progress is being made, more work is needed because the rate of implementation of the new standards is lagging behind the need for economic evaluations of such projects.

Perhaps we can, however, identify an overall role for economics in wildlife management. For one thing, economics can serve the function of providing a framework for decisionmaking in a situation where a vast range of possible management alternatives exists. Hopefully, economists can aid wildlife managers to increase the efficiency of systems where relatively scarce natural resources are used to serve the collective and often conflicting demands of society.

The overall role of economics in fish and game management can be divided into three critical elements. These are:

1. providing a framework for understanding the various factors that affect the distribution of these resources and their relative importance in time and place

2. providing a formal approach to an evaluation of alternative management choices

3. assisting in the implementation of policy objectives.

SOME SPECIFIC ECONOMIC CONSIDERATIONS

Inevitably, any discussion of economics will turn to specifics. In this case, such comments are limited to consideration of the dual elements of supply-costs and demand-benefits.

Supply and Costs

Game and fish managers are well trained to consider the supply aspects and deal continually with the cost aspects of supply. In regard to supply, it is necessary to consider a combination of two potential sources: the public and the private sectors. Private sources of supply are given primary consideration in the eastern United States. In the western United States, however, where a high percentage of the land surface is in public domain, there is a tendency to underestimate the role of the private sector. Shooting preserves, businesses catering to fishermen, and private shooting and fishing clubs are coming on the scene in increasing numbers throughout the United States. We also see an increasing number of people that can be classified as caterers-guides, motel and cabin operators, and others who provide services to hunters and fishermen on both private and public land.

In the eastern United States, where heavy population pressures have existed longer, the role of the private sector in providing a supply of game and fish is stronger. On the other hand, rapid population growth and urban development present some minus factors. The encroachment of urban and industrial interests on ranch and farm land may tend to reduce game and fish populations. Likewise, many choice areas now available to the public are being bought up for summer homes, private fishing and hunting areas, and other purposes.

The probable increase in complexity on the supply side will make the job of game and fish management increasingly difficult. In the past, much of the cost associated with such management has been mainly in the nature of direct costs. More and more indirect cost elements will emerge as the intermixed pattern of public and private supply elements develops.

Demand and Benefits

Consideration of demand for game and fish must be done within the context of a rapidly changing picture of overall recreation demand. Until very recently when total demand began to approach total supply, society found it feasible to pay for the recreation supply base through general taxation and surtaxes on sporting goods. There is nothing wrong with this approach from the financing side, but it has led to a major misconception in the minds of many consumers. This is the idea that access to a hunting and fishing area is not only the right of all Americans but a privilege which is provided free of charge. There is no need to belabor the point that today nothing worth having is free.

Adoption of a "user-fee" approach as part of the financing arrangement for outdoor recreation has forced us to focus more clearly on a significant problem. This is the question of "who benefits?" Consider this problem in the case of wildlife resources. Historically, society has decreed that the primary beneficiaries have been hunters and fishermen, and, therefore, these user groups have had to bear a major share of public management costs.

In most cases, hunters and fishermen are primary direct beneficiaries. It must be pointed out, however, that with an increasing demand for all types of outdoor recreation, other indirect users of game and fish resources are coming on the scene in increasing numbers. These are persons having an interest in "quality" wildlife resources in the overall recreation environment. Many of this group have made a direct payment for access for the first time and now are actively seeking a voice in management of the environment— including the game and fish. Finally, there is also the valid voice of those who hold an interest without any physical presence whatsoever in the wildlife habitat areas. For example, many conservation groups and individual citizens derive pleasure from the maintenance of populations of various species, particularly those in danger of extinction, without finding it necessary to view them in the field. They get tremendous satisfaction in simply knowing the species are still there.

The Significance of Intangible Values

The three resource user groups identified above are often in conflict with one another, but all have one thing in common—they seek out certain intangible values when using wildlife resources. Indeed, the basis of conflict among them usually centers on intangible arguments.

Traditionally, the role of wildlife has been overshadowed by intangibles. For some interest groups, these resources are so often couched in a context of intangible values that the subject has taken on many aspects normally associated with myth and folklore. Therefore, managers of game and fish resources are often faced with the same kind of frustrating situation as is a highly skilled physician who is trying to treat a patient who believes strongly in home remedies and so-called folk medicine.

There is nothing mystic about a consideration of intangibles. Each day all of us make countless value decisions without conscious regard to what degree intangible values are involved. For example, when a person buys a new suit and has his hair styled prior to a job interview, does he really attempt to equate the benefits expected with the price for the overhaul job? Suppose he lucks out and gets the job. Would this somehow balance the scales or result in a favorable "benefit/cost ratio"? Who can say? In almost everything we do, both tangible and intangible considerations are involved. In our daily decisions, we seldom deliberately overshadow one with the other. Why then should we continue to do this in the case of wildlife benefits?

Managers who have had the opportunity to work with multiple-use land and water development proposals are acutely aware of how frequently differences of opinion focus on intangible values. Far too often, we hear a game and fish manager's complaint that he is at a distinct disadvantage when forced to compromise or to plan jointly with the irrigation specialist or flood damage specialist who argues primarily in economic terms. If proponents of these and other project purposes depended on intangible arguments to the same degree as recreationists, conservationists, and game and fish managers, the hope of ever reaching agreeable compromises would be diminished. For example, would it be wrong to justify an irrigation project on the basis that many people derive pleasure from making a desert "bloom"? Conversely, isn't there a sad feeling when traveling through parts of the western desert crisscrossed with unused irrigation channels because a former water supply was depleted?

Few irrigation proponents seriously use intangible values to justify their project purpose because they have developed more effective means of winning arguments. Likewise, for game and fish managers to live in the past by claiming too much in terms of intangible values of wildlife resources misplaces the emphasis when striving to gain a bigger role for these elements in public programs. The measure of tangible benefits and costs, as reflected in economic benefit/cost ratios, should stand on its own. Rapidly accelerating demands by users of game and fish resources, which are occurring in the face of greater pay-as-you-go financing, are ample evidence that some major arguments can be won on the basis of dollar data for these project purposes, too. (The problem, in a nutshell, is that distinction between tangible and intangible benefits is less important than recognition of the division of benefits that relate to market and extra-market means of satisfying consumer demand.)

In addition, however, let us face the question of intangible elements squarely whenever they occur and relate them to all interest groups involved. Aren't we really kidding ourselves when we try to justify some project purposes involving wildlife on the basis of intangible benefits accruing to those relatively few people who utilize these resources on site? Wouldn't it make more sense, say in the case of the whooping crane, to argue that this species should be preserved, not because of intangible recreation benefits, but because it represents a vanishing part of our cultural and historical heritage? The retention of this species, perhaps, as a living part of a largely bygone era has tremendous educational value and in the future may contribute much to bolstering an otherwise sagging national ego. Those who benefit from a preservation effort will, of course, include the recreationists who actively go out to see or use a wild species in a natural habitat. It will also include a vastly larger "audience" that benefits from the confines of a classroom or from the television set that is showing a Walt Disney wildlife movie. My point is to give intangible elements of game and fish their just due, but not to saddle the recreationist with the whole burden when we are fighting for a larger role for these natural resources.

CONCLUSION

We have not yet reached the point of formulating wildlife resource development proposals which begin with an analysis of human behavior and end with ideal site selection and facility installation plans. Such plans should be based on the objective of providing the greatest total benefits per taxpayer dollar spent. However, there is no reason to assume that wildlife and other outdoor recreation resources cannot be subjected to the same rigorous economic analysis in the future that is now afforded to flood control, electric power, municipal and domestic water supplies, and other resource development and management purposes. It assumes, however, that we are willing to strip away the overriding psychic and preservation considerations normally associated with wildlife resources. Game and fish managers should deal with these resources as a truly competitive element in planning for multipurpose development, use, and management. Only by reflecting all public interests can these resources be elevated to the role of full partner in the sharply competitive game of stretching scarce natural resources to fulfill rapidly expanding and competitive demands.

LITERATURE CITED

Ciriacy-Wantrup, S.V. 1969. Dollars and sense in conservation (Circ. 402, Calif. Agr. Exp. Sta., Berkeley, 1951). Reprinted, NRE-7. Dept. of Econ., Colo. State Univ., Fort Collins. 3 pp.

President's ad hoc Water Resources Council. 1962. Policies, standards, and procedures in the formulation, evaluation, and review of plans for use and development of water and related land resources. Senate Doc. No. 97. Washington, D.C. 20 pp.

Water Resources Council. "Water and Related Land Resources: Establishment of Principles and Standards for Planning," *Federal Register*, Vol. 38, No. 174, Part III. Monday, September 10, 1973, Washington, D.C.

SELECTED REFERENCES

Ashton, P. M., R. A. Wykstra and K. C. Nobe. 1973. Optimum supplies of recreation days under conditions of uncertainty: A case study application to wildlife resources, NRE-17. Dept. of Econ., Colo. State Univ., Fort Collins. 74 pp.

Chapman, D. W., K. C. Nobe, *et al.* 1973. Sports fishery economics. Final report to the National Marine Fisheries Service, Idaho Cooperative Fishery Unit, Univ. of Idaho, Moscow. 100 pp.

Gilbert, A. H. and K. C. Nobe. 1969. Annual gross hunting and fishing expenditures in Colorado, NRE-5. Dept. of Econ., Colo. State Univ., Fort Collins. 67 pp.

Lovegrove, R. E. and D. D. Rohdy. 1968. Estimated expenditures, by location, attributable to the 1967-1968 Special Goose Permit Season in North Central Colorado, NRE-2. Dept. of Econ., Colo. State Univ., Fort Collins. 8 pp.

Nobe, K. C. and A. H. Gilbert. 1970. A survey of sportsmen's expenditures for hunting and fishing in Colorado, 1968. Spec. Rep. No. 22, Colo. Div. of Game, Fish and Parks, Denver, Colorado. 83 pp.

Nobe, K. C. and H. W. Steinhoff. 1973. Values of wildlife. Wildlife and the environment, Proceedings of the Governor's Conference, Denver, Colorado, March 30-31, 1973. Info. Series No. 7, Environ. Res. Cen., Colo. State Univ., Fort Collins. 119 pp.

Radosevich, G. E. and K. C. Nobe. 1969. Use of private property for outdoor recreation: Legal rights and liabilities. Bull. 467-A. Coop. Ext. Service, Colo. State Univ., Fort Collins. 13 pp.

Ross, Lee Ann, Dwight M. Blood and K. C. Nobe. 1975. A survey of sportsmen expenditures for hunting and fishing in Colorado, 1973, NRE-20. Dept. of Econ., Colo. State Univ., Fort Collins. 64 pp.

Schaefer, R. K. and K. C. Nobe. 1969. Economic evaluation of the land acquisition program of the Colorado Div. of Game, Fish and Parks, NRE-6. Dept. of Econ., Colo. State Univ., Fort Collins. 57 pp.

PUBLIC RELATIONS AND COMMUNICATIONS

Douglas L. Gilbert

Good public relations may be defined as the successful completion of a necessary task plus the attainment of public understanding and appreciation for the effort. This results in acceptance or good will toward the agency involved and its programs. All good public relations must be founded in truth and honesty.

Public relations are not the same as information and education. The latter terms (I and E) mean that contact with the public is made either directly or through the various media. Public relations implies much more, such as program planning, research relative to the specific publics involved and their stage of adoption or rejection of ideas, and evaluation of the total effort. Public relations people also counsel management and are counseled by management. They are, or should be, part of the decisionmaking process, as public relations should be a constant effort and not a "sometimes" thing.

Communications are not synonymous with public relations. It is well to think of communications as being an important tool, but only one part of public relations.

Most natural resource managers are public employees who work for state or federal agencies. Natural resource management agencies, including fish and wildlife organizations, need good public relations as much as any other business or enterprise. Any business needs to have adequate funds, contented workers, operable rules, and satisfied customers. The natural resource agency also needs adequate budgets and qualified, motivated personnel, good laws, and satisfied, but managed, users. A major difference between these agencies and most businesses is that most of the agencies offer services or opportunities rather than goods.

Most of the problems in natural resource management are people oriented problems. This is true for problems internal to the organization (budgets, policies, laws, personnel), as well as for external issues. Anti-hunting or harvest problems and trespass or access problems are examples of external problems. The only way that problems such as these will ever be solved is through cooperation and understanding resulting from good public relations programs.

PUBLICS

A public is two or more people with a common interest. There are many publics, each different. Internal publics are those which are part of the parent organization; the external publics are not part of the organization.

Gilbert, Douglas L.   Professor and Chairman, Department of Fishery and Wildlife Biology, Colorado State University, Fort Collins

Internal publics of wildlife agencies include field officers, researchers, administrators, and office workers, among others. It is easy to see that these groups are all different, with varying viewpoints. Each contains sub-publics. For example, researchers would be divided into fish, bird, and mammal researchers. A further division of mammal researchers might be into big game, small game, and non-game researchers. Again, each of these publics is different, with different viewpoints, leaders, and goals.

External publics of natural resource agencies are many, including harvesters, outdoor recreationists, community, schools, youth groups, landowners, and many others. Each has a different, but common, interest.

A cardinal rule of good public relations is that the internal publics must accept programs first. How can a program possibly succeed if those within the organization talk against it? It is good to give all employees a voice in making a decision or setting a policy; however, once set, a unified front is necessary, and employees should not publicly oppose it.

Media (radio, TV, newspaper) personnel constitute a special, external public. They are important because of their role in making messages attractive and available to other publics. The media have rules of operation such as time restraints, style, quality, and other regulations. Natural resource agency personnel must know and abide by these rules.

Commissions or advisory boards are a special internal public. They are especially important because of their policy setting responsibilities. Special efforts should be made to communicate with them so that they understand issues and programs. Complete clarity in presenting information to the commission members is mandatory.

Legislators should probably be considered as an internal public. They have responsibilities for budgets and laws that govern an agency operation. It is easy to see that honesty, clarity, and complete understanding again are important. Communications with legislators should be constant, not just when the legislature is in session.

TECHNIQUES

There are many techniques or tools used in public relations programs that the PR person should know and perhaps use. One of these is *empathy*. In a controversial issue, if a person will look at the issue from the viewpoint of the opponents, a common area of understanding may be achieved. This affords a point from which to start further discussions toward solving the problem.

Research should be done to seek out *leaders* of the publics. Each public has leaders; some are formal (elected, appointed, etc.), while others are informal. The public relations practitioner should develop rapport with these leaders. If the leaders understand and are convinced, they can aid in working with their followers or constituents.

Additional research could show the attitude toward possible *adoption* or *rejection* of an idea held by the particular public involved. It is much harder to change a strong belief or opinion held by an individual than it would be to change an incorrect opinion at the early interest stage.

Emotion is a very powerful force in "selling" an idea or convincing people. Natural resource management professionals are prone to use statistics, reams of data, and "the facts." These are important and should be available; but a little emotion associated with dollars, beauty, sorrow, hate, or fear, can make a big difference in successfully promoting a venture.

Publicity is often used and can be positive or negative, good or bad, favorable or unfavorable. It simply is a means of attracting attention. I and E personnel usually take care of agency publicity.

Propaganda is a powerful tool used in influencing people. It can be thought of as a "willing and conscious effort to influence others." Not all propaganda is bad, despite the fact it has an evil or dishonest connotation. For example, it is often difficult to separate propaganda and education. When one side of an issue is stressed, that is propaganda. We are propagandized every day and should recognize it. When we take a group to a drained duck marsh and use that as an example (when all the other marshes may not be quite so dry) we are propagandizing. Again, all good public relations efforts must be founded in truth and honesty.

Natural resource agencies should *act* instead of reacting. It is better to discuss a controversial issue before it happens and try to achieve understanding, than to wait until it is in operation or completed and try to explain it. Relative to an issue, the side that takes the offense early usually wins. Natural resource agencies are too often on the defense.

PUBLIC INVOLVEMENT

"Public involvement" is a phrase presently used by many natural resource agencies. Interest in public involvement has increased due to a tremendous increase in concern for natural resources as reflected in recent federal legislation. Public hearings and presentations are common. This approach has widely been used by the U.S. Forest Service in their "I and I" (Inform and Involve) programs. The Colorado Division of Wildlife used public involvement and subsequent meetings to attempt to "sell" a drastic, proposed change in big game regulations.

A public meeting is not necessarily public involvement. To truly have public involvement, it is necessary to know and to understand the involved publics. The agency should provide leadership by forming advisory groups, task forces, study sessions, etc. These should contain representatives of the interested public. Goals should be set for each group, and personnel of each group should understand the inherent responsibilities and limitations of the agency. The agency should provide all needed data to the groups. Agency personnel also should give professional evaluations of the alternatives as they are usually the best informed on the situation.

Small groups work more efficiently than large ones. The reports of small groups can then be coordinated into a single report. This should give the most popular, and the best, solution to the problem. In many issues, the proposed solution from the advisor groups will somewhat resemble that desired by the agency and may also contain some valuable innovations.

The agency decision then should be made. Hopefully, it will be similar to that advocated by the advisor groups. A public meeting now should be held and should be open to all interested people. Advisor group personnel may be allies and often will support agency proposals, and the meeting should go well.

Public involvement should not be just an occasional, issue-oriented effort. Agency personnel should make continuing contacts with the various publics and/or their leaders so that they understand the agency's programs, policies, and goals.

COMMUNICATIONS

The ability to communicate easily and effectively sets human beings apart from lower animals. More than anything else, this ability is responsible for the leadership position assumed by man in the world. He writes and speaks. He communicates with words, images, and actions.

True communications require *understanding*. Only when an idea is transmitted from one person to another, without a change in meaning, have communications taken place. An interchange of ideas, questions, and answers (called the "two-way" approach) facilitates establishment of the desired understanding.

Thus, communications are more than mere contact. People usually don't have to listen, to read, or to watch. Thoughts may be far away although the people are physically present. It is necessary to gain attention and to retain it during the process if good communications are to be established and if understanding is to be achieved. To this end, it is helpful to involve as many senses as possible during communications. Participation and active involvement should be used.

The essentials for good communications may be diagrammed as follows:

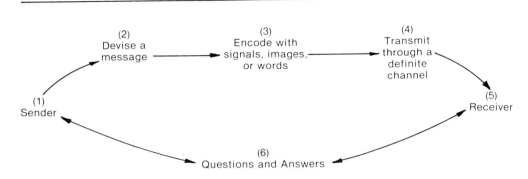

With the two-way approach, the person on the receiving end becomes the sender, and the first sender becomes the receiver. If any link is missing in the process, communications do not happen. Rumors may result; knowledge is not transferred; there is frustration; and understanding does not take place.

Newspapers, magazines, signs, pamphlets, and other written materials all involve the *written word*. Only the sense of sight is involved, and effort is necessary to make the message interesting. Illustrations and use of color can help. The message must be attractive, brief, clear, and direct. It should be kept simple. Too often the professional tends to use "jargon," or terms which are familiar to him but not to his audience. Under such circumstances, the audience understandably becomes "snowed-under" and disenchanted.

The *spoken word* is one of the most popular and frequently used methods of communication. A face-to-face approach, with questions and answers, can be extremely effective and is often the best method where critical issues are involved. Radio is a mass medium which uses only the spoken word. Huge audiences can be reached, but questions cannot be directly asked and answered. Only the sense of hearing is involved, and the involvement frequently is passive while another task is being performed, such as driving a car.

Images include pictures, displays, and exhibits. Images usually are used as an aid and in conjunction with other forms of communication. For example, a slide show, TV program, or motion picture without sound or text might leave much to be desired.

A person also can communicate with *actions*. A gesture, a touch, an expression, a handshake—all can send a message without a word being spoken. Communications may even be achieved when they are not desired. The failure to act or react also can result in a message being sent and received.

These tools of communications (spoken words, written words, images, and actions) should be used in combination to involve the persons receiving the message as much as possible, to stimulate them to use a variety of senses, and to clarify the message. Other senses such as touch, smell, and taste may also be used to increase the likelihood of achieving understanding.

Barriers to communications are many and are always present. Research should be done ahead of the actual communications effort on characteristics of the audience and their state of readiness to receive the message. This research should point out problems and help the sender select the most appropriate method of communication.

There may be social barriers between sender and audience. Among these are political incompatibility, differences in age, money, and status. A difference in level of intelligence or education can be a barrier between the audience and the communicator. The message should neither be too simple nor too complicated. No audience likes to struggle to understand, nor will they do so. If the message is too simple, the audience will feel insulted; if it is too complicated, they will be "turned off."

Speed of the message also can create a barrier. If presented too rapidly, the audience will be lost; if presented too slowly, any challenge is gone, and the attention of those receiving the message also may be lost.

Vocabulary should be adapted to the audience. It must be appropriate to their educational level, but also should be adjusted to specific group experiences of the audience or to overcome stereotypes they may already have formed. For example, the word "conservation" can mean anything from preservation to exploitation, depending on the individual's background and experience. Words also can "wear out," and their real meaning may be lost.

Another important barrier to consider is the illusion that the message has been received. The sender leaves one point and goes on to the next while the audience still is struggling with the first idea.

Physical barriers are not as important as they once were. Virtually everyone has access to radio, television, newspapers, and magazines. Travel has become easier and more common. The communicator can usually find some way to deliver the message. The receiver can have access to the message if the desire to do so is present.

Another problem is the lack of desire to communicate. A person *must* *want* to communicate, or he cannot. An unwilling effort will communicate indifference to the audience. A haphazard, token effort cannot possibly succeed, regardless of the method used. Unfortunately, this is often the result when some agency personnel are "ordered" to give presentations at public meetings.

People naturally resist change. This is especially true of the uneducated. It is human nature to be against what is new or not understood.

Communications constitute a tool of public relations. Good communications will result in understanding, acceptance, motivation, or permission and facilities to proceed. Poor communications will result in adverse reaction, or nothing.

VISUAL AIDS

Natural resource personnel can usually increase their communication effectiveness by using good visual aids. Visual aids are exactly that, "an aid, through visual perception, to any effort of communications." Visual aids are used to increase the possibility of a message being understood and accepted. Visual aids cannot replace good writing or speaking; they are in addition to, not instead of.

Reasons for Using Visual Aids

Visual aids, be they pictures, models, slides, or whatever, employ the use of additional senses or allow actual participation and involvement on the part of the individual.

Visual aids provide other values as they create and retain interest. The average person needs to be attracted. We must have an audience, readers or viewers, to work with. For example, slide shows and motion pictures are more attractive to the average person than a straight lecture. Or a picture story will attract and be read by more people than straight prose. After initial interest, attentiveness needs to be maintained. Clarity and ease of explanation are also aided with good visuals. Closely allied to clarity is the advantage of retention of ideas by the audience. A good chart, cartoon, or photo will be remembered long after the words are forgotten.

A final reason for using visual aids is that they are an excellent outline for the speaker to follow during a presentation. If the slides are in proper sequence or charts in logical order, the oral presentation also will be in proper arrangement.

Types of Visual Aids

Normally, the *actual object* being discussed is the best visual aid to use. However, there are many times when the actual object isn't suitable. It may be too big, such as a watershed, or a forest, or an elk trap. Or, it may be too small, such as an insect or a parasite.

Models can be used to increase or decrease size and to show working parts. A model of a bee can be made large enough so every one within a reasonable distance can see. The watershed can be shown in the form of a papier-mache or styrofoam model. Models can be constructed so segments can be removed, and they also can be animated.

Active graphics are visual aids, such as flannel boards or "hook and loop" boards, where the visual is built up or put together as the talk progresses. Other examples are the chalk board, bar graphs with movable bars, and news pads, where the material is uncovered as the presentation progresses. The use of color and caricatures makes active graphics more effective.

Projected images (slides, motion pictures, opaque projection, and overhead projection) are probably the most popular visual aids used by professionals in natural resources management. Color, sound, and size can all be controlled. Like other visual aids, however, they should be an aid to the presentation and should be of high quality. A motion picture should never be just "shown." There always should be an opportunity for questions and answers at the end, and the film should be properly introduced. Slide shows can be good or bad, depending upon the quality of materials, care involved, and the ability of the speaker. A preview should be routine; there is no excuse for upside-down slides or those out of sequence. The overhead projector is especially good for small audiences in lighted rooms and the speaker can face the audience.

Static graphics are usually the least effective visual aids. These are the maps, charts, graphs, or photos that have no movable parts. They should be simple, colorful, and of appropriate size.

Of course, visual aids can effectively be used in combination. For example, an overhead projector often is used with several overlays in combination with an active graphic. There is no reason why more than one type of visual aid can't be used in a single presentation.

Guidelines

A person should have an important message or something worth saying. Objectives should be definite and well in mind. This is the first step.

Second, it is well to outline the message with the most important points as main headings. The outline also will serve to organize the presentation in a logical sequence.

The last step is to select the aid which will best visualize important points. Many times the actual selection will depend on budgets, time, materials available, and abilities of people involved.

It is well to remember that a person should not use visual aids just to be using them. Too many can clutter. They should serve a purpose and always be of good quality.

Size of material is important. Why show something if it can't be seen? It should be kept simple, yet be colorful and appealing. Pictures, cartoons, and color all help if used correctly.

Generally, there should not be more than six or seven words per line or six or seven lines per visual. Letters should have balance; in other words, be heavy enough but not too heavy, and of one style. The width of letters should be approximately ¼ their height. For a chart or graph, letters ¼-inch high can be easily seen at a distance of 8 feet; ½-inch high at 16 feet; 1 inch at 32 feet; 1½ inches at 48 feet; and 2 inches at 64 feet; line spacing should be about one and one-half as much as the height of the letters. Projected graphics must be designed so that the screen image is large enough to be seen (Fisher 1976). For making slides or overheads from a standard 8½ x 11-inch sheet of paper, letters should be at least ¼ inch high.

Colors can add to, or subtract from, any visual aid. Light colors make things appear wider and larger. Dark colors give the object the appearance of being smaller and narrower. Generally, the smaller the visual aid, the brighter the colors should be. Usually, two to three colors are enough for one visual aid. Black denotes formality, richness, or strength. Green gives the feeling of freshness or youth, while orange is a gay, warm color. Blue is cool and gives a melancholy feeling to most people. Red is the color to use for anger, hate, love, or heat. Yellow denotes ripeness, lightness, or warmth. White is the color to use when depicting purity, cleanliness, or neatness.

Backgrounds are important. Gray or some other low-contrast color is excellent for most work and especially necessary for visual aids to be used on television. Greater contrast may give the best effect in an average exhibit or presentation. Green on white and red on white are good examples.

Selecting the Visual Aid

Which visual aid should be used? This depends upon the subject being discussed, the time and the budget available, the quality of materials on hand, and the ability of the person making the presentation.

If suitable, the best visual is the actual object. A set of deer jaws that can be closely examined is the best way to learn how to age deer. One jaw, however, would not be large enough for a group to see. Instead, it may be wise to use a model, slides, or a graphic type of visual aid. A forest can't be brought into the room, but good visual aids can be used to show characteristics of a forest.

Cartoons and caricatures make a visual aid more interesting, understandable, and attractive. (Courtesy of Cooperative Extension Service, University of California)

So much for the strengths and weaknesses. What sort of material should be presented as a publication and how should conservation agencies use this medium?

TYPES OF PUBLICATIONS

There are several types of publications that can be delineated for clarity. Publications take many forms and serve many purposes. Here are some of them:

Annual Report—primarily a fiscal report on the agency, but has general public relations or promotional functions

Book—in general, "a work of substance," which is bound

Booklet—a smaller book, used to "persuade, demonstrate, or educate"; may be bound in many ways and in a variety of sizes

Manual—an informative handbook, reference, or guide

Brochure or Pamphlet—may be a booklet, but usually a minor effort with fewer pages

Poster—a single sheet, printed on one side, to be posted in a public place

Bulletin—one of a sequence of factual reports, issued at irregular intervals, when new information is available; may be a single leaf, folder, or booklet in format

Circular—a single leaf, folder, or booklet of few pages to announce any event, activity, product, or service

Handbill or Flyer—a single leaf, printed on one side, for distribution by hand

House Organ—a periodical, to promote the interests of an enterprise, usually "internal" to employees or "external" to the public, or both; helps to implement the philosophies and policies of the organization

Magazine—a periodical, published at scheduled intervals to present and implement the philosophies and policies of the organization, but aimed primarily at "external" publics

News Release—message that appears in someone else's publication

There are other types of published materials, but those outlined above are the ones most commonly used by conservation agencies.

Examples of typical publications might be the fish and game regulations (booklet); management data for field men (manual); and "how to . . ." publications (circular or pamphlet). Most states publish an annual report (book or booklet), and 42 states publish some type of periodical or magazine.

The Missouri Department of Conservation, which has one of the largest publication programs, currently has in print some 350 different titles of brochures, books, booklets, leaflets, and manuals, both for use by employees and for distribution to the public.

Agencies work out their distribution procedures in a variety of ways, but some suggestions may be helpful. A listing of publications should be available to interested groups at every opportunity. Teachers' meetings, sportsmen's clubs, and the various youth organizations are obvious targets. Publications lists make handy giveaways at fairs and sports shows, saving costs by not giving away the publications themselves in such situations, but letting the public know they are available. Publications lists also should be tailored to specific publics. For example, there may be one list for educators and a different list for the general public.

Another way to distribute publications is through the organization's personnel, especially field men. In fact, some publications are designed for specific programs and personnel involved in such programs are the best outlet.

In general, all published material falls under two headings: those dealing with information that the organization wants to get into the hands of the public to further its own policies and programs; and second, those things that may be indirectly related to programs and policies, but not of immediate concern or the agency's legal responsibility.

A game and fish department may make available free those publications that it feels further its own programs. A modest charge can be made to recover expenses on those items that are outside its responsibility. As an example, a booklet on wildlife identification is the department's concern, and it is provided free of charge. A booklet on wild game cookery, on the other hand, may be considered outside its management interests, but nevertheless related. A modest charge would be made for the cookbook. In these days of rising costs and inadequate budgets, a charge to cover publication expenses might be justified on all but minor publications.

PUBLICATION PRIORITIES

The monthly magazine, provided that it has adequate distribution, is the best single public relations tools a conservation agency can have. A magazine is the best way to repeatedly sell conservation and the department's point of view. There is no substitute for continued exposure over a long period of time to get a message across.

Next in importance are those publications that must be published to expedite the program, like regulations booklets. From then on, circumstances and priorities should dictate what should be published. Subjects that need elucidation by the department, or those that bring the most inquiries from the public are obvious choices for publications. Most of these need not be elaborate or expensive to produce, but should be attractive to give the reader a good opinion of the department. They should be as brief as possible and still get the message across.

PUBLICATION PRODUCTION

Probably the most expensive publication, and one that involves the most effort, is the organization's magazine. In order to vie for attention and compete with the myriad of other things that occupy a person's time, magazines must be attractive, well designed, and crisply written. This takes professional competency, which is not to say that other publications do not.

The question is often asked whether or not to charge for a magazine. It all depends on the point of view. An argument against charging is that those willing to pay probably are not the ones who need to read the conservation message. In any event, if a charge is made, the product must be competitive with other types of reading matter for which the subscriber pays. This can often mean a subtle pressure to deal with matters other than of immediate interest to the agency. Nevertheless, about one-half the states publishing magazines do charge for them.

A magazine can have only one editor. He should be skilled in his field and should have authority within organizational policy to exercise his judgment and talents. A magazine should have a consistent editorial slant. A committee cannot put out a good magazine. It takes the guiding hand of one competent man.

The cost of printing and mailing publications can be money well spent. Personnel used to produce publications should be professionally competent and imaginative. They should have been trained for their jobs and should be sent to refresher courses occasionally to keep abreast of new techniques.

A department's publishing program cannot be expected to work miracles. It must be viewed as a long-range program to enlist public support. It is an educational program, and education is a long-term and continuous process.

Dissemination of information to the public is an essential component in a good conservation program. Publications are one of the media available, and a good one.

SELECTED REFERENCES

Darrow, R. W., D. J. Forrestal, and A. O. Cookman. 1967. Public relations handbook. The Dartnell Corp., Chicago. 944 pp.

Gilbert, Douglas L. 1971. Natural resources and public relations. The Wildl. Soc., Washington, D.C. 320 pp.

ENVIRONMENTAL POLLUTION— EFFECTS ON FISH AND WILDLIFE MANAGEMENT

Dean E. Arnold

Environmental pollution, and public concerns about it, have had a strong impact on fish and wildlife management. This impact may be separated into two categories: that affecting animals and plants directly and that affecting primarily those scientists and managers who work with the animals and plants.

Pollution may affect animals directly by killing them, by interfering with their food source, by making their necessary habitat untenable, or in more subtle ways such as interfering with the reproductive system. Plants are seldom thought of as "wildlife," but most fish and wildlife managers are deeply involved with them since they furnish food, cover, or both for nearly every animal. Plants, too, suffer from pollution in many ways.

PEOPLE—THE BASIS OF POLLUTION

People, of course, are the primary factor in pollution. As our population continues to grow and becomes more affluent, our total output of waste products increases at greater rates. In addition, we continue to invent, and eventually discharge into our environment, new products and by-products whose effects are poorly understood. Seldom have our efforts to understand and control pollutants kept up with our ability to produce them. Meanwhile, people are rapidly becoming a pollutant themselves. To the average person, the big cities may be the prime example of this, but although the numbers involved are smaller, the effect may be greater in the "great outdoors." Each year there is more crowding in parks, on lakes, and in all the other areas where we traditionally have gone to get away from each other. When this crowding becomes even a little obvious, serious problems for the resources can occur. Furthermore, the more of us there are, the more difficult it is for each person (especially the outdoorsman) to escape and/or ignore pollution and its effects.

A wildlife-related example of these problems is the bear situation in Glacier and Yellowstone National Parks. For years, the illegal, but popular, feeding of black bears has presented problems to managers in Yellowstone and elsewhere, but these problems have mostly been ones of keeping traffic moving and applying minor first aid. Another type of "feeding," the dumping of garbage near campsites and then observing the bears that feed on the dump, was very popular in many areas until the practice led indirectly to several deaths and injuries. These incidents led to a continuing reevaluation of the relationships between parks, visitors, and bears. Although one faction favors strong control measures against "problem" bears, another strong point of view is that more control of bears will lead to their extinction, and that

Arnold, Dean E. Assistant Unit Leader, Pennsylvania Cooperative Fishery Unit, Pennsylvania State University, University Park

parks are in a sense a tool for preservation. Both sides agree that as population pressures (and thus visitor numbers) increase, the number of bear-visitor contacts will increase, and with it the number of serious problems.

SEWAGE

Turning to more "conventional" forms of pollution, we can look first at the one most people think of when the subject is brought up—sewage. Sewage is strange stuff. It is hard to define, since its composition varies from day to day and from source to source. To certain organisms, it is not harmful and in fact is highly beneficial. Its adverse affects, except in the now rare case of waterborne diseases, are indirect. One of these is the consumption of dissolved oxygen from water as organic matter breaks down. Most aquatic animals require dissolved oxygen levels above four to five parts per million. Heavy sewage pollution can easily cause levels to drop below this range, either through decomposition or through the respiration of heavy plant growths that are fertilized by the nutrients in the sewage. If such growths die from natural causes or due to man's efforts to control them, they, too, decompose and use up dissolved oxygen.

We do, fortunately, know how to control oxygen and plant growth problems, although sometimes only at great expense and effort. A problem of this type was largely solved at one fish hatchery in a simple way. This hatchery had heavy weed growths in its supply pond that caused dissolved oxygen (which is produced by plants in light) to be high during the day but critically low at night. By placing lights over the pond and leaving them on all night, the plants were made to produce enough oxygen to balance their own respiration, and the fluctuations were eliminated. Under certain conditions, the nutrients may not promote weeds but rather the tiny, single-celled or filamentous plants called algae. These may produce the same effects on dissolved oxygen, the same clogging of waterways as weeds, and may create other problems as well. They often give the water a "pea-soup" appearance or form large, smelly, and ugly floating mats. The forms most often favored by pollution are the blue-green algae. Not only do these produce some of the worst scums and smells, but recent research has shown that they are often toxic to many types of animals. These algae can affect fish populations through depletion of their food supply, and wildlife that drink from waters containing blue-greens may be sickened or killed.

Runoff water from farm lands, common everywhere, usually contains heavy nutrient concentrations originating from animal wastes or excessive and careless use of fertilizer. This drainage usually produces the same effects as municipal, "domestic" sewage.

EROSION

Runoff often produces another type of pollution in the form of silt and mud. These change the aquatic habitat by filling in ponds and reservoirs. Most sport fish are eliminated, but the habitat may be more suitable for muskrats, waterfowl, or other species. Silt in lesser quantities often interferes with fish reproduction by smothering eggs or filling the spaces in gravel beds, which are essential for successful spawning. In some cases this has necessitated heavy stocking to support fishing in otherwise good habitats. A similar effect is sometimes produced by pulp mill and ore concentrating plant wastes that settle on the bottom, smothering either fish eggs or fish food organisms.

An interesting if rather unusual effect of silt on wildlife populations is seen in the case of the Aswan High Dam in Egypt. For centuries the Nile has been moving silt and associated nutrients into the Mediterranean Sea and, in flood time, depositing them on the fertile plains along its course. Since the closing of the dam, this supply of nutrients has been cut off, as the silt now settles in the reservoir and flooding no longer occurs. This has resulted in both serious harm to agriculture on the plains and a collapse of the important fish populations that formerly existed off the mouth of the river and whose food organisms were dependent on the nutrients carried out during floods.

PESTICIDES

One of the most active areas of pollution research has involved the effect of pesticides, especially the long lasting ones such as DDT (now severely restricted). Often the effects of such pesticides are expressed in reproductive failure of some sort. In the case of eagles, ospreys, and other birds of prey, research indicates that the primary cause of reproductive failure is interference in eggshell formation, causing the shells to break prematurely. Since many pesticides concentrate in fat, and the yolk sac of young fish is high in fat, many fish are killed when they absorb the yolk soon after hatching.

As in the case of birds, it is the "top predators" in the aquatic food chain, such as salmon and lake trout, which most often show the effects of pesticide poisoning or are prevented from sale by government regulations on pesticide content. This is because of the process of "reconcentration" in the food chain, a serious problem with radioisotopes, other harmful pollutants such as mercury and zinc, and pesticides.

Reconcentration occurs because an organism at any level in the food chain eats a great many of the organisms in the next lower level. If the food organisms contain a substance that is not readily eliminated, it will accumulate in the consumer (Fig. 1). Since such pollutants commonly accumulate in certain areas of an organism (Fig. 2), a temporary solution may be to permit the use of only those parts that are low in accumulation. An example from fisheries management is the stocking of Coho salmon, which was widely proclaimed to be the salvation of the Great Lakes fisheries. This generated a huge sport fishery and associated economic boom in western Michigan. Just as the situation was becoming really phenomenal, the state and federal regulatory agencies began seizing shipments of commercially canned Coho because their DDT content was above legal limits. Although DDT contamination has decreased, and sport fishing continues, a definite damper has been put on the entire program. More recently, concern has shifted to PCB industrial products now present in excessive levels in the Coho. In addition to the interference with food value, the pollutants may become a serious barrier to expanding hatchery production of these fish, due to the reproductive problems mentioned earlier.

THERMAL POLLUTION

Another problem, often in the news and now a subject of considerable research, is thermal pollution, usually consisting of the discharge of cooling water from steam-powered electric generating stations. Probably the most likely effect of heated discharges is an increase in biological production in the local surrounding area. This may take the form of "blooms" of weeds or of blue-green and green algae, which are already a problem in many waters. Certain species of fish, mostly the less desirable ones, may be attracted by the warmer water and the increased food supply it promotes.

There is some question about the effect on animal and plant life passing through the cooling system. Even if most of the organisms in the huge volume of water passing through are killed, the nutrients in their bodies will be released and may support increased production, which could more than replace their numbers. It is possible that certain species may be killed and others not, which could produce changes in the local aquatic community. Even for organisms not passing through the system, the locally higher temperatures may cause a selective process to occur, changing the dominant species. This could take the form of direct action through unsuitable temperatures or could act indirectly through interference with growth, behavior, laying

FOOD CHAIN

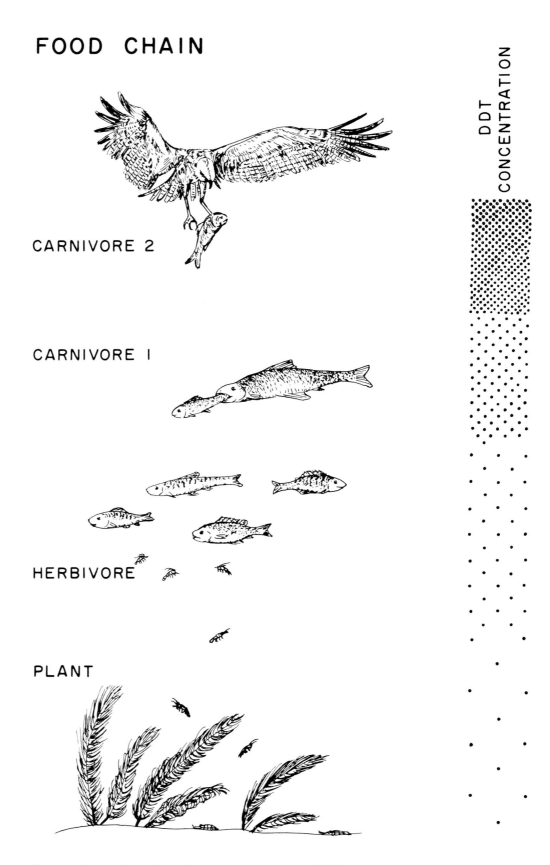

CARNIVORE 2

CARNIVORE I

HERBIVORE

PLANT

DDT CONCENTRATION

Fig. 1. Aquatic food chain, showing concentration of DDT residues in successive levels. The "top predator" (carnivore 2, the osprey) accumulates the highest concentration. (Adapted by permission from *Environment*, Volume 11, Number 6, July-August 1969.)

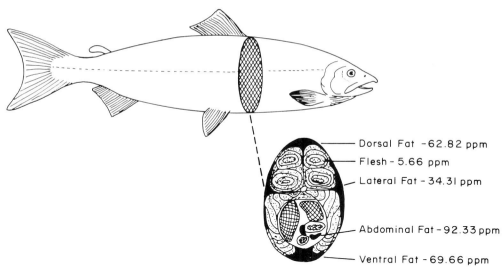

Fig. 2.   Average DDT concentrations in portions of 10 adult coho salmon from Lake Michigan in October 1968, just before their spawning run (when most are caught). The highest values are found in the areas that are high in fat content. The average value for the DDT complex (DDT + DDE + DDD) in whole eviscerated salmon steaks was 14.89 ppm. The average value for the DDT complex in the whole fish was 12.21 ppm (parts per million). (Adapted by permission from *Limnos*. Volume 2, Number 3, Fall 1969.)

or development of eggs, lowered dissolved oxygen levels (warm water holds less dissolved gas than cold), or increased activity of natural or artificial toxins. In general, we can conclude that no desirable effects of heated discharges are likely; that undesirable effects may be produced directly; and that even if this does not happen, undesirable processes already underway may be accelerated.

In an effort to mitigate the effects of thermal discharges, many power plants are now being provided with enormous cooling towers. In addition to their "visual pollution" impact, there is speculation that these towers may have effects on local terrestrial wildlife by producing clouds and fogs. Another "side effect" of power plants and other sources of smoke is the "acid rain phenomenon," by which sulfates, nitrates, and other compounds discharged to the air react with moisture to form acids. These acids can have severe effects on plants and on natural waters when they fall as rain.

Reservoirs, too, may produce "heated" or "cooled" discharges, depending on whether the discharge is from the top or bottom of the dam. Either of these may constitute "thermal pollution" if they are very different from normal temperatures in the stream. Specialized fisheries have been developed in these tailwater situations, but they are dependent on the discharge being maintained continuously, which often is not possible.

There are many other forms of pollution which are, or should be, the subject of immediate research. Some of these are spectacular, like oil spills; others are less obvious, like radiation and most forms of air pollution. The latter types usually affect the environment through long-term degradation so that it gradually becomes unsuitable for the native species. Less frequently, they cause long-term effects on the health, behavior, or reproduction of organisms.

A CASE STUDY

It is rarely the case that only one form of environmental pollution acts on a given aquatic or terrestrial habitat. Usually all or many of the types mentioned above act together in a complex way, producing effects more serious than might be predicted from studies of the individual pollutants.

A case study that has received nationwide attention is the so-called "death" of Lake Erie. This term, of course, is an exaggeration. "Death" in an ecological sense is not a loss, but a change in the biological community occupying a given space. When an organism "dies" in the conventional sense, it and its space are taken over by other communities. This is the process now occurring in Lake Erie. The old Lake Erie may be "dead," but in its place is another which is, in fact, teeming with life. Our problem is that we prefer the old version but have not developed sufficient desire to stop doing the things that caused its loss. From the standpoint of fish and wildlife management, the Lake Erie story is complicated by the results of a long history of underregulation and overexploitation. However, we cannot separate this from the effects of pollution. As H. A. Regier (1966) has pointed out, the more limiting the Lake Erie environment becomes, the more easily overfishing can occur.

For years, the results of pollution of Lake Erie showed up only in the fishery. Seldom, if ever, was it necessary to close bathing beaches or carry out unusual procedures in water treatment plants. This was because the primary pollutant was silt from developing farmlands and homesites. The primary effect of this material was to interfere with the growth of plants, both rooted and floating (phytoplankton). The rooted plants served two functions: provided spawning ground for many species of fish and retarded the flow of silty water at the stream mouths. This caused the silt to settle to the bottom before reaching the main lake. As these plants disappeared, the smothering and shading out of bottom organisms spread, and fish dependent on them decreased in numbers and distribution.

As time went on, the character of the pollution entering Lake Erie changed. Silt loads were still high, and farmers began to use fertilizer to maintain yields from the now-depleted soil. Together with increasing amounts of domestic sewage, the runoff from these fields provided a much greater supply of nutrients to the lake. Not only did this result in increased plant production, chiefly in the form of algae blooms, but it also caused a change of plankton species to forms more tolerant of high-nutrient conditions. This change tended to shift the species composition of the fish community as well, since the previously dominant fish were not able to efficiently utilize the newly dominant plankton. In combination with the poorly regulated fishery, this probably led to the disappearance of such species of the cisco, whitefish, and sauger and allowed the increase of alewives, yellow perch, and other "less desirable" species.

The increased biological production resulting from these nutrients, and the additional organic matter entering from the cities, then began to build up the organic deposits on the bottom, particularly in the western basin. Eventually the oxygen demand increased to the point that a prolonged calm in September 1953 allowed complete oxygen loss in the western basin, wiping out the existing bottom animals, mostly mayfly naiads. Oxygen loss has now become regular in the deeper areas of the central basin and occurs periodically in the western basin. The present fish populations are usually able to move out of low oxygen areas, but their food organisms have been greatly affected. Thick growths of attached algae now appear on the submerged rock reefs that are the main spawning area for walleye, the last of the "high value" fish species. These growths could seriously interfere with egg development.

Industrial wastes, although contributing to the general decline of the Lake Erie environment for some time, have recently had direct impacts on fish and wildlife. In March 1970, Ontario banned commercial fishing in the Lake St. Clair area due to high levels of industrial mercury wastes found in fish. Alerted, Michigan and Ohio followed with fishing bans on the U.S. side of St.

Clair and then in western Lake Erie, into which St. Clair flows. Although action has been taken to eliminate the sources of this pollution, and the bans have been partly relaxed, it may be years before it reaches suitably low levels in the ecosystem. It is a safe assumption that other pollutants, equally as dangerous as mercury, are acting in similar ways but have not yet been studied. The future of fishery management in Lake Erie is thus in some doubt.

Terrestrial case studies are more difficult to document, largely because fewer suitable studies have been done. But investigations of DDT effects on predatory birds, and other pollution discoveries, leave little doubt that other, equally serious effects on wildlife management exist.

POLLUTION AND MANAGEMENT

As mentioned earlier, there is a second group of the effects of pollution—those on the management process itself. In the few years since the first edition of this book was published, the National Environmental Policy Act has appeared and has had tremendous impact on the activities of fish and wildlife managers. Much time is now being spent on the creation and review of "Environmental Impact Statements." These may vary from a few to thousands of pages, and are required to be written for nearly every action by, or with aid or permission from, a government agency. Most such statements

85

deal not only with pollution but with construction of new facilities, with new or old activities, or even with the effect of doing nothing. The statement process has not only provided new work for old biologists and managers but hundreds of new jobs in the fish and wildlife field.

Another effect of pollution is that, because of pollution concerns, many products formerly used for fish and wildlife management, such as disease control chemicals, have become unavailable. One of our greatest challenges is to find new ways to carry out our traditional mandate of managing, producing, and protecting fish and wildlife without becoming polluters ourselves.

TIME TO ACT

Man, of course, is in a sense another member of the wildlife community, and often the one most susceptible to pollutants. It is only recently that we have begun to realize this and to do away with what Barry Commoner has called "The Myth of Omnipotence." It is time for wildlife research to shift away from identifying the effects and causes of pollution damage and to begin studying the ways of ending it. Without such efforts, we can no longer continue to live with our fellow organisms on earth. As Paul Ehrlich wrote: "It is the top of the ninth inning. Man, always a threat at the plate, has been hitting nature hard. It is important to remember, however, that *nature bats last.*"

LITERATURE CITED

Regier, H. A. 1966. A perspective on research on the dynamics of fish populations in the Great Lakes. Prog. Fish-Culturist. 28(1):3-18.

SELECTED REFERENCES

Ehrlich, P. R. 1968. The population bomb. Ballantine Books, New York. 224 pp.

Environment (periodical). Published by the Helen Dwight Reid Educational Foundation, 4000 Albemarle St., N.W., Washington, D.C. 20016.

Heer, J. E. and D. J. Hagerty. 1977. Environmental assessments and statements. Van Nostrand-Reinhold Co., New York. 367 pp.

Hynes, H. B. N. 1960. The biology of polluted waters. Liverpool University Press. 202 pp.

Miller, G. T. 1975. Living in the environment—concepts, problems, and alternatives. Wadsworth Publishing Co., Belmont, Calif. 593 pp.

Wagner, R. H. 1978. Environment and man. 3rd Edition. W. W. Norton and Co., New York. 591 pp.

WILDLIFE
MANAGEMENT

88

Penny Edwards

PRINCIPLES OF
WILDLIFE MANAGEMENT

George V. Burger

Wildlife management has been variously defined. To paraphrase two such definitions (Leopold 1933, Giles 1969), wildlife management is a blending of science and art, aimed at achieving sound human goals for wildlife resources by working with habitats, wildlife populations, and people.

The "science" basically stems from the relatively new discipline of ecology, embodying principles fundamental to understanding and applying the "art" aspects of management.

ECOLOGICAL BACKGROUND

Estimates are that well over one million different living species of plants and animals share this planet with man. Individuals of each species are not scattered about the earth evenly or at random, but rather exist in units or *populations*. Further, each species population typically is grouped with other populations of animals and plants in assemblages called "natural communities," which may be as small as that within a decaying fallen tree or as large as a hardwood forest, of which the fallen tree is but a minute component.

The geographical location, limits, and structure of these communities are determined by the environment, which is the total of all physical and biological factors acting upon the community, from weather, soils, and topography to complex interrelationships between the plants and animals themselves. As a result of evolutionary processes, and through such mechanisms as competition, each species population within a natural community has become fitted to a particular *niche* in relation to both physical and biological factors of that community's environment.

Sounds simple? It is not. Many physical factors influencing the environment change constantly. Temperature, light, wind, and humidity, for example, vary not just from season to season and with long-term climatic changes, but often from minute to minute in any specific location. Species unable to adapt to such change, much less to complex shifting relationships with other species, are destined to vanish from the community.

An ecological principle fundamental to wildlife management is the soil-plant-animal relationship. Through the process of photosynthesis, green plants capture sunlight energy, which—bound with water and soil nutrients absorbed by root systems—is converted to plant tissues. Herbivorous animals, from cardinals to cottontails, incapable of utilizing sunlight energy directly, obtain energy and tissue-building materials from the plants they eat. Carnivores,

Burger, George V.   General Manager, Max McGraw Wildlife Foundation,
    Dundee, Illinois

while not directly consuming plant tissue, are ultimately dependent on the plants that feed their prey.

Since the soil supplies the basic nutrients that pass from plants to animals, the distribution, quantity, and quality of vegetation and, eventually, of wildlife, on a given area depend to a large extent on soil type and fertility. The wildlife manager thus must be vitally concerned with soil erosion problems and with techniques to retain and enhance soil fertility.

The food-energy relationship is the basis of many of the threads that bind different species populations into the fabric of the natural community. In a midwestern farm woodlot, for example, the fertile soil sustains a white oak, whose acorns feed a fox squirrel, who in turn provides a meal for a red-tailed hawk. Such simple *food chains* are but parts of major *food webs*, with myriad ramifications. Insects feeding on leaves of the oak may be trapped by a spider, who falls victim to a toad before the toad is consumed by a snake; the snake in turn is prey for the same red-tail.

Looked at another way, food-energy relationships tell us something about predators and prey. In the long haul, predators depend on prey species small enough to kill and eat, yet large (or numerous) enough to replace more energy than was expended in their capture. Hence the *pyramid of numbers* concept, which depicts a natural community as having a broad base of many small organisms (sustained by plants and, ultimately, by the fertility of the soil), supporting progressively smaller numbers of larger animals, up to a few major predators at the top. It is important to understand that such food pyramids function from the base upward; in normal communities the quantity and quality of food provided by each "layer" determines the number of animals in the next. Thus, the abundance of prey normally determines the number of predators, *not* the reverse.

These are very simple examples of extremely complex relationships. Additional complexity comes with the recognition that the diet of many animals can and does change with age or season, thus shifting the position of that species within the food chain, web, or pyramid. The wood duck that fed primarily on insects as a duckling is basically a mast-eater as an adult; the ring-necked pheasant wintering on waste grain likewise began life on an insect diet.

A number of animals are adapted to feeding on a rather restricted variety of plants. Crossbills, for instance, have bills constructed for extracting seeds from certain conifers. Their range is therefore restricted to areas where these trees grow. Deer, on the other hand, eat a number of different plants. But even here there are limitations; California blacktails seem to do best where a particular buckbrush species is abundant.

Plants also furnish wildlife with cover for nesting, protection from weather, and shelter from predation. And the amount and distribution of such plant cover—especially for nesting—can determine the presence or absence, and relative abundance, of the many animals that are quite selective in their cover requirements. Consequently, animal distribution, in a section or a broad region, is tied closely to plant distribution, and the successful wildlife manager must be concerned with the manipulation of vegetation much of the time.

The manager may often take advantage of, or be frustrated by, an additional factor of complexity in natural communities. The vegetation he works with is frequently unstable over time. Where vegetation has been disturbed by nature or man, as is the case in most areas in modern times, the process of *plant succession* is underway. A typical midwestern farm field, if abandoned, will, for a period of two to three years, be overgrown with annual weeds. These will eventually give way to perennial forbs and grasses and finally will be invaded by such sun-loving, hardy shrubs and trees as honeysuckle, sumac, Siberian elm, and box elder. Later, slower-growing, longer-lived trees, such as oaks, maples, or basswood, may dominate the old field as a mature forest. The rate of change, the number of stages, and the specific plant characters in this sequential drama vary from area to area, dependent upon climate, soils, and other factors.

The wildlife manager must be aware of plant succession. The close, direct dependence of wildlife on plants for specific food and cover means that animal succession accompanies plant succession. The abandoned field whose weeds and grasses are a mecca for cottontails, certain native sparrows, and quail or pheasants early in the game is home to squirrels and woodpeckers many years later. Thus, depending upon the species toward which management is directed, the manager must understand plant succession, and decide how and whether—via management techniques—he should set back, speed up, or attempt to retard succession's "clock."

Relationships between animal species likewise help determine animal distribution. The association of burrowing owls, rattlesnakes, and black-footed ferrets with prairie dog colonies is one case in point. Animals also can cause major alterations in the environment. The reintroduction, protection, and subsequent dramatic increase in beaver is a modern example. When beaver dam a stream, fish and aquatic insect populations change as water flow, temperature, and chemistry are altered. Flooded upland plants die out and are replaced by emergent aquatics and species that can withstand "wet feet," and waterfowl and wading birds appear.

We have looked at a highly simplified picture of some of the extremely complex factors—soil, weather, plant-to-plant, plant-to-animal, and animal-to-animal relationships—that are part of the environment of living natural communities and that determine wildlife distribution and abundance. In this picture, some broader ecological principles are apparent. First is the sheer complexity of community relationships. Second, and a corollary of this complexity, is the fact that a major change in one or more plant or animal species in a community potentially can impact all species, in a shock wave effect. That impact need not be immediately apparent to be long-range and drastic.

Finally, it should be clear that the environment (physical *and* organic) in any one area is constantly changing or subject to change. The play of sunlight on the floor of a woodlot, a woodchuck excavating a burrow, the devastation of a forest by tornadic winds or a budworm outbreak, or a fire in grasslands can alter species populations or whole communities. The "balance of nature" we hear mentioned so often exists at best as constant fluctuation around a changing mean, with a variety of weights and measures.

Thus the extreme "preservationist," who advocates keeping wildlife populations or plant-animal communities "just as they are," lacks a grasp of the dynamic processes inherent in nature and espouses a doomed cause. The management he decries, in reality offers the best chance to maintain, to at least some degree, the status quo he seeks, particularly as regards plant succession.

WILDLIFE POPULATIONS

Since wildlife management normally deals with populations, rather than individual animals, a brief outline of population dynamics—covered in detail elsewhere in this publication—is essential to an understanding of management principles. In our review of ecological fundamentals, we learned that animal species are adapted to niches within natural communities, whose metes and bounds are set in turn by the physical and biological ingredients of their environment. Management at times may be able to modify or create suitable environmental niches to enable introduction or range expansion of wildlife species into new "ground." But more frequently, management efforts aim at increasing numbers of one or more species in areas where such species already exist.

Thus the question of what controls wildlife population size is vital. Leopold (1933) clearly elucidated the interplay between environmental factors and the forces of reproduction and mortality that determine wildlife numbers. First is the *breeding potential*—the maximum reproductive capacity, characteristic of and often unique to each species, and determined by such factors as minimum and maximum breeding age, number of young per brood or litter, and number of clutches or litters per year.

Since we are not inundated by robins or ruffed grouse, forces obviously are at work countering achievement of the breeding potential for each species. Such reproductive factors include sex ratios and mating habits. In monogamous Canada geese, surplus adult males or females beyond a 1:1 sex ratio essentially will be nonproductive. In polygamous wild turkeys and ring-necked pheasants, there are a number of surplus males, which creates the basis for the management practice of spring gobbler and cocks-only hunting seasons.

Weather can affect achievement of breeding potential. Desert quail may not breed at all when there is no rainfall to trigger growth of new, green vegetation. And prairie-nesting ducks may not establish nests when the pothole country is dry.

Diet is a key reproductive factor. Doe deer on prime range with abundant, high-quality food often produce twin fawns and may breed as yearlings. On ranges where available food is scant or of low quality, due to overpopulation, basic soil fertility, or other reasons, yearlings rarely produce young, older does may be barren, and those that do reproduce usually bear but one fawn. While deer present a classic, well-documented instance, food quality and quantity are key determiners of the degree to which wildlife populations—herbivores or carnivores—will reach breeding potential.

Despite the impact of these forces on reproduction, most wildlife species (at least in a reasonably healthy natural community) still are capable of producing enough young to overwhelm their habitats if it were not for what Leopold termed *decimating factors*. Predation is perhaps the most visible decimating factor, but starvation, disease, and parasitic infestations take their toll, either directly or, more often, by interacting with one another or by rendering animals more vulnerable to predation.

The breeding potential of a wildlife species is comparable to a strong flat spring, whose innate tendency is to fly upward. The reproductive and decimating factors act to hold down this spring, cutting down production of new individuals, and eliminating a number of those that are produced. Where the balance is struck between production and mortality is the key to whether a given species population, in any given area, will increase, hold its own, or dwindle. This balance, and these population trends, are crucial to the wildlife manager and are usually the focal point for his management techniques.

WILDLIFE MANAGEMENT PRINCIPLES

Habitat Factors

The stability, increase, or decline of a wildlife species population depends basically on the extent to which the habitat of its range supplies the needs of that species. Those needs are not simple, viewed from the standpoint of the complexities of natural communities.

An adequate food supply is one obvious essential. It must be of the proper kind and available in sufficient quantity at each season and stage of the animal's life cycle. Food quality also is critical; food must be adequate nutritionally to maintain life and reproductive success. Water is important, available as open water, dewdrops, or in succulent plant parts, depending on the needs and adaptations of the animal species.

"Cover," another essential, is such an all-embracing term as to be deceiving and sometimes underrated. Adequate cover at the site where eggs are laid or litters born is important to successful production, and the requirements of most species are quite specific, from tree cavities of certain dimensions for wood ducks and tree squirrels to forbs and grasses of proper density and height for ground-nesting birds. Cover also includes shelter from weather and from predators and varies from adequate roosting trees for wild turkeys to soils suitable for burrowing for woodchucks.

In addition to adequate food, water, and cover—all of the proper type, in the right place at the right time—most wildlife species require certain special habitat ingredients if they are to prosper. These requirements range from a suitable source of grit for many birds to adequate hibernation sites for black bear to "booming" sites for prairie grouse.

It is not enough that a given region supply all these necessities. The spatial relationship of food, water, cover, and special requirements to one another often spells the difference between a healthy and a declining population. Pheasants that must travel long distances over open ground between food and shelter in winter are much more vulnerable to losses from predation and severe weather than are ring-necks where cover adjoins food supplies. The location of key habitat ingredients relative to each other is termed *interspersion*, or edge effect, and is a major principle in wildlife management. The principle is acknowledged, if not fully understood, by most outdoorsmen, from the bow hunter who takes his stand at a woods' border to the bird-watcher who seeks clearings in the forest.

The importance of interspersion is well demonstrated by the impact on wildlife of the growth of crop monocultures. On agricultural land, the old "family farm," with an orchard, pasture, woodlot, and relatively small, fenced fields in a variety of crops, provided a number of cover types and habitat "edges." When this landscape was replaced by modern agriculture's huge, unfenced corn or soybean fields, cover not only was lost but so was variety *and* edge, and farm wildlife populations declined dramatically. A similar effect occurs when a mixed native forest, in various stages of plant succession, and with openings, dead trees, and other variety- and edge-producing elements, is replaced by a single-age, single-species tree farm stand.

As a general rule, then, management should seek to establish a variety of vegetation types, well interspersed with water and those other habitat elements essential to the target species or group of species. Food, water, cover, special needs, and their interspersion are the factors that normally determine where a wildlife species' breeding potential "spring" will be balanced by mortality. This level, for a given land unit, is termed the *carrying capacity* of that land for the species in question. When, as is normal, more animals are produced than food, water, cover, or other key habitat ingredients can accommodate, predation, starvation, disease, and other decimating factors whittle away at this *annual surplus* of individuals. The key fact is that habitat is what determines how many individuals are "surplus," *not* predation or other decimating factors, which are simply nature's tools for removing the surplus in order to maintain the health of the species population and the community of which it is a part. Modern man is an exception; his firearms and technology make him a decimating factor capable of reducing wildlife populations below habitat carrying capacity, even to extinction.

As with all things in nature, carrying capacity is rarely constant for long periods. It can and does change with advancing stages of plant succession, weather and climate, modifications of man's use of the land, and other factors impacting the environment.

Despite its dynamic nature, carrying capacity, for a given species on a given area, normally is determined by the quality and/or quantity of one essential habitat ingredient. In the case of wood ducks, for example, that ingredient may be the number of suitable nesting cavities; for Kirtland's warblers, the availability of jack pines in the proper growth stage; for ring-necked pheasants, the timing of hay mowing. Other essential habitat ingredients may exist in abundance, but the overall population level of the species—the carrying capacity of its range—will be determined by that essential, the *critical limiting factor*, in least supply. Obviously, much of wildlife management hinges on determining and attempting to resolve the effect of critical limiting factors upon specific animal populations.

Basis of Management Techniques

Methods for managing wildlife are discussed in detail elsewhere; we will simply look at how and to what degree these techniques are based on the principles reviewed. Of all the major management approaches, *habitat management* has the best "fit" with underlying ecological factors, population dynamics, and the principle of carrying capacity. Obviously, without suitable habitat, there would be no wildlife. Further, since viable wildlife populations result from an adequate amount and quality of food, cover, and other requirements, properly interspersed, the provision, maintenance, or improvement of these habitat ingredients is essential to the health of those populations.

Artificial propagation and introductions of exotic species enjoyed temporary popularity as a management technique in the 1930s and in more recent times in some cases. The premise that stocking hand-reared wildlife into habitat already occupied by the same species would result in significant, sustained population increases—a major thrust of earlier efforts—does not jibe with current knowledge. Added to existing populations already at carrying capacity, stocked individuals are simply expensive surplus, quickly removed by predation and other decimating factors.

The introduction of exotic species, with some exceptions (notably the ring-necked pheasant), likewise runs counter to basic principles. In undisturbed natural communities, all "niches" are full. *If* a suitable niche should exist for an introduced exotic, the newcomer must be able to out-compete the native species occupying that niche. Even if successful, the result is simply a trade-off of a native for an exotic, with the latter quite likely to be less desirable.

When natural communities are severely disturbed—as were those in North America by man—they are much more subject to invasion by exotics. Checks and balances are disrupted, some old niches destroyed, and new ones created. Introduced into such chaos at the right time (accidentally, more often than not), exotics may be highly successful, fortunately in the case of the pheasant, hardly so with the starling, house sparrow, and many Old World weeds and insects.

Modern management has a place for artificial propagation, stocking, and even introduction of exotics, but on a much more limited basis than in the past and with suitable safeguards. Restoration of rare and endangered native species, stocking wild-trapped turkeys into new or restored range, expanding the range of desirable waterfowl and other species into former or new man-made habitats, and stocking hand-reared game birds on public and private hunting grounds for increased recreational opportunities are cases in point.

Relatively recent times have seen the emergence of hunting-harvest *regulations* as a major thrust of wildlife management. As growing recreational demands were made on a stable or diminishing resource, the setting of seasons, bag limits, and the like developed, for a number of game species, from "guesstimates" aimed primarily at preventing overharvest to scientifically based efforts utilizing all possible surplus individuals. Operating on the principles of species' breeding potentials and the carrying capacities of habitats (plus the variation in carrying capacity from year to year), regulations are based on inspections of existing habitat conditions, predictions of trends in habitat, and surveys of populations and reproductive success. Sophisticated tools used include telemetry, satellite photography, and computer systems.

Arctic-nesting geese provide a classic example of how regulations can be employed to manage for population growth. Restricting bag limits and seasons on several major population units of both Canada and snow geese has resulted in dramatic increases. Locating the breeding and wintering grounds helped to establish that carrying capacity on these grounds was not being reached and laid the basis for predicting nesting success and fall flight numbers. Success of restrictive regulations in this case rested on the principle that man (the one decimating factor capable of reducing populations below carrying capacity for sustained periods) had, through hunting, held these geese to levels below those their breeding habitat could sustain. Further, the creation and active management of refuges and the availability of waste grain from modern farming methods resulted in increased carrying capacity on wintering grounds.

The technique has little glamour; results are rarely immediate or dramatic and are often difficult to document. As one result, management on the land has come to lack the appeal of some other, better-spotlighted facets of wildlife work. However, effective habitat management calls for a thorough knowledge and application of the full range of both the "science" and "art" of wildlife conservation. A good manager must understand all the complexities of natural community relationships, plant succession, and population dynamics, plus the requirements of target species, and the carrying capacity and limiting factors of his area for those species. He must then be able to apply his tools—from fire to mower—to manipulate plant succession, improve inter-spersion, and carry out numerous other applications of his art and science to restore, maintain, or improve the land for wildlife. An expert habitat manager is a virtuoso, and his work (and the principles and methods he develops) is a mainstay of wildlife conservation.

Once applied to all manner of game species, the use of *refuges* as a management technique has been demonstrated over time to be less than effective in many instances. For example, once modern regulations protected resident small-game populations from overharvest, refuges for these species no longer made scientific sense. The idea that small, protected, "seed stock" areas would generate major population surpluses to overflow into surrounding lands in significant numbers is inconsistent with what we know of population dynamics and carrying capacity. Applied to big game, the refuge-protection concept often led to overpopulation and consequent range destruction, still with little "spillover" effect. Today, refuges are used primarily to protect vital habitat for waterfowl for nesting, along migration routes, and on wintering grounds and to preserve areas critical to the survival of endangered species. Even the idea of refuges as sacrosanct "preservation" sites has changed. Habitat management often is employed extensively, and many waterfowl refuges are open, at least in part, to regulated hunting.

Predator control, as a means of increasing numbers of prey species, does not fit with our knowledge of the pyramid of numbers and other principles pointing to the regulation of predator populations by the amount of available prey, rather than the reverse. By and large, when predators are removed or reduced, starvation, disease, and other decimating factors compensate by eliminating, in time, any temporary surplus of prey. Consequently, predator control is usually an unproductive and often expensive technique. Recent studies indicate that nesting success of upland-nesting ducks and pheasants can be improved locally by intensive control of nest predators, which at first glance would seem to refute the principles of predator-prey relationships. However, drainage, grazing, intensive cultivation, and other human activities have greatly restricted the habitat available to upland nesting wildlife in many regions. Crowded into strips and blocks of remaining cover, these species are highly vulnerable to nest predators, who are essentially removing clutches and nesting hens that exceed the capacity of the habitat to provide suitable cover in amounts adequate for good nest distribution. Predator control in such circumstances may offer temporary respite at one stage of the prey's life cycle, but it is hard to imagine any sustained, major growth in the species populations concerned unless suitable nesting habitat is substantially increased.

The spectacular success of management by regulations in the case of Arctic-nesting geese should not blind us to the fact that such opportunities are highly limited. Habitat, not regulations, produces wildlife; most modern wildlife populations are at the carrying capacity of their habitats and are thus incapable of responding significantly to limitations on hunting.

Hunting

Sport hunting is a major factor in wildlife management. The compatibility of hunting with the conservation of game species is based on the principle that the breeding potential of animals produces a surplus of individuals above carrying capacity. This "annual surplus," doomed in any event, can be removed by hunting, as a substitute for other decimating factors. The overall validity of the principle is borne out by the fact that no United States species has become extinct or endangered in modern times by sport hunting. In this context, with the knowledge of the effectiveness of man as a decimating factor, the importance of carefully prepared and adequately based hunting regulations is underscored.

In today's disturbed natural communities, sport hunting is a useful management tool, in addition to furnishing recreation and supplying the major funding source for wildlife management programs. Where natural predators no longer exist in kind or number to serve as a decimating factor for big game, starvation and disease eventually operate, but normally not before major habitat destruction by the overabundant game species. Hunting, having the immediacy of predation, here becomes a key tool for reducing game species to carrying capacity before habitat is destroyed.

The "People Factor"

Although wildlife management is aimed at achieving human goals, the human element largely was ignored until recent years. Early management efforts were directed almost entirely at game species. Yet even here there is little evidence that the hunter constituents were polled or queried as to their wishes; by and large, professional wildlifers and agencies set their own goals for game populations, with at least the implication of "we know best."

The rapid increase in numbers of bird-watchers and other "nonconsumptive users" of wildlife and the growing power of their organizations, combined more recently with the highly vocal resurgence of an antihunting movement, led to recognition of the layman's needs and "goals" vis-a-vis wildlife. As a consequence, the past few years have seen numerous sociological and demographic studies of hunters, antihunters, nonhunters, bird-watchers, and other segments of the public. This effort on the part of professional wildlifers and their agencies is as commendable as it is overdue. But, while it is important to understand varied public goals for wildlife, extreme care must be exercised to avoid a blind rush to fulfill these expectations. "Human goals" must be soundly based on ecological principles; where there is conflict, wildlife management's first and most critical duty is to the well being of the wildlife resource.

Growing urbanization and increased concern with socioeconomic problems is resulting in an increasing proportion of the American public who know little (and could hardly care less) about wildlife. Wildlife conservationists need to recognize this problem and to lend strong support to educational, "urban wildlife," and other programs and policies aimed at its resolution.

SUMMARY

Wildlife management is based on the application of scientific principles to the art of manipulating land, vegetation, and animal populations to achieve certain goals set by man. Fundamental principles include interactions within natural communities of living organisms, plant and animal succession, wildlife population dynamics, and such concepts as carrying capacity and critical limiting factors that aid in understanding the relationships between habitat and population levels.

Techniques of management art, from habitat manipulation to stocking hand-reared wildlife, normally have been successful only to the degree to which they are based on and conform to these principles. Habitat management is the fundamental technique, the only one capable of making sustained increases in wildlife populations. Regulated sport hunting is both a useful management tool and a recreation source compatible with wildlife conservation because it is consistent with principles of population dynamics.

Detailed examination of the human element as it applies to management goals is both useful and overdue. In attempting to fulfill public expectations and human goals for wildlife resources, however, management must remember that its first duty is the welfare of that resource.

LITERATURE CITED

Giles, R. H. (ed.). 1969. Wildlife management techniques. The Wildl. Soc., Washington, D.C. 263 pp.

Leopold, A. 1933. Game management. Charles Scribner's Sons, New York. 481 pp.

SELECTED REFERENCES

Allen, D. L. 1962. Our wildlife legacy. Funk and Wagnalls Co., New York. 422 pp.

Black, J. D. 1954. Biological conservation. The Blakiston Co., Inc., New York. 328 pp.

Burger, G. V. 1973. Practical wildlife management. Winchester Press, New York. 218 pp.

Dasmann, R. F. 1964. Wildlife biology. John Wiley & Sons, Inc., New York. 231 pp.

Gabrielson, I. N. 1951. Wildlife management. The Macmillan Co., New York. 274 pp.

POPULATION DYNAMICS

Richard D. Taber and Kenneth J. Raedeke

WHAT IS A POPULATION?

A population is the number of some species living in a particular area. Yet it is not easy to define because the area a population occupies is not always the same, the total number of individuals changes frequently, and the age and sex composition is constantly shifting. It is dynamic.

In order to understand the ways in which populations change, it is necessary to investigate causes and processes. Once these are known, it becomes possible to predict and manipulate. Reliable information on population dynamics, therefore, is central to all efforts to conserve, manage, and control wild animals. Such knowledge provides both guidelines for accomplishing the desired management objective and yardsticks for assessing the effects of management strategy.

This is the sort of knowledge that permits us to gauge what the optimum harvest rate of a game population may be, where our efforts to control a pest situation should be applied, and why some plausible conservation measures do not work. While a complete understanding of both causes and processes of the dynamics of every population of every species would be most desirable, in real life, we must work with less, often much less. By first developing a model of how a typical population acts, we can often draw valuable inferences from the less-than-total information we obtain about particular populations.

It is almost a truism that each population consists of only one species. While we might refer loosely to "populations of aquatic animals," we can scarcely analyze the productivity, say, of the muskrats, coots, and alligators of the Great Dismal Swamp, without making three populations out of them at the start.

We refer to the continental hunting season population of mallards, or the population of mallards wintering in the Pacific Flyway or the breeding population of mallards in Yellowstone National Park. The same bird could belong in all three. Yet, for management purposes, these are three distinct populations that should not be confused with one another. Many arguments could be avoided if people were more careful about defining populations.

ELEMENTS OF POPULATION DYNAMICS

Some elements we have to work with are: population size or density per unit area, age and sex structure, productivity, and the three things which

Taber, Richard D.   Professor of Forest Resources, University of Washington, Seattle

Raedeke, Kenneth J.   Research Associate, Wildlife Sciences Group, University of Washington, Seattle

combine to control these—reproduction, movement, and mortality.

A model of a population can be used to illustrate the various important processes at work. Every habitat sets limits on the total population it can support, by virtue of its capability to provide food, shelter, nesting places, drinking water, or the other essentials for that animal species. For some species, the limiting factor is space between one individual and another. So, we may think of a given habitat as a box of definite dimensions (which probably change seasonally). Within this box, the population lives. Through reproduction, it tends to become more crowded; but since the box always has a definite capacity, every addition over that capacity means that there is a corresponding death or departure from the box (mortality or movement).

In the spring, where seasons are regular, the box becomes large with the start of the growing season. The young are brought forth in this expanded box. Then, as the box shrinks with the coming of winter, the losses occur.

Movement outside the box is often the same as mortality, since only if the individual—usually the young individual—is lucky, will he find suitable habitat not already occupied.

To manage this situation, we can remove individuals from the box and reduce the amount of natural mortality or movement. This is called hunting harvest.

THE CARRYING CAPACITY CONCEPT

The finite capacity of the box in the example above can be thought of as the "carrying capacity" of the habitat (the box). It might be briefly defined as the number of individuals of a population that can be supported (i.e., "carried") in a given habitat for a period of time. Dasmann (1964) discusses carrying capacity as follows: "Assuming that a species can find the necessary combination of climate, substrate, and vegetation to permit it to occupy an area, the numbers which can then be supported in that area are determined by the amount and distribution of food, shelter, and water in relation to the mobility of the animal. A flying bird can use an area in which these elements are widely separated; a small, ground-dwelling mammal would need to find all of its requirements in a small space. None of these general requirements is simple in itself. Each species requires a particular kind and combination of food. Food in the broad sense, grass, shrubs, or trees, is not enough. The kind, distribution, quantity, and quality are all important, and the needs of an animal will vary with the seasons."

The carrying capacity of an area is influenced by many factors that cause a change in the habitat, such as the progression of the seasons through the year, land use practices, plant succession, weather patterns, and even the number and type of other animals present in the habitat. As a result of these changes, the population levels rise or fall accordingly.

Where there are seasons of marked environmental adversity, such as cold snowy winters or hot dry summers, the carrying capacity will drop accordingly during the unfavorable season. Then as the favorable season is reached again, the carrying capacity rises. Ordinarily, wild animals are quite closely attuned to this annual fluctuation of carrying capacity, bringing forth their young close to the beginning of the season of high carrying capacity. As the habitat-box grows, in other words, the population expands through reproduction and growth to keep it full.

The following graph (Fig. 1) shows actual season population levels for black-tailed deer on both good and poor ranges. In each case, the population is higher in the spring-summer and lower in the winter, but the average population level on good range is much higher than that on poor range.

Carrying capacity may fluctuate around some general level, rising above it in some years and dropping below it in others. This is the usual case where the habitat elements stay much the same from year to year while the

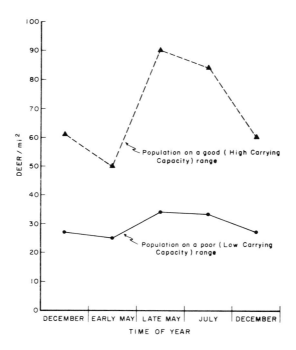

Fig. 1. A comparison of two populations of black-tailed deer; one on good and one on poor range. Seasonal population fluctuations are linked to seasonal changes in carrying capacity (after Taber and Dasmann 1957).

seasonal climate varies. But where key habitat elements change from year to year, carrying capacity reflects their trend.

Short-term changes in important habitat elements can be caused by such periodic events as flooding, drought, and fire. Black-tailed deer populations rise in response to an abundance of nutritious food, such as chaparral sprouts following burning, and quickly decline as forage quality declines (Fig. 2). Long-term changes in important habitat elements, and through them carrying

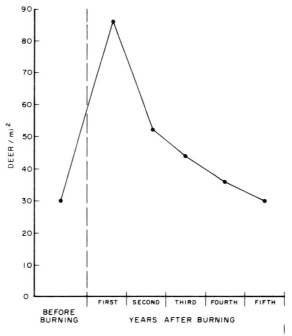

Fig. 2. Black-tailed deer population responds quickly following fire and the increase of good forage. The subsequent deer population decline is the result of the decline in quality of forage (from Taber and Dasmann 1957).

100

capacity, are frequently caused by plant succession and by changes in land-use. A deer population increased rapidly in the west coast Douglas-fir forest following logging (Fig. 3). This was due to the rapid increase in the abundance of nutritious forage. Also shown are two possible subsequent population levels: (1) a rapid decline due to quick reestablishment of the forest and shading of the forage plants, and (2) a continued high due to delayed forest re-establishment which permits continued production of nutritious forage. Such disturbances as logging and burning usually impose a cyclic pattern of population increase and decline, following the vegetational change cycle. Land use changes, in contrast, are often more permanent and, indeed, cumulative. For example, the tendency in agricultural regions is toward larger fields and fewer waste areas, with consequently less and less wildlife cover.

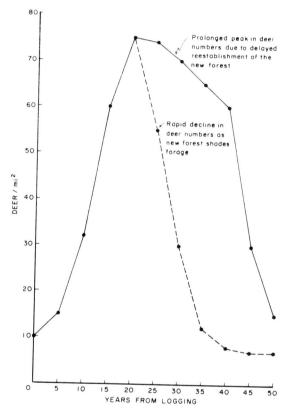

Fig. 3. Black-tailed deer populations may vary regarding their decline after reaching peak numbers. This is due to the rate of reforestation and the rapidity with which the new forest, once established, shades out the forage plants (after Brown 1961).

In the Lake States during the forties, higher corn prices led to more land draining, which reduced winter cover and pheasant populations, and which finally led to a 50 percent decline in pheasant harvest (McCabe, et al. 1956).

On a smaller scale, we can see what happened on a neglected farm (Fig. 4) with brushy abandoned fields, when it was gradually put back into agricultural production. Four species of birds (prairie warbler, white-eyed vireo, yellow-breasted chat, and catbird) that required brush for nesting declined in numbers as the brushy fields were cleared.

The introduction of a new animal species into the habitat box can affect the carrying capacity of the habitat for some members of the original fauna. A common example is the grazing of livestock in wildlife habitat. Often, live-stock compete with native herbivores for food; a current example is the uncontrolled increase of burros in the southwestern deserts, which has

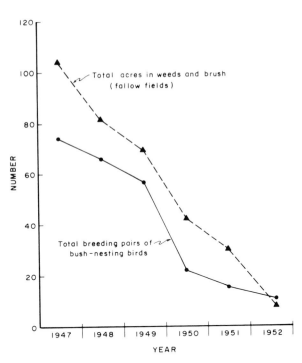

Fig. 4. As an abandoned, brushy, Maryland farm was again brought under cultivation, the carrying capacity for four species of brush-nesting birds (prairie warbler, white-eyed vireo, catbird, and yellow-breasted chat) was progressively reduced (data from Warbach 1958).

reduced carrying capacity for bighorn sheep. On the other hand, when live-stock can be controlled and biological processes are understood, grazing can actually increase wildlife carrying capacity. For example, Anderson and Scherzinger (1974) used moderate spring cattle grazing on elk winter range to cause regrowth and curing of grasses so that winter elk forage was improved.

Some wildlife species can influence the carrying capacity of their own habitat. Beavers flood out trees and encourage willows, which are beaver food; young ospreys use nests constructed by the preceding generations. Conversely, herbivores can continue to eat and increase until the plants on which they depend are weakened and decline in productivity; such a population has reduced its own carrying capacity.

Finally, it is possible that an uncontrolled population can exceed the long-term carrying capacity of the habitat and actually reduce the carrying capacity. It is common for ungulates, when unharvested, and with other natural controls removed, to build up large populations and to overgraze the habitat. Once the habitat has been overgrazed, the carrying capacity is reduced, and the population must decline. It may even decline to numbers well below those before the population increased. When the habitat has been damaged, its recovery is often quite slow, and the wildlife populations will also recover slowly.

These various examples illustrate a single point, that the size of the habitat-box (the level of carrying capacity) varies even on one site due to both long- and short-term changes, and that population levels rise or fall accordingly.

Thinking along these lines, we begin to see that box sizes for desirable species are shrinking right along. Every time that a pothole is drained, the blue-winged teal box shrinks a little; every time the highway engineers straighten a mountain stream, the rainbow trout box shrinks a little; every time a farmer rips out a fencerow, a whole series of boxes—for pheasants, bobwhite quail, cottontails, a whole group of songbirds—gets a little smaller.

But the importance of all these boxes for the wildlife manager is that he can only sample their contents, never measure them totally. Therefore, he must make his managerial decisions on the basis of partial information concerning population levels, structure, and dynamics.

PATTERNS IN POPULATION STRUCTURE AND DYNAMICS

In general, the structure and dynamics of a given population are strongly influenced by the sex ratio, the age distribution, the nutritional state, the effects of crowding or harassment, the stresses of weather and disease, and similar things. The losses—the sum of mortality and movement—are likewise influenced by a host of local events. It is predictable, then, that the dynamic pattern displayed by one population may be quite different than that characterizing another, even though they are of identical species occupying closely adjacent habitats.

To start with a simple example, let us illustrate the pattern of structure, gains, and losses in a population in which movement in or out is not significant. Table 1 describes a black-tailed deer population from which a light harvest of adult bucks is taken and in which there is both summer and winter mortality.

TABLE 1. Differential Age and Sex Distribution and Mortality in a Population of Black-Tailed Deer[1] (Tabler and Dasmann 1957).

Age and sex classes	Adults		Yearlings		Fawns		Total
	Bucks	Does	Bucks	Does	Bucks	Does	
Number per 10 square miles in June	65	133	24	28	50	45	345
Percent of total population	19	39	7	7	15	13	100
Annual mortality: number	19	26	5	2	27	17	96
Annual mortality: percent of class	34	18	21	7	54	38	
Number per 10 square miles the following May	46	107	19	26	23	28	249

[1]Hunting harvest adult bucks only.

Table 1 shows the structure of this population in age and sex classes and brings out the fact that annual mortality is much heavier in some classes than others. In this example, the mortality in the harvested (adult buck) class is only about one-fifth of the total annual mortality in the population. The importance of this piece of information for the wildlife manager is obvious— reduction of competition within this population by reducing population density significantly would have to involve harvesting antlerless as well as antlered deer.

It is helpful, in trying to define or describe the variation that can exist in patterns of population dynamics, to contrast two extreme situations, that in which cropping by humans (hunting or trapping) does not occur and that in which cropping is heavy.

Where there is no cropping by man—say in a park or sanctuary—the population quickly fills its box. Competition between individuals, either for space or some other habitat necessity, is keen. In such a competitive situation, the strong—that is, the healthy, prime adults—have the advantage over the weak—the young, the sick, and the aged. This is reflected in the pattern of mortality, since the heavy losses are among the very young and the very old. It is also reflected in reproduction, since the competitive pressure on the young may delay their sexual development. It may even have an influence on the sex ratio, as in mammals where severe competition bears hardest on young males. In such a population, then, we expect a small annual survival of young, a large survival of the population in the prime years, and heavy mortality among the old.

In contrast, a population from which a heavy annual crop of both sexes is taken has a quite different structure. The annual removal of a substantial proportion of the population reduces competition among individuals. This improves the chances of survival among the weaker members of the population. But, by removing a heavy annual crop, we take many animals in their prime, and so reduce the number surviving to grow old. This throws a greater proportional advantage to the young. They survive well, mature rapidly, and produce young. The structure of such a population will obviously be heavy in young animals. Biologists speak of such a population as having a rapid turnover, that is, a rapid disappearance, through mortality, of each succeeding generation.

Table 2 shows population structure for two elk herds, the Tule elk of Owens Valley, where cows were not hunted, and the Rocky Mountain elk of the White River Plateau, Colorado, where they were. The unhunted population shows high calf mortality and high survival of older individuals; the hunted population shows the reverse.

When the maximum possible harvest is being obtained from a given population, it may still be possible to obtain a higher production and yield by shifting the sex ratio—reducing the proportion of males by heavier hunting pressure and thus increasing the size of the reproductive base, the female component. This will only be possible, of course, in species with polygamous breeding habits.

Beyond this, increases in harvest can be obtained only by increasing the size of the breeding population through habitat improvement, which would increase the carrying capacity of the habitat.

TABLE 2. A comparison of the age structure in cow elk from an unhunted and a hunted population. The 1x column is the age class structure, and the percent column is the percent of the population in each age class.

X	Unhunted*		Hunted**	
	1x	Percent	1x	Percent
0-1	1000	31.1	1000	27.3
1-2	376	11.7	831	22.7
2-3	363	11.2	654	17.8
3-4	341	10.0	477	13.0
4-5	314	9.8	291	7.9
5-6	279	8.7	179	4.9
6-7	230	7.2	108	2.9
7-8	177	5.5	66	1.8
8-9	115	3.6	37	1.0
9-10	18	0.6	23	0.6

*McCullough (1969)
**Boyd (1970)

RELATION OF POPULATION DYNAMICS TO ANIMAL CONTROL

An understanding of population dynamics is not only useful in attempts to increase the production and yield from a wildlife population, it is also desirable when the objective is to reduce the number or productivity of some population causing problems.

When a population is too high to tolerate, man often responds by attempting direct control—say, by offering a bounty. But killing part of a population only improves reproduction and survival for the rest. We may even kill a very high proportion, especially if we concentrate on males, and have more than ever. Suppose that elephants in East Africa damage crops and are controlled by shooting. If the shooters chivalrously spare the cows and concentrate on bulls, they will shift the sex ratio toward a greater proportion of cows. The population will consequently have a larger annual calf crop, thus aggravating the control problem.

While it is sometimes possible to reduce populations by direct control, it often requires substantial continued effort. Controlling the population by reducing the carrying capacity through habitat change may have long-lasting effects at little cost. For example, cleaning up backyard garbage cuts the rat population down more cheaply and effectively than a trapping campaign.

MODELING POPULATION DYNAMICS

From our various examples, and from common experience, we see that there are various ways in which man may influence population dynamics so as to attain his particular objectives. Under favorable circumstances he can change sex ratio, age structure, density, food quantity, food quality, nesting cover, escape cover, season of harvest, size of harvest, structure of harvest, and so on. In any particular situation, these attempts by man to achieve his

Ralph
Oberg

objectives will be affected by other things such as whether to produce some outcome in terms of population level or yield. The workings of these various influences on populations, singly and together, are often so complex that it is difficult to assess the specific effects of some particular manipulation. The solution of the mathematical problems involved in such an assessment of managerial strategies has been so difficult in the past that it was often not attempted. Over recent years, however, the development of computers has provided us with a tool for the rapid solution of such complex calculations.

This has opened the possibility of problem simulation. That is, the development of a mathematical model that can then be used to discover the population consequences of a wide variety of managerial manipulations. Such models are constructed from real data, so that they will provide reliable answers to real problems. The more closely the model corresponds to the actual situation, the better. Fortunately, the very process of model construction brings to light the need for specific pieces of information. If these are unknown, research on the actual population in question must be carried out. Thus, there is a continual interplay between the model and the real population, with the model demanding accurate information, and the population providing it up to the limits of research capability. The more important the population is, the more time, money, and expertise we can concentrate on research concerning it. Thus, a whole new era in the understanding and manipulation of population dynamics is beginning to unfold.

LITERATURE CITED

Anderson, Wm. E. and R. J. Scherzinger. 1975. Improving quality of winter forage for elk by cattle grazing. Jour. Range Manage., 28(2) March pp. 120-125.

Boyd, R. J. 1970. Elk of the White River Plateau, Colorado. Colo. Div. Game, Fish, Parks, Tech. Publ. 25:1-126.

Brown, E. R. 1961. The black-tailed deer of western Washington. Washington State Game Dept., Biol. Bull. No. 13. 124 pp.

Dasmann, R. F. 1964. Wildlife biology. John Wiley & Sons, New York. 231 pp.

McCabe, R. A., R. A. MacMullan, and E. H. Dustman. 1956. Ring-necked pheasants in the Great Lakes Region, pp. 264-356. *In* D. L. Allen, ed. Pheasants in North America. The Stackpole Co., Harrisburg, Pennsylvania. 490 pp.

McCullough, D. R. 1969. The tule elk, its history, behavior, and ecology. Univ. of Calif. Publ. in Zoology 88.

Taber, R. D. and R. F. Dasmann. 1957. The dynamics of three natural populations of the deer *Odocoileus hemionus columbianus*. Ecology 38(2): 233-246.

Warback, O. 1958. Bird populations in relation to changes in land use. J. Wildl. Manage. 22(1):23-28.

SELECTED REFERENCES

Caughley, G. 1977. Analysis of vertebrate populations. John Wiley & Sons, New York. 234 pp.

Eberhardt, L. L. 1969. Population analysis, pp. 457-496. *In* R. H. Giles, Jr., ed. Wildlife management techniques, 3rd ed. The Wildl. Soc., Washington, D.C.

Pianka, E. R. 1974. Evolutionary ecology. Harper & Row, New York. 356 pp.

ANIMAL BEHAVIOR

Aaron N. Moen

The behavior of an animal "has gradually come to be recognized as the overt expression of the coordinated life processes of the animal . . ." (Emlen 1955). Behavior, thus defined, is an expression of the effect of the factors that are influencing an animal. Consider the depth of that definition! It includes both external and internal stimuli that cause an animal to react; it recognizes an external environment and an internal environment. Environment is best considered in a functional way, an ecological complex of relationships that exists only because these relationships have become a part of the coordinated life processes of an organism.

How can we ever understand or even recognize all of these relationships? Some are quite easy to recognize, because they affect us humans, too. A strong and turbulent wind makes it difficult for us to walk, and we note that small birds have difficulty flying. We find it relatively easy to interpret their overt behavior, because we can relate to the problem. We must be very careful, however, not to make the mistake of thinking that animals are affected to the same extent that humans are. The effect of the wind on us may be somewhat similar to that of a small bird—at least the air exerts a mechanical pressure on both of us, and both man and bird might reduce their exposures to it—but the functional relationships between man and wind and bird and wind are quite different because of our different anatomies, masses, and adaptations to the effects of wind. Thus, it is well to keep in mind that the basic characteristics of stimuli, the basic characteristics of the organisms receiving the stimuli, and changes through time in stimulus-response interactions—both short-term and long-term—are all a definite part of the total organism-environment relationship. Keeping that in mind, let us take a brief look into some relationships between behavior and wildlife management.

Factors that affect an organism, called stimuli, cause changes in the life processes of the organism. The changes are called responses. Organisms are constantly receiving potential stimuli from their environment, but only some of them cause changes in the life processes of the organisms. Many stimuli are filtered out because experience has shown that they are relatively unimportant. For example, a deer is grazing in a meadow in the spring as a male songbird sings from a nearby fence post. The deer will likely filter that noise out; it is relatively unimportant to the deer that the bird is singing from that post. Another singing male of the same species, however, will likely recognize the song, and this may elicit an aggressive reaction as they determine territorial boundaries. It is clear that responses to a particular stimulus vary from

Moen, Aaron N.   Associate Professor of Wildlife Ecology, Cornell University, Ithaca, New York

species to species, and through time as well. After the breeding season is over, the once territorial male birds may be quite gregarious.

The singing male is providing an auditory stimulus for other singing males of its own species. These males have the ability to receive and respond to the sound energy that makes up the song. Many species other than song-birds use vocalizations for communications. Elk vocalize by bugling, and wolves have a rather highly developed repertoire of howls. Coyotes howl, too, and prairie dogs and ground squirrels emit warnings that sound like a "bark."

Some sounds used to communicate are not vocalizations but are produced by mechanical means. Male ruffed grouse "drum" by rapidly beating their wings. Male pheasants vocalize by "crowing" and then beat their wings rapidly immediately afterwards. Two bighorn sheep deliver rather resounding blows to each other's horns, and this sound has meaning to other sheep, and white-tailed deer may be attracted to the sound of antlers striking each other.

In general, the sounds of birds have meaning to other members of the species without being learned, while many of the sounds made by mammals seem to have little meaning until an association between the sound and the circumstances is learned. It is very difficult to determine how much information is conveyed by sound stimuli emitted and received by lower animals, because our human evaluations must always be indirect.

Sound stimuli are often accompanied by visual stimuli. Male birds in breeding condition are often brightly-colored or have some recognition marks that are recognized by other members of their own species. Sometimes these are conspicuously displayed as a part of intimidation displays that may precede or preclude aggressive behavior. Turkeys, for example, communicate by altering feather contours, body posture, and head movements; threat displays are marked by sleeked feathers, and courtship displays by ruffled feathers (Hewitt 1967). There are definite social orders in groups of animals, and these are often maintained by visual communications, though the positions in the ranks may have been established by aggressive action.

Mech (1966) discussed several of the facial and postural expressions used by wolves in communicating. Many of these are very subtle to humans and can only be discerned by comprehensive observations of interactions. Since many animal-environment actions change through time as reproductive and social functions proceed through annual cycles, it is important that research scientists devote continuous attention to all aspects of a species' ecology over several years so patterns may be detected.

While visual and auditory stimulus-response relationships are generally more highly developed in birds than in mammals, chemical interactions as a result of olfactory capabilities are more highly developed in mammals than in birds. It is very difficult to study olfactory interactions because man has a poor sense of smell, and there is no indirect way to quantify olfactory characteristics. So much of what we learn about the sensory capabilities of lower animals must come indirectly through interpretation of behavioral responses. Carnivores seem to communicate quite extensively by olfactory means. Individual wolves smell each other, especially in the head and neck region and in the anal-genital area. A pack of wolves marks out its territory by establishing scent posts. These may be logs, stumps, rocks, clumps of grass, or other conspicuous objects that are used as targets for urination. Red foxes use the same kind of objects to establish scent posts that define territories, and these are visited and maintained regularly.

There is another aspect to chemical stimulus-response combinations that is easily overlooked. This is the internal chemical balance of the individual—the hormone balance—and it is often the very basis for the kinds of responses to visual, auditory, and olfactory stimuli. The hormone balance, for example, determines whether a female will stand for breeding, or deter the male from interactions. In fact, when the female is in heat, she *must* stand, for her hormone balance dictates that behavioral response. The response need not be initiated by a male of its own species; female white-tailed deer in heat in a laboratory herd will freeze and remain rigid in response to a human hand placed on their hindquarters just superior to the anal-genital region.

The hormone balance that is such a vital part of internal stimulus-response relationships is usually a response to stimuli from external sources. The effect of light on reproductive behavior provides one of the most striking examples of a chain of events that includes both internal and external stimuli. When pheasants are exposed to longer periods of daylight, their reproductive organs reach a functional condition. The testes and ovaries become active, males begin to crow and display, sperm and eggs are produced, and mating occurs. The actual time of mating depends on external stimuli that the males exchange with the females, including displays of color, body posture, and other signals that inform the mate that conditions are right for copulation. Thus, a chain of events begins with the effect of light on the reproductive organs, changes in the release of reproductive hormones occur, and finally external behavioral responses result in successful matings.

The series of events continues as mating is followed by nest building and egg laying, and then by incubation and brood rearing. This sequence, rather rigidly programmed, results in a very distinct biological chronology. In fact, biological chronologies of five species of duck (Moen 1973) illustrate how migration begins at a fairly determinable time, arrival on the nesting grounds can be accurately forecast, and the amount of deviation in the timing of nesting activities is quite predictable from year to year. The biochronology of individuals is more precise than that of populations, of course; the incubation period for each nesting female is likely to be within a day of the characteristic length for that species, while the peak of hatching in a population varies from year to year by a few days. Female birds will lay eggs whether or not they have been fertilized, and incubation will continue beyond the normal time period if hatching does not occur. Eventually, gonadal regression occurs, the hormone balance changes, and new responses occur.

Biochronologies for mammals may be determined on the basis of reproductive readiness that is mediated by variations in day length, by the lengths of gestation periods for each species, and by the nutritional and social interactions between parents (sometimes only the mother) and offspring that follow. Thus, a female white-tailed deer that is exposed to a changing light regime in the fall will likely breed in the middle of November. She is then committed to nearly seven months of gestation and about three months of lactation. After the young are weaned, she has two to three months before being bred again, a period of time when she gains weight, primarily fat, to use as a reserve during the winter when range resources are limited and conditions rigorous.

Similar patterns may be described for other mammals too, with differences in the timing of the events but not in the pattern of events. Such reproductive responsibilities dictate many of the behavioral characteristics of a species. Lactogenesis, for example, is a very costly biological process, and lactating females spend most of their active time foraging. Rigorous range conditions at a time when range resources are limited dictate behavioral responses that are very definite adaptations for survival. Thus conservation of energy is practiced by many mammals, with hibernators, such as ground squirrels and woodchucks, carrying this to an extreme. Some animals are less extreme, being very inactive for extended periods of time—bears and raccoons, for example—while still others that are not considered hibernators at all do reduce their activity and metabolism, with reduced thyroid activity, in the winter. The reduction of energy expenditures by a "homeotherm" (warm-blooded animal) may seem contrary to the responses required in the cold, but

109

there is a considerable body of evidence that many northern species reduce both their level of activity and their metabolism when range resources are limited. Behavioral and metabolic responses of deer are quantified in a paper describing the results of several thousand hours of electrocardiogram and behavioral observations at the Wildlife Ecology Laboratory, Cornell University (Moen 1978) and in northern Minnesota (Moen 1976).

It might be easy to conclude that the behavior of an organ in the body, such as the thyroid gland, which regulates metabolism, is more properly classified as physiology. Physiology and behavior cannot be separated, however, for they are linked together in a functional way—the thyroid gland releases thyroxine that regulates metabolism, which then affects the activity level—and both must be considered before one can understand how an animal lives under natural conditions.

There are many stimulus-response relationships that determine the distribution of individuals and populations. Visual, auditory, and olfactory relationships are significant determinants of the distribution of animals with its range. Such relationships result in populations with social structures that often limit the number of animals in a population, the age structure of the population, and even the gene structure of the population. The gene structure of the population may be regulated by very nonrandom breeding activity in those species with distinct male rankings. This occurs in wolf packs (Mech 1970), elk (Murie 1951), turkey (Watts and Stokes 1971; Moen 1973), and other species.

110

Wind is a mechanical force that affects the flight activities of birds. Sometimes it is strong enough to be inhibitory, preventing flying activities, and at times it is beneficial, as a tail wind in migration, increasing the birds' ground speed. Free convection over differentially-heated land areas results in thermals that are used by soaring birds such as hawks, eagles, and vultures.

Mechanical characteristics of soil also affect the distribution of individual animals that burrow. Soil depth, density, and water-holding characteristics are three very important factors affecting the distribution of woodchucks, ground squirrels, and other burrowing animals. Snow is a mechanical barrier, too; travel is much more difficult when the animal sinks to its belly. When deer must bound through deep snow, energy expenditures go beyond a reasonable upper limit and rapidly drain energy reserves. Wild turkey in the northeast sometimes have to plow through soft, deep snow, and this is energetically costly, though the costs of such travel have not been determined yet.

Thermal stimuli affect the distribution and activities of animals as well. Some escape cold weather by migrating, others adapt to it by reducing energy expenditures. A general pattern of thermal stimuli-responses has emerged from recent research in energy exchange. As temperatures rise, radiation exchange becomes important, and at high radiation loads and ambient temperatures near body temperature, heat losses due to evaporation become most important. Every animal must live within the framework of energy transfer by radiation, conduction, convection, and evaporation, altering its metabolism and behavior to maintain variations within tolerance limits that are characteristic, in general, of the species, and specifically, of individuals through time. Thus, there is a repertoire of thermoregulatory behavior patterns that animals employ, involving habitat selection, posture, and orientation, as variations in energy balance are kept within the tolerance limits.

Stimuli may cause conflicting responses. When a prey animal sees a predator, for example, the prey may have a tendency to remain hidden or to run, and the response the prey animal makes is dependent on the many stimuli being received at the time and on the past experience of the prey. Deer that are hunted have a greater tendency to run farther from a person (a predator) than deer that are not hunted. Thermal and metabolic relationships are somewhat dependent on the size of the animal, with smaller animals being in a less favorable energy balance than larger ones. Yet there are social ties that may override thermal relationships. Mechanical factors affect animals, even of the same species, differently. A six-month-old white-tail fawn may be forced to bound through 40 centimeters of snow, while a three and one-half year old adult can walk. The two experience very different responses to the same conditions. The behavioral responses of animals, then, are a complex integration of many factors or stimuli.

The stimulus-response combinations discussed thus far include: thermoregulatory behavior, gene structure, inhibitory mechanical forces, auditory and visual cues, and similar functions. There is another type of behavior that is characteristic of most animals, and that is play behavior. Deer will frolic, running in circles for no apparent reason, butt heads, splash in the shallow water of a lake, and do other things that have no immediate survival value. Fox pups play near the entrance to the den, growling, biting, fighting with considerable aggressiveness, sometimes annoying the parents with their playfulness. Play behavior is likely to be very useful in establishing social bonds and in teaching prey capture techniques, effective escape techniques, and copulation postures. It is clearly a natural part of the life of many animals.

Most behavioral responses are the result of the basic drive of individuals to survive, which results in the survival of the species. Individual survival depends on the ability of the animal to get food, to find enough protection from the forces of the weather, and to escape death from predators, parasites, or diseases. The survival of the population depends on the abilities of the animals to mate successfully and produce offspring and rear them to the age when they are self-sufficient members of the population, capable of reproducing. The presence of these basic drives in all animals leads to some definite patterns of behavior with animal populations that are characteristic of the species.

Relationships between animals of the same species (intraspecific relationships) or different species (interspecific relationships) can be classified into three general categories: competition, cooperation, and a neutral type of relationship where neither animal is affected by the other. It is frequently difficult to assign a behavioral relationship to a single category, and it is very important to understand that the relationships between animals change with the season. Some examples will illustrate these points.

Competition results when two animals are after the same component of their environment when the supply of that component is limited. A most obvious type of competition is for a limited food supply where a dominant animal (who might be the largest, oldest, or most aggressive animal) will usually be in the best position to consume his portion of the food supply first. This is frequently observed in groups of deer—the adult male is often the dominant animal in a winter concentration area. Scientists have known about dominance patterns and social ranks in animal populations for some time, and have given it the name "peck order" because it was first described in chickens.

The social hierarchy or "peck order" develops from several factors, including experience, age, physiological condition, and physical size. Experiences may be very important; the work of Silver and Silver (1969) on canids has shown that the dominant animals assume that role very early in life. Establishment of a social order in a group of animals does not necessarily result in a perfect dominance hierarchy. The dominant animal and the most repressed animal may remain in their position, but those between these two extremes may change positions, or at least give that appearance to the human observer. Mech (1966) pointed out that the most conspicuous wolf in a pack of 16 was one who was clearly the most repressed individual. The leader was not always in the front of the pack, however; its dominant position was maintained without the necessity to physically lead in every case.

It is interesting to note that the maintenance of social orders is not necessarily dependent on physical conflicts between individuals. Wolves recognize leadership by the posture of the animal, particularly the erect tail. Red fox establish territories without physical contact between foxes; scent posts are used to outline an individual's territory. Birds sometimes fight between themselves, but very often the conflict over territorial boundaries is resolved by aggressive displays that are not accompanied by actual physical contact.

Cooperation between members of a species is observed in many kinds of animals. Pronghorn frequently associate in bands, bison live in herds, caribou travel on long migrations together, and musk oxen live in a group that functions together as a unit when danger approaches by forming a circle with each member facing outward. This type of cooperation among members of the same species may be beneficial to their survival under natural conditions. The presence of several pronghorn in a band makes it more likely that one member of the group will spot danger before a single animal would when traveling alone. On the other hand, dependence may also result in competition since more animals are crowded together.

The amount of intraspecific, or "within species," cooperation varies at different times of the year. Many species are quite gregarious at some times of the year, while at other times, individuals may compete with each other, as during the breeding season. Waterfowl are good examples of this; they migrate in groups as they move northward in the spring but tend to disperse as they select nesting sites. Indeed, the competition for territory may be so keen that a pair of blue-winged teal will simply not tolerate the presence of another pair on a small midwestern pothole.

Neutral types of relationships between animals of the same species are difficult to recognize in the wild. Complete neutrality implies that the relationships between different animals is a random one, with no cause and effect relationships whatsoever. This would seldom occur under natural conditions. There are times, however, when relationships between individual members of a population appear to be very loose. Male deer in late winter may have little contact with female deer, but they may have some kind of loose "males only" organization. The degree of competition, cooperation, or neutrality between animals depends on a number of factors, especially those related to the reproductive cycle.

The presence of interactions between animals of the same species and of different species has resulted in the formulation of some principles of behavior that are common to most animals. First, let us consider the concept of home range. Many animals spend most of their lives in a given area. Red fox, for example, once they have ceased to be transients or wanderers in search of a home area, settle in a home range where they secure their food and raise their young. The home range of one pair will not likely include any other resident fox. When this competitive exclusion occurs, the home range is appropriately called a territory; this concept is discussed later in the chapter.

Home ranges of several individuals of the same species may overlap. This is common in field mice, and it is tolerated until certain population densities are reached. It is very difficult to drive animals out of their home ranges if population densities are not high enough to cause emigration. It was thought, at one time, that deer could be driven out of a winter concentration area to better range, but that is not practical. Rather, deer are more gregarious in the winter than the summer, balancing the benefits of an area containing established trails in the deep snow with the effect that confinement to these trails has on the diminishing forage supplies. The calculation of energy costs demonstrates the benefits from such adaptation (Moen 1976, 1978).

Although the idea of home range is quite a simple one, there are many things that are yet unknown about how or why the home range has its own unique shape and size. Certainly seasonal food supplies are fundamental since food is necessary for life purposes. Topography, vegetation, and other features must also play a role in the geometry of individual home ranges.

The term "territories" was introduced earlier when the idea of competitive exclusion was attached to the concept of home range, as for red fox. The basic difference between a home range and a territory is that the home range is not defended against intruders of the same species, but a territory is. Several different types of territories have been described by behavioral scientists working with different species. Songbirds, for example, defend an area where they feed, mate, and produce their young. There is an active defense of the territory from the time it is established before or during breeding to the time when the young are born and reared. Waterfowl defend a mating and nesting area, but they may feed in flocks with little or no conflict. Upland game birds, such as pheasants and grouse, defend the mating area. Crowing areas are set up by cock pheasants and drumming logs by ruffed grouse. The smallest kind of defended territory is characteristic of colonial nesting gulls that defend but a square meter surrounding their nest site. The largest kinds of defended territories are characteristic of larger mammals that maintain a high level of activity and move over large areas of land regularly. Thus, the sizes of territories may vary from a square meter to several square kilometers, depending on the species and on the local characteristics of the habitat. Normally, males are most conspicuous in defense of territories against other males of the same species. This behavioral characteristic is used by man in censusing populations.

What biological benefits are associated with such things as social hierarchies, home range, and territoriality? Several possible benefits may be considered. A social order that is recognized by members of a population of animals will result in a reduction of fighting between individuals. This isolation of individuals during the breeding season tends to disperse the population and provide for a more even use of the available resources, especially food. The more or less organized dispersal of the population may result in a more stable productivity because range resources are used more evenly; the spacing will also result in a faster growth of the individuals in a population. The more aggressive and dominant animals, often the larger ones, may be more successful as breeders, especially if the population is high, and food or space on the range is in short supply. The above factors minimize the tendency for population oscillations, as high density populations are less likely to occur under these conditions. Moreover, even population distributions may cause more evenly distributed predation, since predators cannot take advantage of a high concentration of prey, resulting in greater stability in the predation rates.

MANAGEMENT IMPLICATIONS

Analyses of patterns of behavior and stimulus-response relationships provide insights into the need for and the effectiveness of management policies and actions. Decision-making in natural resource management can be effective only when it is made within the biological framework of possibility. This may sound so logical that it need not be said, but the fact is that many policy decisions are made with little or no knowledge of biological relationships. Snowmobile trails, for example, are often laid out where it is most convenient to do so, using old logging roads, railroad beds, and other existing pathways. The relationships between deer and snowmobile activity are largely unknown. Research, as yet unpublished, at the Wildlife Ecology Laboratory at Cornell University using heart rate transmitters indicates that cardiac responses often occur without overt behavioral responses; one cannot say, "I did not disturb the deer at all—they just stood and watched me," because there is an internal response that is part of the animal's overall behavior. Further, since deer exhibit very definite energy conservation adaptations in the winter, any disturbance by snowmobiles and other mechanical devices is contrary to their long-term adaptive strategy. A snowmobile is, to a deer, a potential predator with unlimited kinetic energy.

Behavior relationships limit the densities of many populations, especially of those species that are highly territorial. Thus, red fox populations will likely never explode to where there is a fox behind every tree, because fox do not tolerate each other that well. Often the most important stimulus in an animal's environment is another member of its own species. Pheasant hens, for example, may abandon their own nest in the final days of incubation in response to the sights and sounds of newly-hatched chicks. Such a response suggests that there is a relationship between pheasants, broods, and nesting success. Such situations do not lend themselves to analyses by simple arithmetic; pheasant production is not as simple as multiplying the number of eggs per nest times the number of nests.

Some species are very gregarious and need to have sufficiently large areas for certain behavioral activities. Prairie chickens, for example, need "booming grounds" that are more than little patches of grass; they do not thrive in areas that are farmed intensively.

Animals exhibit many behavioral options in their responses to different kinds of stimuli. If some of these are denied, other responses compensate. Deer in temperature-controlled chambers, for example, exhibit a rise in metabolism when lower temperatures are reached. Other species exhibit a rise in metabolism as a variety of thermoregulatory behavioral responses are employed under natural conditions that were impossible to obtain in the chamber. Such different potential responses may result in erroneous conclusions from experimental work when results are applied to the field.

Patterns of behavior and stimulus-response interactions are understood best when underlying physiological rhythms are also understood. There is a real need for behavioral research that is accompanied by physiological analyses as well, and both behavior and physiology should be studied throughout the year, with as little intrusion into the lives of these animals as possible. Thus, remote-measuring techniques—radio telemetry, radioactive isotopes, nondisturbing visual observations, and others—should be used in an effort to understand the total picture through time. Behavior—the total expression of an animal's condition—is a most difficult science because an understanding of so many underlying relationships is essential. Difficult, yes, but good ecological research is expected to be difficult since so many variables are involved.

It naturally follows that many difficulties exist in managing biological resources. Many of these arise because it is so hard to recognize the environments of animals. There are, to be sure, many components of a habitat, but

115

the recognition and understanding of those components that have a beneficial or detrimental effect on populations is extremely difficult. Without such an understanding, management decisions might be good, they might be bad, or they might be irrelevant. Wishful thinking, fond memories of boyhood days, or even democratic action will not change the basic biology of living organisms.

LITERATURE CITED

Emlen, J. T. 1955. The study of behavior in birds. Pp. 105-153 *in* Recent studies in avian biology. A. Wolfson, ed. Univ. of Illinois Press, Urbana.

Hewitt, O. H. 1967. The wild turkey and its management. The Wildl. Soc., Washington, D.C. 589 pp.

Mech, L. D. 1966. The wolves of Isle Royale. U.S. Govt. Printing Office, Washington, D.C. 210 pp.

———. 1970. The wolf: the ecology and behavior of an endangered species. The Natural History Press, Garden City, N.Y. 384 pp.

Moen, A. N. 1973. Wildlife ecology: an analytical approach. W. H. Freeman and Co., San Francisco. 458 pp.

———. 1976. Energy conservation by white-tailed deer in the winter. Ecology 57(1): 192-198.

———. 1978. Seasonal changes in heartrates, activity, metabolism, and forage intake of white-tailed deer. J. Wildl. Manage. (In press.)

Murie, O. J. 1951. The elk of North America. The Stackpole Co., Harrisburg, Pa. 376 pp.

Silver, H. and W. T. Silver. 1969. Growth and behavior of the coyote-like canid of northern New England with observations on canid hybrids. Wildlife Monograph No. 17, The Wildl. Soc., Washington, D.C.

Watts, C. R. and A. W. Stokes. 1971. The social order of turkeys. Sci. Am. 224(6): 112-118.

WILDLIFE NUTRITION

Louis J. Verme

For any animal, nutrition controls the complex processes vital to its welfare—its reproduction, growth, and survival. Hence, any shortage in the amount or quality of food could result in ill health of the animal and, ultimately, in a greatly reduced population. Unfortunately, most sportsmen are quite apt to blame a decline in game abundance on factors other than proper nutrition. To better appreciate the biological aspects of the problem, a brief review of the basic constituents, or building-blocks, of foodstuffs is in order.

FOOD COMPOSITION

All living plant and animal tissue is made up of water, organic matter, and certain minerals. The organic compounds are composed of chemical units, which we label as proteins, carbohydrates, and fats. Life requires protein, which come directly or indirectly from plants. The proteins are exceedingly complex chemically, each molecule consisting of a considerable number of different nitrogenous compounds called amino acids. The specific mixture of the various amino acids comprising a protein determines its relative nutritive value. For many animals, the quality or kind of protein eaten is fully as important as the amount. The factor of adequate diet is especially important among simple-stomached animals. They have only very limited ability to change (through digestion) any amino acids, of which there is an excess, into other forms that are lacking but essential for life. On the other hand, animals with complex stomachs (ruminants) have many types of microbes in their paunch that can make all the amino acids necessary from the plants eaten.

An animal's minimal protein requirement depends on how fast it is growing, its relative body size, and activity level. The protein needs of young animals are great, because they are building new tissues rapidly. Mature animals require protein mainly for maintenance and repair of body cells. When there is not enough protein in the diet for growth and maintenance, growth slows or stops. Pregnancy and lactation increase considerably the demand for protein. Protein can also supply energy during periods of stress.

Most of the energy animals need to sustain them comes from carbohydrates. All plants manufacture carbohydrates and store them in the form of sugars, starches, and cellulose. In contrast, an animal's body contains very few carbohydrates as such, although these are readily converted into fat, which is then stored for reserve energy. The digestion of sugars and starches is accomplished rather simply by specific enzymes in the digestive tract.

Verme, Louis J   Wildlife Research Biologist, Michigan Department of Natural Resources, Cusino Wildlife Research Station, Shingleton.

Utilization of cellulose and related compounds rests primarily on the action of bacteria in the digestive tract. In the paunch of ruminants, specialized bacteria break down the cellulose and form (synthesize) it into amino acids and vitamins that the animal can then utilize for food.

The fats, oils, and related substances are very important both for plants and animals. Fats and fatlike substances are soluble in ether. The materials dissolved by this solvent are termed ether-extract, also known as lipids. Fats furnish about two and one-quarter times as much energy per pound as do carbohydrates. They, therefore, have a correspondingly higher food value per unit weight. Aside from its energy value, certain "fatty acids" in fat are necessary for life. Some fats and oils serve as important sources of vitamins. Fats increase the efficiency of utilization of protein and carbohydrates in the diet.

Certain mineral elements are essential for proper bodily function, plus bone formation, and therefore must be present in the diet. Some minerals are needed only in small amounts and, thus, are referred to as "trace" elements. A lack of cobalt in the diet of hoofed game (ruminants) could result in a vitamin B_{12} deficiency, for example, as this vitamin is not present in the plants that comprise their food, although it can be synthesized by the bacteria if cobalt is ingested. Whether any wild animal is faced with mineral deficiencies to the point of sickness is yet to be adequately determined.

FOOD DIGESTION

Metabolism is the term used to indicate the chemical changes constantly taking place in living matter. Metabolic rate, or heat production, is a measure of an animal's energy requirements. The potential nutritive value of foodstuffs is measured in calories, which signify the gross energy that may be released as heat when food is digested. The oxidation (burning) of food by the body provides the energy, which serves in a manner somewhat like that of fuel in a

furnace or machine. This "machine" must continue to run 24 hours a day throughout life, even when no food is available. At such time the energy comes from oxidation of body tissue. Since fat is a readily available source of reserve energy, it is used continuously in metabolism, especially when an animal is fasting. Obviously, heat production must equal heat losses from all causes if body temperature is to be maintained. The relative efficiency with which food is converted into heat energy by an animal can be accurately measured in the laboratory by means of a "metabolic chamber."

The nutritive value of plant foods can be approximated by analyzing their chemical composition. Generally this involves the determination of such factors as crude protein level, fat content, crude fiber, minerals, and other elements. Unfortunately, the results of these studies are not always too meaningful. The trouble is that the nutritional needs and digestive processes of most wild animals are so poorly understood that we often cannot appraise how they will respond to a particular ration, or why. In the Lake States region, for example, white-tailed deer manage to survive the winter on a sole diet of white cedar browse, whereas they will die when fed balsam fir alone. Chemical analysis reveals little difference in food value between the two conifer species. Their protein content, for instance, is rather similar. Recent study has indicated that the rumen microbes are unable to break down certain nutritive units in balsam fir to form compounds that the deer can assimilate for energy. Consequently, even though they continue to eat balsam fir, they eventually die. Technically speaking, the cause of death is malnutrition, the term "starvation" being inappropriate since the stomach is usually full of undigested browse when the animal dies.

The nutritive value of plants commonly varies appreciably, depending upon many complex and interrelated factors. To begin with, the basic fertility of the soil affects the chemical composition of forage. Unfortunately, the soil's nutrient levels may affect the food quality of plants in a manner not readily detected by methods of chemistry now employed. The actual quality of forage can best be determined from feeding trials, or by evaluating the physical condition of free-roaming animals from a certain range. Compared to poor soils, fertile land usually supports a greater assortment of vegetation. More important, rich soils also produce more forage per unit area. In arid regions, soil fertility usually is overshadowed by rainfall as the controlling factor.

Protein is mainly a constituent of actively growing tissue in plants; thus the leaves and tips (current year's growth) are much richer in this nutrient than are the hardened stems. As the plant matures, there is a movement of protein from the vegetative parts to the seeds. Fat is also higher in the leaves than in the stems and generally is greatest in the seeds. The nature of carbohydrates differs markedly according to whether it is serving as a reserve (in seeds) or as a structural (stiffening) part. Since cellulose and related compounds, collectively called crude fiber, are much less digestible than starch, the various portions of a plant vary widely in nutritive value according to their relative digestibility.

FOOD SELECTION

Given a free choice, all wildlife probably eat foods that provide an optimum diet for the species. Deer, for example, have been observed to feed heavily on fertilized forage in preference to untreated growth nearby. Similarly, they prefer to browse on sprouts as compared to slower growing stems of seedlings. Although the greater "succulence" or moisture content of sprouts may be attractive to deer due to better digestibility, sprouts also are very nutritious because they can draw abundant nutrients from the parent root system. The protein content of sprouts produced as a result of fire, herbi-

119

cide application, or cutting is considerably higher than that in the current growth of older (residual) stems.

Animals probably determine differences in the nutritive value of plants by taste, although to us the items superficially may look alike. The term "palatability" is commonly used to denote the ranking of food preferred by animals. Highly palatable foods, therefore, are those that are readily eaten when a wide assortment is available. However, the palatability scale of a species varies considerably from one region to another, evidently depending upon the local situation. It would seem that palatability and nutritive value of food are one and the same thing. That is, an animal eats certain vegetation because it is the most nutritious, and not just because it tastes "good."

The feeding behavior of wildlife is often puzzling to us. However, it is becoming clearer that the foodstuffs selected best satisfy the animal's basic physiological requirements. Recently it was noted that during late winter and early spring, ruffed grouse in Minnesota seek out the male flower buds of aspen trees; whereas, the female flower buds are practically ignored. Chemical analysis suggests that the male flower buds are more nourishing than the female buds of aspen. The extra energy gained by such selective feeding during this period of bitter cold weather might, in fact, spell the difference between success or failure in reproduction when the breeding season gets underway. Eating habits of most animals change with the seasons, according to the nutritive quality of the food supply and the species' metabolic needs. If there is a plentiful mast crop, for instance, many birds and mammals will gorge on acorns or beechnuts in autumn. Since these starchy foods are readily converted into fat, this stored energy helps tide the animal through the pinch of winter.

In their evolution, some animals have developed rather limited feeding habits; whereas, closely related species are not nearly so food-specific. Thus, in the winter the spruce grouse dines almost exclusively on a diet of spruce and jackpine needles, while the ruffed grouse diet is more varied. Chicks of both species, as well as other birds, feed heavily on insects that provide the protein so essential for rapidly growing young. Among hoofed game, the caribou subsists largely on lichens; whereas, moose eat a variety of plants. In both cases, the food provides a well-balanced diet. Deer can live over winter by consuming an assortment of browse plants, each of which is of low digestibility. In all likelihood, the combined ration is satisfactory because each plant supplies some nutritive unit that is absent or deficient in the other species.

Bears and raccoons are omnivorous, being able to digest virtually anything that is available. The nutritive needs of the carnivores are fairly simply satisfied. It has yet to be shown, for instance, that a pound of field mice is not nutritionally equivalent to a pound of cottontail rabbit. Carnivores may consume the entire carcass, obtaining from the internal organs some vitamins and minerals not present, or in small amounts, in muscle flesh. Predators generally are opportunistic feeders, eating whatever is most abundant and easiest to catch.

MANAGEMENT IMPLICATIONS

As a rule, the problem in managing herbivorous game animals arises when overpopulations are allowed to exist. At this point, virtually all of the nutritious browse has been eliminated due to the excessive pressure. The animals are then forced to subsist on second-rate forage, which does not provide enough energy or the proper nutrient balance essential for their well-being. Symptoms of malnutrition are perhaps first noted in a lowered reproductive rate. This comes about in several ways. The juvenile females may not become fertile at the normal time, while adult females might not produce any offspring or give birth to smaller litters. In this instance, the caloric intake simply is not sufficient to trigger ovulation. Pregnant females require ample food to adequately nourish the developing fetuses. If fetal growth is retarded by lack of sustenance, the young may die prematurely or at birth. Because the energy demands incurred by lactation are very great, undernutrition of the mother could lead to reduced milk production. Hence, the nursing young may be stunted in growth or die from starvation. Finally, prolonged food restriction frequently results in individuals that are abnormally small at physical maturity. Among antlered game, poor antler development occurs in males that are in subpar physical condition in spring. Energy from food consumed goes primarily into skeletal growth and body maintenance, the vital considerations for survival.

The link between available food and population levels of animals holds true for all herbivores. The density of predators, whether birds or mammals, also fluctuates in response to prey availability. The lynx population in Canada, for example, hinges on the cyclic abundance of snowshoe hares. Generally, a species increases in numbers to the limit of its food supply. On the other hand, an "explosive" increase in population followed by severe depletion of the food resource inevitably leads to a "crash" decline. The widespread die-off of muskrats, after they have eaten out the marsh vegetation, is a notable example of this situation. In that event, unfortunately, the habitat often is ruined for years to come. The solution to this vexing problem lies in controlling the population by hunting or trapping, or allowing predators to take the annual surplus of animals produced. If this is not done, then disease, stress, and starvation will take their toll.

Determination of range carrying capacity is, at best, difficult. Biologists commonly rely on an examination of the animal itself for clues. Since the animal is subjected to the daily stresses and strains imposed by the environment, its general physical condition reflects a "computerized" version of the sum influences. The relative nutritional state of an animal can be evaluated from its size or weight, reproductive status, blood analysis, and fat storage. Big game, particularly deer, have been studied frequently. Examination of carcasses of hunter-killed animals provides a good index to range quality. A deer's vigor during the crucial winter months in colder regions depends on its energy budget. The food consumed must compensate for the energy lost as body heat due to chilling weather, as well as that expended in struggling through deep snow in search of forage. A negative energy balance develops when the available browse is comparatively indigestible or in short supply. Consequently, deer must then call upon their stored fat reserves to stay alive. Fat depletion, especially in the femur bone marrow, indicates that the animal is on the verge of death from malnutrition.

A final word is in order concerning artificial feeding of game during winter. This practice is often advocated by well-meaning, but misguided, sportsmen. Emergency feeding usually is ineffective, and actually may do more harm than good. Haphazard piling of such food as corn, hay, or other supplements within a small area tends to concentrate the animals. Social strife frequently results, because it is the nature of beasts to form a decided "pecking order" when crowded together. The possibility of predation is greatly increased when animals are concentrated. Beyond that, half-starved deer being fed hay often cannot digest the unnatural forage, and they die anyway. Feeding them corn is extremely dangerous because they will often overeat and bloat.

Needless to say, the goal of sound game management is to control the population and to manipulate the habitat so that acute shortages in key food and cover components do not occur. Given a fair chance, game animals are well endowed by instinct and physiology to face the rigors of a harsh environment. It is only when man upsets the biological mechanisms that control the population's dynamics that serious management problems arise.

SELECTED REFERENCES

Dietz, D. R., R. H. Udall, and L. E. Yeager. 1962. Chemical composition and digestibility by mule deer of selected forage species, Cache La Poudre range, Colorado. Colorado Dept. Game and Fish. Tech. Pub. No. 14. 89 pp.

Maynard, L. A. and J. K. Loosli. 1956. Animal nutrition. McGraw-Hill Book Co., New York. 454 pp.

U.S. Department of Agriculture. 1959. Food. Pp. 39-100 *in* The yearbook of agriculture. Washington, D.C. 736 pp.

DISEASES
OF WILDLIFE

Lars H. Karstad

Disease has been defined as any condition that jeopardizes the survival of an animal in a particular environment. This is a broad definition but one most useful in considering diseases of wildlife. Too often we confuse the terms "disease" and "infection." They are not the same. There are many diseases that are not caused by infection. Consider injuries, birth defects, changes due to malnutrition, and certain tumors; all of these are examples of disease conditions that are not infections. I had an opportunity to investigate a serious disease of caribou calves in Newfoundland, a disease that killed up to 50 percent of the newborn calves in some seasons. This disease was characterized by the development of large abscesses in the necks of very young calves. Detailed pathological studies of affected calves did not uncover the cause. The cause was finally found by a combination of field observation and common sense. The abscesses that killed the calves were the result of wounds caused by lynx! The watchful doe caribou were able to drive off the attacking lynx, but usually not before they had caused the wounds, which eventually resulted in death.

EFFECTS ON WILDLIFE

The impact of disease on a wildlife population is usually difficult to measure. One of the reasons for this is that it is difficult to find wild animals that are sick or dead. It is the nature of a sick animal to be secretive and to "crawl away to die." As a result, the first indication of trouble may be a sudden marked reduction in the number of animals seen. A population crash is obvious, but the cause may be difficult to determine. The periodic sudden decline of a peak population of snowshoe hares is a prime example of this. The carcasses of large animals are most easily found. Deer, dead of epizootic hemorrhagic disease, may be found, necropsied, and the cause of the high mortality diagnosed.

Often the effects of disease are subtle and of long duration. Pesticides, for example, may slowly accumulate in a food chain until the effects are expressed as reduced fertility or a lowered reproductive rate. The end result may be just as destructive as the more dramatic acute diseases. Other examples of chronic insidious diseases are malnutrition, which may result when overpopulation leads to destruction of habitat, or to buildup of excessive loads of parasites when too many animals use the same range. Problems of this kind are seen in some of our big game ranges, for example, with certain deer and bighorn sheep populations. Parasite problems may become acute when deer, elk, or bighorn sheep are forced to share crowded winter range with each other, cattle, or domestic sheep.

Karstad, Lars H.   Head, Section of Wildlife Diseases, Veterinary Research Laboratory, Kabete, Kenya

PARASITES AS CAUSES OF DISEASE

Some people believe that parasitism is normal, that all wild animals have parasites; therefore, parasites cannot be causes of disease. This attempt to generalize is an example of faulty reasoning. True, it is natural to find some parasites in any wild animal. However, an excessive number of almost any parasite can cause disease, and it should be recognized that some animals have evolved a rather amiable host-parasite association with certain parasites. Yet, the same parasite in another species of animal may be very destructive. The brain worm of deer, *Parelaphostrongylus tenuis*, does little harm to its accustomed host, the white-tailed deer, but it is highly destructive to moose, elk, and caribou. These species may not have had an ages-long exposure to the worm. The meningeal worm is now recognized as the cause of "moose sickness," a fatal neurologic disease of moose caused by migration of the worm through the tissues of the spinal cord and brain. "Moose sickness" occurs only where deer and moose inhabit the same range, where deer are the reservoir hosts, and moose suffer severe disease. This disease may be an important reason for the failure of moose to increase in numbers in moose-deer areas of Minnesota, Maine, and New Brunswick.

DISEASE CONTROL

"Why study wildlife diseases? If you find their causes you cannot treat the animals." This is the question often asked and the defeatist attitude too often taken. There are ways to deal with problems of disease other than treatment of the individual animal. Treatment of the individual is possible in diseases of captive wildlife. Preventive medicine is a far more effective means of dealing with disease in free-living animals.

Disease in a wildlife population is rarely a simple, one-cause, one-effect situation. Usually it is the product of profound changes in the environment. In the Newfoundland calf caribou problem, it was observed that the disease ran a cycle that coincided with the cycle of lynx abundance. Lynx numbers in turn were dependent upon numbers of their basic prey species, the snowshoe hare. Control of this caribou disease was successfully carried out by reduction of lynx numbers in the immediate vicinity of the calving grounds.

Botulism is one of the most destructive diseases of wild waterfowl, particularly in the western parts of North America. The causative agent is a very powerful poison produced by a bacterial organism, *Clostridium botulinum*. This bacterium multiplies in rotting vegetation and animal matter. Its growth and toxin (poison) production requires certain conditions of warmth and moisture. These conditions are met when summer drought lowers the depth of water along the shores of shallow lakes and sloughs. The carcasses of birds dead of botulism provide more decomposing organic matter for growth of the bacterium.

Clostridium botulinum produces resistant spores that live in the soil from one disease outbreak to another, leaving the area permanently seeded and waiting for the optimum conditions of weather to set the stage for another die-off of ducks. Control is aimed at prevention of the disease: by changing the environment; by control of water levels to maintain depths so that decomposing vegetation does not warm to temperatures suitable for toxin production; by draining certain problem areas; or by preventing access by waterfowl. In the summer of 1969, an effort was made to prevent losses from botulism in waterfowl in the central valley of California by driving the birds away with aircraft. It is obvious that control of diseases in wildlife may be very expensive.

CONTROL BY ERADICATION

Control of disease may also be costly in lives of the wild animals involved. Some diseases can be controlled best by eradication, the detection and slaughter of every infected animal. This sounds like harsh treatment, but the method is still the best means of control of certain infectious diseases. Twenty-two thousand black-tailed deer were slaughtered in 1924 in the Stanislaus National Forest of California to eradicate foot-and-mouth disease. Similar methods were used to eradicate the disease from livestock in the nearby range areas. Complete eradication was successful. This destructive disease of worldwide notoriety has not since gained a foothold in livestock or wildlife in the United States. In this instance, control of the disease in deer was paid for on the grounds of protection of the livestock industry.

Wildlife has benefited from at least one other large scale livestock disease control program. Until recently the screw worm was a great killer of deer in the Southern states. Screw worm larvae were laid on accidental wounds and, most significantly, on the navels of newborn fawns. In the late 1950s the United States Department of Agriculture mounted a massive screw worm control program in the Southeastern states, particularly Florida and the Gulf Coast. Control was effected through the release from aircraft of millions of male screw worm flies sterilized by irradiation. Females mate but once, and sterile flies so outnumbered the normal males that little reproduction took place. Gradually the parasite was eradicated from its entire range in the Southeastern states. A similar program in the Southwestern states has been almost equally successful. Eradication of the screw worm has helped the livestock industries, but as a by-product it has had a dramatic effect in increasing the rates of survival of deer fawns.

SIGNS OF DISEASE

How do we know when an animal is diseased? Any dead wild animal, unless the cause of its death is obvious, should be examined for cause of death; even animals killed accidentally. For example, road kills are fruitful sources of specimens for examination by a wildlife pathologist.

Signs of disease in a live animal may be any change from normal appearance, behavior, or movements. A sick animal may have dull or inflamed eyes; rough or soiled hair, fur, or feathers; or difficulty with the normal movements of walking or running. Loss of fear or aggressive behavior may indicate rabies. Abnormal lumps (Fig. 1) or discoloration of the skin or internal organs are signs of various diseases. Small whitish spots scattered through the liver or spleen tissues are seen in several diseases. One of them, a common disease of rodents and rabbits, is tularemia.

DIAGNOSIS

The gross outward signs of some diseases are obvious, and with experience, a diagnosis can be made. An example of such a disease is the scaly or horny malformation of the skin, which results from certain mite infestations (Fig. 2). More often there is little or no change in the external appearance of the diseased animal, and even necropsy may not reveal tissue and organ changes visible to the unaided eye. In such cases it may be necessary to undertake detailed, laborious and often expensive laboratory tests to make a diagnosis. Often the diseased wild animal must be examined for microscopic tissue changes and for parasites and microbiologic agents before a diagnosis can be made. If the disease is infectious, it may require special methods to isolate, cultivate, and identify the infectious agent before the diagnosis can be stated with certainty. Some cases require use of that most powerful tool of the microbiologist, the electron microscope.

SPECIMENS FOR DISEASE DIAGNOSIS

It is not necessary for every wildlife biologist or conservation minded citizen to be acquainted with all of the laboratory procedures listed above in

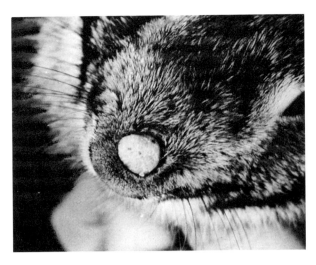

Fig. 1. A small tumor (fibroma) on the nose of a cottontail rabbit, caused by a virus infection.

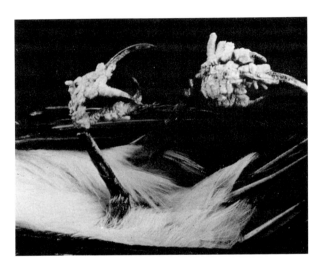

Fig. 2. Mite lesions on the feet of a yellow-crested flycatcher.

order to contribute to the understanding of wildlife diseases. He need only know what specimens to take and how to take them. Necropsy methods and the methods for collection and preservation of specimens for disease diagnosis are described in Chapter 16 of *Wildlife Management Techniques* (Cowan and Karstad 1979), published by The Wildlife Society. Some of the more important points will be presented here:

Specimens must be fresh or properly preserved. A diseased animal still living is the best kind of specimen to bring to the laboratory. This is not always possible. Live diseased animals should not be sent by post or commercial carrier. If the live specimen cannot be taken to the laboratory, the pathologist should be contacted so that he can advise on proper handling.

If body size permits, an animal that is found soon after death should be brought to the laboratory intact. The pathologist will then be given the best possible opportunity to make a diagnosis. If the carcass cannot be transported to the laboratory intact, the body may be opened and specimens taken for laboratory study. Portions of all major body organs (or whole organs, if size permits) should be taken. These can be placed in plastic bags and chilled on ice during transportation to the laboratory. If there will be more than a few hours delay between the taking of the specimens and their delivery at the laboratory, small pieces (about one inch or less in diameter) should be immersed in a solution of 10 percent formalin at least 10 times the volume of the tissue. The formalin-fixed tissue is thus preserved for microscopic examination, while the cooled organs can be used to test for living infectious agents. If specimens must be held for several days before delivery to the laboratory, portions should be placed in formalin and the remains of the major organs frozen in individual plastic bags. However, freezing is destructive to tissues and should be avoided if possible. Decomposition, on the other hand, renders animal tissues useless for laboratory examination.

Blood samples in glass vials, blood smears on glass slides, and blood dried in special paper discs are useful in diagnosis of some diseases. The pathologist should be consulted for special instructions.

Special preservation methods may be used for parasites. Here again, it is best to seek advice from a pathologist or parasitologist.

HUMAN HEALTH HAZARDS

Because many wildlife diseases are also transmissible to man, precautions must be taken in collecting specimens to prevent human exposure. Carcasses, and portions of carcasses, should be placed in moisture-impervious containers. Plastic, since it is unbreakable, is better than glass. Metal may rust or tarnish. Rubber gloves should be worn in handling diseased animals and tissues. In handling live animals, avoid bites and scratches. Wash with soap and apply disinfectants if accidental contamination occurs.

IMPORTANCE OF WILDLIFE DISEASE STUDIES

In summary, studies of wildlife diseases are important not only to insure survival of the wildlife species, but also to safeguard livestock industries and the health of man. An abundance of healthy wild animals denotes a high quality environment. Conversely, diseases in wild populations can serve as an early warning system of problems in the environment.

SELECTED REFERENCES

Page, L. A., ed. 1976. Wildlife diseases. Plenum Publ. Corp., New York. 686 pp.

Cowan, I. McT., and L. Karstad, 1979. Post-mortem examinations. *In* S. Schemintz, ed. Wildlife management techniques. 4th ed. The Wildl. Soc., Washington, D.C.

PREDATION— PROBLEMS AND PRINCIPLES

Roger M. Latham

The problem of predator control is as old as man, for in the early stages of evolution, he was an important prey species himself. Until perhaps 50 years ago, predators were to be killed at every opportunity. Even game managers discussed ways and means for exterminating certain of the more destructive species. And in their zeal they came close to accomplishing their goal in a few cases.

But in more recent years, particularly since about 1940, predators have been viewed in a new light. With the development of the science of ecology and the modern-day concern for the total environment, carnivores are recognized as occupying an important place in nature. With this has come a new assessment of wildlife values.

Those responsible for formulating the philosophy of wildlife conservation now dare suggest that an individual mountain lion has far more aesthetic appeal, scientific interest, recreational value, and economic impact than an individual mule deer or a white-faced steer. Today those men can call for the protection of the birds of prey without fear of censure from game managers, sportsmen, farmers, and the general public. In other words, the old adage "the only good predator is a dead predator" is no longer in vogue.

PRINCIPLES

The principles of predation may be stated as follows:

1. The term predator does not necessarily denote a destructive animal. Some of the animals most beneficial in respect to man's economy are predators.

The barn owl is capable of killing as many as 8,000 rats and mice in a single year. Weasels work furiously 365 days of the year destroying mice and other rodents to the benefit of man.

2. Generally speaking, predators live on the annual surplus produced by a prey species. Their influence seldom causes a serious reduction in succeeding breeding populations.

The "law of diminishing returns" preserves the prey species from serious decimation. Except in rare instances, the predator turns to other prey when a species becomes sufficiently reduced to be difficult to find.

3. Except under the most extenuating circumstances, no predator except man is capable of exterminating a prey species.

Only man with his sophisticated equipment and materials (guns, traps, nets, poisons, etc.) can reduce animal populations to extermination. Only man, sometimes with the aid of his domestic animals, can destroy the habitat

128

Latham, Roger M. (deceased). Outdoor Editor, Pittsburgh Press, Former Chief, Wildlife Research Division, Pennsylvania Game Commission.

of animal species. Only man can utilize biological methods, such as sterilization, to accomplish total control.

4. The most destructive predators, when occurring only sparsely, can have little effect upon the total numbers of desirable prey species. However, an only slightly destructive predatory animal, if it occurs in sufficient abundance, can become a potent decimating agent.

It is obvious that neither the rare peregrine falcon nor the equally rare black-footed ferret would be likely to exert much pressure on prey populations when the numbers of each are so very low. On the other hand, the ground squirrel or the cotton rat, occurring by the millions, could be tremendously destructive if each took only one bird egg during the entire year!

5. A reduction in the number of predators on a given area does not necessarily mean a reduction in predator pressure on a specific prey animal.

A certain segment of a prey population appears to be vulnerable to predation. Conversely, another segment appears to be relatively secure. The vulnerable animals can be removed quickly by many predators or more slowly by a lesser number. The end result may be much the same in either case. Those predators that survive the control efforts merely live better!

6. Because herbivorous animal populations tend to increase toward self-destruction, if not held in check by various counterforces, predation may be considered a beneficial service for most prey species of this type. Predators may be an important factor in the survival of some prey species.

Hoofed animals and rodents are inclined to overpopulate their habitat when effective controls are absent. The end result of this overpopulation is usually a "crash" brought on by starvation, disease, or emigration. The famed Kaibab Forest deer herd is a classic example of a browsing animal destroying its own habitat because its normal large predators (including man) had been eliminated or not allowed to operate.

The hypothesis has been advanced that egg predation might be responsible for the prosperity and survival of many game birds in the temperate zone. If there were no second and third nesting attempts by upland game birds and waterfowl, brought on by the loss by predation of the first nests, then it is conceivable that reproduction on certain years could be an almost complete failure. Unseasonal freezes or prolonged cold rains could destroy almost every egg and chick, if these periods of adverse weather coincided with egg-laying or hatching.

7. The net effect of predation upon a particular prey species is measured, not in terms of its percent occurrence in the predator's diet, but rather in terms of the numbers lost to predation in relation to the total population of the prey species.

Too many predator control programs have been instigated on the basis of predator food habits studies, rather than upon ecological studies in the field. Why should a game department pay bounty upon great horned owls, simply because cottontail rabbits occur regularly in their stomachs, when hunters and owls together may be harvesting less than 30 percent of the total cottontail population?

8. Availability, above all else, governs the diet of most predatory animals. The availability of prey animals may be regulated or controlled by cyclic influences, weather conditions, presence of protective cover, adequacy of nutrition, parasites or diseases and probably other factors. Usually, a predator transfers its pressure to other species when the primary prey species become relatively or totally unavailable. Only in the Arctic regions does the predator commonly concentrate on a single prey species. In this case, it emigrates or starves when its source of food becomes unavailable.

9. Predator control may benefit a desired species on areas where other environmental conditions are favorable for increase, especially when the numbers of the prey species are well below normal. This applies particularly

to big game species and large predators. Seldom has predator control produced startling, or even measurable, results where an effort has been made to control smaller predators (foxes, hawks, owls, weasels, etc.) for the benefit of small game animals (rabbits, pheasants, grouse, quail, etc.).

10. The need or value of predator control in game management is proportional to the intensity of the game harvest.

Predator control efforts can be considered worthwhile only where any considerable portion of the increase generated is utilized by man for food or recreation.

PROBLEMS

Problems in regard to predation and predator control are:

1. There is a need for a proper definition of the word predator and a better identification of predators to be classified as truly destructive and requiring control. Additional research is required to determine the exact relationship between predator and prey. A philosophy of giving the carnivore the "benefit of the doubt" should be adopted until studies prove its total ecological relationship. Too often a predator is suspected without proof.

2. Control efforts need to be specific for the target predator. Extreme caution should always be exercised to prevent loss of other wildlife, including certain predators, and to prevent the contamination of the environment in general. Such methods as pole traps, poison bait stations, and sometimes even regular steel trap lines can be notoriously nonselective.

3. The cost of predator control to protect livestock has often cost more than the livestock is worth. On much of the sheep range in the western states, coyote control efforts have exceeded the value of the meat and wool produced by the sheep grazed in the region. Adequate estimates are seldom, if ever, available of the number of livestock "saved" by predator control.

4. Emphasis should be upon control or alleviation of the damage, rather than upon control of predators. Traditional predator control programs are just that—they concentrate their attention upon killing predators. In many situations, there are other more suitable ways of controlling the damage presumed to be done by predators.

5. The bounty system is most often inefficient, nonselective, and noneffective. Other, more practical methods should be substituted in almost every instance. Bounties are too often paid on animals that would have been killed otherwise. Bounties encourage indiscriminate killing, with the hope that the bird shot or the animal trapped will be the bountied species. It is rare that effective control is achieved through bounty payments. Normally, the governmental agency is merely paying for a good portion of the normal, annual population turnover.

6. A need exists for the recognition of the many values of the predator. Civilized men cannot afford to permit or condone the extinction of predatory animals. They are too valuable for scientific and aesthetic purposes and perhaps for ecological values yet undetermined. Because of their great worth as a hunter's trophy, big cats, wolves, and others may have tremendous economic value within the region where they are found. Also, abundant predators, such as foxes, coyotes, and native cats, have largely unrealized recreational values for hunting, photographing, predator calling, and for students of nature. Some of this activity, especially for those hunters who run hounds or use calling devices, can be profitable as well.

Trapping has become an important recreational pursuit for many individuals. Thousands use a portion of their vacation time to run a trapline for beavers and other fur bearers, almost totally as an "escape" from the pressures of their civilized world. Trapping is "big business" in the United States and Canada, with a net annual income to U.S. trappers in excess of $200 million (Sisson-Lopez and Cringan 1979). A substantial percentage of this amount is realized from the sale of furs from predatory mammals.

7. There is a need to provide people with biological information concerning the benefits and values of predation and the need for caution and careful direction in control. This can best be done in the schools and universities and through the efforts of federal, state, and private conservation agencies and organizations.

SUMMARY

Historically, survival of man has been severely tested by environmental pressures. These include competition with other animals for food, space, and life itself. Predators have been one of the chief competitors with man. This relentless conflict has continued into the twentieth century where different cultures, new knowledge, and a change of values have placed predators in a new perspective. The science of ecology (the study of interrelationships among living organisms and their environment) has provided us with a sound basis for management, rather than elimination, of predator populations. One of the greatest challenges facing educators and researchers today is that of providing adequate information to establish wise public policy and implementation for both selective predator control and species preservation.

SELECTED REFERENCES

Errington, P. L. 1967. Of predation and life. Iowa State Univ. Press, Ames. 277 pp.

Leopold, A. S. 1964. Predator and rodent control in the United States. Trans. N. Amer. Wildl. Conf. 29: 27-49.

U.S. Department of the Interior. 1967. Man and wildlife: a policy for animal damage control. Bureau of Sport Fisheries and Wildlife, Washington, D.C. Processed. 12 pp.

Sisson-Lopez, J., and Cringan, A. T. 1979. Analysis of U.S. fur trade. Report to U.S. Forest Service (in preparation). Colo. State Univ.

D. Delany

HABITAT IMPROVEMENT

James D. Yoakum

Wildlife management has been defined as the science and art of the interrelationships between wild animals, habitats, and man (Giles 1969). Therefore, the maintenance or manipulation of habitats is a major component of the wildlife biologist's responsibilities. This responsibility cannot be slighted, because wildlife habitats in North America are undergoing tremendous changes. These changes are primarily due to man's activities: grazing rangelands for red meat; logging forests for building materials; or constructing towns, cities, and highways for concentrated human activities. Man's manipulation of the environment for his needs is the most prevalent factor affecting wildlife habitat and, consequently, wildlife populations. Often it is not the *act* of using natural resources, but the *way* man uses these resources that determines the total impact on wildlife.

There are many examples of how the manipulated environment can be beneficial or detrimental to wildlife. For instance, logging dense, old-growth forests may be disastrous to the spotted owl's nesting and feeding requirements, but could greatly increase preferred forage for elk. Wildlife biologists must recognize the factors that affect wildlife habitat, specifically those not designated or implemented for wildlife, and understand the habitat and animal interrelationships. The wildlife biologist has the responsibility to show how such practices can be modified to increase habitat diversity for the benefit of wildlife and man. These interrelationships are well documented by Thomas et al. (1976) for habitats in the Northwest and Holbrook (1974) for habitats in the South.

PRINCIPLES

Wildlife habitat management is basically concerned with two major objectives: (1) maintaining quality habitat as it exists in a natural ecosystem and (2) providing quality habitat where it has deteriorated or where a specific habitat component is lacking water, food, or shelter. The following basic principles should be included in planning and implementing habitat manipulation practices:

1. Projects must be justified according to biological needs based on intensive investigation.

2. Proposed practices must be evaluated for their effect on other natural resources and land uses.

3. Projects must be economically practical and should specify if the objective is to maintain, improve, or completely alter the existing habitat character.

Yoakum, James D.   Wildlife Management Biologist, Bureau of Land Management, Reno, Nevada

4. Improvements must simulate natural conditions. Generally native flora and fauna should be perpetuated.

5. Manipulation projects must be designed to follow natural topographical features rather than geometrical squares or strips.

6. Projects must be evaluated at intervals to determine if the objectives have been accomplished.

PRACTICES

Aldo Leopold's (1933) list of "axe, plow, cow, and fire" as major habitat management tools has expanded with new knowledge and technological advances. All of the land-use tools available to the farmer, forester, and construction engineer have been used to manipulate wildlife habitat. However, all the habitat manipulation techniques cannot be described in one chapter; consequently, a guide for selection of projects and ways to "accomplish management goals" is presented. Each method must be judged critically for each site and for the goal to be accomplished.

This chapter concentrates on methods and techniques of habitat manipulation specifically designed to increase food, water, or cover for wildlife. The primary objective is to provide the basic principles for the variety of techniques available. It is not a complete summary of all techniques but shows the tremendous variety of methods available for improving food, water, and cover. The wildlifer is cautioned to become familiar with proven methods, for poorly planned or executed habitat projects can be harmful to wildlife.

FOOD PRODUCTION

Improving food production is the most frequently used technique to manipulate habitat for wildlife. This may be accomplished by (1) mast or fruit production, (2) browse plantings, (3) herbaceous plantings, and (4) aquatic plant development.

Mast and Fruits

Mast is the fruit of oak, hickory, beech, gum, cherry, ash, and other tree and shrub species. Mast occurs on a wide variety of shrubs, such as flowering dogwood, wild grapes, haws, crabapples, persimmon, serviceberry, sumacs, wild plums, wild cherries, and many others. The three major methods of improving mast and fruit production are propagation, release, and protection. Propagation is the direct planting of desirable seeds or transplants. Release involves the removal of competitive plants through such practices as mechanical crushing, controlled burning, or chemical means. Protection includes the preservation of mast producers until they reach mast producing age and protection of the mast itself from consumption by undesirable organisms.

Experience in developing shelterbelts, windbreaks, living fences, and gully or waterway plantings has provided much helpful information on propagation. It is suggested that the person interested in plantings consult the local office of cooperative extension or Soil Conservation Service.

Browse Plantings

Browse is defined as the shrubs and trees, and especially their leaves, shoots, and twigs, used by wildlife for food. In some situations, such as a range recently burned by wildfire, there may be a need to plant browse species to restore forage.

Browse manipulation practices can be grouped into the following categories:

1. Release through thinning to reduce competition from less desirable species.

2. Rejuvenation through breaking, crushing, herbicide spraying, pruning, or burning.

3. Planting in areas of need, either to introduce seed stock or to provide for additional browse production.

Browse manipulation is occurring in every western state today. These practices are mostly aimed towards improving forage for livestock, but similar manipulation techniques can definitely improve deteriorated ranges for the benefit of wildlife. Here are a few of the major types of conversion practices currently being implemented:

1. Chaining consists of dragging a heavy anchor chain between two crawler tractors through undesirable vegetation in order to break off or uproot plants. Following chaining, the area is aerially planted with a seed mixture, then chained again to cover the seeds. Such practices are frequently used in sagebrush and pinyon-juniper types. This technique has proven successful on winter deer areas in the Great Basin Region.

2. Cabling is a technique used in areas where the need exists to increase residual stands of desirable shrubs and herbaceous cover. Cabling practices are conducted essentially the same way as chaining, except that a one and one-half inch diameter cable, 150 to 200 feet long, is used.

3. Spraying of selective chemicals may be used to reduce stands of undesirable browse. Basal sprouting of shrubs that have grown too high or dense to provide for deer and elk forage can be stimulated by killing the aerial crowns with chemicals. The sensitivity of different species to the chemical concentration and time of application should enable discriminating manipulation of the habitat. However, the habitat manager must have a thorough knowledge of this treatment as it affects the total environment, both on a short- and long-term basis.

4. Burning in a planned or controlled manner is one of the more economical procedures for removal of vegetation. It can be used as a first step in seedbed preparation to reduce competing plants, to create openings in dense stands of brush, to break seed dormancy in some species, or for other purposes.

5. Seeding can follow any of several procedures commonly used, including: deep-furrow drill, Hansen browse seeder, cutout disk, seed dribblers, aerial broadcasting, and hand broadcasting. The kinds of equipment and methods of use are described in the Range Seeding Equipment Handbook (USDA Forest Service 1965) and Habitat Improvement Techniques (Yoakum et al. 1979).

Herbaceous Plantings

Alert habitat managers may seek opportunities to improve herbaceous plantings along with other land management activities such as timber stand improvement, type conversion, soil stabilization after wildfire burns, restoration of roadside cover, ski-slope or skid-tail stabilization, patch cutting of timber, and range reseedings. It is often possible to recommend desirable wildlife foods for inclusion in the seeding mixtures for these areas (Fig. 1).

Ordinarily, regular farming methods provide the best chance for successful establishment of grass or forb plantations. Given adequate soil moisture, the three essential steps needed for herbaceous seeding are: (1) removal of other plant competitors, (2) planting seed at proper depth, and (3) good cover of seed. The species to be chosen will vary by region, climate, elevation, and soil type. Desirable native seed, when obtainable, reduces the gamble on most sites.

Mixture Seedings

For most western range rehabilitation projects designed to improve habitat for wildlife, seed mixtures should be used rather than straight browse or grass plantings. Native ranges containing a wide choice of grass, forbs, and browse usually support the most abundant wildlife populations. Therefore, habitat rehabilitation projects should be designed not only to increase the quantity of grass, forbs, and browse, but to provide a well-balanced variety as well.

Mixture seedings are best accomplished when the following basic principles are followed (Plummer et al. 1968):

1. Reduce other competitive plants to allow moisture and soil nutrients for planted seed.

Fig. 1. Wild turkeys feeding in opening created in continuous forest habitat. (Courtesy of Pennsylvania Game Commission)

2. Plan the project using the right method for the specific habitat needing improvement.

3. Eliminate or control grazing by livestock, rabbits, or rodents to allow young seedlings an opportunity to grow and reproduce.

4. Determine whether annual precipitation is adequate.

5. Decide whether the terrain and soil can support the desired forage species and permit restoration treatments.

6. Plant adapted species and strains.

7. Plant mixtures, especially on variable sites. A major reason for using mixtures is to put different species on the site conditions to which they are best suited.

8. Use sufficient seed to insure a stand.

9. Make sure that proper planting and coverage of seed is carried out.

10. Seed usually in late fall and early winter, but transplant in early spring.

WATER DEVELOPMENTS

The supply and quality of water throughout the year often can be improved for wildlife use. Also, water can be "removed" to reduce animal numbers or use of areas. Although usually developed for uses other than wildlife, when properly designed, water developments can provide additional values directly to wildlife.

Following are some methods of improving waters specifically for wildlife:

1. Natural waterholes are often found in "playas" and rocky areas where runoff waters are accumulated in a depression. At times, such holes can be improved by deepening the catchment or by trenching runoff water directly to the basin.

2. Springs and seeps can be developed, but before attempting to improve natural water sources, one should consult an experienced water

developer, as it is possible to do more damage than good by improper practices. A good development, however, can be of tremendous value to wildlife.

3. Reservoirs and small ponds may be formed by building a dam directly across a drainage or by enclosing a depression to one side of a drainage and constructing a diversion ditch into the resulting basin. The assistance of professional engineers is often needed for projects of this type.

4. Water catchments during the past two decades have involved many types of self-filling watering devices utilizing precipitation and designed for the use of wildlife in semiarid areas. Probably the greatest number have been constructed primarily for the use of quail. These are called "gallinaceous guzzlers" or just "guzzlers" (Fig. 2). Water catchments of various designs have also been constructed for the benefit of deer, elk, antelope, bighorn sheep, sage grouse, rabbits, songbirds, etc. (See the references at the end of this paper.)

5. Other water developments that the habitat manager may construct include such items as tanks, troughs, or wells for wildlife. Generally, these projects are constructed for other purposes; that is, livestock, campground water storage, and fire suppression. Often a slight modification or addition to the design will provide water for wildlife.

6. Safety devices in water developments should always be considered. Some water developments planned for other uses are designed in such a manner that they attract and entrap wildlife. The hazard of drowning can be reduced by the addition of floats, ramps, or ladders in the facilities, thereby allowing avenues of escape for wild animals.

Fig. 2.   Chukar partridge using "guzzler," a water catchment device used in arid West. Rain falling on cement apron (center) is collected in tank underneath. Birds have access to water by sloping ramp at lower right. (Courtesy of D. L. Gilbert)

COVER IMPROVEMENT

Cover is as important to wildlife as food and water. The absence of cover, its sparseness, or its poor distribution can limit the use of an area by wildlife. When manipulating food or water, care should be taken to assure that enough cover of various kinds is retained to meet wildlife needs.

Following are two categories of cover, with suggested methods for their improvements:

136

1. Vegetation is protective cover, offering hiding places from the sun in the summer, or from driving rains, winds, or snow in the winter. Vegetation from which game cannot be driven by predators or hunters constitutes protective cover.

Examples:

a. Planted hedgerows provide desirable escape, refuge, and travel lanes.

b. Brush piles of small trees, tree limbs, or shrubs can be loosely piled into heaps. Grass, forbs, and vines will grow up through the brush and add density and permanence to the pile.

c. Natural and artificial roosts can be provided for some species of wildlife, such as quail, turkeys, and many songbirds, that require adequate perching or roosting sites. Such cover can be provided through natural vegetation plantings or artificial roosting structures.

2. Specific recommendations to maintain or improve nesting cover are:

a. Such cover must be protected from excessive grazing, fires, and mowing during critical nesting and rearing periods.

b. Provide cover in ample amounts, as this is the most critical problem for many ground nesting game animals.

c. Existing den or nesting tree areas need to be preserved, while artificial nest structures should remain primarily a secondary technique.

d. Artificial nest structures can substitute for natural sites in otherwise suitable habitat (Fig. 3).

Fig. 3. Wood duck nesting structure used in areas lacking natural tree cavities. (Courtesy of Pennsylvania Game Commission)

Nest boxes have been useful for wood ducks, squirrels, and songbirds. The nest boxes must be properly designed, located, erected, and maintained for beneficial results. They must be durable, predator proof, weathertight, lightweight, economical to build, and convenient to erect and maintain.

Nesting platforms have been constructed for the benefit of birds of prey and geese (Fig. 4). Their value to geese is greatest in areas where lack of

Fig. 4. Elevated nesting structures have been provided for Canada geese in areas of fluctuating water levels. (Courtesy of Colorado Division of Wildlife)

high nest sites requires nesting on the ground and predation becomes a major mortality factor. Nest cones have proven successful in increasing mourning dove survival. These cones are made of wire and placed in the forks of trees.

WETLAND IMPROVEMENT

Techniques for improving wetlands will vary with water management, soil, climate, topography, and plant succession. Some areas may best be developed primarily for waterfowl, others for fur bearer production.

The habitat manager can often use a variety of practices to create interspersion of open water and marshland. A few suggested techniques follow:

1. Shallow marshes provide nest sites, cover, and food. A marsh should have open areas for maximum wildlife values. Artificial impoundments are a common practice used to improve existing marshes or to create new ones. The objective is to control water levels as a method of increasing desired food and cover vegetation. Ditching and dredging techniques are frequently needed to control water levels.

2. Potholes or sumps may be created as a means of increasing water surface acreage in areas of heavy plant cover. Draglines and bulldozers have been used to develop new potholes. The use of a blasting agent may be the most expeditious and economical method in many regions.

3. Green tree reservoirs are bottomland hardwood areas flooded during the dormant tree growth periods for the purpose of attracting waterfowl. The practice is mainly used in the South.

4. Water level controls are often needed for the production of submerged aquatic vegetation that requires stable water levels. Such structures include dikes, embankments, spillways, level ditching, and plugs. Needless to say, it is highly advisable to utilize engineering assistance.

5. Plantings for food and cover should be undertaken only after thorough surveys of existing conditions. The important native plants should be managed first. Desirable vegetation that has been successfully planted includes pondweeds, smartweed, duck potato, duckweeds, coontail, grasses, cereal crops, and alkali bulrush.

6. Nesting and resting sites are often needed. Ridges and islands can be constructed with bulldozers or draglines during dry periods or during the con-

struction of ponds. Floating islands can be anchored in shallow, low water ponds.

SUMMARY
The techniques described are only a few of many available to the habitat manager. Information regarding additional improvement practices or greater detail on improvements described in this chapter may be found in the chapter entitled "Habitat Improvement Techniques" published in the fourth edition of the Wildlife Society's book, *Wildlife Management Techniques* (Yoakum, et al. 1979). This chapter also contains various mitigating measures for wildlife habitat management; for example, raptor roosts on power lines, livestock fence specifications best for allowing big game access, road and highway construction, and other measures. This report is the most current information on habitat principles and practices available to the wildlife manager. It is used in course studies for colleges and universities, as guidelines for state and federal wildlife management agencies, and as evidence in court cases on the values and procedures for wildlife habitat improvement.

LITERATURE CITED
Giles, R. H. 1969. The approach. Pp. 1-4 *in* S. Schemintz, ed. Wildlife management techniques. 4th ed. The Wildl. Soc., Washington, D.C. 623 pp.

Holbrook, H. L. 1974. A system for wildlife habitat management on southern National Forests. The Wildl. Soc. Bull. 2(3): 119-123.

Leopold, A. 1933. Game management. Charles Scribner's Sons, New York. 481 pp.

Plummer, A. P., D. R. Christensen, and S. B. Monson. 1968. Restoring big game range in Utah. Utah Div. Fish & Game, Salt Lake City. Pub. No. 68-3. 183 pp.

Thomas, J. W., R. J. Miller, H. Black, J. E. Rodick, and C. Maser. 1976. Guidelines for maintaining and enhancing wildlife habitat in forest management in the Blue Mountains of Oregon and Washington. North Amer. Wildl. and Nat. Res. Conf. Trans. 41: 452-476.

U.S.D.A. Forest Service. 1965. Range seeding handbook. Washington, D.C. 150 pp.

Yoakum, J., W. P. Dasmann, R. Sanderson, C. M. Nixon, and H. S. Crawford. 1979. Habitat management techniques. *In* S. Schemintz, ed. Wildlife management techniques. 4th ed. The Wildl. Soc., Washington, D.C. 623 pp.

SELECTED REFERENCES
Atlantic Waterfowl Council. 1972. Techniques handbook of waterfowl habitat development and management. Bethany Beach, Delaware. 2nd ed. 218 pp.

Shoman, J. J., B. L. Ashbaugh, and C. D. Tolman. 1966. Wildlife habitat improvement. National Audubon Society, New York. 96 pp.

U.S.D.A. Forest Service. 1969. Wildlife habitat improvement handbook. Washington, D.C. Looseleaf, n.p.

U.S.D.I. Bureau of Land Management. 1964. Water development: range improvements in Nevada for wildlife, livestock, and human use. Reno, Nevada. 37 pp.

WATERFOWL AREAS— DEVELOPMENT AND MANAGEMENT

C. J. Barstow and Dale E. Whitesell

Two of the primary objectives of waterfowl management in North America are to maintain sufficient habitat to support desired populations of waterfowl and to maintain the wide distribution of the waterfowl resource. Acquiring control (purchase, lease, or other means) of suitable waterfowl areas and, in most cases, enhancement through development and management have been the principal means of attaining these objectives. Recreation, especially hunting, has been a basic purpose in the establishment of waterfowl areas. Hunting interests, in fact, are responsible for a major portion of the existing areas through private clubs, state programs, Ducks Unlimited projects, and federal acquisition via duck stamp funds.

Destruction of wetlands is continuing to occur at an alarming rate (Sanderson and Bellrose 1969). Coupled with the general trend in land use and degeneration of existing habitats, these factors are progressively narrowing the base for waterfowl. A majority of the existing waterfowl habitat is on private property. This represents a tremendous potential for development and for the future of the birds—*if* interest can be stimulated to save and enhance these habitats.

Although the general public shares the responsibilities of maintaining the waterfowl resource, the following have traditionally been the principals involved in developing waterfowl areas: (1) private individuals and groups, (2) citizen organizations such as Ducks Unlimited, and (3) government (county, state, provincial, and federal).

The future of this resource is dependent upon creating and maintaining public interest, keeping existing projects, retaining threatened habitat, and enhancement of areas through sound development and management.

GENERAL HABITAT REQUIREMENTS FOR WATERFOWL

Waterfowl (ducks, geese, swans, coots, gallinules, and rails) comprise an extremely diverse and unique group of birds. They vary widely in physical characteristics, behavior, distribution, and, therefore, habitat requirements. For all this diversity, they share an important similarity—dependence upon specific kinds of wetland environment. Because of migration and other factors, these needs often change geographically with the seasons—even for a given species. Waterfowl areas are thus designed to provide one or a combination of the following basic needs or kinds of habitat: (1) nesting and production, (2) molting and staging (premigration requirements), (3) migration, and (4) wintering. These divergent habitats and requirements of various species of waterfowl may be attained through a very wide range of land and

Barstow, C. J.   Regional Director, Ducks Unlimited, Inc. Stoddard, Wisconsin
Whitesell, Dale E.   Executive Vice President, Ducks Unlimited, Inc., Chicago

water manipulation. Examples might include upland cover for ground nesting birds, creation of large, deep marshes for certain species of divers, maintenance of timbered swamps for wood ducks, or provision of pastures for geese. These programs would include the essentials: a place for water related birds to live, breed, feed, loaf, and prosper—in other words, space, food, cover, water, and some degree of protection.

A basic understanding of the above complexities—the birds, their habitat requirements, and wetland systems—is absolutely necesary to provide a sound foundation for area development and management. Two excellent sources of general information on habitat requirements are *Ducks, Geese and Swans of North America* (Bellrose 1978) and *Waterfowl Tomorrow* (Linduska, ed. 1964).

PLANNING THE DEVELOPMENT OF WATERFOWL AREAS

A completed waterfowl area may look rather simple—possibly a dike, control gate, and a flooded area, but this simplicity is misleading. The planning, development, and operation of a wetland can be one of the most complicated and expensive of all wildlife management endeavors. The work involves applying knowledge of soils, water chemistry, hydrology, plant succession, engineering, construction, and other specialties. A waterfowl area is generally a lasting environment. The benefits or mistakes can be obvious for a long time. For these reasons, the planning and operation of an area should include the use of the above skills. Otherwise finances will be wasted and success jeopardized. Local and regional experience and expertise should be utilized.

What can go wrong if good planning is not executed and followed? Flooding of adjacent property, adverse changes in water quality, inability to fully manipulate water levels, depredations, rapid sedimentation, inadequate supplies of water, excessive hunting pressure or other uses, washed-out dikes and spillways, public hostility, and a basketful of other headaches can occur.

The following sequence of planning should be appropriate in considering and designing both small and extensive wetland developments.

Reconnaissance

1. *Collection of available support information.* This might include soil surveys, hydrological data, topographic maps, aerial photographs, land-use records, biological reports, local knowledge, and other related information. This should also involve experienced consultation specifically related to all aspects of wetland/waterfowl management.

2. *Determination of objectives of the project.* Is the area to be for breeding, postbreeding, migration, or wintering? Is it to be used for hunting, research, nature observations, general recreation, and/or other purposes? Will it include a refuge? In government projects it should be determined whether the area fits into flyway programs, needs, and priorities.

3. *Determination of scope and potentials.* A generalized concept of the scope, potentials and problems of the area should be possible through limited field inspection and use of the above support information. This tentative information will be necessary to determine if the project should be pursued further.

What are the initial and long-term potentials for development, management, number and kinds of birds, hunting, and other uses; i.e., for reaching the determined objectives? How large an area, total and flooded, will be needed? Is control of the necessary lands possible? If several potential areas are being considered, how do they rank as to capabilities and relative costs? Are sufficient funds available to carry out the program? What are the major projected problems?

Earth fill dam and water control structure under construction. (Courtesy of Ducks Unlimited)

Site Investigation and Development Plans

If the reconnaissance indicates that the area is suitable, intensive site investigation and detailed development plans will represent the next stage.

1. *Site investigations.* This will involve intensive investigation of the same basics that were considered generally in the preliminary reconnaissance—topography, soils, water supply, water quality, vegetation, animals, etc. This detailed information is essential in the development of sound engineering and biological aspects of the area development.

2. *Development plans.* This should include design of water control facilities (dams, control structures, water supply, and ditches), roads, accesses, parking lots, blinds, buildings, islands, shoreline modification, and food and cover programs. The following publications offer good guidelines for development of wetland areas: *Waterfowl Habitat Development and Management Techniques Handbook* (Anon. 1963); *Managing Farm Fields, Wetlands and Waters for Wild Ducks in the South* (Davidson and Neely 1959); and *Ponds and Marshes for Wild Ducks on Farms and Ranches in the Northern Plains* (Hamor, et al. 1968).

3. *Cost/benefit analysis.* Analysis of costs (including annual operating costs) versus benefits of the proposed project may be helpful, especially if several areas are being considered for development.

4. *Legal review.* There are many laws (state, federal, and other government units) now in effect that relate to floodplains, wetlands, use of water, and, in some cases, dam construction (safety). A thorough investigation of these laws and associated requirements should be involved in planning. Public hearings may also be required.

5. *Public relations.* Public relations can make or break a project. It is an absolute necessity for government programs, especially since many must successfully pass review in public hearings. It can be critical for private areas as well. Through good communication programs, the public should understand the reasons for projects and hopefully back them. Local support can minimize poaching, draining of impoundments, destruction of facilities, and other forms of vandalism, which can seriously jeopardize the success of an area.

PLANNING THE MANAGEMENT OF THE WATERFOWL AREA

Preliminary management considerations were probably designed as a common process to development planning, i.e., in the determination of potentials of the area and overall project costs. Detailed management plans will be needed to form annual and long-term operational programs on the area. Management, like development, is expensive; thus planning must be sound, and the results evaluated on a continuing basis. The initiation and maintenance of records will be essential in this evaluation and in long-term management planning.

Management will probably include a mix of operations involving habitat, wildlife, and people. The following represent management potentials that might be considered, depending on the objectives of the area:

1. *Habitat.* Water level manipulation is the most effective and efficient tool available to enhance the productiveness and attractiveness of an area and therefore help to assure its continuing success. It can normally be used to provide optimum food and cover requirements. Mowing, burning, soil disturbance, planting (natural and agricultural varieties), fertilization, chemical control, timber management, and grazing can also be used to increase the productivity of the area. Nesting islands, boxes, rafts, and level ditches may be appropriate on some projects.

2. *Wildlife.* Management of wildlife and habitat management are almost the same, but not quite. A slight difference in water depth or location of a refuge boundary can be attractive for certain species and restrictive to others. Some species such as Canada geese may be desired but only at given population levels. Flight and use patterns can be predetermined by coordination of habitat and hunter management operations. Predator control, depredation management, and the introduction of breeding stock (Giant Canada geese, for example) represent other problems and potentials that might be considered. Special area regulations can be very important in regard to planning management of wildlife on the site.

3. *People.* Management of human use of the waterfowl resource and area is essential to the success of a project. This is especially critical where multiple use is a special consideration. Hunting, trapping, fishing, nature study, research, and possibly special land use, such as grazing and sharecropping, might all be involved. Without proper planning, these uses will be in conflict and result in adverse public reaction. Planning may involve time-and-place controls on the various activities and the design of necessary support facilities such as roads and access.

Waterfowl hunting management is a very important and often neglected phase of area operation. The success of some projects with high potential has been minimal due to lack of controls. The program can include management of number of hunters, time of hunting, spacing of activity, and establishment of refuges. Special features such as blinds, boat launching facilities, parking areas, toilets, and other use facilities may be necessary. These can be important tools in the control of numbers and distribution of hunters.

4. *Administration.* Managers often fail to provide themselves with sufficient time and resources (equipment and facilities) to permit proper administration of an area. This problem should be recognized and prevented through good planning. The size of the area, scope of management, and basic project objectives should provide guidelines to the level of administration required.

DEVELOPMENT AND MANAGEMENT OF WATERFOWL AREAS

Development, large or small in extent, should follow the prescribed plans and be of high quality. Otherwise, the area will be plagued with maintenance problems and related additional costs. This is not a place for amateur work. Engineering and biological specialists should be involved. Continuous supervision will be especially critical where contractual services are used.

Management requires implementation and maintenance. Thus, managerial service will be necessary to operate the area on a sound basis. It will help to assure success and to protect the initial and ongoing investment. Depending on the size of the area and the level of management applied, this may involve a part-time caretaker or perhaps a full staff. It is often valuable to have such personnel on the site during development.

Development and management are only briefly discussed here. This does not imply lack of importance. These phases of area operation bring a project to life. Applying knowledge and work to water, vegetation, and land and seeing the results in waterfowl usage can be extremely challenging and personally rewarding.

Fig. 2. Stoplog water control structure. (Courtesy of Ducks Unlimited)

EVALUATION OF SUCCESS

Evaluation of the success of the development/management program is essential. It is required to compare results to the original projected potentials, to assess management practices (results and costs), and to strive to improve the project. The following types of information are normally basic to this important phase of operation:

1. water level records
2. notes on vegetation species and abundance—analysis of transects
3. phenological notes—migration dates, spring breakup, freezeup
4. inventory of species, production, and/or abundance
5. records of human usage—hunters, harvest and success; fishing; trapping; nonconsumptive activities; demographics
6. photographic records of development and habitat management (especially to note changes in programs and results)
7. notes on effects of changes in management techniques (probably involving all of the above).

The challenge is to have adequate evaluation and not an excess. It is not uncommon to find the situation where evaluation is conducted for the sake of evaluation and not for the reasons mentioned above. This can cause a drain on financial resources and jeopardize the success of the area.

SUMMARY

Due to the continuing destruction of wetlands, the development and management of habitat is extremely important to the future of the waterfowl resource. The realization of this potential will be dependent upon the sharing of mutual interest, concern, and action by private and government sectors.

Besides the obvious and critical benefits to waterfowl, the creation or improvement of wetlands can provide numerous other products—economic, general recreational, hunting, and habitat for numerous other species, etc.

Due to the relatively high costs, and the complexity of both wetlands and waterfowl, a development and management program must be planned and executed in a sound manner.

LITERATURE CITED

Anonymous. 1963. Waterfowl habitat development and management handbooks. Habitat Management and Development Committee, Atlantic Waterfowl Council. 164 pp.

Bellrose, F. C. 1978. Ducks, geese and swans of North America. Stackpole Books, Harrisburg, Pennsylvania. 544 pp.

Davidson, V. E. and W. W. Neely. 1959. Managing farm fields, wetlands, and waters for wild ducks in the South. U.S. Dept. of Agri. Farmers Bull. No. 2144. 14 pp.

Hamor, W. H., Hans G. Uhlig, and Lawrence V. Compton. 1968. Ponds and marshes for wild ducks on farms and ranches in the Northern Plains. U.S. Dept. of Agri. Farmers Bull. No. 2234. 16 pp.

Linduska, J. P. (ed.). 1964. Waterfowl tomorrow. U.S.D.I., Bureau Sport Fisheries and Wildlife. 770 pp.

Sanderson, G. C. and F. C. Bellrose. 1969. Wildlife habitat management of wetlands. Suplemento dos An. Acad. Brasil. Cienc. 41: 153-204.

PRIVATE LAND WILDLIFE— A NEW PROGRAM IS NEEDED

Keith W. Harmon

Land management decisions, while seldom noncontroversial, become most complex on the 1.3 billion acres of private land in the United States. This is particularly true when uses conflict with social values such as wildlife. Legal concepts of ownership have evolved over centuries, and, while ever changing, the right to use land as the owner sees fit remains the cornerstone of the law. Nowhere is the cornerstone more solid than for agricultural land. Maintenance of social values while working within the structure of ownership rights is the problem to be resolved. A solution is critical.

The value of wildlife associated with private land cannot be overemphasized, if for no other reason than that a significant portion of recreational hunting takes place there (U.S. Fish and Wildlife Service 1977).

TABLE 1. Hunting on Private Lands in the U.S.—1975 National Hunting & Fishing Survey (U.S. Fish & Wildlife Service 1977)

Type of game	Number of Hunters	% Hunters Using Private Lands	
		Residents	Non-Residents
Small game	16 million	71	80
Big game	13 million	58	37
Migratory game birds	9 million	69	57

Unquestionably, without this land resource, hunting space would be drastically reduced. The issue, however, is not solely one of space. Equally important are wildlife population levels and the role they play in hunting. The fabric of hunting is woven from a number of self-fulfilling experiences. From that premise, several philosophies emerge. One states that aesthetics, companionship, and communion with nature are paramount, even to the exclusion of "game in the bag." Stankey, et al. (1973) took a somewhat different view. While recognizing hunting as a multifaceted experience, they said, "Success represents a major component of quality; thus, when designing programs to provide satisfactory hunting experiences, we need to insure hunters some reasonable expectation of success." This philosophical treatment dovetails with Leopold's definition of game management—making land produce sustained yields of wild game. The same logic is valid for nonconsumptive wildlife. Hunting (bird-watching) without game (birds) is not hunting (bird-watching) regardless of how much land is available or how readily accessible it is.

Harmon, Keith W.   North Central Representative, Wildlife Management Institute, Firth, Nebraska

Acceptance of the first theme, related to aesthetics, dictates that a wildlife agency's resources need not be used for producing wildlife. Its role becomes one of directing moral and ethical standards. The second interpretation places the agency in the wildlife management business. Protecting, preserving, and producing wildlife for all its values become the major functions. If this responsibility is not fulfilled, there is no need for hunting ethics.

WILDLIFE—A PRODUCT OF THE LAND

A fundamental requirement for producing wildlife, or any commodity for that matter, is control and/or influence of a piece of land. In an economic society, private land-use is selected by the owner, who is influenced by potential return on investment. Very simply then, wildlife levels that provide a reasonable expectation of hunting success or quality (the definition is left to the reader) must be achieved through programs that influence land-use decisions, meeting the owner's objective of highest potential income. Wildlife agencies control about 35 million acres nationwide. Even so, statewide and regional populations of agricultural wildlife have not been maintained and continue to decline.

It has been commonly, hopefully not irreversibly, accepted that wildlife on private land is a by-product of the dominant use. This may prove acceptable at certain times. However, with today's farm technology, by-product management is yielding one result—less wildlife. As an example, eight Midwestern wildlife agencies watched annual pheasant harvests plummet from 10 million birds in the 1940's to fewer than 4 million by the 1970's (Harmon and Nelson 1973). If a reasonable expectation of success (birds bagged) is indeed a major component of quality, that likewise diminished.

The reasons for declines in farm wildlife are well documented—larger farms and fields, fewer odd areas, drainage, monoculture cropping systems, and other reasons. Cumulatively, they are expressed as increased commodity output. No tract of land can produce all products at maximum levels, economically or biologically. And as landowners increase agricultural outputs, wildlife must decrease. This straightforward relationship works equally well in reverse. That is, a habitat-related increase in wildlife produces a decrease in agricultural output (income) and is out of tune with the owner's primary objective of earning money.

ECONOMIC CONSIDERATIONS

Given the economic truism that landowners tend to devote land resources to uses that provide the greatest potential dollar return, it becomes academic, as well as unproductive, to argue whether farmers have a moral or social obligation to produce wildlife. If they do, they have generally rejected it. Until economically competitive, wildlife will continue to receive token consideration.

That farm wildlife is noncompetitive is irrefutable. A simplistic comparison, at the risk of offending the economic fraternity, illustrates this fact. In 1975, hunting leases and fees on 153 million acres grossed $225 million, an average of $1.47 per acre (U.S. Fish and Wildlife Service 1977). Crops and livestock are the major outputs from private agricultural land. Gross income was $102 billion in 1975 with production costs of $82 billion. There were approximately one billion acres being farmed, leaving a net income of $20 per acre. This was nearly 14 times greater than the gross income from wildlife. For those who insist on comparing net incomes, the disparity becomes absurd.

Certainly, cases where income from hunting is lucrative can be cited—in the vicinity of national wildlife refuges and dove hunting fields in the southeast, for example. But several points are important: (1) large concentrations of migratory birds are present, (2) normal cropping systems seldom are

147

adjusted (causing additional cost of operation) except to provide for easier bird harvests, and (3) the farmer has not modified his agricultural practices to aid wildlife or hunting. These, or any other exceptions, in no way invalidate the general contention that, for the most part, wildlife is not competitive. This single fact should be the overriding consideration in designing wildlife agency programs.

Wildlife agencies have sometimes attempted to close the money gap. Federal Aid in Wildlife Restoration (P-R) programs are cases in point. Up until the 1960's, in 14 Midwestern states, monies were earmarked for habitat work on private land. Since then, the money allocated for such work has declined with fewer and fewer states being involved. By 1970, for all practical purposes, the effort had ceased.

As the states were bowing out or severely scaling down private land efforts, emphasis was shifting to the acquisition of land. Acquiring land in fee peaked in the late fifties or early sixties. Since then, although acquisition budgets have increased, it has only been possible to purchase fewer acres due to increasing land prices. It would appear that land values have escalated more rapidly than agency income, another indication of wildlife's noncompetitive status.

The retreat from private land efforts and a fading acquisition program placed many wildlife agencies in a status quo position by the early seventies, but agriculture was unwilling to assume a similar posture. Agricultural activities varied; however, a few are particularly noteworthy. Acreages of corn for feed grain remained nearly stable, although intensive management pushed yields from 53 to nearly 88 bushels per acre. Acreage expansions did not occur because the price between 1959 and 1972 only rose 49 percent and because federal feed grain controls were in effect through 1974 and prevented an acreage increase.

Two major acreage adjustments did take place, however—a decrease in oats and an increase in soybeans. The 1959 oats crop of 35 million acres dropped to below 13 million in 1976. Although the average price had risen from 65¢ to $1.55 per bushel (138 percent), average yields only increased from 38 bushels per acre to slightly over 45 (20 percent), indicating a limited reaction to management. On the other hand, soybean production climbed from somewhat over 23 to slightly more than 50 million acres. The major incentives were a 273 percent price increase and no government controls.

The foregoing discussion indicates why wildlife production has not been competitive with traditional agriculture production. Factors of land ownership, wildlife ownership, capital sources for development and management, and management technology are all different.

U.S. Department of Agriculture (USDA) programs have a significant influence on land use. The primary goal is higher commodity prices for farmers, and to achieve this, land is removed from production to bring supply in line with demand. In this case, the federal government substitutes for the market. Several program variations have been used over the past two decades, all important, or potentially so, to wildlife on agricultural land.

The Agricultural Act of 1956 provided for long-term land retirement— five to ten years—with permanent cover required. Enrollment peaked in 1961 with nearly 29 million acres taken out of production into the "soil bank." From that point, a rapid decline took place until by 1970 all contracts had expired. Two other programs with similar features were authorized by the Food and Agricultural Acts of 1962 and 1975—but, due to a reluctance on the part of Congress to appropriate funds, only 4.6 million acres were contracted.

These programs benefited wildlife, especially the soil bank. Pheasant populations in South Dakota, for example, made spectacular gains. According to Dahlgren (1967), "The value of good habitat to the pheasant population can be seen by comparing the population of the mid-fifties, four to six million birds, with that at the height of the soil bank, eight to 11 million. Good cover nearly doubled pheasant numbers."

For various reasons, mostly political, long-term land retirement, with required permanent cover, expired in 1961 except for outstanding contracts. Surpluses of farm commodities still plagued agriculture, however, and land retirement continued. A major program change was implemented, i.e., the annual contracts. Under this approach, acreages retired nearly doubled, averaging 40 million acres annually between 1961 and 1972. Then a devaluation of the dollar, crop shortages in other countries, and a balance of payment deficit dropped retirement to 19 million acres in 1973 and to zero from 1974 to 1977. But, as has always been the case, surpluses of feed grains and wheat again became an issue. These crops were again eligible for retirement programs in 1978 and 1979, the yearly average expected to approach nearly nine million acres.

USDA's Environmental Impact Statement for the 1972 program stated, as have subsequent ones, "This program has important environmental aspects in that the set-aside acreage . . . is put to a public-benefiting conserving use on an annual basis." A survey by 13 Midwest state wildlife agencies found otherwise, the real situation being: (1) no cover on 57 percent of the retired acres (90 + in some states), (2) new seedings on about 20 percent, and (3) previous year seedings on another 20 percent. Plowing and mowing of the new and established seedings commenced early. By August, 66 percent of the total acreage had no cover, and this number rose to 85 percent by December (Harmon and Nelson 1973).

The value accruing to wildlife is illustrated by a look at South Dakota. In 1972, over three million acres were retired under annual agreements, nearly double that during the soil bank. The state wildlife agency found that 67 percent of the land retired had no cover, and of that having any wildlife value, 9 percent was judged fair, 10 percent good, and 14 percent excellent (Erickson and Wiebe 1973). Thus, even with a two-fold increase in land out of production, pheasant populations dropped below those of the pre-soil bank years.

An exhaustive review of USDA programs is not feasible here, but the foregoing example is not unique. Other programs—the Small Watershed Program (Harmon 1976) and the Agricultural Conservation Program (Harmon 1974), to name two—lack desired wildlife benefits.

At times, USDA legal compliance has been questionable. Through the combined efforts of wildlife interests, the 1973 Agriculture and Consumer Protection Act authorized multi-year retirement with cover required. During the five years this act (amended in 1977) has been in effect, not once has the USDA chosen to use multi-year agreements. In a letter to the Wildlife Management Institute (9/7/78), the secretary of agriculture stated, "While the annual set-aside contract is not the ideal from the standpoint of wildlife management, we believe that the restrictions that we have placed upon the uses of the set-aside acreage do contribute significantly to soil conservation and to habitat preservation" (per. comm.). Another survey in the Midwest was conducted in 1978, and the results showed that summer fallow (no cover) was a common practice—11 percent in Minnesota, 76 percent in Nebraska, and 95% in North Dakota. Most of the remainder was in stubble or green manure crops that were plowed down in short order.

In spite of these problems, potential benefits for wildlife could exist with minor modifications. For this reason, wildlife agencies have a responsibility to work for needed changes.

It is clear that, regardless of the adjustment—shifts in acreages or crops or participation in farm programs—decisions are made with one overriding consideration, maximum return on investment. From a habitat standpoint,

149

more intensive management of monoculture row-cropping systems interspersed with retired land devoid of cover, except during the soil bank era, resulted in lower wildlife populations. Concurrently, wildlife agencies reduced acquisition efforts by more than 70 percent and nearly halted private land programs. It can only be supposed that these programs were underfinanced, noncompetitive, politically constrained, and/or insignificant influences on land-use decisions.

The diminished activity on private land, as conducted, may have been justified. Through Indiana's effort, 2,872 wildlife areas containing approximately 20,000 acres were established on private holdings prior to 1961. After evaluating 273 areas, Bushong (1961) concluded that low wildlife populations had not been increased to any measurable degree. In a similar vein, de Vos and Mosby (1963) stated, "Small stands of a desirable plant scattered here and there may not replace the larger loss of a changing land-use pattern that eliminates the intermixture of various cover types found under more primitive farming."

ARE THERE WORKABLE SOLUTIONS?

A workable alternative, adequately funded, still eludes wildlife agencies. In fact, there is not even common agreement on whether a program should be conducted, much less how. One faction advocates eliminating private land programs entirely, contending that they are impractical and beyond the monetary capabilities of wildlife agencies. This relegates wildlife management to a passive role, thereby abandoning a valuable resource. Nothing in state statutes appears to give agencies this option, although it may be argued with some logic that lack of funds is a legislative mandate to curtail this activity.

Others reason that high production cropland is, and will remain, something wildlife can't compete with, but that certain less fertile land may have management possibilities. Yet a third group supports a realistic cost to the beneficiary that permits agencies to finance and launch realistic programs commensurate with willingness to pay.

Several wildlife agencies have resurrected private land programs in recent years. While technical assistance and planting stock are often program elements, some major philosophical changes are evident. Recognizing that wildlife, as a free good, continues to decline on private land, funds have been obtained to compensate the landowner for protecting and/or providing habitat.

The Nebraska Game and Parks Commission, in facing this fact, obtained funds in 1977 from increases in existing license fees and a new $7.50 habitat stamp. Farmers then are given annual per acre payments of $25 for establishing permanent cover, $20 for growing sweet clover, and $15 for protecting wetlands and woody vegetation in 1978. The costs are shared by the commission (75 percent) and by local natural resources districts (25 percent) from their local tax levies.

South Dakota also recently (1958) secured additional revenue from a $5.00 pheasant restoration stamp. Here as well, the program's fundamental feature is annual rent for land taken out of crop production. Goals are to establish 6,500 acres of nesting cover and to improve or expand 500 acres of shelterbelts annually. Payment rates for cropland range from $12 to $15 per acre per year. Rates (one-time payment) for shelterbelt renovation are 25 percent of the cost or up to $30 per acre.

Within present funding levels, both programs are progressing well, indicating a latent market demand. While these earmarked funds will potentially generate substantial revenues over a period of years, they are only large relative to past budget increases and are thus only initially impressive. In reality, they are low considering needs and they are fixed unless the number of hunters increases substantially. Within time, the affected acreage will become stabilized, since contracts were for specified periods—three years in South Dakota and two to ten in Nebraska—and all funds eventually will be encumbered. At that point, future funds will be used for existing contracts or for replacing those that expire, not additional acres.

Further progress pivots on new sources of money. Authorization and acceptability would be conjecture. Up to some limit, however, when new dollars are targeted to identifiable benefits, they appear to be more easily obtained. This was evident in Missouri recently where the electorate passed a 0.8 percent sales tax that would generate $20 million annually to finance the conservation department's "Design for Conservation," that displayed specific goals.

Other agencies concentrate on access to private land with habitat development a minor feature, usually consisting of the traditional free assistance and planting materials. McConnell (1977) reviewed several examples. Among them, North Carolina issues a voluntary $8 game-lands permit. Half the funds derived are used to reimburse landowners for allowing access. The remainder covers enforcement, posting, development, and map costs. Under this program, nearly two million acres were available for hunting. However, not all were private, as about one million acres of U.S. Forest Service land were included.

Pennsylvania, a pioneer in providing access, has 172 on-going farm game projects in which landowners, owning 1,000-plus acres, enroll their lands for a minimum of five years. No monetary compensation is offered, but landowners receive posting material and enforcement protection. In exchange, about two million acres are opened to hunting. For smaller acreages, a safety zone program is available that furnishes access to additional acreage. Services provided are similar.

Some states still conduct day-old pheasant chick programs wherein the state resource agency gives the landowner newly hatched pheasants for release on his land, with the only consistent feature being the inconsistency with which they are started. The reasons for such programs vary from public relations to public pressure. Rarely is the primary goal increased bird populations, as field studies have shown poor chick survival. In an attempt to produce some tangible benefits, some states have required that habitat be available. Colorado, for example, made one year of habitat development a condition for receiving checks. Some excellent habitat sites resulted; however, retention becomes uncertain once the individual is no longer in the program (Schmidt, per. comm.). Seldom have such programs been large in scope or applicable to large areas of private land.

Throughout wildlife management's short history, agencies have periodically stocked birds before the gun. Present efforts are small relative to those of the past, Michigan being a recent exception. When voters approved the Recreation Bond Program, the legislature directed the Division of Wildlife to supply pen-reared pheasants for hunters from, or in the vicinity of, urban areas. With this constraint—pen-reared birds—the division concluded that the most cost-effective method was a put-take program that yielded a high rate of return.

Through a special appropriation for capital investment, a $1.2 million hatching and rearing facility was constructed that produced 116,000 birds for release in 1976, of which about 70 percent were harvested. The cost per bird released or retained as a breeder was $4.40. Michigan's program is not directed toward improving habitat on private land. It merely provides those willing to purchase a $10 permit an opportunity to participate in the harvest of some 80,000 birds on state-owned property. Without doubt, the legislature reacted to a three-decade decline in the pheasant harvest of one million birds. Whether that body acted with great wisdom can be debated. It does, however, substantiate the contention made earlier that dollars targeted to specific benefits are often more easily obtained. In that regard, the put-take program has replaced about ten percent of the decline while servicing six percent of the 500,000 hunters. Only half the costs are recovered, a not uncommon situation in wildlife programs.

The history of Michigan's private land program has been identical to that of most states. Beginning in 1949, nearly $85,000 was earmarked for private land habitat development. Funding dwindled to $45,000 by 1963, and ceased in 1964. In the same period, funds increased from $43,000 to nearly $600,000 for development on state-owned lands. The increased attention to agency land did not prevent the loss of a million pheasants in the annual harvest. This is neither new nor unpredictable; for without sound biological programs that meet public demand, the decisions will be made in the political arena.

It is difficult to make an in-depth comparison of Michigan's put-take program and one for habitat development that yields similar outputs. The data are simply not in hand. Working with those available, however, produces some interesting results. First, assuming it were physically possible to replace the one million bird deficit artificially, program costs would be $6.3 million ($4.40 per bird released with 70 percent recovery) annually. An initial capital outlay of $15 million would be required to construct 12 hatcheries with a 120,000 bird capacity each.

The second alternative is natural reproduction from habitat on private land. MacMullen (1957) defined a "good year" as 10 cocks per 100 acres with an 80 percent harvest. To duplicate these conditions, management on 19,600 square miles (12-plus million acres) would (theoretically) yield the one million bird harvest. Assuming that use on five percent of the land (600,000 acres) needed to be controlled, and could be for $20 per acre, annual program costs would be about $12 million. To finance this venture, each of Michigan's half-million small game hunters must purchase a $25 license. The answer to the question "Would they pay the price?" is uncertain. Unquestionably, the $10 permit, first required in 1975, dropped more than 60 percent of the put-take hunters from the ranks. On the other hand, Nebraska's new $7.50 habitat stamp had little or no impact on sales.

From this rather primitive comparison one would conclude that, on a per bird basis, stocking for the gun is cheaper than manipulating habitat on private land. This is not a new or revolutionary statement in wildlife circles. To be sure, birds in the bag are important and a valid program objective. From a hunting standpoint a well managed system of rearing, preflighting, and releasing can do a creditable job of duplicating natural conditions.

Too many factors are involved, however, to make decisions on such a straightforward cost-effective analysis, even if completely accurate. Wildlife agencies in their expanded roles have more responsibilities than just birds bagged, and while extremely important in planning programs, other factors must be considered. An entire array of wildlife, both for consumptive and nonconsumptive uses, depends on private land for their welfare. In fact, wildlife is only one of many values flowing from a habitat program and herein lies the weakness in the above comparison. All costs of a habitat program cannot be charged to pheasants or small game.

As discussed earlier, accomplishments have been limited, and new, economically sensitive approaches are needed. Some states have taken the first faltering steps on a course that is unexplored. Although underway only for a short time, some early conclusions are possible. First, the fact that funds are being encumbered in states like Nebraska and South Dakota is evidence that private land for habitat is a negotiable item. Second, the acreage affected will be small. Much higher funding must be obtained with the costs distributed among all beneficiaries. And third, while local wildlife populations should benefit, no major statewide increases can be expected. To effect changes of this magnitude, costs will be high, and the consumer's willingness to pay will be severely tested when full costs are displayed.

Farley and Hamor (1977), in an imaginative proposal, estimated costs and benefits of providing pheasant habitat on a 100-square mile area in South Dakota at three levels of production and harvest, all achieved under natural conditions. Costs for habitat (payments, planning, etc.) were $921 per section (640 acres) per year. With high production (137 cocks/mi^2), high harvest (82 cocks/mi^2) and the economic value of a bird harvested ($26.50, the amount of money a hunter expends on equipment, food, transportation, etc.), benefits were $2,174 per section per year. They determined that for each dollar expended on habitat, $2.40 would be pumped into the state's economy. Such a benefit-cost ratio is taken as clear evidence in federal circles that a project is justified and feasible.

Annual costs for the 100-square mile area ($92,139) are well within the state wildlife agency's budget capabilities. South Dakota's prime pheasant range, however, encompasses 51,000 square miles, and statewide costs consequently became $47 million annually. Funding a statewide program at the level of management envisioned by Farley and Hamor, with all costs charged to pheasants, would require a $245 hunting license.

Undoubtedly, a $245 license fee would be neither acceptable nor justifiable. A substantial increase is realistic, however, considering the level of management needed and benefits produced. Other direct beneficiaries exist such as cafes, motels, and sporting goods stores, and a method of collecting proportionate funds from these entities is needed. Also, if, as economists claim, society in general benefits from economic activity, appropriations from the general fund are defensible. In financing public programs, the principle that the beneficiary pays the costs is becoming widely accepted. Based on this concept, those who benefit from other outputs—soil erosion control, agriculture supply and demand control, water quality, and nongame wildlife—should share in the costs. Procedures for such analysis are used extensively in federal water projects. They can, and should be, refined for financing habitat programs on private land.

The states, for the most part, have yet to utilize a systematic planning approach in addressing private land habitat problems and solutions. Several basic steps are needed:

1. identify the problem
2. develop practical solutions
3. establish costs at various levels of output
4. designate beneficiaries and their respective costs, and
5. identify funding sources.

With this in hand, the agency can approach the beneficiaries, letting them decide what they desire and how much they are willing to pay. This logically places the burden squarely where it belongs—on the beneficiaries. The agency's role becomes one of supplying a service commensurate with willingness to pay. As it now stands, the agency is in the untenable position of attempting to provide a high level of service with funding that permits an emaciated private land program at best. The result is legislative tinkering and continuous criticism by a dissatisfied clientele.

The foregoing becomes academic unless the question, "Can hunters afford to pay for an adequately funded habitat program on private land?" is answered. Some insight as to ability to pay can be gained by looking at some historical expenditures. From 1960 to 1975, license income averaged only five percent of the hunter's expenditures. This minor investment in wildlife programs has permitted the continuous erosion of an important resource—habitat on private land.

Data from the *1975 Survey of Hunting and Fishing* (U.S. Fish and Wildlife Service 1977) indicate that hunters can afford to make a greater contribution toward maintaining habitat. In 1975, more than 20 million hunters spent nearly $6 billion, of which $277 million (5%) was for licenses. By comparison, they spent over four times as much on food and drink, nearly eight times more for transportation, and about seven times more to purchase equipment. None of these funds, with the exception of the 11 percent excise tax on firearms and ammunition, produced a single acre of habitat.

Cash outlays of this magnitude would indicate that hunters are not destitute; even with a four-fold increase in costs (1960-75), there were almost nine million more hunters in 1975 than 15 years earlier. Even though the majority of this group's expenditures are not being reinvested in habitat, there is no question about the availability of increased funds. Neither is there a question concerning the ability to pay. Any group that spends nearly three times as much on hunting dogs as it does on wildlife programs (U.S. Fish and Wildlife Service 1972) has little to look forward to in terms of quality hunting in the future. The "wildlife is free" syndrome has crippled wildlife management on private land. For those who care to look, the evidence of that is on the land.

LITERATURE CITED

Bushong, C. 1961. Evaluation of farm game habitat restoration efforts in Indiana. P.R. Bull. No. 5. Div. Fish and Game. Indianapolis, Indiana. 104 pp.

Dahlgren, R. 1967. The pheasant decline. S. Dak. Dept. Game, Fish and Parks. Pierre, South Dakota. 44 pp.

de Vos, A. and H. S. Mosby. 1963. Evaluation of habitat. *In* Mosby, H. S., ed. Wildlife investigational techniques. 2nd ed. The Wildl. Soc. 419 pp.

Erickson, R. E. and J. E. Wiebe. 1973. Pheasants, economics and land retirement in South Dakota. Wildl. Soc. Bull. 1(1): 22-27.

Farley, J. and W. Hamor. 1977. A plan for pheasant habitat development and management, one hundred square miles, Brown County, South Dakota. U.S. Dept. Agric., Soil Cons. Serv. Huron, South Dakota. 50 pp.

Harmon, K. W. and M. M. Nelson. 1973. Wildlife and soil conservation in land retirement programs. Wildl. Soc. Bull. 1(1): 28-38.

———. 1974. Do incentives to protect soil and water benefit fish and wildlife? Proc. 29th Annual Meeting. Soil Cons. Soc. Amer. pp. 39-43.

———. 1976. Improving fish and wildlife habitat and recreational opportunities. 23rd Nat. Watershed Cong. pp. 99-103.

McConnell, C. A. 1977. Strategies for improving wildlife habitat and access on private lands. Proc. 32nd Annual Meeting. Soil Cons. Soc. Amer. Pp. 62-67.

McMullen, R. A. 1957. The life and times of Michigan pheasants. Game Div. Mich. Dept. Cons. Lansing, Michigan. 63 pp.

Stankey, G. H., R. C. Lucas, and R. R. Ream. 1973. Relationships between hunting success and satisfaction. Trans. 38th N. Amer. Wildl. and Nat. Res. Conf. Wildl. Manage. Inst. pp. 235-242.

U.S. Department of Agriculture. 1973-77. Agricultural statistics. U.S. Govt. Printing Office. Washington, D.C.

U.S. Fish and Wildlife Service. 1949-76. Federal aid in fish and wildlife restoration. Wildl. Manage. Inst. and Sport Fishing Inst., Washington, D.C.

———. 1972. 1970 national survey of hunting, fishing. U.S. Govt. Printing Office, Washington, D.C. 108 pp.

———. 1977. 1975 national survey of hunting and fishing, and wildlife-associated recreation. U.S. Govt. Printing Office, Washington, D.C. 91 pp.

THE SHOOTING PRESERVE CONCEPT

Edward L. Kozicky and John B. Madson

One of our most critical needs is quality outdoor recreation, especially in heavily populated regions. Some of this desperately needed recreation can be provided by various public agencies—but the bulk of it must come from private enterprise.

Certain types of commercial recreation efforts dovetail with those of state wildlife departments and should be licensed and supervised by those agencies. Of these, none is more important to state wildlife departments than the shooting preserve industry, for one of the most significant features in tomorrow's recreation will be the lack of good places to hunt near metropolitan areas. It is a deficiency that can be well filled, however, by a good shooting preserve.

For the record, a shooting preserve is simply an area owned or leased for the purpose of releasing pen-reared game birds for hunting over a period of five or six months. This has been called "fee hunting," "pay-as-you-go hunting," and "put-and-take shooting." There may be a better term than "shooting preserve," but this is the accepted name that originated in New York in 1911 (Kozicky and Madson 1966). In Texas, a shooting preserve is a "shooting resort."

GETTING STARTED

The shooting preserve concept was slow getting started. Traditionally, wild game has been relatively abundant and much of our population was rural; there was plenty to hunt, and plenty of places to hunt it. As the nation grew, game habitat shrank and urban areas expanded. There was less small game and fewer places to hunt it, and the need for shooting preserves became more apparent.

At first hunters were suspicious of the shooting preserve concept and did not favor legislation to permit the operation of preserves. Game had always belonged to the commonwealth, and there seemed to be something unAmerican about putting a price tag on a game bird. Some hunters condemned it as a return to the "European System," although shooting preserves have been around for about seventy years and are as American as quail and cornpone.

The attitude of state wildlife chiefs toward the shooting preserve concept has been a mixture of resentment and endorsement, depending on the vision of the administrator or his lack of same. Writing in the foreword of *American*

Kozickey, Edward L. Director of Conservation, Winchester Group, Olin Corporation, East Alton, Illinois

Madson, John B. Assistant Director of Conservation, Winchester Group, Olin Corporation, East Alton, Illinois

Game Preserve Shooting (Smith 1937), Seth Gordon, former executive director of the Pennsylvania Game Commission, stated:

> The sportsman who has a desire for more shooting than is afforded by public administration and who has the means for developing shooting should be given every reasonable aid. It can easily be done without adversely affecting public game or public shooting. On the contrary, a substantial percentage of the birds . . . produced or liberated escape to adjacent areas open to the public.

One of the greatest problems in the early days of the shooting preserve movement was lack of suitable legislation. Good shooting preserve legislation protects the operator and permits him a chance to earn a fair profit, helps assure his customers of quality sport, and protects natural wildlife resources from any exploitation. Michigan is a good example of what happens when the original legislation is shaky: shooting preserves were closed down, and it was most difficult to legalize their operation a second time.

A major breakthrough came in 1954 when a model statute for the establishment and operation of shooting preserves was developed by the Sporting Arms and Ammunition Manufacturers' Institute (Kozicky and Madson 1966). This has been a guideline for state legislation throughout the country, and opened up a bottleneck in the shooting preserve concept.

At the same time, several other factors were sparking the young shooting preserve industry:

1. An expanding human population, with shorter work weeks and higher pay scales has more time and money for hunting, as well as more men of retirement age with time and money to spend on hunting.

2. The mechanization of game propagation, the improvement and control of quality game feeds, and development of effective medications for various diseases have all permitted game to be produced at a lower cost per bird in spite of a rise in our economy.

3. Increasing restrictions of public hunting opportunities by wildlife agencies in an effort to fit the harvest to the game supply have resulted in reduced hunting seasons and bag limits.

4. A growing number of people and industries have wanted to do something about increasing the chances to enjoy a day afield with dog and gun.

BOTH PUBLIC AND PRIVATE MANAGEMENT NEEDED

After a certain point, a state wildlife department can do little to provide more public hunting. It can acquire some public hunting areas, research game needs, and set regulations that provide equitable chances for the public to harvest game.

Since little can be done to provide actual places to hunt, the hunting public will always be dependent on the private landowner for most of its sport. We need areas near home where hunting is not only available, but warmly encouraged.

Some state wildlife departments do acquire and manage public hunting areas. However, these are expensive and there is a definite limit to the number of areas that can, and should, be bought and maintained with hunting license fees. There is also a definite limit to the amount of wild game that can be produced on such areas. Since total acreage of such state areas, and the wild game supplies on them, will never meet the public need, hunters will always be dependent on the private landowner for the bulk of their hunting.

Such public hunting areas are good as far as they go—they just do not go far enough. They must be reinforced by private shooting areas, and the development of the one will benefit the other.

Private enterprise is still the most efficient system in the world for providing a service or a product. It is also in a position to cater to various

The standby of the shooting preserve is the ring-necked pheasant. Beautiful, big, and always wild, it is a fine table bird as well as a sporting species. (Courtesy of Conservation Department Winchester-Western)

economic levels—tailoring its product to the customer. Public areas, on the other hand, must deal with a broad citizenry and be heavily subsidized.

It has been said that nothing good "just comes"—if it is any good, it has to be "fetched." This is certainly true of good hunting in general, and of good shooting preserves in particular. Some short-sighted preserve operators wonder why (since their birds are reared in captivity and are private property) the state wildlife department should have anything to do with them. There is some thin logic in this, but the truth of the matter is that the industry will grow and prosper best when working in conjunction with the state wildlife agency.

STATE AND PRIVATE COOPERATION ESSENTIAL

State wildlife departments must be the arbiters of quality in hunting wherever it occurs. On shooting preserves, a high level of quality can be achieved with the cooperation of good operators who know that quality is the key to survival and success. They should know, even more than the state wildlife department, that a substandard preserve hurts their industry and their future. Subquality operators eventually go broke, but they leave bitter memories with their patrons, and a blot on the shooting preserve industry. A good way to prevent this is a mutual willingness of the shooting preserve operator and the state wildlife agency to work together.

The shooting preserve industry attracts potential operators from a wide background of experience and education. These people envision shooting preserve management as an ideal way of life. They may think that all they need is a tract of land and a crate of birds and the world will beat a path to their front gate. They will be earning a living from the sport of hunting—a dream to stir the heart of any outdoorsman! Without guidance, however, this is not only a dream but a dangerous one. These are good, sincere people,

158

and they need all possible assistance when they apply for a license to operate a shooting preserve.

A responsible state wildlife department should be ready to guide and advise these new operators with *qualified* men. The potential shooting preserve operator needs assistance with the economics, management, and promotion of his enterprise. A lot of people have a lot at stake.

Nothing succeeds without enthusiasm, and the enthusiasm of the freshman shooting preserve operator must be matched with the enthusiasm of seasoned professionals within the state agency. At least one man within the wildlife department should become thoroughly familiar with the problems and potential of shooting preserves. Such a job should not be palmed off on someone who lacks ability or desire to work with private enterprise, or who just happens to be on the payroll but has shown little ability to do any other jobs. One good man is more important than three or four who lack the right attitude, or who are already overloaded with duties.

One of the wildlife agency's most useful services may be in discouraging certain individuals from getting into the shooting preserve business. It is better to head off a potential failure than to have it happen—in such cases, the state wildlife departments are protecting both the hunting public and the shooting preserve industry.

The wildlife agency's liaison man should also be able to guide the preserve operator into related recreational projects. Few shooting preserves provide an adequate annual income. The successful operators are those who obtain a year-round income from a combination of projects: farming, game breeding, camping, fishing in late spring and summer, and hunting and certain winter sports in fall and winter.

Wildlife department personnel can also stress such important points as a market survey to the potential shooting preserve operator. Where will customers be found? What are their hunting likes and dislikes? Will it be necessary to provide lunches or overnight lodging? Does the potential preserve operator have sufficient financial backing to operate without a profit for the first two to three years? The wildlife department "extension man" will do the potential shooting preserve operator a great service by stressing the importance of family help on the preserve and the fact that the preserve operator must be a jack-of-all-trades and master of most. A good preserve operator understands hunters and hunting, dog training and handling, game breeding and rearing, farming, shooting preserve management, public relations, business administration, and shotgun shooting.

To introduce state wildlife managers to the shooting preserve concept, the conservation department of Winchester-Western holds a short course, upon request, on the management, economics, and promotion of shooting preserves. The course is conducted at Nilo Farms, Winchester-Western's demonstration and experimental shooting preserve near Alton, Illinois.

State wildlife department personnel assigned to work with shooting preserves can benefit from close association with the North American Game Breeders and Shooting Preserve Association and their annual meetings (address: Arrowhead Hunting and Fishing Club, Goose Lake, IA 52750). The NAGB and SPA publish a monthly periodical and provide a constant flow of information on game breeding and shooting preserves.

As the shooting preserve industry grows within a state, the operators should be encouraged to form an association. Annual meetings of such a group can afford an excellent opportunity for shooting preserve operators and state wildlife personnel to get their heads together and work on common problems. The most urgent of these—and the one of most continuing importance—is the maintenance of quality sport on the shooting preserve. To insure this, one of the first jobs of a shooting preserve association is to

Chukar partridges are new to most eastern and midwestern shooting preserves. These exotics are becoming increasingly sought after game birds. (Courtesy of Conservation Department Winchester-Western)

develop a set of workable, practical, and reasonable minimum standards of operation.

To begin with, such standards may be on a voluntary basis and should be widely publicized. Eventually such minimum standards will become mandatory for the good of the sport, the protection of the public, and the growth of the enterprise, and they will be enforced as regulations by the state wildlife department with the cooperation of the state association members.

Since all shooting preserves within a state are licensed (or should be) and are well known to the state wildlife department, one of the great services the department can offer the sportsman is to develop and distribute a state directory of daily fee shooting preserves. This helps the young industry, gives sportsmen a list of places to hunt, and is an expression of good faith to the shooting preserve operators. It is not an endorsement of any particular preserve, but of the industry in general. It also helps to dispel the notion that the state wildlife department is just another government office to which to send endless reports and money for licenses and bands.

To sum it up, privately operated shooting preserves are about the only way we can ever have quality hunting near metropolitan areas where access to private lands is highly restricted; however, preserve operators need encouragement and technical help. And if the state wildlife department is the official arbiter of hunting quality that it should be, it is the logical source of such help.

The standard game management efforts of yesterday, or even today, will not be sufficient tomorrow. Open minds, leadership, and statesmanship were never more essential for state wildlife commissioners and administrators. Our state wildlife agencies must adapt with imagination, accept change, and form new alliances. If one of these new alliances is the shooting preserve concept, the future of our hunting tradition will be assured even in the shadows of our growing cities.

LITERATURE CITED

Kozicky, E. L. and J. Madson. 1966. Shooting preserve management—The Nilo system. Conservation Dept., Winchester-Western, Olin, East Alton, Illinois. 311 pp.

Smith, L. 1937. American game preserve shooting. Garden City Publ. Co., Inc., Garden City, New York. 175 pp.

WILDLIFE ENTERPRISES ON PRIVATE LAND

Richard D. Teague

Private land can, and must, provide more wildlife for recreation. Professional wildlife administrators, biologists, and commissioners must consider the role of private land managers as full partners in the important business of managing our valuable wildlife resources.

National authorities acknowledge that outdoor recreation needs cannot be met by the combined efforts of local, state, and federal governments. It is not economically feasible for states to purchase enough land to handle increasing recreation requirements. In addition, much public land is incapable of high wildlife production.

Three needs are evident: (1) more places to hunt and fish, (2) an increase in the yields of wildlife crops, and (3) a maximum harvest of annual increases in game and fish populations. Private enterprise can assist materially in serving these needs. It is estimated that 85 percent of the wildlife habitat that it is economically feasible to improve is on private land.

Encouragement for landowners to provide wildlife must be more than a simple pat on the back. The farmer cannot stay in business giving away his personal resources or the produce of the land. At present, less than four percent of national hunting expenditures goes to the private land manager. If wildlife is to compete for space with corn, cotton and cows, then it must provide an appropriate economic return. It is inconsistent, and illogical, to continue spending the major part of our money and efforts in wildlife management programs on public lands when nationwide, 80 percent of the game is harvested on private land.

BENEFITS

Under certain circumstances, wildlife enterprises on private land can be of value to the landowner, the sportsman using private or public lands, the nonconsumptive user, the state resource agency, and the business economy of the area.

Briefly, here are some of the values each of those groups or individuals receives:

The Landowner
Less vandalism, property damage, and better control of hunters
Retention of land in private ownership
Better use of all land, capital, and labor resources
Direct financial gain

The Resource Agency
Improved overall wildlife habitat
Landowner understanding and support of state management programs

Teague, Richard D.   Assistant Director, Wildlife Specialist, Cooperative Extension, University of California, Davis

More license sales and more federal aid funds

Relief of hunter congestion on state management areas and public lands

The Sportsman (private land user)

Quality hunting conditions (a result of managed habitat and high game populations)

Reduced travel distance and time investment

More total days hunting (licensed preserves have several more months' hunting than regular state seasons)

The Sportsman (public land user)

Less competition for space on public lands

Increased wildlife population on private lands migrating to public areas for harvest

The Nonconsumer (e.g., photographers and bird watchers)

Increased activity for wildlife will provide more game and nongame species for this group to enjoy. Historically, many refuges, habitat improvement projects, and other programs to enhance wildlife populations have been financed by hunters and fishermen. Many game management areas are available on a multiple-use basis for other recreationists to enjoy.

The Local Economy and Recreation Industry

Every dollar spent on wildlife is usually at least doubled by the economic activity generated.

Tax revenues are increased.

A study in Colorado revealed that 67 percent of the private land surveyed was posted against free public uses (R. C. Rounds, unpublished data). Reasons given included property damage, fire danger, vandalism, and theft. Many landowners leasing their land to hunters received greater benefit from control of hunters than from the financial gain. In Michigan it was found that hunters were not the only public segment causing harassment of landowners (Burger 1964). Land closures resulted from year-round problems with fishermen, berry-pickers, mushroom and nut gatherers, hikers, and others. Many California landowners have found that hunting club members zealously patrol their hunting grounds and assist the landowner in protecting himself from such intruders.

TYPES OF WILDLIFE ENTERPRISES

The Cooperatives

Many landowners open their land to hunting and fishing in return for protection from random trespass and property damage. Users may be a group of friends or local sportsmen who provide posting and patrol and do other minor chores. In Richvale, California, rice growers have formed a pheasant cooperative with money from hunting permits going toward community projects. A Grange Co-op of 22,000 acres in Washington State charged $10 each for 610 pheasant hunting permits, the proceeds going toward a new Grange hall (Graham 1965).

Such arrangements may be handled by the state resource agency. This usually involves posting of the co-op area and controlling ingress, egress, and possible property damage. Examples are the Williamson Plan in Michigan and California's Cooperative Pheasant program. Similar efforts of "cooperative programs" have been tried in other states, including Pennsylvania, Virginia, New York, Wisconsin, and Utah.

Such cooperative arrangements aid in providing open land to hunting and are relatively inexpensive to administer. However, such programs are usually short lived. This is due to change in land ownership, whims of human nature, or development of the land into a commercial venture. Protection and patrol may serve to encourage landowners to allow hunting, but they almost never provide sufficient incentive for the landowner to consistently produce more game or even to curtail the agricultural practices that limit wildlife numbers. Even state programs that provide free plant materials for wildlife cover have not materially improved wildlife habitat or animal populations.

As hunting demands increase and more hunters are willing to pay for their sport, cooperatives are replaced by commercial ventures. Information from one western state revealed that five out of every six ranchers preferred sole landowner development. Eight out of nine preferred owner management. Further, eight out of nine landowners wanted remuneration in the form of "fees" rather than tax incentives, concession rights, patrol efforts, etc. (California Cattlemen's Association survey, unpublished data).

Private Preserves and Clubs

In some parts of North America, private clubs or preserves have been developed by groups of hunters who are landowners. Habitat work is carried out and farm-reared birds released for the benefit of club members only. In some sections of the West, ranches have been purchased for fishing and hunting solely for the owners. This type of program benefits few people but is better than nonuse of the wildlife resource.

Exclusive waterfowl clubs in the Pacific flyway may be considered in this category. There are some differences, however, as they are operated in harmony with state and federal waterfowl areas. Game farm birds are not normally released, but habitat is improved to provide wintering areas for birds and to reduce depredation to agricultural crops. These private duck clubs also serve the valuable function of retaining wetlands as waterfowl habitat. Of the historical wetlands saved for waterfowl in California, 75 percent are under private management. However, only 41 percent of the waterfowl are killed on these club lands (F. M. Kozlik, personal communication). Obviously, private waterfowl clubs in the Pacific flyway are providing birds for hunting on lands outside their boundaries.

Commercial Wildlife Enterprises

Commercial wildlife enterprises certainly are here to stay. "Package" plans for hunting and fishing are available for a price from Alaska to Alabama. Some large California ranches provide hunting of a variety of game, including pheasants, valley quail, chukars, doves, band-tailed pigeons, wild turkeys, waterfowl, black-tailed deer, and wild pigs, plus trout and warm water fish. In many cases, shooting preserve operations, with their long hunting seasons, make the wildlife enterprise a year-round operation. Some landowners have found varmit hunters and "coon hound" enthusiasts who are willing to pay to pursue their sport on private land. Quail-cattle and deer-cattle management programs are complementary operations.

Southern farms and timber operators provide hunting and fishing in several ways. Green tree reservoirs are formed by cutting timber in a grid pattern and then flooding from November to March for waterfowl shooting. One operator increased waterfowl use from 1,500 to 100,000 ducks in three years' time using this technique. An excellent variety of game hunting is provided by planting millet for doves and then flooding the areas for waterfowl. Freshly plowed fields provide good snipe shooting.

Guides and outfitters are available almost anywhere their guide services are needed. It is possible to obtain guide services for a day's fishing on the Madison River in Montana or for several weeks of big game hunting in remote portions of Alaska. A few guides make their sole livelihood from this occupation, while others spend most of the year operating a livestock ranch and guide only during the fall elk season. Many part-time guides in the West use the home ranch for base camp, but utilize mostly public lands for hunting and fishing. On large Texas ranches and other similar operations, guiding may be entirely on private land.

Another way to provide hunting and fishing on private land is being promoted by special sportsmen's corporations. One such operation leases nearly 5 million acres nationwide, paying the landowner from 85¢ to $1.50/acre depending on its wildlife value. Wildlife habitat improvement work depends on the length of the lease and the landowner's desires and cooperation. Annual individual dues run about $375.

There are numerous private professional wildlife and fishery management consultants and state and federal personnel available to assist landowners with enterprise development.

Exotic and Native Big Game

Texas has probably had more experience with marketing exotic big game than any area in North America. As early as 1900 several species of exotic game birds and mammals were released. Leases for commercial hunting of white-tailed deer and wild turkey were negotiated as early as 1939. Net income from ranching has declined steadily over the past years until hunting of deer can now provide a higher income for some than raising domestic livestock. Ramsay (1965) found that an adequately harvested deer herd on the Edwards Plateau region brought $38.60 per animal unit as opposed to $28.82 per animal unit of livestock. Even under today's economic situation, where good management is practiced, the value per animal unit of deer is greater than that per animal unit of livestock. Exotic big game bring even higher prices to the landowner. One large Texas ranch lists their 1979 prices:

Axis deer (India)	$ 900
Blackbuck antelope (India)	$ 800
Corsican rams	$ 400
Wild Spanish goat	$ 200
Mouflon rams (Europe)	$ 750
Sika deer (Japan)	$ 600
Fallow deer (Europe)	$ 750
Aoudad sheep (N. Africa)	$1,200
Ibex (Asia)	$1,200

The same ranch lists native whitetail deer (bucks) at $600 and wild turkeys at $200.

A 1974 survey of exotic game ranches in the United States (J. T. Attebury, et al. 1977) yielded national average trophy fees and average invested cost by species. Some of these are:

	Average fee	Average investment
Axis deer	$621	$308
Blackbuck antelope	600	295
Corsican rams	236	55
Mouflon sheep	338	149
Sika deer	408	246
Fallow deer	398	212
Aoudad sheep	632	293

Native game provide hunting for the 45 to 50 days of the regular hunting season in Texas. Exotics, which can be hunted anytime, provide use of facilities the other 10 months of the year.

Many exotic species of wild ungulates can enhance the sport hunting value of land and increase meat production from such areas. It is recommended, however, that such introductions be preceded by proper study to minimize conflicts with domestic livestock and agriculture.

Native big game provide income to landowners throughout North America. Harvest of the annual increase is of economic importance both as direct income to the landowner and to reduce agricultural crop damage.

FEES

There are few criteria for establishing "access" prices to hunt and fish on private land. Many factors are involved, including regional economics, local demand, kinds and numbers of wildlife, size and accessibility of the area, and facilities provided, such as campsites, cabins, horses, etc. The following are some scattered examples based on 1979 prices.

Pheasant clubs in California receive an average of $500 for 40 birds. This price varies across North America depending on the intensity of cover management and facilities.

Package hunting and fishing may range from a $250/person fly-in drop hunt to Alaskan trophy fishing with deluxe accommodations at $1,500/person/week. Virtually every state in the United States and every province of Canada has enterprising private land-resource managers catering to outdoorsmen.

Some typical big game, upland game, and waterfowl fees for California are interesting.

Waterfowl: $200-$2,500 per blind annually
Deer: $200-$450 per season
Quail: $150-$200 per season up to $100/day with dog and guide
Doves and wild pigeons: $250 per season or $25 per day
Rabbits: Usually part of a package deal
Wild pigs: $500 for two-day trophy hunt; $375 non-trophy hunt.

CONSTRAINTS TO DEVELOPMENT

It is logical to question why more landowners do not enter into wildlife enterprises if they are as lucrative as they appear. The truth is, numerous wildlife ventures have gone broke for many reasons. Space does not allow detail, but some of the more important constraints need to be listed.

1. Many people still believe wildlife enterprises on private land to be "commercialization" of the public's fish and game. This attitude is moderating.

2. Some large timber companies in the Southeast fear that fee programs may provoke public reaction in adverse public relations, property damage, and liability problems (L. R. Shelton, personal communication).

3. Inability of resource agencies to recognize the private sector as a full partner in wildlife management is still prevalent in some sectors. Although gun clubs have existed for decades in California, it wasn't until December 9, 1966 that the California Fish and Game Commission formally recognized, as written policy, the value of the private wildlife manager. That policy encouraged landowners to participate in fish and wildlife management, recognized landowner prerogative to select users, to levy user fees, and to receive technical guidance from the Department of Fish and Game.

4. Landowners fear unrealistic tax assessments.

5. Lack of good economic data is a formidable restriction to planning a new wildlife enterprise.

6. The lack of low-cost credit to small landowners is a constraint on wildlife development.

7. Antiquated laws and public misunderstanding restrict realistic game harvests in many states. There are numerous examples of unnecessary legal shackles to flexible management and harvest on private (and public) lands that can make the difference in enterprise survival. Some species could be harvested at a rate many times that now realized without harm to the breeding population.

8. The lack of an efficient marketing channel is the greatest restraint in many parts of North America.

SUMMARY

"Fee" or "paid" hunting, meaning direct reimbursement to the landowner for the right to hunt, is a growing practice in virtually every state and province. Leopold (1956) summarized the situation well, "When free hunting is no longer available, sportsmen will pay for it, and ranchers will provide it. . . . We can ignore it, fight it, or work with it. My opinion is that we will get farther if we work with it."

Private wildlife enterprises are legally and ethically justified in the legitimate marketplace. Wildlife is a crop of the land that responds to scientific animal husbandry and cannot survive under abuse and exploitation. Private land managers have already proven their ability to perpetuate our valuable wildlife resources for everyone's enjoyment.

LITERATURE CITED

Attebury, J. T., J. C. Kroll, and H. L. Michael. 1977. Operational characteristics of commercial exotic big game hunting ranches. Wildl. Soc. Bull. 5: 179-184.

Burger, G. V. 1964. Is there a "case for paid hunting?" New York Sportsmen's Cons. Workshop, Ithaca, New York. (mimeo) 8 pp.

Graham, C. T. 1965. Fee hunting in the state of Washington. Game Bull., Wash. State Game Dept. 17(1): 8-9.

Leopold, A. S. 1956. Hunting for the masses—can game departments supply it? Proc. Western Assoc. State Game and Fish Comm. 36: 59-64.

Ramsey, C. W. 1965. Potential economic returns from deer as compared with livestock in the Edwards Plateau Region of Texas. J. Range Manage. 18(5): 247-250.

SELECTED REFERENCES

Rockefeller, L. S., et al. 1962. Outdoor Recreation Resources Review Commission. A report to the President and to the Congress. U.S. Government Printing Office, Washington, D.C. 246 pp.

Smith, C. R., L. E. Partain, and J. R. Champlin. 1966. Rural recreation for profit. The Interstate Printers and Publishers, Danville, Illinois. 303 pp.

Shelton, L. R. 1969. Economic aspects of wildlife management programs on large private landholdings in the Southeast. Unpub. M.S. Thesis, Mississippi State Univ., State College. 88 pp.

Caesar Kleberg Research Program in Wildlife Ecology. 1968. Symposium. Introduction of exotic animals: Ecological and socioeconomic considerations. Coll. of Agr., Texas A & M Univ., College Station. 25 pp.

WILDLIFE DAMAGE PROBLEMS

Maynard W. Cummings

At some time, every wildlife biologist, manager, and administrator encounters a wildlife damage problem. Action taken depends upon his knowledge of wildlife damage principles, his proximity to or his receipt of accurate information about this particular problem, and his position and degree of responsibility.

To insure proper interpretation of damage problems and appropriate recommendations for their solution, it is obvious that the first basic requirement is accurate problem identification. Many damage situations are appraised too superficially, or by someone not experienced in reading the symptoms of damage. Even experienced professionals must often make detailed examination, repeated observations, or technical analysis to positively define the cause of damage by wildlife.

Consider, for example, the widespread problem of tree bark damage. This may occur on any tree species, in any geographical location, and at practically any point on the tree. It is comparatively easy to sort out antler-rubbing damage by deer from that caused by mice at and below the groundline. But more specific determination may be needed. Is it really mouse girdling, or could it be pocket gopher damage? What appears to be porcupine damage to small trees or, in deep snow country, on the trunk and lower limbs of larger trees, also can be caused by pocket gophers during their winter foraging from snow tunnels. Predation is an entire topic in itself. Precise identification of the predator involved is essential, as identification is the first step in treating all wildlife damage.

The scope of damage also is important. The major facts needed are the seriousness of the damage—how many orchard trees by age and kind are damaged and to what extent, or how many acres of alfalfa, beans, or grapes have been affected, or how many sheep were killed or beehives destroyed—and in how many areas the damage is repeated. Complete reporting also includes severity of damage (whether total destruction or only temporary setback in the case of growing crops), all facts regarding how the damage was inflicted, probable cause and time of the offense, if damage is continuing or is likely to reoccur. Only then can proper control measures be planned and carried out.

This last decision is the most vital. Control is not justified just because damage occurred, but only when human interests are significantly more valuable than the wildlife involved. This is both a moral and economic decision. Economic evaluation must determine if effective control can be accomplished for less cost than the appraised damage.

Cummings, Maynard W.   Unit Director, Wildlife and Sea Grant, and
    Extension Wildlife Specialist, University of California, Davis

Regardless of the details at issue or the wildlife species involved, the professional damage appraiser should bear in mind the wide and often divergent social views related to the problem. An increasing segment of the public is interested primarily in the positive values of wildlife and questions the necessity of control programs that result in reduction of wildlife populations. A different view is held by land resource managers and supervisors of land use industries who are responsible for a total resource operation. To form a proper policy of wildlife damage control, it is necessary to recognize fully these often varying viewpoints.

Public attitudes toward animal control have changed and so have those of control personnel. Formerly, numerous mammal and bird species were grouped as pests, and control programs were aimed at their eradication. Some insects and lower animal forms still are regarded as wholly injurious, but this is generally not true for mammals, birds, and most other vertebrates.

Today extermination is not the goal of damage control programs. Indeed, it could not be attained because of economic, technical, or biological limitations. Wildlife damage control programs then should not be based upon animal population figures. Rather, the aim is to eliminate or reduce damage to a tolerable level. The amount of control to be applied should be the minimum necessary to achieve that objective.

The most frequent damage problems, wildlife groups, and control methods involved may be classified in several ways.

1. Nature of the damage
   a. To other wildlife
   Examples: predation on game species, such as coyote-antelope, bobcat-wild turkey, raccoon-duck nesting; indirect damage, such as beaver activity making water temperature unsuitable for trout
   b. To surrounding natural resources
   Examples: rodent and big game damage to native vegetation
   c. To agricultural crops or other interests of economic value
   Examples: deer-livestock forage competition; rodent damage to orchard and timber trees; migratory bird damage to cereal, fruit, vegetable crops, etc.; beaver and muskrat damage to water structures
   d. In wildlife-livestock disease transmission
   Examples: anaplasmosis, deer-cattle; tuberculosis, wild pigs-cattle; Brucellosis, elk-cattle
   e. Endangering public health or safety
   Examples: wildlife-human health, rabies (skunk, fox, bat); bears or rattlesnakes at campgrounds; bird hazards to aircraft; deer-automobile collisions
2. Nature of the animals and their habits
   a. Local or wide-ranging in feeding habits
   b. Migratory or non-migratory
   c. Native or introduced species
   d. Seasonal or year-round activity
3. Legal status of the animal (under federal or state jurisdiction, or both)
   a. Fully protected mammal or bird
   Examples: sea otter (competes with abalone industry); bald and golden eagle (livestock or fish predation)
   b. Game mammal or bird
   Examples: deer (timber and crop damage); ducks and geese (crop damage, especially cereals);
   c. Furbearer
   Examples: muskrat (canal and stream bank damage); beaver (causes flooding, cuts trees); weasel (kills poultry, game birds)
   d. Nonprotected, classed as pest or depredator
   Examples: rats (health hazard, crop and property damage); starling

(city nuisance, crop damage)
e. Wild domestic
Examples: feral house cat (kills game birds); feral dog (kills game, livestock)

4. Control technology
a. Lethal control, most direct method
Examples: gassing and shooting woodchucks, poisoning orchard field rodents, special deer hunts to lessen damage to vineyards, alfalfa fields, and Douglas-fir plantations
b. Preventive methods such as fencing, frightening devices, chemical repellents, and trapping-transfer of offending animals
Examples: deer- and rabbit-proof fences, carbide exploders and distress calls to repel blackbirds, bird roost repellents, live-trapping and transplanting bears and beavers
c. Environment control for reduction of animal damage by making the damage areas less attractive to the offending species or by improving habitat for them on alternate areas
Examples: vegetation removal in airport vicinity to prevent starling concentration hazard to aircraft, weed control in orchards to remove cover for mice at base of trees, waterfowl refuges to offer attractive resting and feeding areas as an alternative to croplands
d. Physiological control to modify the offending animal's ability to survive, resist other control measures, or reproduce
Examples: in control of blackbirds and starlings the use of wetting agents to induce exposure symptoms and chemosterilant application in pigeon control.

Crop damage insurance has been used in Canada in mitigating grain damage by waterfowl and has been suggested for certain livestock predation situations. However, compensation for wildlife damage is not a control but an alternative to control. The compensatory approach to game damage may have a place, but it cannot be regarded as an ultimate solution as it ignores the reason for the wildlife conflict.

In many wildlife damage situations, a combination of control approaches is most successful. For example, orchard damage by deer may be best alleviated by fencing, repellents, and special hunting seasons. Such conditions occur when natural wildlife habitat has been converted to income crops, often highly attractive to certain wildlife. Utilizing the man-made habitat is natural and necessary from the animal's standpoint. Defending against this use when it creates serious economic loss is essential to human interests.

Table 1 lists some wildlife damage problems and their control.

CONCLUSION

Optimum control of wildlife damage problems may include most of these procedures:

1. Some reduction in animal numbers to immediately alleviate damage
2. Fencing or other mechanical barriers to prevent access to the crop
3. Frightening techniques
4. Encouragement of adequate game harvest by hunters
5. Adjustment of agricultural practices
6. Establishment of feeding and resting areas on noncrop lands

Since man's alteration of the environment has created many wildlife damage problems, ecological principles must be considered in their solution.

TABLE 1. Some Wildlife Damage Problems and Their Control

Species	Type of Damage	Usual Damage Pattern	Factors Creating Conflict	Control Methods
Deer	Browsing and antler damage to orchard and forest trees; browsing field crops and ornamentals; livestock competition; and highway hazard	Orchard, forest, and vineyard damage may be year-round with resident deer; migratory herds and annual crops are seasonal factors	Habitat loss to highway, farm, urban, and water project development; lack of management, range overuse, under-harvest	Fencing, repellents, alarm devices, capture and transplant, shooting permits, hunter harvest
Elk	Browsing of orchard and forest trees; grazing of standing and stacked hay; livestock competition	Seasonal damage in migratory patterns; tree damage year-round in some areas	Range loss to farm, water and urban project development; forestry practices may intensify damage to young growth	Fencing, repellents, shooting permits, range improvements, livestock reallocation, hunter harvest
Pheasants	Pecking and eating corn plantings, tomatoes, berries, grapes	Localized in pheasant concentration areas	Habitat change by intensifying agriculture	Repellents, scare devices, special hunts, increased hunter harvest
Blackbirds (also grackles, cowbirds, starlings)	Feeding on corn, rice, milo, grapes, soft fruits, and at feedlots; noise and filth at city roosts (starlings)	Migratory concentration	Change in native habitat and increased single-crop farming	Alarm devices, protective nets, repellents, crop rotation, poisoning
Finches and sparrows	Feeding on fruit, planted seeds, disbudding of orchard trees	Widespread seasonal attacks in migratory concentration areas	Favorable cover but lack natural food in proximity to agricultural crops	Alarm devices, protective nets, repellents, crop rotation, poisoning
Waterfowl	Feeding on corn, rice, vegetables, pasture crops	Heavy feeding by huge flocks; pulling of sprouting grains by geese and pasture use by coots	Replacement of natural food in concentration areas by extensive farming of attractive crops	Exploders, scare devices, fireworks, aerial herding, refuges as alternate feeding areas, hunting pressure, special hunts
Eagles	Sporadic, isolated killing of domestic lambs and young of big game	Localized killing of lambs on migratory routes	Coincidence of lambing with migratory eagles	Closer watch at lambing time in areas prone to eagle attack
Raccoon	Feeds on corn, other crops, poultry, raids fish ponds, and is suburban nuisance	Persistent, year-round attack by resident animals on any available food source	Expansion of animal range, adaptability, and ability to eat almost anything	Livetrapping, night hunting
Jackrabbits and cottontail rabbits	Feeding on forage and vegetable crops; girdling of young trees, vineyards, ornaments	Seasonal with crop pattern and lack of natural food; fluctuates with population cycles	Lack of effective population control methods, increased agricultural plantings, and suburban developments	Repellents, fencing, shooting and poisoning of jackrabbits
Field rodents, gophers, mice, ground squirrels	Feeding on crops and ornaments; girdling of forest and orchard trees	Damage to field crops may be heavy and widespread; cyclic pattern with species such as meadow mice; resident year-round problems	Agricultural crop and rangeland offers favorable habitat; rodent productivity high	Repellents and screening for orchard tree and ornamental protection; trapping, fumigation, shooting; poisoning in organized control programs
Muskrat and Nutria	Burrow damage in levees and banks; crop damage (rice); flooding and erosion are secondary effects	Bank burrowing may lead to washouts, flooding, bank erosion; debris clogging water structures	Year-round activity; overpopulation by lack of fur trappers	Habitat control (vegetation removal and drainage); fur trapping; traps, poison in bait boxes
Skunks	Public health hazard (rabies); poultry, game bird, and turf damage, odor nuisance	Resident, nocturnal predation on birds and poultry; odors from residence under buildings	Suburban development in skunk habitat; skunks are a primary rabies carrier, and undesirable because of odor	Live traps, screening, trapping and shooting; organized control in suburban prevention programs

TABLE 1. Continued.

Species	Type of Damage	Usual Damage Pattern	Factors Creating Conflict	Control Methods
Porcupine	Girdling orchard and forest trees; gnawing buildings, equipment, and signs; feeding on hay crops; livestock injury	Forest damage most severe in young trees; costly damage to buildings, equipment, and trail signs; quill injury to grazing cattle and horses	Migration and over-wintering may concentrate damage	Screening ornamental plants; trapping and shooting; poison at dens, roost trees, and travel routes
Beaver	Tree cutting: riparian softwoods, orchard, and ornamentals; dam building may obstruct water structures, flood roads and meadows, create washout hazards, affect fish habitat	Migration into new irrigation areas; pond building may be beneficial or detrimental to fish habitat depending upon fish species and pond site	Road and canal building, summer home and orchard development near beaver waters; underharvest	Livetrap and transplant, fencing; fur trapping, shooting in damage areas
Foxes	Poultry and game bird depredation; rabies carrier	Local predation year-round; rabies transmission to dogs; game bird predation not generally decisive population factor	Suburban development; lack of sport hunting, fur trapping	Fencing and building for poultry protection; traps, shooting, fur trapping
Bobcat	Depredation on birds, poultry, lambs; rabies carrier	Resident, year-round damage to poultry and livestock; may be locally important in game bird introductions	Range poultry and sheep operations offer available food	Sport hunting, traps, shooting
Coyote	Sheep, goat and game depredations; some crop damage; public health hazard	Seasonal migration may spread damage over wide area; local losses of deer, sheep, and poultry; melon and fruit crops may be damaged; rabies transmission to dogs	Agricultural and suburban growth may provide favorable habitat; coyote adaptability	Fencing, traps, shooting, poison in supervised control programs
Mountain lion	Livestock and game depredation	Individuals may cause local losses to sheep, calves, colts, and deer	Mountain lions protected or big game in most states	Sport hunting, traps and dog hunting for depredation control
Black bear	Livestock killing, beehive, cabin, and forest tree damage; camp nuisance and safety threat	Individual bears may require control	Inadequate natural food; habitat change and increased human activities create conflict	Sport hunting, livetrap and transplant; traps and dog hunting for damage control or adjustment of conflicting uses

This table presents only a few representative examples of animal damage, possible causative factors, and suggested controls. Each damage pattern varies by area and with individual animal behavior.

SELECTED REFERENCES

California Vertebrate Pest Committee. 1962, 1964, 1967, 1970, 1972, 1974, 1976, 1978. Proceedings. Univ. of California, Davis.

Giles, R. H., Jr. (Ed.). 1969. Wildlife management techniques. The Wildl. Soc., Washington, D.C. 623 pp.

Leopold, A. S. (Chairman). 1964. Predator and rodent control in the United States. Trans. N. Amer. Wildl. Conf., 29:27-49.

National Academy of Sciences/National Research Council. 1970. Principles of plant and animal pest control. Vol. 5. Vertebrate pests: Problems and control. Washington, D.C. 153 pp.

INTRODUCTION
OF EXOTIC ANIMALS

James G. Teer

From his earliest beginnings, man has taken plants and animals with him wherever he went. In exploratory and colonial periods of history, and certainly with nomadic peoples, movements of cultivated crops and domestic livestock from one place to another were essential to his welfare and survival. The geographic exchange of food crops and animals still continues and often is desirable.

Justification for the movement of wildlife from one place to another or between continents is not so clear. The results of translocations of plants and animals of wild character and wild environments sometimes have been highly beneficial to man. In other situations and times, their impact has been detrimental, or even catastrophic. For the most part, man has thought only about the good that could come from his introductions. He has not always considered other consequences of his efforts. Nonetheless, man and nature, by accident and design, have mixed and are still mixing the earth's inhabitants.

SHOULD EXOTIC GAME ANIMALS BE INTRODUCED?

Opinion has always been divided on the propriety and prudence of introducing and moving animals from one place to another. Most Americans— biologists and conservationists, land operators and agriculturalists, private citizens and sportsmen—have an opinion about the matter of bringing in new game animals or the stocking of foreign animals in native game ranges. Their opinions have been fashioned by past experience and the results of "trying" new animals.

On the one hand, introductions of desirable game animals have succeeded in a few cases and have provided hunting recreation and enjoyment to millions of Americans. Few people are impressed when told that only a very small fraction of the trials of hundreds of species have successfully established themselves. Successful and desirable animals introduced in the United States include the Chinese or ring-necked pheasant, Hungarian partridge, chukar partridge, brown trout, axis deer or chital, blackbuck antelope, nilgai antelope, and a few others.

On the other hand, many introduced animals have become serious economic pests, have brought diseases and parasites with them that are harmful to native game animals and domestic livestock, or have succeeded at the expense of desirable native animals. The English sparrow, European starling, European carp, sea lamprey, and gypsy moth are but a few of the well-known, successful, but highly undesirable introductions into North America. Small wonder, then, that differences exist about the matter of introducing exotic animals.

Teer, James G.   Director, Welder Wildlife Foundation, Sinton, Texas

The reasoning presented in defense of or against moving wildlife about is usually founded on aesthetic or practical considerations. Some simply do not wish to tamper with nature for fear of upsetting nature's balance or changing the environment from the way it was originally constituted. However, most objections to introductions of exotic animals stem from the undesirable results that have occurred. No one wants an agricultural pest in the United States like the European rabbit in Australia or the red deer in New Zealand.

Other people want introduced animals in their lives. In the early days of settlement and development of our country, nostalgic immigrants wanted familiar animals from their homelands. Unquestionably, the average person is fascinated by animals, and he enjoys seeing creatures of other lands. Our numerous zoos attest to that fact. Today, some people want additional and different kinds of animals to hunt. They see a possibility of having additional animals by stocking foreign species. Probably the greatest stimulus to the introduction of big game species, particularly in the southwestern United States, is the growth of commercial shooting preserves and the potential for economic gain through the sale of trophy heads to sportsmen.

ECOLOGICAL MORALITY AND SAFEGUARDS

The role of the biologist and administrator of our conservation and natural resource agencies—for that matter, the role of all of society—is to see that our wild environments and game ranges are not prostituted by the introduction of exotic animals. Such areas must be protected as national treasures. Where man's cultural, industrial, and agronomic activities have reconstructed or changed natural communities, opportunities for exotic animals exist.

Second, careful assessments must be made of the need, desirability, probability of success, and possible impact of the introduced animal on native plants and animals before the exotic species is brought in. Such evaluations might require months of study of the candidate animal in its native range. The evaluations surely must involve intensive studies of the range where it is to be stocked and of the requirements of the animal in that new range.

SOME ECOLOGICAL PRINCIPLES TO CONSIDER

Probably no single game management activity practiced by private citizens as well as conservation agencies has had as many failures and been as expensive as programs of liberation of exotic game animals. Literally millions of dollars have been spent in trying this or that game animal. One courts failure when he simply "tries" an animal. The probability of an animal becoming established can be increased if preliminary studies of the biology and requirements of the species are made in its native range and in the range where it is to be stocked. Moreover, there are at least five ecological principles that should be considered when decisions are being made about the efficacy of introducing a particular animal and about the probability of its becoming successfully established.

Every Habitat Tends to Be Full

Nature abhors a vacuum, and there are few vacant spaces in natural communities. There is some evidence to suggest that large herbivores were numerous in North America in geologic history, but these became extinct following the last glaciation. Whether the loss of these animals left vacant niches is not clear. In any case, the grasslands, prairies, and plains where many of these animals lived have been changed drastically by agrarian man. Thus, vacancies may exist for selected grazing ungulates. However, the communities have been changed so completely in many habitats that they will no longer support any kind of grazing animal.

The ring-necked pheasant and Hungarian partridge are examples of introduced animals occupying habitat totally different in character and com-

Free roaming herds of *aoudad* (barbary sheep) can be found in New Mexico, Texas, and California. (Courtesy of Jim Yoakum)

position from what it was in pristine times. The pheasant and partridge are largely birds of farmland, and they reach their greatest abundance in farmlands of the Lake States and Dakotas. Originally, these farmlands were grasslands and plains with prairie grouse as important members of the habitat. Thus, with the ax and plow, man destroyed niches for birds of the grassland and created niches for birds of cultivated lands.

The desert areas of the Southwest have been viewed by many as places where nature has been stingy with her animals. The Chihuahuan and Sonoran Deserts support sparse populations of big game and game birds when compared with other ranges in the United States. Efforts to improve the habitat by providing water in catchments for dry times have not been successful in increasing game numbers. As has been noted by those familiar with the deserts, game animals could be increased if we could find animals that could eat and thrive on creosote bush! The point is that space alone does not constitute a vacancy. Nature usually has provided and stocked her habitats.

Each Species of Animal Has a Specific Set of Tolerances

Some animals prefer wet habitats; others prefer dry. Some can live in hot deserts; a few can live on Arctic ice packs. This is to say that all animals have evolved to interact and meet the impact of their environments through morphological, physiological, and behavioral adaptations. When they are put into situations in which they are not adapted, they will die.

The late Ding Darling once said during the duck depression of the 1930's, "Ducks do not nest on fence posts." The habitat must contain the animal's requirements and must be such that the animal can fulfill its needs under conditions found there. Even one factor not suited to it can cause the animal's failure.

The chukar partridge was first tried in 1893 in Illinois. It failed there, as it did in practically every state where it was liberated. It finally became established in the semi-arid west of the Rocky Mountains where it is hunted today. A climatograph depicting monthly averages of rainfall and temperature in its native land and in the United States showed that these states west of the Rockies were most like its native land in these two important climatic features.

It follows that ecological homologues are probably good candidates for introductions. An ecological homologue is an animal (or plant) with an identical counterpart often found on another continent. Such animals are often look-alikes, have the same habits, and occupy very similar habitats. But here logic in introducing an ecological homologue ends. There is simply no need for it; the habitat now contains a similar species. Efforts could best go into improving conditions for the native form.

Genetically Plastic Species Have Higher Probabilities of Succeeding

Many thousands of ring-necked pheasants were turned loose in trial transplants in North America before they finally became established in 1881. These transplants comprised individuals of several races including Mongolian, Chinese, Japanese, and English forms. It is likely that the race of pheasants that finally succeeded, and the one which we hunt today, is a genetic deviate from original stock tried unsuccessfully dozens of times.

A plastic species is one that has large variation in its appearance as indicated by large numbers of races. While there is no real problem in recognizing a North American ring-necked pheasant for what it is, there are subtle differences in coloration and other attributes. The pheasant which finally caught on simply had high variability in its genetic make-up which aided in its success. Hybridization between the races of the pheasant probably played a role in developing a bird more tolerant of or more adapted to conditions in North America.

Non-plastic, specialized forms are poor choices in transplant programs. Rarely are conditions similar enough or their ability to change to meet different conditions great enough to risk them in stocking programs.

Competition

The old adage, "two tigers cannot occupy the same ant hill," holds true when animals with the same, or even nearly the same, requirements are put together in a habitat. They likely will compete for some resource in the environment which is limited or in short supply. The result will be either complete elimination of one of the species or perhaps an adjustment in their numbers so that some kind of equilibrium is reached where both populations operate at low numbers.

Usually one or the other fails. The native species can usually be figured to have the advantage in such a competitive situation because it evolved in place and is the result of a part of that environment. The exotic may be able to find most of its requirements, but it may be less skilled or at a disadvantage in using them. Dislocations of native species can and have occurred, but the greatest probability is that introduced species in competition with closely related animals will fail.

Animals Taken from Complex to Simple Communities

Transplants of animals from continental to insular habitats have been eminently successful. Except for two species of bats, New Zealand had no indigenous land mammals. Now over 30 species of mammals have been released and have succeeded. The oceanic islands generally have experienced the same results.

One of the reasons for successful introductions of animals and plants into farmlands is that farmlands are much simplified in form and in numbers of living organisms. Natural communities are much more complex than farmlands, and many of the checks may not be present in farms.

SOURCES OF EXOTICS AND QUARANTINE LAWS

While it is not the purpose of this report to list all of the sources of exotic animals, it seems important that the usual sources be identified.

The Bureau of Sport Fisheries and Wildlife in cooperation with the state game and fish departments had a program of investigations and introductions of exotic game birds. The Bureau had personnel in foreign lands investigating likely candidates for introduction. The states and the Bureau cooperated in choosing release sites and in following the transplants. Birds were usually trapped from wild stock in native ranges and shipped to the United States by air freight. Before shipment, they were held in quarantine for about two months, where they were carefully examined and watched for diseases and parasites. They were also held in quarantine in the United States by the Animal Health Division of the United States Department of Agriculture for several weeks after arrival. After passing quarantine, the birds could be released directly into wild environments. This program is no longer in effect.

Big game animals are available from many animal dealers in practically every continent of the world. Zoos are also other sources of the big game species. Shipments of the animals must undergo several weeks of quarantine in the country of origin and also several weeks of quarantine in the United States by the Animal Health Division. Only the offspring of the introduced animals may be released into wild environments. Usually the animals are allowed to reproduce in captive conditions, often in zoos, and after sufficient young have been produced, they are released in wild environments. This sometimes requires years before enough young are available for stocking. The total operation can be an extremely expensive one.

Gemsbok (Kalahari oryx) have been successfully established in the White Sands area of New Mexico. (Courtesy of New Mexico Game and Fish Department)

CONCLUSION

It is apparent that interest in introductions of exotic animals for sport hunting has increased since World War II. Interest remains high, and there is no reason why carefully selected exotics cannot be safely introduced and be beneficial to man and his sport hunting. But if society demands and accepts the promises of exotic animals, it surely must accept rigid standards of safeguards and ecological morality in programs of stocking exotics. This responsibility rests not only with conservation agencies, but with all of society.

SELECTED REFERENCES

Caesar Kleberg Research Program in Wildlife Ecology. 1968. Symposium. Introduction of exotic animals: ecological and socioeconomic considerations. Coll. of Agr., Texas A & M Univ., College Station. 25 pp.

Craighead, F. C. and R. F. Dasmann. 1966. Exotic big game on public lands. Bur. of Land Manage., U.S. Dept. of the Int., Wash. 26 pp.

Decker, E. 1978. Exotics. Pp. 249-256 *in* Big game of North America. Wildl. Manage. Instit., Washington, D.C.

de Vos, A. and G. A. Petrides. 1967. Biological effects caused by terrestrial vertebrates introduced into non-native environments. 10th Technical Meeting, Int. Union for the Conserv. of Nature. IUCN Pub. New Series No. 9, pp. 113-119.

Elton, C. S. 1958. The ecology of invasions by animals and plants. Methuen and Co., Ltd., London. 181 pp.

Petrides, G. A. 1968. Problems in species' introductions. IUCN Bull. 2(7): 70-71.

Teer, J. G. 1975. Commercial uses of game animals on rangelands of Texas. J. Animal Science 40(5): 1000-1008.

NONGAME WILDLIFE

Bruce J. Wilkins and Steven R. Peterson

Each year more people become interested in wildlife, yet the proportion of the population hunting is on the decline in the United States. More people visited waterfowl refuges last year than ever before, but duck stamp sales are below levels reached in the 1950s. How can this be? How can interest be up, but hunting down? Simple, people are becoming more interested in watching, hearing, seeing, and otherwise enjoying wildlife without harvesting it.

THE HUNTER AND NONHUNTER

It should be recognized that hunters have been responsible for most of the pioneering work, and much of the money, that halted the rapid decline of many game species in the 1900s. Thus, the existence of large numbers of many wild animals is the result of hunter interest. Populations of wild animals can have the annual surplus cropped without harm. Indeed, failure to take the surplus has often been viewed as wasteful, and sometimes detrimental, to the species itself. To recognize nongame values, then, is not to say hunting is bad, but rather to suggest that wildlife can also be managed for other values.

How widespread is this nongame interest? Nearly 15 million people spent time photographing wildlife in 1975 and over 49 million people spent time observing wildlife in that year (U.S. Department of Interior 1977). The same study found less than half as many people (20 million) hunted (all data refer to residents nine years of age or older). Earlier studies are not strictly comparable to the 1975 survey, but most observers would agree there has been a steady increase in the number of people involved in observing and photographing wild animals, and clearly they represent a substantial portion of the nation's population. Even lands purchased with hunting license money are used predominantly by people who enjoy wildlife through observation.

STAND STILL OR MOVE AHEAD?

Professional wildlife biologists and managers can take different stands. One would be to view wildlife managers as only interested in serving hunters and their interests, as this is the source of most wildlife financial support. Also, the training of most professional wildlife managers has historically focused on game animals. That view is gradually losing preeminence to an alternative view that: "Professional wildlife managers should try to help people get wholesome enjoyment from wild animals. Some people will hunt them; some will feed them; some will just look; and there will even be some

Wilkins, Bruce J.   Associate Professor of Natural Resources, Department of Natural Resources, Cornell University, Ithaca, New York

Peterson, Steven R.· Associate Professor and Chairman of Wildlife, College of Forestry, Wildlife and Range Sciences, University of Idaho, Moscow

who only listen to them. The professional wildlife manager should help folks get enjoyment in any of these ways."

This may seem a logical change, but it has major effects. By choosing to serve all the people, a natural resources agency will employ biologists to do research on animals not hunted, manage habitat for songbirds, and increase interpretive services, thereby helping people better understand what they see.

Evidence of just such a change is widespread. State fish and game departments have established positions for mammalogists, ornithologists, and herpetologists, and have assigned biologists to work on bats, raptors, and endangered species.

Concurrently, state and federal agencies have adjusted their budgets to initiate or expand nongame programs, and to purchase habitat important to such animals. In a recent year over $2.3 million was spent by federal agencies on management and over $10 million was devoted to research on nongame animals. The bulk of these funds were concentrated on species with endangered, threatened, or "undetermined" status. The commitment that individual states have made to such work varies, but California, Colorado, Oregon, Utah, and Washington each has a nongame wildlife budget exceeding $100,000 annually. The majority of the states have now made a commitment to nongame programs.

Several states have purchased land specifically for nongame animals. Since 1968 California has established 18 ecological reserves for endangered species, such as the Morro Bay kangaroo rat. Michigan has purchased several hundred acres of habitat for a specific warbler, and Washington purchased part of an island to protect a breeding seabird colony.

There are numerous examples where management efforts by state and federal agencies have helped nongame species. Alligators, exploited almost to the point of extinction in Florida and Louisiana, have made a remarkable comeback and now are considered a nuisance in a few areas. A second population of whooping cranes is being established to augment the Wood Buffalo-Aransas population. Peregrine falcons are now being propagated successfully in captivity and reintroduced to areas where they once bred. Breeding populations of trumpeter swans have recently been reestablished in several of the lower 48 states.

Many rare or endangered species in our country are benefiting from recent federal and state legislation. The Tennessee snail darter, the Devil's Hole pup-fish, and the Houston toad have benefited from such pioneering legislation. But restoration or protection of historically hunted species (wolves, for example) has also been aided by legislation that applies to "game" and "nongame" animals alike.

DIFFERENCES IN MANAGING NONGAME WILDLIFE

What is so different in managing nongame wildlife? Some agencies have made the transition so it must not be a very difficult shift—or is it? Do new concepts, new approaches become desirable, perhaps necessary, when a commitment is made to nongame aspects of wildlife management? Only the differences are emphasized here. It is recognized that the basic influences on game populations—behavior, population dynamics, and habitat—also apply when managing nongame populations.

Ease of Viewing

A major difference in managing for the nonhunting user is the need to reduce the difficulty of viewing wildlife. Nonhunters are not as aggressive in seeking out animals. Managers must use new knowledge, skills, and techniques to make wildlife more available, and thus of maximum value, to the nonhunter.

Speaking in broad terms, the more animals present the more likely we are to observe them. Therefore, maximum populations would seem desirable. We find some conflict between nongame interests, wildlife managers, and the hunter in this regard. A difference exists in attitude between those desiring maximum possible populations and those desiring maximum naturally sustainable populations.

With imagination, some of these conflicts can be minimized. Michigan's elk herd needed to be reduced to remain within the carrying capacity of their range. Resort owners felt the large bulls with their royal racks had high appeal to tourists. How could they keep the bulls, yet reduce the herd? In this case, the answer was a cow only season! This did not require new knowledge but rather an ability to look at this new dimension in wildlife use to see how it could meld with the traditional hunting interest.

We can also concentrate animals or make them more readily observable. The bird feeders that millions of families enjoy, and the bird concentrations on waterfowl refuges are examples. Salting, baiting, and other concentrating methods are reasonable techniques for the nongame user. Construction of marshes, tanks, or ponds are means to attract and concentrate or expose animals so we may better see them.

Education of the User

The location of wild animals and the people interested in them also has an important influence on the ease of viewing. On an isolated northern lake or on the Chicago waterfront, a loon is a loon. The bird's potential value to humans may be greater near Chicago, if only because many more persons have ready opportunity to enjoy it near that city.

Many urban citizens do not want to travel great distances to observe wildlife, nor do they need to. Numerous bird and mammal species tolerate close association with urban dwellers as long as this wildlife is provided with suitable food and protection.

Acquiring and establishing urban areas dedicated to wildlife will provide nearby areas for observation, relieve public pressure on nearby management areas, and preserve critical habitat that would otherwise be lost to urban expansion. To acquire habitat in an already developed area is extremely expensive, but the long-term benefits to the state and the resource may make it worthwhile. Where additions or redevelopment areas of cities or suburbs are occurring, dedication of areas for wildlife should be an integral part of the planning process. Wildlife habitat in urban areas adds to the value of the land, the quality of life, and to the betterment of the species. Perhaps as important, people who ultimately influence decisions affecting wildlife can acquire a closer and better understanding of nature.

Educating the nongame user may also have very direct value to persons and agencies interested in game species. Many of the difficulties that natural resource agencies have experienced in recent years stem from the fact that urban people have lost contact with the land and the wildlife it supports. Yet, virtually every wildlife management principle utilized by resource managers can be demonstrated on nongame populations within a city. In the future, urban wildlife demonstration areas will be one of the keys in helping to combat public ignorance of the basic principles of wildlife management. Most of the species involved will be nongame or nonharvested game species and these animals, as well as the conditions under which they survive, will leave lasting impressions, especially on children.

Teaching persons to identify major wildlife species and habitats and to appreciate the interrelationships existing among living organisms should be an important concern of those responsible for wildlife management. With the recent trend toward species management in waterfowl hunting, such knowledge can yield a special bonus to hunters. Special instruction in Michigan enabled hunters to improve their ability to identify ducks, and the hunters generally approved qualification tests (Martz et al. 1969).

Seeing New Animals

As his view of nature is broadened, the nongame user may discover smaller vertebrates, a management variation that can yield him great value. Turtles, frogs, mice, snakes, and ground squirrels are present in numbers and variety in most areas. Persons can learn much about natural history through observation of these readily available forms of wildlife. In a very real sense new species are added when people see what was always there.

The wildlife biologist's innovation can expand those opportunities. One reported example concerns a Canadian group committed to helping individuals gain more from wildlife. People walking trails actually see few of the animals because animals are often active at hours when most humans are not. Further, the probability of a given animal being within the view of a given visitor is low. But most land animals leave some record of their passing—tracks. How could this be capitalized on? Thought and experimentation lead to a "sand trail"—several inches of moistened sand spread over plastic and paralleling the trail for a considerable distance. Smoothed several times a day, the sand trail provides a clear record of passage of ground-moving animals including amphibians, reptiles, and even some insects! The person walking the trail may still see a fox or a pheasant, but many more are likely to see their tracks, in some cases tracks left "just since we passed here a half hour ago."

This kind of thought, testing, and action has been directed to managing game animals for well over 50 years. Such attention to nonhunting aspects is much more recent, and thus would seem to be a fertile field for new ideas.

WORK WITH LANDOWNERS

Wildlife agencies have long worked with private landowners to maintain or increase wildlife populations. Relief from damage caused by deer or elk, additional income from federal programs for retaining wetland habitat, and advice on leaving crops for game are a few such programs.

In recent years, federal and state agencies have increasingly used their ecological expertise to aid nonfarming rural landowners. Millions of acres in this country have shifted from traditional agriculture because these areas could not return a satisfactory income to the owner. A new phenomenon is occurring with all classes of land—it is being purchased by families avidly seeking a rural home while working in town, or by those desiring a vacation spot for use on weekends and holidays. This clientele finds wildlife one of its prime interests.

Where rural land is owned primarily for these leisure uses, wildlife agencies can develop programs to assist families in achieving a frequent goal—more wildlife and a greater variety of wildlife. New York State, for example, has legislation enabling close cooperation between the state and the private landowner. Other states may wish to seek such legislation.

WHO SHOULD DO IT?

Some people question how deeply the historic game agencies should become involved in concerns for nongame species. In some regions, federal or state park agencies are meeting the needs of the nongame user. While it is true these groups have a major role in aiding nonhunters, wildlife agencies, too, must be involved.

With interest in wildlife growing, but space limited, we must use all possible areas as efficiently as possible. It is not very efficient to manage land to be used for only a portion of a year when nearly year-round use could be tolerated and encouraged. This means game lands also attractive to nongame wildlife can be used most of the year, if nongame users are encouraged. It also should mean awareness on the part of historic park or forest land management groups of the opportunities for positive wildlife management. In some areas this may include opening portions of park lands to hunting, but at a minimum, it should include nature interpretation in parks. Skilled personnel already employed by wildlife agencies are well qualified to aid those land managers in their changing wildlife emphasis. If those seeking to harvest game, and those interested in nongame species are to coexist, the old-timer in the neighborhood, the wildlife agency, must help the newcomer understand in many different ways, how the natural world works.

WHO PAYS

The major deterrent to nongame fish and wildlife programs is the lack of an adequate financial base. Monies for these new efforts must come from some source, and the usual approaches have been to stretch the old source a little further, or obtain money from a general fund. Recently, states have tried some new funding schemes including tax write-offs, "vanity" car license plates, decals, and stickers. These methods have met with varying success.

The surest, simplest, and most politically expedient course of obtaining funds seems to be an excise tax on items used by those interested in nongame species, items such as birdseed, binoculars, or hiking equipment. Since many persons interested in nongame wildlife do not buy a fishing or hunting license (the traditional financial support base of state fish and game agencies), this seems a fair way to assess the nongame user a nominal fee. Such an excise tax has been considered by Congress. Recent studies have indicated a small tax on certain recreational items can generate large sums of money. For example, Payne and DeGraaf (1975) have found that direct expenditures for enjoying nongame birds in 1974 exceeded $500 million and 95 percent of this money was spent on birdseed, binoculars, and camera equipment.

Until a decade ago, state wildlife agencies were funded largely with revenue from hunting and fishing license sales, and these funds were used to manage game species. With the increasing demand for wildlife agencies to devote more time and money to the nonharvested species, many hunters and fishermen have become concerned over the diversion of "their" money into nongame programs. If state wildlife agencies are truly "natural resource" or "wildlife" (rather than "fish and game") agencies, then it seems reasonable for nonharvest users of wildlife to pay a portion of the bill for nongame activities.

THE OPPORTUNITY

Management of wildlife resources has indeed advanced since the days of Aldo Leopold, who wrote the first American text on game management. In another pioneering book, he considers five ways through which persons may enjoy nature. The individual may be interested in a trophy; be interested in isolation; seek fresh air and change of scene; seek perception (including nature study); and, finally, attempt to attain a sense of husbandry.

His view of these activities is reflected in this statement:

It would appear, in short, that the rudimentary grades of outdoor recreation consume their resource-base; the higher grades, at least to a degree, create their own satisfactions with little or no attrition of land or life . . . (Leopold 1966:269).

We find ourselves in a time when more people are more broadly interested in our wildlife populations. A major question for the future is one which can only be answered from within ourselves: Are we bound by our heritage of hunting, or can we orient our thinking to that ultimate objective—providing the greatest satisfaction from wildlife for all of the people?

LITERATURE CITED

Bureau of Outdoor Recreation. 1967. Outdoor recreation trends, U.S. Govt. Printing Office. Washington, D.C. 24 pp.

Leopold, A. 1966. A Sand County Almanac. Oxford Univ. Press. 260 pp.

Martz, G. F., G. L. Zorb, and M. K. Johnson. 1969. Qualifying to hunt waterfowl through testing and training. Res. and Devel. Rep. No. 173. Mich. Dept. of Nat. Res.

Payne, B. R. and R. M. DeGraaf. 1975. Economic values and recreational trends associated with human enjoyment of nongame birds. Pp. 6-10 *in* Proc. Symp. Manage. For. Range Hab. Nongame Birds. Gen. Tech. Rept. WO-1. 343 pp.

U.S. Department of the Interior. 1977. 1975 national survey of fishing and hunting and wildlife-associated recreation. Fish & Wildl. Serv., Washington, D.C. 100 pp.

SUGGESTED READING

Hendee, J. 1969. Appreciative versus consumptive uses of wildlife refuges: studies of who gets what and trends in use. Trans. N. Amer. Wildl. Conf. 34: 252-264.

Leedy, D. L., R. M. Maestro, and T. M. Franklin. 1977. Planning for wildlife in cities and suburbs. Urban Wildl. Res. Center, Ellicott, Maryland. 64 pp.

URBAN WILDLIFE— NEGLECTED RESOURCE

Larry W. VanDruff

Human use of land for residential, commercial, industrial, and agricultural needs has drastically reduced the acreage of undisturbed land. Although most people are aware of this trend, ecologists and environmentalists in North America are especially concerned about the loss of certain wildlife habitats such as wetlands. Especially prominent among man's alteration of the natural environment are the artifacts of civilization and the concentrated human populations of urban areas.

Currently, over 70 percent of the residents of the United States live in cities and towns, and the percentage will increase in the foreseeable future. An accompanying trend has been for the use of more land to support a given population. An increase in single family dwellings, wider transportation corridors, satellite shopping centers, and service facilities have all resulted in the increasing acreage needed for an urban population.

The picture is clear—an urbanizing environment is a dominant feature of most areas of the country. Cities, towns, and connecting suburbs, as well as the associated commercial and industrial areas and the corridors for transportation, utilities, and services, are conspicuous. A new environment of artificial structures, disturbed soils, modified vegetation and climate, and altered competitive relationships among the plants and animals has largely replaced the former natural environment.

Within this new environment native wildlife and some species introduced by humans make up the urban fauna. Currently the term "urban wildlife" refers to the nondomestic vertebrates and often the attractive, conspicuous invertebrates found in an urbanizing environment.

OCCURRENCE OF HABITATS AND WILDLIFE

Although most urban areas contain only vestiges of their former natural communities, these remnants and a multitude of altered and man-made habitats supporting wildlife populations exist. The largest, most prominent, and often most utilized tracts are city and county parks within or between municipalities. Cemeteries and institutional grounds, such as college campuses and hospitals, occupy relatively large areas within cities, while unmanaged or neglected areas of private and public ownership also add to the total open space of most villages, towns, and cities. Industrial tracts, landfills, and watershed-reservoir areas, having relatively low human usage, may support sizeable natural areas with resident populations of native wildlife. Large green spaces in urbanized areas form "islands" that may boast densities of certain wildlife, especially of migrating birds, far greater than rural or wilderness areas of comparable size.

VanDruff, Larry W. Associate Professor of Wildlife Biology, College of Environmental Science and Forestry, State University of New York, Syracuse

Within more urbanized areas wildlife find an abundance of private lawns, yards, and gardens with a large array of native and ornamental vegetation. Even a porch or window box with flowers may attract hummingbirds, butterflies, and pollinating insects. While vegetation is noticeably reduced in the central business districts of cities, wildlife do utilize the space. These urban habitats are often interconnected by vegetation associated with transportation and utility rights-of-way, stream and river banks, waterfronts, and steep geologic formations. The resulting pattern offers a diversity of habitats juxtaposed for those species of wildlife able to exist in close association with humans and their activities. Thus, wildlife habitat exists literally everywhere within a city and in the immediate surroundings. The forms that it takes are numerous, but it is always the diversity and types of vegetation that are of key importance in influencing the kinds of wildlife present.

House finches at feeder with peanut butter. Such observations of birdlife provide many hours of enjoyment for city dwellers. (Courtesy of G. A. Swanson)

When considering urban wildlife, one immediately thinks of the nonnative species such as pigeons, rats, house sparrows, and starlings that are abundant because they are supremely adapted to life in close association with humans, utilizing the artificial habitats and altered competitive relationships that are created by urbanization. But other species are found living within cities, often thriving and often unnoticed by most urbanites. Fish and their invertebrate food items are associated with all but the most polluted waterways. Resident populations of amphibians usually are restricted to bottomland or holding-basin sites where standing water and a fringe of cover are available. Most reptiles become noticed only when they venture across a road or into a backyard or gain access to a basement, although turtles may contribute to the attractive fauna of urban ponds or impoundments. A surprising diversity and abundance of birds either reside within or seasonally visit urban areas. Bird observations in London revealed that 67 percent of the avian species of the United Kingdom visited the London area over a 10-year period (Gill and Bonnett 1973).

While larger tracts of green space provide suitable habitat for resting and foraging by migrant birds and their avian and mammalian predators, mowed lawns and their borders frequently are used for foraging by robins, chipping sparrows, mourning doves, and flickers. Urban waterfowl flocks, conspicuous and readily observable by urbanites, can be a recreational and educational asset to a community. With the arrival and lingering of migrants, local populations on duck ponds, reservoirs, rivers, and waterfronts usually swell during fall and winter.

Less conspicuous are the numerous mammals that inhabit the urban environs. While the Norway rat and house mouse are ubiquitous, and often abundant, tree squirrels are more conspicuous in the urban forest. Gray, red, flying, and fox squirrels have urban populations over their respective ranges. Although viewing the gray squirrel is considered a pleasure to most urbanites, this species has a high nuisance potential. The raccoon is another mammal that often thrives in an urban setting, given its predilection for securing food from human refuse and seeking shelter in artificial structures. Skunks, rabbits, opossums, deer, shrews, mice, moles, bats, and an occasional fox are common urban wildlife, although weasels seem noticeably scarce in urban areas. In the Northeast, the beaver is appearing more frequently in urban areas, and muskrats can usually be found straying from watercourses through the city in the spring. Conspicuously absent from the more populated areas of our country are those species with extensive home ranges or those species whose habits have long been in strong conflict with human interests.

Generally, the diversity of vegetation and habitats in cities meets the needs of numerous wildlife species. Individuals—usually viable populations—are found in cities and suburbs dispersed among man's modifications of the natural environment.

SIGNIFICANCE AND VALUES

Undeniably, the sights, sounds, and activities of such colorful and conspicuous animals as cardinals, nuthatches, jays, robins, mallards, squirrels, and chipmunks add an element of stimulation and delight to urban life. Desirable wildlife in one's neighborhood can engender a positive, wholesome attitude toward one's surroundings, and surveys have revealed higher values for property that includes natural vegetation and associated wildlife. Indeed, the wildlife of an area may serve as an indicator of the quality of that environment in terms of human perceptions, values, and desires.

The educational value of wildlife in our midst is important. Birdwatching, a most popular pursuit, is both enjoyable and educational to people of all ages right in their own backyards or in a nearby park, cemetery, or natural area. Teachers find the local fauna invaluable in demonstrating the natural history and biology of various species, as well as ecological principles and environmental events at all seasons of the year.

In cities and towns many people have lost their awareness of the natural world of which they are a part. The presence of conspicuous, desirable wildlife may serve as a daily reminder of the symbiotic relationships between man and nature. Wildlife is an ideal tool for demonstrating the significance of the biological component and the complexities and interrelationships within our ecosystem. Only when these interrelationships are recognized and promoted will humans achieve fulfillment as part of the natural world.

A greater abundance and diversity of wildlife in the urban ecosystem may contribute to greater enrichment of the human environment. Where monoculture of vegetation and retarded ecological succession are prominent, such enrichment is desirable.

Urban wildlife populations may serve as a reserve for resupplying surrounding rural areas following habitat restoration, excessive population decimation by predators or disease, or local overharvest by hunting. High populations of rabbits, squirrels, raccoons, doves, pheasants, and quail in our suburbs, for example, may provide such reserves.

The negative aspects of wildlife in urban areas cannot be overlooked. Problems range from the mild nuisance of an occasional offending animal to the outright destruction of property and threats to human health and safety. The close association between humans, pets, and wildlife in an urban setting facilitates contacts and disease transmission. Gulls and other wildlife attracted to the open expanses of airport runways or the refuse available at nearby dumps may create serious air traffic hazards. Conversely, the urban environment presents hazards to wildlife from pets, people, pollutants, and automobiles.

WILDLIFE'S REQUIREMENTS AND MEETING THOSE NEEDS

The basic survival and welfare needs of wildlife are the same in urban, rural, and wilderness areas—food, water, and cover providing undisturbed den or nest sites and security from overexploitation by predators, pets, or people. Obviously the specific food items, preferred cover type, and choice of home site vary with species, but populations of several wildlife species can exist in the same area. For most urban areas, the greatest diversity of wildlife is found in the urban-rural fringe where there still exist relatively large green spaces with access corridors and interconnecting links. The larger mammals, those with more extensive home ranges, such as coyotes, foxes, and white-tailed and mule deer, occasionally reside there. The preservation, maintenance, and creation of tracts of natural vegetation in all stages of ecological succession, interlaced with corridors for escape, foraging, and exploratory movements, will aid wildlife populations inhabiting or traversing the green spaces.

Closer to the center of the city or within villages and towns, more attention may be directed toward meeting the habitat requirements of specific wildlife groups (for example, songbirds), certain species, and certain individuals. Natural vegetation supplemented by ornamentals can serve both food and cover needs. Especially useful for songbirds and small mammals are the heavily fruiting varieties of cherries, apples, elderberries, mulberries, hawthorns, viburnums, and dogwoods. Those species with persistent fruits will benefit wintering birds and mammals. A lack of available, clean water for wildlife can be alleviated by the use of inground pools, bird baths, and other drinking devices. A source of grit or crushed shells and a bare spot for dusting may entice birds to a backyard, away from hazards at a roadside.

187

MANAGEMENT AND UTILIZATION OF THE RESOURCE

Many argue that humans have a moral obligation to manage nature once we have disrupted it. This management need seems especially acute in our urban areas where human populations (potential benefactors) are high, desirable wildlife already occurs, and political-economic values dominate ecological concerns in land-use decisions. For management of wildlife as part of a physical-biological-cultural system, it is helpful to identify three geographic areas.

Rural - Urban Interface

The first step toward management of the wildlife resources of an urban area is a consideration of the historical and current fauna of the region beyond the urban center. Information on species distribution and habitat affinities, centers of population abundance, predator-prey relationships, roles of endemic diseases, and human utilization of local fauna is desirable. Management of the total wildlife of an urban environment first requires a plan for management of the green space in the rural-urban fringe. It is here that natural areas are being most rapidly destroyed or severely altered. The goal should be to preserve a good diversity of physical and natural landscapes of appropriate sizes, which are connected to one another and the surrounding countryside by open space corridors. Some cities are fortunate in having a desirable mosaic of physical, natural, and cultural features throughout the urban areas. Planning and managing for a beneficial relationship among these features requires the combined talents of perceptive urban and regional planners, landscape architects, urban foresters, and urban wildlife biologists. Plans should be long-range and comprehensive, even for this rapidly changing, transitional zone. The wildlife manager will be concerned with providing access corridors, reducing the impact of large-scale development (e.g., shopping centers, airports, and beltways) upon local populations, and promoting desirable human-wildlife interactions in a natural, attractive setting such as at a marsh, duck pond, river front, or other ecosystem with conspicuous wildlife. Human utilization of the wildlife resource will mostly be by visiting urbanites—outdoor recreationists, bird-watchers, visitors to nature centers or viewing areas, and an occasional sportsman beyond the city limits.

Suburbia

The most extensive land-use type in urbanized areas, commonly referred to as urban sprawl, is characterized by single or two-family detached dwellings and supporting facilities such as playgrounds, churches, schools, sidewalks, and streets. A diversity of wildlife occurs in remnants of former natural systems and interspersed among human modifications of the landscape. Humans and resident or transient wildlife are in close association; the potential for beneficial or nuisance values of the wildlife is high. Successful management of the resource should enhance the positive values of the wildlife to residents. The wildlife manager must continue to consider the fauna as a part of the total ecosystem. Excessive encouragement of particular species may lead to harmful imbalances. Participation of enlightened residents is necessary for successful management of individual species, wildlife groups, or the total fauna of a neighborhood. Conservation information and education must accompany recommendations that may be implemented by individual lot owners.

More specifically, the following suggestions may be offered to the suburban homeowner who wishes to better understand and benefit resident wildlife.

1. Obtain field guides and subscribe to conservation and wildlife magazines to learn more of the natural history of the wildlife of your area.

2. Become observant of wildlife in your neighborhood and record observations to note seasonal and annual changes.

3. Provide nest boxes for those bird and mammal species that you wish to encourage.

4. Select and add annual and perennial native and ornamental plantings with wildlife specifically in mind; increasing the diversity of vegetation on your lot should attract more wildlife. The presence of flora with abundant fruits (dogwoods, viburnum, hawthorns, crab apples, cherries, etc.) will increase the appeal of your lawn and garden to numerous wildlife.

5. Supplement the natural food supply with artificial feeding of the desirable wildlife species; restrict accessibility of the feeder to undesirable species; provide a source of grit and a dusting spot for birds.

6. Maintain a dependable source of water at ground level and a bird bath on your property, especially during midsummer.

7. Restrict free-roaming pets and educate youth to avoid disturbing wildlife.

8. Include evergreens and multiflora roses for wildlife travel lanes along property edges; inform neighbors of your interest in encouraging wildlife; solicit their participation in providing a larger managed area or an area of planned neglect where grasses, weeds, vines, and shrubs are permitted to seed and grow naturally.

9. Be vocal in your support of urban habitat preservation in your community. Within the needs for law enforcement and human safety, many areas can be set aside to permit natural succession to occur.

10. Visit local, county, state, and federal agencies responsible for fish and wildlife conservation to obtain information and encourage them to address the issue of urban wildlife. Do not be discouraged—the concern is very contemporary and available information is sparse.

Metropolitan Centers

Traditionally, the city's central business district and the surrounding ring of multistoried buildings have been the stronghold of nuisance wildlife, usually the pigeon, house sparrow, and Norway rat. Such problems will continue; their reduction will require more effective pest population control measures, strictly enforced refuse containment, thorough rubbish removal, and modification or renovation of ornate or decaying architecture. In addition to alleviating pest conditions, great opportunity exists for encouraging a richer diversity of native fauna in the inner-city ecosystem. In cooperation with urban foresters, the wildlife biologist may strive to increase the diversity of urban flora and fauna. Such changes in metropolitan areas may reduce the competitive advantage provided exotic species, permitting native fauna to become reestablished. Also, attention must be directed toward human interaction with the wildlife present. Viewability of wildlife and type of interactions may become more important than diversity.

THE FUTURE

Some 75 percent of Americans now occupy villages, towns, and suburbs. The acreage devoted to urban use has nearly doubled in the past 25 years, with most growth in the suburbs. This explosion of suburbia attests to a desire for open space with its accompanying vegetation and wildlife. The environmental movement of the past decade has heightened this awareness of the natural world, and interest in wildlife is high. The stage is set for conservation organizations and governmental agencies to utilize and manage the wildlife resource of urban areas to enhance the quality of human life. Efforts to reverse the degradation of large cities and increase the quality of life there should include programs to benefit urban wildlife and promote the positive aspects of the resource. The relationship of urbanites to wildlife in their midst may affect their attitude toward and support of conservation programs directed toward wildlife in rural and wilderness areas as well. It is likely that federal and state monies will be allocated to urban and nongame wildlife programs for the benefit of the citizenry. Such funds are already being spent to inventory the resource and research the possibilities of incorporating urban wildlife into urban areas.

LITERATURE CITED
Gill, D. and P. Bonnett. 1973. Nature in the urban landscape: a study of city ecosystems. York Press, Baltimore. 209 pp.

SELECTED REFERENCES
Bourne, R. and A. MacConomy, eds. 1974. Gardening with wildlife. National Wildlife Federation. Washington, D.C. 190 pp.

Euler, D., F. Gilbert and G. McKeating, eds. 1976. Proceedings of the symposium—wildlife in urban Canada. Univ. of Guelph, Guelph, Ontario. 134 pp.

Leedy, D., R. Maestro and T. Franklin. 1978. Planning for wildlife in cities and suburbs. Off. Biol. Serv., Fish and Wildl. Serv., USDI, Washington, D.C. 64 pp.

Martin, A., H. Zim and A. Nelson. 1951. American wildlife and plants: a guide to wildlife food habits. McGraw-Hill Book Co., New York. 500 pp.

McKeating, G., ed. 1975. Nature and urban man: proceedings of a symposium. Spec. Publ. No. 4, Canadian Nature Fed., Ottawa. 134 pp.

——— and W. Creighton. 1974. Backyard habitat. Ministry of Natural Resources, Ontario, Canada. 10 pp.

Noyes, J. and D. Progulske, eds. 1974. Wildlife in an urbanizing environment. Planning and Resource Development Series, No. 28. Univ. of Mass., Amherst. 182 pp.

Terres, J. 1968. Songbirds in your garden. Thomas Y. Crowell Co., New York. 256 pp.

Thomas, J., R. Brush, and R. DeGraaf. 1973. Invite wildlife to your backyard. Reprinted from Apr.-May Nat. Wildl. Mag., Nat. Wildl. Fed., Washington, D.C. 12 pp.

NATURAL AREAS AND NATURAL HERITAGE AREAS

Richard H. Thom

Conservation agencies are placing increasing emphasis on the identification, protection, and management of natural areas and other types of natural heritage lands as land management professionals and the public recognize the importance and vulnerability of this natural resource. Natural areas are areas of land or water that have essentially retained (or recovered) their primitive conditions. Natural areas exemplify typical or unusual ecosystems and their associated biotic, edaphic, geologic, and aquatic features. Both common and unusual wildlife species live in natural areas, which can serve as benchmark ecosystems for wildlife studies.

Undisturbed natural forests, prairies, marshes, glades, estuaries, alpine meadows, and streams, and their natural successional stages are examples of natural areas. For example, Ohio's Hueston Woods Nature Preserve protects a 200-acre American beech-sugar maple climax forest as one of the last, best examples of this eastern deciduous forest type. In Illinois, the 1,100-acre Heron Pond Nature Preserve contains a remnant of the cypress-tupelo gum forests that once covered a small swath of the southern tip of that state. This area harbors wildlife species that require swamp forest communities, including swamp rabbit, Swainson's warbler, great-blue heron, and bird-voiced tree frog.

Natural heritage areas (also called natural history areas) include natural areas, but they also include areas that are not natural areas but deserve special management because of some significant natural feature, such as an endangered species of plant or animal, an outstanding geological display, or an archaeological feature. To guarantee the scientific, educational, and cultural benefits of natural areas for the future, natural area systems have been developed that aim to set aside examples of every type of significant natural feature within a geographic area. Wildlife professionals often become involved in these natural area programs.

VALUES

Natural areas are control areas against which man-modified environments may be compared. Most natural ecosystems are vastly complex and relatively stable and self-maintaining. In contrast, most man-modified ecosystems are less complex and require human effort to maintain. Research in the functioning of natural ecosystems has application in wildlife and forest management, agriculture, and even in problems associated with pollution and urban environments. Wildlife research on the natural role of predators, population ecology, habitat and food preferences, and many other subjects can be conducted on natural areas.

Thom, Richard H.   Natural Areas Coordinator, Missouri Department of Conservation, Jefferson City

Natural areas and their components are important resources for basic scientific research for virtually every branch of science; they are useful as educational areas; and they may be sources of aesthetic appeal and inspiration.

Natural areas are genetic reservoirs of living species and of natural diversity. Wild species have potential usefulness in horticulture, agronomy, animal science, medicine, and other fields. For example, wild plants and animals can be sources of genetic improvement of the domestic varieties.

Natural areas often provide habitat for rare, threatened, and endangered species that deserve protection for both moral and utilitarian reasons. Aldo Leopold, a wildlife biologist and advocate of natural areas protection, thought that the seemingly insignificant components of natural communities should be preserved simply because their roles in the ecosystem are not well understood. He likened these organisms to the cogs and wheels of a complicated mechanism and wrote: "To keep every cog and wheel is the first precaution of intelligent thinking" (Leopold 1953).

Natural areas are part of our cultural heritage, since they represent the primitive condition of the land as it was encountered by explorers and pioneers. Culture and history are influenced profoundly by the natural environment in which they develop.

Natural areas, when established within wildlife management areas, can be integrated into the overall management program for the areas. The natural area can serve as a refuge or can provide a special habitat type to increase habitat diversity of the management area. Many of the same values of natural areas apply to the other types of natural heritage areas that will be discussed later.

EVALUATION

The quality of a natural area is determined by the degree of man-caused disturbance (or degree of recovery from past disturbance). Natural areas should represent original conditions of a region prior to settlement. Although man's influence on earth has been pervasive, the degree to which an area approaches the undisturbed condition is the measure of its natural quality. A forest that has never been logged, grazed by livestock, burned by man-caused fires, influenced by pollutants and pesticides, or invaded by imported plants, animals, and pathogens would be a high quality forest natural area (and one that would be difficult to find!).

Evaluating the natural quality of an area requires a knowledge of the region's original character and its land-use history, as well as the ability to recognize man-induced changes. The best indicators of disturbance and original character depend on the ecosystem being evaluated; parameters for evaluating a cave would be different from those for evaluating a bog. The vegetation and soil are the most important indicators of natural quality in forests, prairies, tundra, glades, and most other terrestrial ecosystems. Aquatic areas such as marshes, lakes, estuaries, and streams may be evaluated on the basis of past water level changes, shoreline disturbance, water quality, and aquatic life.

A few natural areas represent unique (one-of-a-kind) natural types, such as an unusual grouping of geological features forming environments occupied by a unique combination of plant communities in a small area. Most natural areas, however, represent natural communities that were once common for the region in which they occur. An area need not be unique to be significant.

Size is not so important in evaluating the quality of a natural area as it is in determining the practicality of maintaining the area in its natural state. A natural area and any protective buffer land must be large enough to maintain its ecological integrity. As little as one acre could protect a small sinkhole pond and its entire watershed, but a one-acre forest would be insufficient. For example, an abandoned pioneer cemetery in northern Illinois, the Beach

Cemetery Prairie Nature Preserve, is only two acres in size. Yet it is a significant island of native prairie with rich plant diversity in an agriculturally developed region.

Generally, smaller areas are less able to support certain animal species, including insects and other invertebrates, than larger areas of comparable quality. While a prairie chicken flock could not survive on the tiny cemetery prairie remnant, the 1,360-acre Taberville Prairie Natural Area in southwestern Missouri is sufficiently large to support a population of the greater prairie chicken as well as other species such as upland sandpiper, grasshopper sparrow, Henslow's sparrow, northern harrier, and dickcissel.

Although in the strictest sense natural areas are undisturbed natural ecosystems, state and federal natural area programs usually include other types of natural heritage areas as well:

1. *Habitats of rare or endangered species* may be natural areas, but sometimes they are greatly disturbed, or require modification to create optimum conditions for survival of the target species. Such areas would better be termed rare species management areas.

2. *Habitats of relict or peripheral species* support plants and animals that are relicts of a past climatic period or are near their natural range limits.

3. *Geological* areas have important geological features regardless of the amount of disturbance. Some of the most valuable geological areas, such as roadcuts and quarries, have become important because of the disturbance. Some geological areas are also natural areas, such as an undisturbed cave ecosystem or a sandstone bluff with a natural plant community.

3. *Natural history* study areas are used for nature study and research, although they may not qualify as natural areas. Their greatest value may be proximity to an educational institution or population center.

4. *Archeological* areas contain features such as Indian village sites or burial mounds.

5. *Scenic* areas are recognized for their aesthetic appeal even though they may have been greatly altered by man. (While many natural areas are scenic, scenic attributes are not considered in evaluating natural quality.)

6. *Wilderness* areas are usually large areas (several thousand or more acres) where natural forces predominate or can be restored. A primary purpose of these areas is to provide wilderness recreational experiences. They often contain natural areas within their boundaries.

When dealing with these various types of natural heritage areas, the term natural area should be reserved for undisturbed natural ecosystems. Other more appropriate terminology should be applied to other types of areas unless they are also natural areas.

INVENTORIES

Natural area inventories (or natural heritage programs) vary in scope and methodology according to their objectives and the resources available for their implementation. Comprehensive inventories are important in building a natural area system that adequately represents the natural diversity of a region and in considering natural areas in land use decisions.

Some agencies conduct inventories using in-house expertise or expand their staffs for inventory capability. Another option is to contract the job with universities or private organizations such as the Nature Conservancy. The Department of Interior's Heritage Conservation and Recreation Service supplies technical assistance to states on developing inventories.

Information for natural area inventories is obtained by contacting knowledgeable individuals and organizations, searching published records, reviewing soil and topographic maps and aerial photographs, conducting aerial surveys, and inspecting and evaluating potential natural areas in the field.

MANAGEMENT, USE, AND PROTECTION

Natural area management aims to maintain or enhance the natural quality of the ecosystem. This is accomplished by allowing natural forces to operate, by simulating natural processes that have ceased to operate, and by removing man-caused influences and exotic species from the natural area. Natural area management is essentially native ecosystem management, and in this way it differs from the type of wildlife management aimed at benefiting a certain desirable species or group of species, whether game or nongame. Rather than optimizing conditions for a certain species, natural area management maintains a natural ecosystem as a complex, functioning unit with no particular concern for optimizing conditions for any given species (except that certain species may be monitored as indicators of the natural quality of the ecosystem). Natural area management may create suboptimum conditions for some wildlife species, especially those preferring early successional habitats (although natural areas may also represent successional communities). On the other hand, species that prefer less disturbed habitats in later stages of succession are often benefited. The effect of a natural area on wildlife in the vicinity is influenced by the shape and size of the area and the management of the surrounding land.

Correcting the results of human influences and disturbances often requires active management. Establishment of nonnative species, interruptions of natural processes such as fire or flooding, and man-caused changes in the water table are problems that may require positive corrective efforts. An area with these problems, if simply left alone, may improve very slowly or may continue to deteriorate. Thus, eradication of exotic species, controlled burning, selective cutting, and water level manipulation all can be tools for natural area management. Often, as an area improves in natural quality, less active management is needed to maintain its condition.

Gathering baseline information and monitoring the natural area help to reveal changes that occur in the area and aid in evaluating management. Plant inventories, ecological sampling, permanent photographic stations, and aerial photography all contribute to the understanding of an area.

Use and development of natural areas should be consistent with the perpetuation of the features for which they are protected. Observation, nature study, research, and hiking are the types of activities allowed on most public natural areas. Walking trails, parking areas, and interpretive facilities are sometimes provided.

Development and allowable uses vary with the philosophy of the controlling agency. Some states prohibit sport hunting on all of their recognized natural areas, while this activity is permitted in other states on areas where it is not detrimental to the natural conditions. Analysis of the potential impact of an activity will determine whether the activity is compatible on a particular natural area. Recreational activities usually are not promoted.

Natural areas are vulnerable to a variety of threats. Areas in private ownership and with no special protection can be destroyed at will by the owner. But even recognized public natural areas are vulnerable to problems such as reservoir construction and stream channelization, utility and highway development, timber theft, grazing trespass, and inadvertent mismanagement.

Some threats are of a type against which there is little defense. Among these are problems of air and water pollution originating from sources outside the natural areas, noise from a nearby highway or airport, pest introductions from other regions, and the visual intrusions of powerlines and smokestacks.

Methods used to give protection status to natural areas, listed in the approximate order of the level of protection achieved are:

1. *Environmental impact statement analyses* inform developers of the existence of natural areas so they can be avoided.

2. *Notification and management assistance* informs an owner that he has

a natural area (many a natural area has been destroyed because the owner was unaware of its significance).

3. *Registration* places the natural area on an official registry by non-binding agreement between the owner and the resource agency. Registration formalizes the owner's intent to maintain an area in its natural state and gives an area some protection by public recognition of its significance.

4. *Designation* normally involves public land and is accomplished by administrative action of the managing agency.

5. *Dedication* is a legally binding commitment between a public or private owner and the state to permanently set aside a natural area. Dedication gives a very high level of protection even if the area is in private ownership.

6. *Less than fee acquisition* is the establishment of a protective agreement such as an easement without actual acquisition by the managing agency. Depending on the arrangement, protection may be permanent as in a dedication.

7. *Fee simple acquisition* acquires full title ownership of a tract for the purpose of designation or dedication as a natural area.

STATE, FEDERAL, AND PRIVATE

State natural area programs are usually administered by the conservation department or its equivalent, but many states also have separate boards, councils, or commissions with authority ranging from strictly advisory to that of the lead agency for the state program. State natural area systems have been developed both legislatively and administratively. Units of these systems are variously called natural areas, scientific areas, nature preserves, and by other names. Areas that are included in a formal system are given some level of protection. Designated natural areas are usually recognized as being in their highest and best use and to divert them to another use would require critical public need for which there is no alternative. Official state natural areas can be owned by government agencies, educational institutions, private organizations, commercial corporations, and individuals depending upon the particular system.

The objective of a state natural area system is to establish, maintain, and protect natural areas (and often other natural heritage areas) representing all significant types of natural features in sufficient quantity and with adequate geographic distribution to assure the lasting benefits of these areas. The best remaining example of each type of natural feature is sought for inclusion, with some duplication of features to assure protection of the type. For example, Black Tern Bog Scientific Area is preserved as an example of a bog ecosystem in northern Wisconsin. In addition to its interesting flora, the bog is a nesting habitat for black terns, mallards, black ducks, and killdeer.

The classification of a state's natural features and its bio-geographic regions provide the framework on which its natural area system is built. For example, the best available oak-hickory forest can be included for each geographic division of the state in which this feature occurs. Obviously, a comprehensive inventory using the state's classification scheme is invaluable in developing the state natural area system.

The federal government in 1966 established the Federal Research Natural Areas System, which is coordinated by a Federal Committee on Ecological Reserves. Agencies such as the Forest Service, the Fish and Wildlife Service, and the Bureau of Land Management had designated 4.4 million acres of land in 389 areas into this system by 1977. Some federal agencies had recognized and protected natural areas long before this system was formed.

A partial list of congressional actions that have affected protection of natural areas includes the Wilderness Act of 1964, the Land and Water Conservation Fund Act of 1965, the Fish and Wildlife Conservation Act of 1968, the National Environmental Policy Act of 1969, the Endangered Species Conservation acts of 1969 and 1973, and the Resource Planning Act of 1974.

In 1978 the Interior Department began the National Heritage Program, which created the Heritage Conservation and Recreation Service (out of the former Bureau of Outdoor Recreation) for identifying and protecting natural and cultural resources, provided for funding of natural heritage and cultural heritage preservation, and recommended legislation to address the objectives of the National Heritage Program.

Several private organizations are devoted to the protection of natural areas. The largest, the Nature Conservancy, works closely with state conservation departments in building state natural area systems by including its own areas in such systems, by advance acquisition of areas for later resale to public agencies, and by developing and implementing state natural heritage inventory programs.

Professional organizations such as the Society of American Foresters, the American Society of Range Management, and The Wildlife Society have had long interest in natural areas establishment.

CONCLUSION

Public support for natural areas and other types of natural heritage areas continues to increase with the recognition of their importance and vulnerability. Natural resource professionals should appreciate the many ways in which natural areas contribute to their fields and to the public welfare. Wildlifers, in particular, should prepare themselves for increased involvement in natural areas programs.

LITERATURE CITED

Leopold, A. 1953. Round river. Ed. by Luna B. Leopold. Oxford Univ. Press, Inc., New York. 173 pp.

SELECTED REFERENCES

Arkansas Department of Planning. 1974. Arkansas Natural Area Plan. Little Rock, Arkansas. 248 pp.

Heritage Conservation and Recreation Service, USDI. 1978. Draft natural heritage classification systems. Washington, D.C. 144 pp.

The Nature Conservancy. 1975. The preservation of natural diversity: A survey and recommendations. Arlington, Virginia. 212 pp. plus appendices.

———. 1977. Preserving our natural heritage, Vol. I, federal activities and Vol. II, state activities. USGPO, Washington, D.C. 323 pp. Vol. I, Vol. II.

Whittaker, H. 1975. Communities and ecosystems. MacMillan, Inc., New York. 385 pp.

WILDLIFE MANAGEMENT
FOR WILDERNESS

John C. Hendee and Clarence A. Schoenfeld

The Wilderness Act of 1964, recorded as Public Law 88-577 (P.L. 88-577), allows Congress to classify roadless tracts of 5,000 acres or more in the national forests, national parks, and fish and wildlife refuges as wilderness, thus making them part of the National Wilderness Preservation System (NWPS). The Eastern Wilderness Act of 1975 (P.L. 93-622) extended wilderness eligibility to smaller tracts of roadless land in the eastern United States. The BLM Organic Act of 1976 (P.L. 95-579) made lands managed by the Bureau of Land Management eligible for wilderness classification, following a roadless area inventory to be completed within 15 years. Regardless of the management jurisdiction—Forest Service, Fish and Wildlife Service, National Park Service, or Bureau of Land Management—a separate act of Congress is required to add an area to the NWPS, and wilderness area classification legislation continues to be among the most controversial congressional actions affecting natural resources. Many of the affected interests, including wildlife users such as hunters and fishermen, object to the restrictions on use and management that accompany classification of an area as wilderness. Other wilderness buffs object to the absence of more restrictions on wilderness use and management.

As of March 15, 1978, nearly 17 million acres of federal land in 175 areas in 42 states had been classified by Congress as wilderness under the Wilderness Acts of 1964 and 1975. Another 250 million acres of the remaining roadless lands are potential wilderness and will be or are being evaluated by federal agencies to determine whether they should be recommended for wilderness classification. Whatever the final decisions, the future land base of the National Wilderness Preservation System will be substantial, including perhaps as many as 100-200 million acres.

Associated with all of this wilderness, if not dependent on it, are varied species of wildlife, including some that are threatened or endangered. The presence of wildlife is one element that renders wilderness valuable to millions of Americans today and attracts their support for its classification. Thus, management to protect and enhance the wildlife values of wilderness is an important policy issue concerning public land today.

The major theme of this chapter is the need for a clear wilderness philosophy to serve as the foundation for a wilderness wildlife management policy.

Hendee, John C.   Assistant Director, Southeastern Forest Experiment Station, U.S. Forest Service, Asheville, North Carolina

Shoenfeld, Clarence A.   Joint Professor of Journalism and Wildlife Ecology, Chairman of the Center for Environmental Communications and Education Studies, University of Wisconsin, Madison

DEFINITIONS AND DIRECTIONS

Wildlife and wilderness indeed go together. Ecologically they are symbiotic; culturally they are firmly linked in the minds of humankind. On the other hand, the terms "wilderness wildlife" and "management" may appear antithetical to some people. Yet, it is essential to manage our last strands of wilderness and its wildlife if only to keep human influences from destroying the naturalness and solitude that are legally required wilderness qualities. The natural ecosystems that we have left, with their associated wildlife, are "perhaps the most vulnerable and fragile of all our resources" (Allen 1966).

When we talk about "wilderness wildlife" we refer to those species, large and small, found naturally in the NWPS and thus set aside by Congress under official criteria spelled out in the wilderness acts. These criteria emphasize that each area be essentially roadless, retain attributes of naturalness, and provide outstanding opportunities for solitude or primitive and unconfined recreation. For purposes of discussion we also recognize as wilderness those roadless areas that are being or will be reviewed, studied, or otherwise considered for possible congressional classification as wilderness. Under agency policies and court decisions, these areas are managed so as to maintain their wilderness character pending congressional action; otherwise their crucial qualities of naturalness and solitude may be lost or diminished.

Wildlife management in wilderness may be one of the more complex and controversial parts of wilderness administration. How do we preserve "naturalness" on only one side of a man-made boundary? How do we balance "solitude" against growing forms of "primitive recreation," including hunting, fishing, wildlife observation, and photography? How do we husband "endangered species" in wilderness while minimizing "permanent visible evidence of human activity?" How do we reconcile the sometimes divergent wildlife management philosophies of four federal agencies and 42 state wildlife departments under broad strategies that comply with the wilderness acts and still maintain ecological soundness and political viability?

A Central Philosophy

One central theme is particularly important in wilderness wildlife management: That in congressionally-classified wilderness, wildlife management should be governed by an attitude that seeks the preservation of total natural ecosystems of which wildlife species are an important part, but only a part; a view recognizing that wildlife values and uses in wilderness affect and are affected by a variety of activities—natural and unnatural—within or near designated wilderness; a view that acknowledges that wildlife management and wildlife uses in wilderness are appropriate only when they harmonize with the special wilderness environment. Thus a strong wilderness philosophy is the most important ingredient of wilderness wildlife management policy.

For instance, hunting is allowed in National Forest, Bureau of Land Management, and some wildlife refuge wilderness areas, and in such settings the sport can achieve its finest quality. In wilderness man can most vividly relive his predator past, removed from unnatural disturbances such as roads, traffic, domestic crops, and people. In wilderness, hunting should be part of a larger "wilderness experience," emphasizing the naturalness and solitude and not just a quest for game. Likewise, fishing is a traditional wilderness activity and can be a means by which many users obtain wilderness values (Hendee et al. 1977). Wilderness is a place where one can indulge in the primitive myth that one can live off the land. Catching a few fish and eating them in camp with family and friends contribute to the overall quality of many a wilderness experience and are the goals of many users. Under a wilderness ethic managers would stress those aspects of the experience that depend on the wilderness setting and harmonize with all other aspects of the environment (Schoenfeld and Hendee 1978).

The importance of synthesizing wildlife management and use with the larger wilderness scheme has made us cautious about even using the term "wildlife management in wilderness" rather than speaking of "wilderness management for wildlife." The distinction is subtle, but the latter phrase is an important reflection of the holistic approach that is required in wilderness, where wildlife is but one part of the composite wilderness resource. The wilderness resource itself takes precedence over all uses.

Wilderness areas are unique in that there is a legal commitment to preserve their naturalness and solitude. Even though it may be a part of the Wildlife Refuge System, a wilderness is not a game range to be managed for maximum sustained yield of a particular sport species. Even though it may be part of a national park, a wilderness is not simply an extension of the tourist attraction. Even though it may be a part of a national forest, a wilderness must be protected to every extent possible from the impacts of conventional multiple use management. Even though it may come under the jurisdiction of the Bureau of Land Management (BLM), a wilderness cannot be subject to intensive range management and unregulated mineral development although grazing and mining are allowed in BLM wilderness. If congressionally classified wilderness stands for anything, it stands for "natural," and that goal is the thread that must run through all wilderness management strategies. The issue of how natural—how "pure"—wilderness management must be, is fraught with many practical and political problems, but a line has to be drawn. The flavor of wilderness wildlife management—whether it is to be mere fish-and-game keeping inconvenienced by lack of roads or fish and wildlife conservation in a truly natural setting—depends on the strength of the wilderness ethic among wilderness wildlife managers and their constituencies.

Categories of Wilderness Wildlife

While not intending to willfully exclude any creature large or small, our focus is on those larger mammals, birds, and fish that clearly reflect the legally defined characteristics of classified wilderness. While it is true that in wilderness salamanders and butterflies are as important as mountain lions and eagles, as a practical matter the ungulates and carnivores serve as indicators of the health of lower trophic levels in the ecosystem. The relative stability of a pine marten population, for example, reflects the stability of the rodent population, and the rodent population in turn reflects the stability of the vegetative components of the particular wilderness ecosystem (Koehler et al. 1975).

In a more refined sense, wilderness wildlife may be usefully categorized as (1) wilderness-dependent wildlife, (2) wilderness-associated wildlife, and (3) common wildlife found in wilderness. Of course, it is difficult to pinpoint the status of any particular species within any single category, at least for the entire NWPS, because of overlap, regional and local variation, and exceptions that do not fit neatly into any compartment. However, these three categories are useful because they suggest something about the relationship of the species to the relatively unaltered habitat found in wilderness or the relationship perceived by the public. As an illustration, in roadless area inventory and evaluation of the Forest Service during the late 1970s, known as RARE II, the presence of "wilderness-associated wildlife" was one criterion suggested by the agency and favored by the public to be used for proposing additions to the NWPS.

Wilderness-dependent wildlife includes species vulnerable to human influence, whose continued existence depends on and reflects the relatively wild, extensive, and undisturbed habitat characteristic of wilderness. Inspection of lists of threatened and endangered species suggests that more than a hundred such mammals, birds, fish, reptiles, and amphibians may appear—at least seasonally—in classified or proposed areas of the NWPS. In the case of any particular wilderness area, many locally or regionally rare species might be dependent on the area's continued naturalness and, thus, would be placed in the wilderness-dependent category for that area. For example, in or near proposed wilderness areas in Idaho's Panhandle National Forests are such locally or regionally rare species as grizzly bear, mountain caribou, native cutthroat trout, Canada lynx, wolverine, mountain goat, Richardson's blue grouse, fisher, pine marten, bald and golden eagles, osprey, mountain sheep, and northern white-tailed ptarmigan.

Wilderness-associated wildlife includes species commonly associated, in fact or in human perception, with habitat characteristics of classified or proposed wilderness. This category features wildlife common in the high-elevation habitat that marks much western wilderness, as well as wildlife associated with wilderness swamps and roadless hardwood forests in the East. An illustrative, not exhaustive, list of wilderness-associated species might include hoary, Olympic, and yellow-bellied marmots; pika; heather moles; Clark's nutcrackers; grey jays; golden eagles; grey-crowned rosy finches; deer; bear; elk; moose; mountain sheep; mountain goats; rainbow, cutthroat, and golden trout; and grayling.

Clearly, there are regional variations in the public's perception of which animals are wilderness-associated. For instance, while black bear and bobcat are not strongly associated with wilderness in the West, in the minds of Easterners they are impressive indicators of wild conditions. Some species generally perceived as wilderness-associated may be in fact wilderness-dependent.

Common wildlife found in wilderness includes species that happen to make their homes in the NWPS but which also live in many other more modified environments. Their relationship to wilderness is incidental; they are not dependent on nor even associated in human perception with wilderness. Yet when found in wilderness, these common species are no less important in their natural role. In fact, since they are widespread, the common species may reveal through their places in the wilderness scheme the extent to which they have adapted elsewhere.

The ptarmigan finds its home in high alpine country and is thus a wilderness associated species if not wilderness dependent. (Courtesy U.S. Forest Service)

These three categories are not black-and-white, of course. Certain wildlife species seem to need climax communities; in other places those same species can do quite well in disturbed habitat. For example, good populations of elk exist on cutover lands of western Washington and Oregon. Caribou may do well in mixed boreal forest maintained by fire. Grizzlies range over nonwilderness Montana. Some of the highest populations of cougar on the continent are on cutover lands on Vancouver Island. Eagles occur or have occurred in good numbers on heavily grazed western ranges.

Yet, with its inherent limitations, categorizing wilderness wildlife can be an important management aid. Following the classification of an area as wilderness, a first step should be an inventory of all the seemingly wilderness-dependent species found in the area and of all the characteristics of the natural habitat on which they apparently depend. Wilderness management would then assign a high priority to monitoring and preserving these natural conditions. In many cases a good start on such an inventory may have been accomplished during the study preceding the area's classification. Indeed, the presence of wilderness-dependent species may have been a factor leading to an area's classification.

Following this, an inventory should be made of wilderness-associated species and their habitats. Low priority would be accorded to common species found in the wilderness. Ultimately the aggregation of inventories will define more completely the role and relationship of wildlife to wilderness and help to establish wilderness wildlife management needs and priorities.

WILDLIFE VALUES AND PROBLEMS

Wildlife serves as a barometer of wilderness quality. Wilderness is crucial to the survival of many animals, particularly those with highly specialized natural habitat needs. Wilderness and its wildlife are a standard of comparison for measuring human impact on other biotic communities and are a natural "laboratory" for the development of ecological knowledge and theory. They also provide recreational, cultural, and aesthetic values that are no less real even if difficult to measure in dollars. Wilderness wildlife has helped stimulate the political "lobby" responsible for the wilderness acts and related legislation.

There are many problems related to wilderness wildlife. These include different management approaches of the federal and state resource agencies, poor funding for wildlife management programs, and conflicting laws. Endangered species legislation, for instance, appears in conflict with the thrust of wilderness acts because of limitations as to what managers are allowed to do in wilderness areas. Any habitat manipulation for an endangered species in a wilderness area must blend ecologically and aesthetically with the wilderness environment; yet for the good of the endangered organism a more radical intervention by man may be in order.

Furthermore, the larger wildlife species require a considerable home range to which arbitrary wilderness boundaries may not be related. Wilderness areas are ecological islands subject to numerous external influences, including resource management practices and uses in adjacent multiple use areas. People-wildlife contacts are not necessarily benign for either party, perhaps best illustrated by grizzly bear problems in the northern Rockies and the shaky truce between man and the eastern timber wolf in northern Minnesota (Mech 1977). Hunting and fishing may complicate wilderness management because they attract use and may have an impact on naturalness and solitude. The wilderness wildlife research base is inadequate. Concepts of what constitutes wilderness and its wildlife differ, sometimes sharply. In the management and use of wildlife are some of the greatest pressures for compromising the naturalness of wilderness.

MANAGEMENT OBJECTIVES AND GUIDELINES

Effective management of any resource depends on clear management objectives. The manager must know what he is trying to accomplish before he can consider what actions are needed. Wilderness management must be aimed at goals and objectives derived from the wilderness acts. Such management objectives for all aspects of wilderness—including fish and wildlife—must be spelled out clearly in area plans as criteria for formulating management actions. What should wilderness management objectives for wildlife be?

There is only one direct reference to fish and wildlife in the 1964 Wilderness Act, reserving to state governments their accustomed responsibility "with respect to wildlife and fish in the National Forests." Nor does the 1975 Eastern Wilderness Act specifically include wildlife among the values that are to be promoted and perpetuated. But the basic wording of the acts has clear implications about goals for wilderness wildlife management. Wilderness is to be protected and managed so as to preserve its natural conditions, its primeval character and influence, and its untrammeled community of life. It is to remain free of permanent improvements and permanent evidence of human activity and so will offer outstanding opportunities for solitude or primitive recreation. Each federal agency administering wilderness can continue to manage each area "for such other purposes for which it may have been established," *but* so "as also to preserve its wilderness character," except for various exceptions specifically provided for in the acts. This means, for example, that while fishing and hunting are to be allowed in National Forest, Bureau of Land Management, and some Wildlife Refuge wilderness, the activity must be conducted in such a way that the wilderness character of the area is also preserved.

Management objectives for wilderness wildlife may vary in specifics between administering agencies, but some broad objectives seem applicable to most areas in the entire National Wilderness Preservation System. The following proposed wildlife management objectives for classified wilderness are statements of conditions to be sought through wilderness management, and they serve as criteria for formulating management strategies, guidelines, and actions to achieve them.

Proposed Wilderness-Wildlife Management Objectives

1. To seek natural distributions, numbers, and interactions of indigenous species of wildlife

2. To the greatest extent possible, allow natural processs to control wilderness ecosystems and their wildlife

3. To keep wildlife wild, their behavior altered as little as possible by human influence

4. To permit viewing, hunting, and fishing where such activities are biologically sound, legal, and conducted in the spirit of the wilderness experience

5. Whenever appropriate, to favor the preservation of rare, threatened, and endangered species dependent on wilderness conditions

6. Within the constraints of all transcending legislation applicable to wildlife in a particular wilderness, to seek the least possible degradation of the qualities that make for wilderness—naturalness, solitude, and absence of permanent visible evidence of human activity

To be achieved, these general wilderness wildlife management objectives require appropriate management guidelines or strategies. The following is a summary of wilderness wildlife management guidelines that we have fully discussed elsewhere (Schoenfeld and Hendee 1978, Hendee and Schoenfeld 1978a, 1978b):

Consider wildlife as but one component of the composite wilderness resource. Recognize the necessity for wilderness management because nature alone is powerless to prevent the impact of ever-present human influences. Plan only for the actions necessary to meet wilderness wildlife objectives, in management plans prepared for each individual wilderness area. Follow a principle of non-degradation in area management; that is, strive to prevent further degradation of the naturalness present in individual areas, but seek restoration of naturalness in areas where it is below a minimum standard. Allow natural processes to shape wilderness habitat, encouraging fire and avoiding predator and plant disease controls. Where natural processes must be supplemented or simulated, employ the minimum tool necessary to do the job. Insulate wilderness areas with compatible management practices on adjacent lands. Manage for indigenous wild plant and animal species.

Regulate user impact in keeping with carrying capacity principles, but not in such a way as to degrade wilderness experiences. Promote a wilderness ethic among users so that more people can enjoy wilderness while minimizing their impact. Cultivate hunting and fishing practices that protect the wilderness environment and foster experiences that depend on wilderness conditions. Step up wilderness wildlife research, using methods that do not degrade the wilderness environment or the experiences of other users. Accept the practical realities that dictate varying approaches by different agencies on individual areas, but work toward a consistent, if broad, framework for managing wildlife in all wilderness areas.

The management guidelines summarized here provide a general framework for wilderness management for wildlife. Because of unavoidable constraints on the administrative agency and area concerned, sensitive and perceptive wilderness wildlife management is essential on the part of all assigned agencies, and a wilderness philosophy is a basic ingredient.

Wilderness areas were "born" in the national forests, and as of March 15, 1978, the national forests contained about 90 percent of the 16.6 million acres of classified wilderness. Hence, the evolution of Forest Service wilderness management policy should be instructive. In 1977, Assistant Secretary of Agriculture Cutler explained that policy to Congress (Weaver and Cutler 1977): "Forest Service wilderness management actions are guided by four basic principles: (1) Is it necessary to protect the resource and manage the use? (2) Is it the minimum action or facility required to accomplish the objective? (3) Does it protect wilderness values? (4) Does it pass a test of reason and common sense?"

These principles, and the recent "Policies and guidelines for fish and wildlife management in Forest Service and BLM Wilderness and Primitive areas" (IAFWA 1976), are a good starting point for future discussion of wilderness wildlife management policy. We hope these discussions will become more frequent among wildlife professionals in the future.

The rapid growth of areas designated as wilderness and the prospect of many more to come signify that public attitudes toward natural resources can and do change (Trefethen 1976). Such progress provides hope that we may in the future achieve a balance between economic development and environmental degradation. Our management of wilderness for wildlife will be one measure of our success.

LITERATURE CITED

Allen, D. L. 1966. The preservation of endangered habitats and vertebrates of North America. In F. Darling and J. Milton (eds.), Future environments of North America. The Nat. Hist. Press, Garden City, New York. Pp. 22-37.

Hendee, J. C., R. N. Clark and T. E. Dailey. 1977. Fishing and other recreation behavior at high mountain lakes in Washington State, USDA For. Serv. Res. Note PNW-304 Pac. N.W. Forest and Range Expt. Sta., Portland, Oregon. 27 pp.

—— and C. A. Schoenfeld. 1978a. Wilderness management for wildlife: Philosophy, objectives, guidelines. Trans. N. Amer. Wildl. and Nat. Res. Conf. 43.

—— and C. A. Schoenfeld. 1978b. Wildlife in wilderness. *In* Wilderness management, by J. C. Hendee, G. H. Stankey, and R. C. Lucas. U.S. Dept. of Ag. Misc. Pub. GPO (in press). 425 pp.

——, G. H. Stankey, and R. C. Lucas. 1978. Wilderness management, U.S. Dept. of Ag. Misc. Pub. GPO (in press). 425 pp.

International Association of Fish and Wildlife Administrators. 1976. Policies and guidelines for fish and wildlife management in Forest Service and BLM wilderness and primitive areas. Washington, D.C. (mimeo). 23 pp.

Koehler, G. M., W. R. Moore, and A. R. Taylor. 1975. Preserving the pine marten. Western Wildlands. 2(2):13.

Mech, L. D. 1977. A recovery plan for the Eastern Timber Wolf. National Parks and Conservation Magazine 51(1):17.

Schoenfeld, C. A. and J. C. Hendee. 1978. Wildlife management in wilderness. Wildl. Manage. Inst. Boxwood Press, Pacific Grove, California. 172 pp.

Trefethen, J. B. 1975. An American crusade for wildlife. Winchester Press and the Boone and Crockett Club, New York. 909 pp.

Weaver, J. and M. R. Cutler. 1977. Wilderness policy: A colloquy between Congressman Weaver and Assistant Secretary Cutler. J. Forestry 75(7): 392-393.

oberg.

ANALYSIS OF WILDLIFE DATA

Dale Hein

You need to read this if you are *not* a statistician, biometrician, or computer programmer. My objective is to help persons interested in wildlife improve their understanding of the limitations and applications of quantitative methods for wildlife problems. If you are already competent in this subject, perhaps the following discussion may remind you of what is essential for non-specialists to understand about your science and what properly remains your domain as a specialist in biometry. My theme is not that "every wildlifer must be a statistician and computer programmer," but that *every* wildlifer needs to understand enough about quantitative methods to be able to read scientific literature, converse with statisticians and computers, and know when more highly trained assistance is needed.

Wildlife scientists gather mountains of data. Sometimes these are narrative and descriptive, such as the interesting writings of early naturalists. Today, however, wildlife managers must frequently deal with data that are primarily numerical and with problems concerning the quantitative analysis of these data.

Data should be collected with a clear purpose. The uncritical, miserly acquisition of data indicates unclear objectives and fuzzy thinking. The methods of analysis should be decided and stated before data collection starts. Here is a good test of the adequacy of planning for a project that will require data anslysis: Can the final tables and figures be sketched and titled with only the numbers to be entered lacking? Data "packrats" with files stuffed with ancient, unanalyzed data can seldom contribute to modern wildlife management.

Data should be collected in standard fashion for easy analysis and comparison with data from other sources. Increasingly, the metric system will be used. Some applications of metric are more difficult than others, for example, land survey and legal description of land. We shall have to be fluent in two languages of measurement throughout our lives, but we should ease the task for future wildlife managers by using metric wherever practical.

Many terms have dual meanings—explicit and narrow when used by biometricians but much broader or different in general use. Some examples are: bias, variance, significance, error, statistic, population, consistent, and regression. A few definitions will be suggested here, but there is no substitute for an intensive course in statistics to clarify many terms. Also, different texts in biometry use somewhat different symbols. The apparent chaos is similar to some other peculiarities in our wildlife field; for example, *Bonasa umbellus* is

Hein, Dale.   Professor, Department of Fishery and Wildlife Biology, Colorado State University, Fort Collins

partridge, pat, native pheasant, ruff, timber grouse, drummer, and ruffed grouse in vernaculars of different regions.

PROBLEMS OF MEASUREMENT

Humans seem compelled to quantify and classify in precise manner those characteristics of nature, including wildlife populations, which are really continuous, variable, and changing. We should deal realistically with problems of measurement, and as one biologist warned, "Beware of the dangers of misplaced concreteness."

What are the major problems of measurement? How may they be handled?

The act of measurement may affect the data. We must question data such as counts of animals which may respond to the presence of observers, the opinions of persons who know they are being surveyed, and the observations of animals that have been captured and perhaps had markers or instruments attached. These problems can be reduced to acceptable levels by recognizing their nature and improving techniques of data collection.

Accuracy and *precision* of measurement are often related. The first concerns the average closeness of the measurement or estimate to the true value; the second refers to the repeatability of the measurement or estimate regardless of whether or not it is close to the actual value. Absolute accuracy and perfect precision of data are usually unachievable and unnecessary. However, knowing the degree of inaccuracy or imprecision is desirable.

Generally, we seek *point estimates*—one value to represent a *parameter* (population characteristic) of interest. However, an *interval estimate*, giving a range of possible values for the parameter, may be more realistic and safer. A "rough estimate" often becomes an accepted fact, much to the dismay of a biologist who was pressured to produce a number that was then eagerly grasped and used by others. An interval retains the uncertainty that is too easily lost for a single point estimate.

Problems of "rounding off" and significant digits are dealt with in dreadful detail in mathematics texts. The most important rule is easy—round off or drop nonsignificant digits in the final answer, not in the intermediate calculations. Percents are especially susceptible to absurdity; 56.3% implies accuracy of one part in 1,000—rarely achieved in wildlife data!

Data are really of two kinds. *Attributes* (sex, age-class, color, status, etc.) are qualitative and assignable to categories (male, juvenile, green, dead, etc.). *Measurements* are quantitative and assignable to numbers. And measurements are of two kinds—*continuous*, which may be decimals or fractions of whole numbers, for example, weight, length, etc.; and *discrete*, which are usually counts or whole numbers, for example, the number of eggs in a clutch, the number of fish in a creel, etc.

The most frequent problem of data collection is "how large should the sample be?" This is a problem because of variation. If all hunters shot the same number of ducks, then you would only need a single sample of one hunter from a list of all duck hunters to estimate total harvest. Unfortunately, wildlife-related data tend to be among the most variable of all data in biology or natural resources. A simple answer to "how large of a sample?" is "all you can get!" In practice there are general levels of sampling that should be considered. In my experience, these are samples of 1, 5, 20, 100, 1,000, or "all possible." Frequently, the interval for an estimate can be decreased by half by increasing the sample size from 5 to 20 or from 20 to 100, but the gain is negligible for an increase from 5 to 7 or from 20 to 30. Costs, time available, and purposes of the data collection are major considerations. Previous reports in the scientific literature and a biologist's knowledge of his/her study material are main resources for determining sample size. Of course, there are formulas in most statistics books that help. However, the formulas require some knowledge of the variation expected, the amount of acceptable error, and the degree of confidence demanded in the estimate. Thus, a smaller "pilot study" is sometimes necessary to answer the question of sample size for a major investigation.

DESCRIPTION OF DATA

How can large collections of data be reduced to their simplest and most important facts? *Descriptive statistics* is the answer. The most frequent use of statistical analysis is to summarize the main features of numerous data. Whether the data are survival rates of mallards, expenditures by hunters, or aerial counts of moose, there are two features of a set of data that most often need description. These are central tendency, or clustering around a middle value, and variation, or dispersion. How are they described?

To express central tendency, an average, typical, or representative value is needed. The *mean* is an arithmetic average and is most often used. However, the most representative value may be the *median*, halfway down the list of numbers ranked lowest to highest. The median is especially useful when a few unusually high or low values would greatly influence the value of the mean. The *mode*, or most frequent value, might be the most typical measure of central tendency of a set of data. There are other, less frequently used measures of the center of a collection of data.

The *range*, the difference between largest and smallest value in the data, is an easily understood descriptive statistic to express variation or dispersion. The *standard deviation, variance*, and *standard error* are related measures of dispersion that are routinely calculated as described in any statistics text. Standard deviation and variance describe the dispersion of individual observations (data) about their mean value; the standard error describes the variability of sample means about their average value for repeated samples. Simply, the standard deviation is the number, which when added to and subtracted from the mean, gives an interval that will include nearly two-thirds of the individual observations in a sample of normally distributed data. The standard deviation is also the square root of the sample variance, and the standard error is the standard deviation divided by the square root of the number of items of data in the sample.

A useful but curiously ignored descriptive statistic is the *coefficient of variation* (C.V.), which is simply the standard deviation divided by the mean. This may be expressed as a decimal or multiplied by 100 and expressed as a percent. For many kinds of wildlife data in large samples, the C.V. will be 0.15 ± 0.1 (5-25%). For example, a study of repeated censuses of wood ducks on three rivers yielded a C.V. of 0.29 (29%) for counts made during canoe float trips compared to C.V. of 0.08 (8%) for flight counts made at mouths of the streams. Thus, flight counts were more precise even though float counts gave larger numbers. A coefficient of variation greater than 50 percent indicates serious problems, perhaps errors in measurement or in data handling, insufficient sample size, or abnormal uncontrolled variation. Notice that the coefficient of variation has no specific units. Thus, it may be used to compare the variability of quite different samples, for example, variability of hunters' bags of quail versus variability of the number of trout in creel checks. Coefficient of variation is a particularly useful statistic for a nonstatistician.

Entire books are written on graphic methods used to describe large sets of data. *Pie diagrams* presenting proportions or percentages as wedge-shaped segments of a circle have maximum impact. *Bar graphs* often make data from tables easier to grasp; they aid in comparing many categories of similar data. *Scatter diagrams* of data points plotted on both a vertical and a horizontal axis retain more of the precise, scientific content of the original data than does any other graphic method (Fig. 1). Therefore, scatter diagrams are most used in scientific journals and technical books.

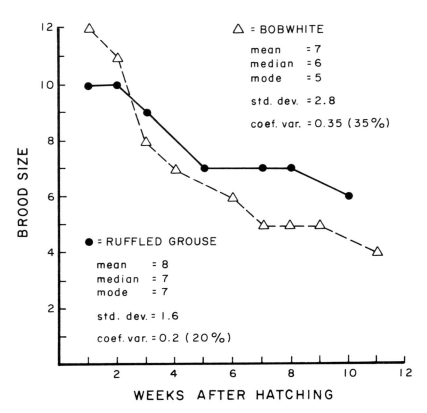

Fig. 1. Example of a scatter diagram.

Dice-Leraas diagrams present comparisons of several samples (Fig. 2). Each sample is described by locating its mean with a short line on a scale. A perpendicular, longer line shows the range from lowest to highest value. A bar parallels the range line in each direction from the mean to show either the standard deviation or the standard error. At a glance, one can see which sample is most variable, has the largest or smallest mean, and overlaps any other sample.

More complex descriptive methods are sometimes called analytical methods. The calculations yield statistics that describe relations among factors. Correlation and regression are related methods of analysis. Scientists often

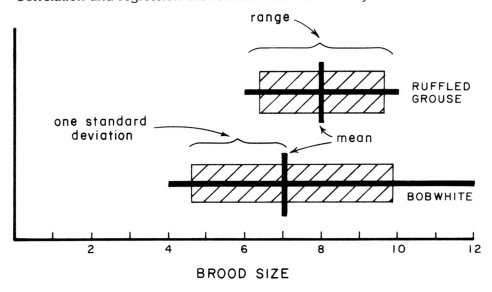

Fig. 2. Example of a Dice-Leraas diagram.

report *regression coefficients* (b) describing the relation between an independent variable factor, for example, snow depth, and a dependent variable factor, such as the number of elk surviving winter. The *correlation coefficient* (r) indicates the strength of the association between the two variables. The values of r range from -1 to +1, and high absolute values (+ or - sign ignored) of r indicate that one of the variables has high predictive value for the other. When r is squared (r^2, R, R^2 of various authors) and multiplied by 100 it is called the *coefficient of determination*, and it indicates the percent of total variation in the dependent variable that is due solely to variation in the independent factor. For example, an analysis of many habitat factors that might be correlated with abundance of mountain cottontails showed that elevation was strongly negatively correlated (r = -0.7) and amount of bitterbrush was positively correlated (r = 0.3). Together these two factors accounted for more than one-half of the total variation ($R = 0.7^2 + 0.3^2 = 0.58$) in abundance of the rabbits.

Computations and interpretations for regression and correlation get complex when many factors and their interactions are considered simultaneously in their effects on the data. Consider all of the independent variables such as weather, hunting regulations, number of hunters, and farming practices that may influence the single dependent variable of total hunting harvest of pheasants. Analysis of covariance, analysis of variance, and multiple and partial regression are topics that deal with increasing complexity in description and analysis of data.

In summary, descriptive statistics are almost always applicable to wildlife data. Descriptive statistics transmit information concisely and precisely. The center point of the data and amount of variability are especially important. Graphic techniques offer useful choices for describing data collections. Most descriptive methods and many analytical techniques are easy, and they should not be ignored by wildlife managers and biologists.

PROBLEMS OF STATISTICAL INFERENCE

The second application of statistical methods to wildlife data is to provide a systematic way to decide whether or not to accept a hypothesis. *Inferential statistics* permits scientists to use inductive reasoning to generalize about populations or larger situations from the basis of a sample or smaller specific case.

Inferential statistics seems to be one of the most intimidating but most useful subjects for wildlife workers. In my experience, few persons succeed in learning inferential statistics by self-teaching. However, persons who missed statistics or never really understood the subject in college need not despair. Many colleges and natural resource agencies offer short courses, workshops, or training seminars in "cram-course" statistics that give a wildlife manager adequate proficiency in the subject. The purpose here is not the impossible task of teaching statistical calculations in a brief chapter, but instead to outline some applications and interpretations of "decision-making" or inferential statistics.

The most common inferential statistics for testing hypotheses are t, F, and Chi-square. They are useful because they have known distributions of values for any sample size. Thus, a t-value can be calculated from experimental data and compared to a published table of values to decide whether the t-value was likely or unlikely if the hypothesis being tested was true. Most descriptive statistics (mean, variance, etc.) are worthless for testing hypotheses because their distributions are unknown, and any particular value of a sample mean or sample variance cannot be judged likely or unlikely with a known probability of being right or wrong.

In order to determine the optimum length of future hunting seasons, we might want to test a hypothesis that successful goat hunters hunt more days than do successful sheep hunters, on the average. It is conventional to restate such a hypothesis and test the *null hypothesis*; that is, there is *no* difference in the average number of days hunted by successful goat hunters compared to successful sheep hunters. We would then try to reject this null hypothesis and accept an alternate (the original) hypothesis on the basis of reasonable evidence from a survey of hunters in a past year. A *significance level* (or alpha-level) is selected by the scientist. Conventionally, these are either 1%, 5%, or 10% (0.01, 0.05, or 0.10). These may also be called confidence levels (99%, 95%, or 90% confidence). If a calculated value of the test statistic, for example, "t" turns out to be a "significant" at the 0.05 level, it means that there are only five chances out of 100 that a true null hypothesis was incorrectly rejected. Or one may say with 95 percent confidence that the alternate (original) hypothesis was supported adequately by the data and that the null hypothesis was false.

The convention of using the 0.05 significance level is based on accepted reasons. Intuitively, most persons seem to agree that something that happens against odds of twenty to one is rare enough to require some explanation other than "random chance." Thus, null hypotheses of no effect or no difference tend to be rejected at this significance level. However, if the consequences of erroneously rejecting a true null hypothesis are judged minor, a wildlife scientist may choose a 0.1 or even 0.2 level of significance *prior* to conducting the test.

With increasing frequency, some scientists prefer not to state whether a test statistic was significant or not. Instead, they report the value of the test statistic and the probability (P-value) associated with it in the table of values. For example, a Chi-square value of 130 calculated from a very large sample has a P-value of 0.02. This means that the outcome of testing the hypothesis would have been significant at the five percent level but not at the one percent level, or the likelihood of getting a Chi-square value this large or larger just by random chance alone was only two percent. This puts the burden on a reader to decide whether the evidence for or against the null hypothesis was adequate. However, the investigator usually is the person best qualified to make the decision and should not shirk that responsibility.

You can use several criteria to judge the value and trustworthiness of inferential statistics in scientific literature or technical talks. First, sample size—do you believe that the data are reasonably numerous and adequate?

Second, does the scientist identify any weaknesses or questionable assumptions in the investigation? Whoever uses statistics should be the most severe critic of possible deficiencies.

Third, do the results make sense biologically? Only rarely will analysis yield completely surprising or unexplainable conclusions.

Finally, did the investigator clearly have a hypothesis before the data were analyzed? This is probably the most common serious error in wildlife research—testing a hypothesis with the same data that suggested it.

ROLES OF COMPUTERS

We are emerging from an awkward decade of data handling. The computer specialists arrived just in time to save us from submerging in data. A few years ago, wildlife workers had to write their own computer programs. Now "canned" programs are as numerous and available as are maps that the previous generation of wildlifers finally escaped making for themselves. I seriously doubt the value of more than an introductory course in computer science for most wildlife biologists, although there are a few exceptions. After all, who does their own soil analysis or engineering plans? They are done by specialists, just as programming should be done by specialists. How many wildlife managers *ever* need to write a FORTRAN statement?

What wildlife biologists and managers need is availability of a computer specialist and ability to communicate with that person. They need to learn to read computer printout, what facilities and services are available, the format in which data can be handled by their computer, and costs for computer services.

Modern wildlife management is drawing closer to systems ecology and systems management, and the computer is becoming the primary physical tool of wildlife management. Computers contribute to all phases of wildlife management—administration, law enforcement, habitat evaluation, population inventory, communications, education, and other branches. This revolution is not finished just because pocket calculators have replaced slide rules. Interactive computer terminals are decreasing the need for "batch processing" of data cards. Computer languages are approaching common English. Costs are declining as availability increases.

There is a tendency to overbuy computer equipment. Many of us have pocket calculators with numerous expensive features that we never use and have not learned to use. Agencies often buy expensive computers for prestige, when a lease to share someone else's would be far cheaper. One bit of advice concerns desirable features of a small office computer to be shared by many persons. A computer with separate program storage can be reprogrammed instantly for each user. Also, paper printouts give a permanent record of entries and outputs; many errors occur in copying numbers by hand off a display panel.

Finally, I wish to reassure wildlifers who are apprehensive about computers in our field. Computers are freeing managers and biologists from much drudgery so that there is more time to practice our science. They are reducing mistakes, saving money, and improving management, not by eliminating jobs or by replacing professional expertise, but by making each wildlife employee more effective.

EDUCATION IN WILDLIFE BIOMETRY

Some readers of this may be students or educators who ask what formal course work in biometry is desirable as part of the training of a wildlife student for professional employment. I recommend a solid foundation in mathematics including college algebra, logarithms, exponential functions, and introduction to matrices and linear programming. This should be followed by a calculus course that introduces concepts of limits, derivatives, difference equations, and integration of simple functions. The standard college course in computer programming is not as useful as a more practical course in using canned programs and computer services. If this course can emphasize applications to natural resources, it will be more effective than if it is a business course. The basic course in statistical methods should not be a "watered-down" survey course that leads nowhere. It should introduce Chi-square applications, regression, and analysis of variance. It should logically lead many students to additional courses such as multiple regression and especially sampling. A chance to apply statistical methods to one's own data seems almost essential to mastering the techniques.

CONCLUSIONS

Persons interested in wildlife usually find that the diversity, uncertainty, and variety of wildlife and management activities are challenging and intriguing. These persons are seldom as interested in quantitative topics, such as wildlife biometry. With virtually no calculations, symbols, or technical terms, I have outlined and discussed some basic concepts of wildlife biometry. From this, I hope that you see the scope and general applications of quantitative methods to wildlife biology, and I hope that you appreciate the importance of statistics, mathematics, and computer science to wildlife management. Every wildlife worker should try to understand basic biometry, but only a few specialists need to stay familiar with many computational methods. In general these are not topics that a casual student can master in his/her spare time. They require rigorous college-level courses. But we can all learn enough to communicate adequately with a specialist in wildlife biometry. Probably the most important message for you in this chapter is the last sentence: Seek the advice of a staff specialist or consultant in wildlife biometry as early as possible in the planning stage of any project that will involve collection, calculations, or presentation of data.

SELECTED REFERENCES

Snedecor, G. W. and W. G. Cochran. 1967. Statistical methods. Iowa State Univ. Press, Ames. 593 pp.

Sokal, R. R. and F. J. Rohlf. 1967. Biometry. W. H. Freeman, San Francisco. 776 pp.

Steel, R. G. D. and J. H. Torrie. 1960. Principles and procedures in statistics. McGraw-Hill, New York. 481 pp.

POPULATION AND HARVEST STUDIES

Aelred D. Geis

Information on the size of game animal populations and the number of each kind harvested plays an important role in game management and research. Included in this section are discussions of the various sources of population and kill information, the importance of such information, and some problems affecting this information's accuracy. Subsequent sections on wildlife management principles and wildlife population dynamics will present the important implications revealed by population and kill statistics.

Though seemingly different, population and harvest data are closely interrelated. Often the best source of information on the size and productivity of a wildlife population and its ability to provide recreation through hunting comes from a knowledge of the size of the kill and its age and sex composition. Aware of this fact, federal and state conservation agencies routinely collect data on population levels of important species and conduct surveys to measure the size of the harvest and, often, age and sex composition. I will not discuss the many methods that wildlife biologists have devised to measure game populations and harvest individually, but will group these into related approaches in an attempt to develop a general description of this vital part of the game management picture.

COMPLETE COUNTS

In some cases, it is feasible to make a complete count of a wildlife population. This is particularly true when the number of animals involved is relatively small, if they are found in specific known areas, and if they are fairly visible. The most extensive attempt at a complete wildlife count is the annual winter inventory of waterfowl throughout North America. This survey tries to examine all known waterfowl areas and record the total number of each species present. The degree to which it succeeds depends upon the area and species involved. Reasonably good counts of many goose populations are obtained; nevertheless, widely scattered species using secluded areas, such as the wood duck, have only a part of their population recorded. Under some circumstances, big game species, such as antelope, can easily be counted using complete counts. However, because most wildlife populations are distributed over vast areas, are difficult to see, and the expense is often prohibitive, this approach has lost favor to the procedures about to be discussed.

SAMPLE AREA COUNTS

Probably the most common approach now followed to estimate wildlife populations is to make counts on areas distributed in a representative way

Geis, Aelred D.   Urban Wildlife Specialist, U.S. Fish and Wildlife Service, Patuxent Wildlife Research Center, Laurel, Maryland

throughout the total range occupied by the population. Since the area included in the sample count is known as well as the total range under consideration, it is possible to expand the counts so that they estimate the population of the entire range. Thus, if 1,000 deer are observed on drives conducted on sample areas comprising five percent of the total range, it is assumed that five percent of the deer were counted, and therefore, the total population is 20,000.

The use of sampling techniques is very important in wildlife management and research. The most extensive survey of this type is the annual waterfowl breeding population survey in North America. Ducks are counted from aircraft along 32,000 miles of linear strips, one-fourth mile wide, distributed throughout the major waterfowl breeding areas in North America. Many states conduct aerial counts of big game on representative samples of the total range. Aircraft are used in order to obtain a sample large and representative enough to obtain reliable estimates.

A problem associated with waterfowl and most big game surveys is that neither all ducks nor all big game present are recorded by observers in aircraft. Thus, to fully interpret such counts, it is necessary to have a measure of the proportion of the animals present that are recorded from the air. In regard to breeding ducks in North America, sample areas are counted both by ground and aerial crews to determine the proportion of the birds present that are recorded by aerial survey crews (Martinson and Kaczynski 1967). A similar approach has been applied to evaluating aerial counts of deer (Gilbert and Grieb 1957).

Small game population estimates are often based on roadside counts made according to specific rules concerning dates to be conducted, starting time, and other factors possibly affecting the count. The survey routes are selected at random within the total area of interest. Annual mourning dove, woodcock, and breeding bird (all species) surveys in the United States and portions of Canada are examples of surveys based on counts made along a representative sample of roads.

Many sample area counts of birds are based upon the conspicuous calling behavior of males during the breeding season. Such counts are made of crowing cock pheasants, calling quail, drumming ruffed grouse, "peenting" woodcock, cooing doves, singing song birds, and others. It is important to recognize that these counts do not necessarily reflect fall population levels since they relate to the number of adult males present in the area in the spring. A species such as the pheasant having many "hens per cock" and raising large numbers of young per hen can have a poor relationship between the number of calling males in the spring and the number of birds available for harvest the next fall.

Counts of calling males of a species having a more even sex ratio and a lower and more uniform production rate, such as woodcock, are more likely to indicate probable fall population levels than is the case for a species like the pheasant. Counts of calling male birds, when expanded to reflect the total area being sampled, only provide an index to the size of the population, since the resulting numbers do not indicate the actual number of birds present. However, we assume the size of the counts represents the same part of the population each year and in all areas. Probably the most valuable use of a population index based on calling males is to reflect regional differences in breeding population levels. However, their obvious value in this regard should not be confused with an ability to predict year-to-year changes in fall population levels.

It is extremely important that sample area counts be distributed throughout the entire area in a representative manner. This can be done easily when the counts are made from aircraft. However, this is more difficult in regard to roadside counts because, even though the survey routes are randomly selected, they are still on roads that may not sample the total area in a representative manner. The potential seriousness of this problem depends on the species involved and the geographic area. In the Midwest where roads occur in a grid pattern at one mile intervals and when the species counted can be heard for a long distance, surveys conducted along roads probably produce a representative count. In contrast, roadside counts in mountainous areas could be misleading when the only counts made are along roads through farmland occurring in valleys. Despite this problem, distributing survey routes at random throughout existing road systems represents a big improvement over counts made along roads selected because they were in an especially good area or were convenient to the counter's home, as was frequently done in early census work.

Sample area counts can be made of anything relating to the species of interest, such as track counts, muskrat house counts, or the like. The "sign-count" probably receiving most widespread use is big game fecal pellet group counts. These counts, combined with information on the average number of groups deposited by an animal each day and how long these groups remain visible, provide a basis for estimating the number of animals in an area.

TREND COUNTS

Trend counts result in a population index figure relating to relative population levels and changes in these levels between years. They differ from the sample area counts in that they are usually not conducted on carefully defined sample areas nor according to rigidly prescribed rules. Perhaps the best example is the pheasant or quail count made by rural mail carriers during a portion of the year while delivering the mail. Sometimes conservation agency personnel record the game they see during their normal activities, and these values are used to calculate such things as the number of deer or doves seen per hundred miles driven. Care must be taken in interpreting the results of such counts. In the case of counts made by rural mail carriers, these are often so extensive and involve so many people that there is little doubt that the average counts accurately reflect population levels. However, such counts as informal roadside counts or the number of deer hit by cars can be influenced by many things other than the game population present in the area.

POPULATION ESTIMATES BASED ON MARKING ANIMALS

There have been many wildlife studies in which population estimates have been obtained by marking a sample of the animals present in an area and then determining the fraction of the total population marked by either observing the population, by capturing a sample in traps, or by shooting. For example, assume that 100 rabbits are live-trapped, ear tagged, and released on a study area. If a sample of rabbits shot on the area indicates that one-fourth of the population was tagged, then the total population would be 400. A basis for roughly estimating the size of the Tall Grass Prairie Canada Goose Flock was obtained by MacInnes (1966), who color-marked a sample on the breeding grounds in northern Canada and then determined the fraction of the population marked by observing these birds during migration and on wintering areas in the United States. To obtain reliable population estimates using this method, it is essential that the proportion of the population originally marked be accurately determined. The calculation for this method would be:

$$\frac{\text{Marked and released animals}}{\text{Total population}} = \frac{\text{Recaptured marked animals}}{\text{Total recaptured animals}}$$

HARVEST ESTIMATES

Many states annually estimate the size of the harvest of the resident species from the response to questionnaires mailed to a representative sample

215

of license buyers. Since the number of license buyers is known, the results of the questionnaire survey can be expanded to estimate the total kill. Similar mail questionnaire surveys are conducted by federal agencies in Canada and the United States to measure the waterfowl harvest. It was discovered long ago that reliable harvest estimates could not be based on hunters checked in the field. Mail questionnaire surveys permit a representative sample of hunters to be contacted with relatively little expense. There are some complications in the interpretation of the response to mail survey questionnaires. These problems are caused by the tendency of respondents to exaggerate their success and/or nonrespondents having a different success than those who respond. Nevertheless, procedures have been developed to correct these problems. Information obtained by mail questionnaire surveys about the characteristics of the harvest and hunters plays an important role in making management decisions. For example, this information makes it possible to predict the size of the duck kill in the United States and Canada under various proposed hunting regulations.

The size of the harvest of big game species, turkeys, and Canada geese is often determined from a registration system where hunters are required by law to present their kill at checking stations where it is recorded. The accuracy with which the kill is measured by this approach varies. It is often excellent for big game but is less reliable for turkeys or Canada geese.

POPULATION ESTIMATES BASED ON HARVEST ESTIMATES

The size of the hunting kill of many species depends on population levels. Thus, changes from year to year in the size of the kill reflect population trends. For example, annual fluctuation in population levels of pheasants and ruffed grouse causes marked changes in the size of the kill. However, the size of the kill is not always dependent on population levels. Other factors, such as changes in hunting regulations or hunter numbers, can contribute to changes in kill.

Widely dispersed resident species, such as pheasants, quail, and rabbits, are good examples of species for which the size of the kill is likely to be strongly influenced by population levels. On the other hand, gregarious species, such as waterfowl, that use a limited and well-known type of habitat often are harvested in a way that does not depend on overall population levels. In interpreting kill data, however, one fundamental truth emerges. Animals cannot be harvested that do not exist. Thus, some years ago when improved duck kill surveys in the United States established that the wood duck was the second most abundant duck in the harvest in the Mississippi Flyway and ranked third in the Atlantic Flyway, it was clear evidence that wood ducks were not as scarce as some feared.

If estimates are available on both the size of the kill and fraction of the population harvested, it is possible to estimate population levels. For example, if a kill of 100,000 represents one-tenth of the population, the total population must be one million. Mathematically this procedure is identical to population estimates based on marking, since the proportion harvested usually must be estimated from the proportion of marked animals that are harvested during the hunting season. This procedure has its greatest potential when migratory game bird band recovery rates, adjusted to recognize the proportion of bands taken by hunters that are not reported, provide a basis for estimating the harvest rate. In this way it has been estimated, for example, that the prehunting season wood duck population in the eastern United States, from 1963 through 1965, ranged from 2.3 to 3.0 million (Geis 1966)

Sometimes when kill data are available, but harvest rate information is lacking, it is helpful to assume a harvest rate in order to make a population estimate that can be used to judge the plausibility of other population estimates that are offered. An example of this may be given with regard to the common snipe where the annual harvest in North America is estimated at about 900,000, yet the total population is cautiously indicated as possibly exceeding five million birds (Saunderson 1977). The cited publication also emphasizes that the snipe are very lightly harvested. Thus, if as many as five percent of the fall preseason population is harvested, which is liberal, the North American population would be eighteen million! Information on the size of the harvest can much more easily be obtained than information on population levels. Thus, harvest data provide an important insight into probable population levels.

ESTIMATES OF THE KINDS, AGES, AND SEXES OF ANIMALS HARVESTED

Detailed information about the age and sex composition of the kill of each species is important for many reasons. Although mail questionnaire surveys often provide estimates of the number of various kinds of game taken, this information is usually very general. For example, mail questionnaire surveys in Canada and the United States provide estimates of the size of the duck and goose kill but do not indicate the number of each kind of duck and goose taken. Therefore, in both countries, representative samples of hunters are sent envelopes prior to the season and asked to return a wing from each duck and the tail from each goose taken during the season. The approximately 100,000 wings and tails received each year are examined by biologists to determine the species composition of the harvest. Also, for most species, the age and sex of each bird can be identified. Thus, knowledge relating to reproduction rate and the sex must be interpreted cautiously since all ages and sexes frequently are not equally vulnerable to shooting.

For waterfowl, the extent to which immature birds are more likely to be shot than adults is indicated by a comparison of band recovery rates from adult and immature birds banded before the season. If 10 percent of the banded immature birds are reported as taken by hunters, while only 5 percent of the banded adults are reported, then immatures are judged to be twice as likely to be shot as adults. Therefore, a ratio of two immature ducks to one adult in the kill would mean there was one immature duck per adult in the preseason population.

Difficulty in interpreting the age and sex composition of small game kill due to age and sex differences in vulnerability has led to the abandonment of pheasant leg, grouse wing and tail, rabbit leg, and quail wing collections in some states. However, such information is still gathered in some areas to monitor major changes in production.

The sex and age of big game animals harvested are often determined by biologists examining these animals at checking stations or in meat processing plants. The use of such information on the age structure of a population to draw conclusions about its well being is most helpful to wildlife managers.

CONCLUSION

Any sound business requires an accounting of the size and nature of its assets as well as its annual profit. Sound game management also requires knowledge of population levels and harvest in order to efficiently conduct its business of providing maximum continued recreation. Population and harvest data provide the background upon which sound management decisions can be based.

LITERATURE CITED

Geis, A. D. 1966. Establishing the status of wood duck populations—successes and problems. *In* Wood duck management and research: a symposium: 183-191. Wildl. Manage. Inst., Washington, D.C.

Gilbert, P. F. and J. R. Grieb. 1957. Comparison of air and ground deer counts in Colorado. J. Wildl. Manage. 21(1): 33-37.

MacInnes, C. D. 1966. Population behavior of eastern arctic Canada geese. J. Wildl. Manage. 30(3): 536-553.

Martinson, R. K. and C. F. Kaczynski. 1967. Factors influencing waterfowl courts on aerial surveys, 1961-66. U.S. Bur. Sport Fisheries and Wildl. Serv., Spec. Sci. Rept. Wildl. 105. 78 pp.

Sanderson, Glen C., ed. 1977. Management of migratory shore and upland game birds in North America. Inter. Assoc. Fish and Wildl. Agencies in coop. with U.S. Fish and Wildl. Serv., Washington, D.C. 358 pp.

RESEARCH TO MEET FUTURE MANAGEMENT NEEDS

Robert H. Giles, Jr.

Wildlife management, like other management, is a decision science (Giles 1979). Decisions can be well made or poorly made, but that usually depends on some outside criteria of what is good. The decisions can be studied and worked with—that is the point—and in so doing, ways can be sought to improve them (or at least relieve frustrations by knowing why some decisions were so poorly made).

There is growing acceptance that ignorance of environmental facts, like ignorance of the law, is an unjustifiable excuse for resource abuse. All important decisions now have components that need research results. With the accelerated growth in human power over the environment, there is an accelerated need for facts, for guidance in how best to use such power. A strong research arm is necessary for guiding modern wildlife agencies. For those who play the game of bio-politics, there is political advantage in having competent research and thus information superiority.

Wildlife research is a system for producing inputs to management decisions. Inputs to managerial decisions, typically called wildlife decisions, are measurements, counts, lists, and estimates about populations, habitats, and people. This follows naturally from my definition of wildlife management: The science and art of making decisions and taking actions to change the structure, dynamics, and interactions of habitats, wild animal populations, and people to achieve specific human goals by means of the wildlife resource.

Research itself does not manage wildlife. Neither habitats nor populations are changed by a conclusion. Research must be carried into practice by means of decisions made and actions based on these decisions. Research results are only one of many things that converge in the instant that a manager makes a decision and sets its consequences in motion.

Wildlife management research is the action of qualified researchers to provide useful information, explanations, and predictions to allow more rational decisions to be made. Such research seems to cross all of the scientific disciplines and includes the physics of laser beams for bird control, the brain chemistry of rabbits, the economics of wildlife meat production in Africa, the psychology of game poachers, and computer systems for minimizing wildlife impacts on high-voltage power transmission corridors.

"Research" is used broadly, contrary to the above effort to make it fairly specific. Research is an idea, a process, a program, scientists, and the scientific method. It may be theoretical or very physical. It may be national, state, or individual. It may be basic or applied.

Giles, Robert H., Jr.   Professor, Department of Fisheries and Wildlife Sciences, Virginia Polytechnic Institute and State University, Blacksburg

After the research system operates, conclusions and findings emerge. These are the outputs of that system. Unless they are pressed into service, are fed into the decision-making system, they are isolated, no different than a thousand conclusions arrived at by any other branch of scientific endeavor. A greater union can exist (but does not always do so) between research and practice. The union can be improved by an understanding of the role of research in generating inputs to decisions.

BASIC AND APPLIED RESEARCH

Much has been written about the difference between basic and applied research. What is or is not basic is critical because of the wording of certain laws providing funds for research. A major difference, perhaps the only one of significance, is the time between the final report of the research and the application of the findings. The longer the time, the more clearly the research is basic; the shorter, the more applied. The other often-cited difference is that basic research need not have a purpose—no application of the results need be seen when starting. Applied research is the imaginative application of the scientific method to a particular problem, the solution of which can strongly influence a decision. In applied research, the investigator knows what is being sought before starting; in basic research it may not be known. There are higher risks to be taken in basic research than in applied, but the more progressive wildlife agencies usually display a willingness to take such risks. Failure to probe the barriers of knowledge is also risky. There may be extremely great payoffs. The results of basic research may change someone's whole way of looking at things.

The superficial difference between basic and applied research is not important. There are no fundamental differences—only the time of application and the attitudes of researchers separate the ideas. Communication among researchers and those who allocate research funds can be restored if the differences are minimized.

THE RESEARCHER

By concentrating on objectivity, research technology, and the achievements of the scientific process, it is easy to lose sight of the very personal nature of research, its sociology, and the humanness of researchers.

Researchers, like most other humans, are less than they can become. They need encouragement, incentives, opportunities, as well as checks and controls. They can become very busy repeating work (for there is pleasure in performing a task well), but repetition beyond a limit does not produce useful inputs to decisions. There are some problems for which no more effort will produce any more useable results. There are some projects for which a good hypothesis or methodology has not been advanced. Until they are advanced, delays are very rational. There are some problems that are not researchable (e.g., some related to threatened animals in which research may destroy the population or habitat). Many readily researchable problems have already been completed. The cream has been skimmed off. The remaining problems are more difficult, often requiring advanced technology, large amounts of manpower, transportation, and regional cooperation. Often these are less appealing to the researcher for they are more difficult to control, more variable, and produce administrative problems often exceeding the scientific ones. These situations require the most judicious management of research personnel and the development of especially well-conceived, well-integrated, and well-communicated research programs.

Lyon (1965) studied industrial research project selection and found these criteria:

1. Scientists should have the freedom to select their own research problems subject to the criterion of relevance and the probability of potential

personal competence to solve them.

2. Creative individuals should have freedom of action and the freedom to choose the paths they take within their field of interest.

3. Each scientist should be allowed to determine his own method of attacking a problem.

Other conditions needed to create an environment for an effective wildlife research program are:

1. Clearly stated organizational objectives (These provide limits often needed to focus research and avoid administrative and interagency conflicts.)

2. Specialization of a degree by individuals and agencies (No one can master the literature in one field any longer; knowledge of several fields is impossible. No agency can solve all the problems encountered in wildlife management.)

3. Team efforts on projects

4. Reduction in "trouble shooting" and emergency problem solution tasks (Some may be desirable for generating ideas and improving relevance of research findings.)

5. Removal of major administrative and public relations activities

6. Long-range plans with orderly progression, foundation building, and use of all possible resources (e.g., literature) to achieve the planned objectives

7. Opportunities for researchers to sell their programs and results

8. Assurances against arbitrary termination of projects

9. Assistance from consultants or staff in using computers

10. Ample technicians, aids, and transportation (including efficient scheduling)

11. Atmosphere conducive to the exchange of ideas

12. Widespread contacts throughout the wildlife management field, including access to short-term consultants

13. Appropriate salaries and recognition of achievements based on explicit criteria for evaluations

14. Programs of continuing education

15. Excellent library facilities and access to information retrieval systems (Failure to use information now available or to seek it through efficient searches remains a blot on higher education in, and thus the practice of, wildlife management.)

BUDGETS

No imaginative scientist has as much money for research as ideas for how money can be spent. Nevertheless, it is essential that enough money be available to remove the major constraints to creativity and hypothesis formation.

The massive tools of modern research (e.g., the nuclear reactor, computer, electron microscope) are out of the financial reach of wildlife agencies. Affiliation with universities or industrial research centers becomes necessary to assure that agencies stay at the leading edge of scientific research.

Far too little is spent on basic wildlife research. The amount allocated, by any categorization, is far below the gross average of 10 percent budgeted by many industries and public agencies. Wildlife managers, alone, cannot produce all the answers for basic information needs. The field is too great; the interactions are uncountable. The wildlife researcher needs the contributions of molecular biologists, biochemists, biometricians, geneticists, taxonomists, and radio biologists. When their contributions to questions are not available, it may be wise to wait for them. If waiting seems too risky, the wildlife researcher must forge ahead, knowing the hazards and inefficiencies of entering a new field without ample time for educational retooling.

Remarks are often made that more research is needed to develop wildlife management techniques. There is some truth to these remarks, but many

221

very good techniques now exist that have failed because of poor experimental design, inadequate funding, and misapplication. Half-jobs have been done and the poor results blamed on the technique rather than on execution—planning, manpower, supplies, or time. It is far better not to allocate any money for research than to allocate insufficient amounts and then scrap techniques, employees, or even good hypotheses because the research "did not show anything."

There are cases where a good research design indicates that a specific sample size is needed. Field staff may indicate that it is impossible for any number of reasons to take or process that many samples. Rather than canceling the study, fewer samples are taken, the study completed, and the only conclusion that can be reached is that no conclusion could be reached and further studies are needed. As much as was known at the beginning of the study before any funds were used! Greater reliance must be placed on good design and unpleasant cancellations made when sampling procedures cannot be executed.

WHO SHOULD DO RESEARCH?

It becomes increasingly evident that all individuals are not equally competent researchers. Not only are there differences among individuals, but also among groups. The perceptive research administrator will exercise great care in hiring researchers and will insist on their continued training. Poorly educated people must not be thrust into research. The experimental designs of even superior researchers will be reviewed by competent judges. A high proportion of reported current wildlife research is conducted by graduate students, who, relatively speaking, are neophytes. Increased efforts by experienced researchers, both in reporting as well as conducting research, is likely to improve wildlife management action.

Research findings (usually reports published in journals) need to be compared against costs. The costs of knowing are now so high and the statewide and national consequences of not knowing are so great that any inefficiency or duplication cannot be afforded. It is cheaper to predicate management programs on research than costly field trial-and-error.

One way to improve efficiency is to become involved in interstate or regional research efforts.

What agencies should do wildlife research? There are so many problems that there is room for everyone. Efficiency can be gained by discussing competence and interest and formulating gross areas of specialization (but not exclusively). The state efforts will probably remain focused on needs unique to the states. In many cases, however, by orienting experimental designs, results may be widely applicable. The states need to conduct in-house research, encourage particular federal research, and fund support university and corporate research to meet needs that cannot be achieved by in-house efforts.

The federal wildlife research agencies need to direct research at problems common to many states; energize, coordinate, and assist in regional research programs; and pursue problems associated with migratory species, disease, law enforcement, water, and pollution. There are problems so large that even state cooperatives cannot fund them. Federal assistance is needed.

EXAMPLES OF SPECIFIC NEEDS

The following list is intended to present several scales of dominant wildlife research needs. Priorities will vary widely for agencies, regions, and researchers. The topics are important, but they are only relevant if they are skillfully planned, well supported, artistically investigated, widely reported, and rapidly converted into improved management of the wildlife resource.

Man

1. Identify and rank wildlife values held by major socioeconomic groups in North America.

2. Identify the explicit objectives associated with each type of wildlife resource use (e.g., the squirrel hunt, the photography trip).

3. Ascertain by socioeconomic and age categories the numerically ranked esthetic appeal of certain plant communities and the associated quality of successful hunts or recreational experiences in different plant communities.

4. Evaluate the influence of wildlife laws and regulations on the quality of the user's experiences.

5. Evaluate the influence of trails, roads, signs, bridges, hunting lanes, and cultural activities on hunter behavior and utilization of the wildlife resource of an area.

6. Study the relation of hunter density to hunter satisfaction and kill per hunter.

7. Study the influence of nonhunting recreational use of an area on wildlife populations. Conversely, evaluate the contribution of wildlife presence to the satisfaction of recreational use of areas.

8. Test whether computer-based simulation games can significantly improve the decisions and capabilities of environmental managers.

9. Conduct nationwide studies of higher education in wildlife management to assure the best possible long-run professional resource management. This includes evaluation of the employment market, the effects of urbanization on the wildlife management recruit, and the needs for technicians and advanced degree holders.

10. Conduct studies of the needs for postgraduate "updating" of professional educational services and requirements.

11. Study the influence of license fees on hunter numbers, activity, and satisfactions.

12. Determine for each species the relative satisfactions derived from it by hunters and nonhunters, and identify intensities of use with minimal conflicts.

Habitat

1. Determine predictive equations for food production over time on various sites.

2. Continue on-site studies to determine the best kinds and amounts of fertilizer, proper seeding rates, and proper scheduling of treatments (such as mowing, pruning, or flooding) to achieve previously specified goals.

3. Conduct economic studies of crop and forage production to enable rational judgments for livestock-wildlife use.

4. Build improved mathematical models of the habitat to enable comparisons between sites, explanations of changes, and predictions of how future plant communities will look.

5. Determine the nutritional character of plants used by wildlife. Amounts of energy and protein are particularly critical in evaluating food quality and, thus, how much wildlife it can support.

6. Improve knowledge of the year-round food habits of wildlife, relating amount of food eaten to quality of food eaten and to the availability of the foods eaten within the environment.

7. Gain knowledge of the relative protection that cover gives wildlife and how vegetation can be manipulated to reduce the drains made on wildlife energy during exposure. Determine the balance between the food energy intake and the environmental energy drain.

8. Develop automated systems for analyzing a minimal number of biological and physical samples of an area. The concept of automated diagnostic services in hospitals has utility for habitat or population "diagnoses."

9. Conduct research on the effects of climate modification, highways, dams, suburbs, even campsites, on plant or animal communities.

10. Study and develop with engineers and economists new technologies for improving resource use at equal or reduced costs to users but increased wildlife benefits.

11. Describe in great detail a few select natural and relatively undisturbed areas as check areas or controls. These are needed to allow comparisons to be made with the functions and structure of disturbed areas.

12. Conduct basic research into the physiology of reproduction of wildlife fruit or seed-producing plants.

13. Continue improvements in habitat inventories, particularly those available through aerial photographs and satellite-based studies.

14. Increase cost and production studies of habitat manipulation.

15. Test the influence of manipulating nesting and breeding cover on populations.

16. Study plant-insect-wildlife disease relations.

17. Improve knowledge of controlling bird and animal impacts on plant communities.

Wildlife Populations

1. Improve computer models of the characteristics and functions of major species to be intensively manipulated.

2. Predict the influence of various population manipulation practices such as length and season origins, allowable weapons, and license fees on game kill and benefits derived by resource users.

3. Explain and predict the influences of climatic changes on population changes and on hunter harvests and success.

4. Identify further the crowding stress syndrome of animals and its interaction with reproduction, nutritional requirements, and disease.

5. Improve techniques for sexing and aging wildlife species.

6. Study influences of ecological additives, such as pesticides, on wildlife, particularly chronic effects on biochemical and physiological systems.

7. Study the ecology of diseases of wildlife associated with man.

8. Relate wildlife population behavior to habitat manipulation and to hunter or user behavior.

9. Improve radio-telemetry and data analysis systems for animal behavioral studies.

10. Improve sampling methods and systems for analyzing and reporting the results of hunting seasons.

LITERATURE CITED

Giles, R. H., Jr. 1979. Wildlife management. W. H. Freeman Co., San Francisco, California. In press.

Lyon, L. T. 1965. Administration of natural resources research: some lessons from industrial research. Amer. Inst. Biol. Sci. and Colorado Dept. Game and Fish, Washington, D.C. 62 pp.

NEW TOOLS
IN WILDLIFE
RESEARCH

Tony J. Peterle

The old cliche "as difficult as finding a needle in a haystack" is no longer appropriate in view of our twentieth century technology. If the needle were made of radioactive iron or nickel, it would be a simple matter to take a portable Geiger-Mueller counter and find the needle. In fact, using modern analytical methods of assaying low levels of radioactive elements, you could easily find a kernel of corn in 60 carloads or locate a single, marked person in a city the size of New York.

In current studies of pollutants in the environment, particularly pesticides, detection of residues in the part per billion or part per trillion range is not uncommon. The quantity one part per billion is one drop in 16,000 gallons. This might seem biologically insignificant, but an insecticide, endrin, can kill catfish exposed to 0.29 part per billion. In order to gain an understanding of how persistent toxic compounds are transferred in natural environments, it is necessary to be able to measure these low levels. As our approaches to understanding and managing biological systems become more sophisticated, so must our research approach and equipment be more refined and exacting. The development of sophisticated and expensive laboratories must not be an end in itself; it must be the means to an end, a better understanding of biological functions in the individual organism as well as in the population and the ecosystem.

Advantages of automated and costly equipment must be balanced against personnel costs, the availability of trained, competent technicians, and the ultimate goal of the research program. Modern techniques for the study of biological systems are being developed very rapidly. Consequently, in most instances, training new personnel or retraining experienced biologists is necessary to adapt these new methods to ongoing research and management programs.

RADIATION

The great impetus in the use of radioactive materials in biological research came in the post-World War II period as a result of nuclear armament production. Many radioactive isotopes became available in sufficient quantities, and it became economically feasible to use them in research. Some isotopes are stable, and others are unstable and release energy in a distinctive pattern for a specific period of time. These time periods are referred to as half-lives, and the energies are described as alpha, beta, and gamma. An example of a radioactive isotope frequently used in biological research as a tracer is Phosphorus 32 (P^{32}), which has a half-life of 14.2 days and emits

Peterle, Tony J.   Chairman, Department of Zoology, Ohio State University, Columbus

pure beta energy. This means that if you began an experiment with 1,000 atoms of P^{32}, 500 of them would have released their energy and returned to the stable isotope of sulfur in 14.2 days.

Radioactive isotopes are unique in that they react biologically and chemically as stable elements but give off energy. Isotopes are used as tracers in biological systems in the individual animal as well as in the environment. Many physiological studies of the metabolism, digestion, blood composition, and reproduction of animals involve isotope tracers. In field studies isotopes have been used to mark individual animals for later recovery and to detect the progeny of isotope-treated females. The use of isotopes for locating animals in the field is not too practical since the high levels of radiation necessary to detect an animal at distances over five or ten yards would be harmful to the animal.

Recently, isotopes have been used to study pollutants in the environment, primarily insecticides. Various insecticidal compounds are "labeled" with isotopes and the subsequent assay of physical and biological samples from the treated environment is by radio-assay techniques rather than by normal chemical methods. Radio-assay analyses are quicker and cheaper, costing only one-fifth to one-tenth as much as chemical analyses. A second advantage is that only the compound utilized in the experiment is measured. This is important now that essentially the entire earth is contaminated with DDT. The isotope-labeled DDT accumulated by a mallard in a treated area could easily be detected and quantified when compared to the DDT already present in the test bird, which was accumulated from "natural" exposure. Isotopes also can be used to study pesticide spray distribution and the subsequent accumulation in plants and animals.

Neutron activation analysis (NAA) is another technique that has application to biological problems. This is a nondestructive sampling method that provides an assay of minute quantities of various elements contained in biological materials. An oft-quoted and unique application of the method was the detection of arsenic in a small sample of Napoleon's hair. As a result, the suspicion is that he was slowly poisoned to death while in exile. Neutron activation analyses were used to determine which ruffed grouse were shot along roadsides; those birds with a higher lead content in their feathers were those found adjacent to roads because of contamination from automobile exhausts. Some preliminary work has been done with migratory waterfowl that suggests that gamma-ray spectra from bird feathers might be unique to the bird's natural area. Feathers from geese, which apparently came from a marine environment, had higher manganese levels. Only small quantities of such material can be inserted into high-flux nuclear reactors, and the subsequent analysis of some radioactive elements can be determined to part per billion levels. Current projects using neutron activation analysis are related to the determination of mercury residues in the body tissue of pheasants, fish, and other wildlife. Residues apparently accumulate from fungicide seed dressing applied to cereal grains and from industrial pollution.

Transmission and scanning electron microscopy (TEM and SEM) are now being used to investigate pathological and structural aspects of organisms at the subcellular, cellular, tissue, and appendage level. Photographic resolution is down to two or three microns. The SEM in concert with an X-ray gamma analyzer is also being used to quantify chemical elements in the surfaces of small portions of biological material.

Radiation is measured with a variety of instruments, from the rather simple field survey meters to complex and expensive multichannel gamma analyzers. Specific types of assay equipment are more efficient for measurement of the various types of alpha, beta, or gamma radiation. Costs vary from several hundred dollars for a field survey meter to $20,000 or more for a multichannel gamma analyzer. Isotopes can efficiently and economically be

226

used in many types of research with a minimum investment in equipment. The advantage of using radioactive compounds or elements in any project should be carefully assessed to be sure that other normal methods are not applicable. The U.S. Atomic Energy Commission licenses all users above a certain minimum level, but restrictions and licensing are not a hindrance to proper use. Some experience or training is necessary prior to application for a user license.

POLLUTANTS

Considerable research effort has been devoted to residue analyses of pollutants as they influence wildlife. Most residue determinations have been for pesticides, primarily chlorinated hydrocarbons (DDT, dieldrin, heptachlor, endrin, and others). Other important compounds and elements that are considered pollutants include heavy metals such as cadmium, mercury, and lead and polychlorinated biphenyls (PCBs) and in some areas of the nation polybrominated biphenyls (PBBs). The heavy metals are frequently determined using an atomic absorption spectrometer and the pesticides, PCBs, and PBBs utilizing an electron capture gas chromatograph. The tissues of the animal being sampled, first extracted by some suitable method, are cleaned up in a filtration process prior to injection into the chromatograph.

As the pesticide passes through the chromatograph, the flow of electrons is altered, and the alteration is recorded as peaks on the chart. The various time periods (retention time) necessary for the compounds to flow through the device is characteristic of the compounds. Isomers and metabolites of DDT, for example, produce peaks in different positions on the chart than those from other pesticides. Peak heights on the chart are subsequently quantified by using injections of pesticide standards, and the quantity of pesticide in the biological sample can be calculated.

The U.S. Food and Drug Administration is responsible for establishing residue tolerances on foodstuffs. In many instances this is at three ppm (parts per million) for some meat products, one ppm for many vegetable crops, and in some instances it is established at zero (for mercury). Many state fish and game agencies are currently assessing residues in fish and game consumed by sportsmen.

REMOTE SENSING

A recent approach to aerial photography and satellite imagery, as it might be adapted to censusing animals and to providing unique photographs of various vegetative types, has been the use of infrared film. Much of the methodology for using remote sensing has been developed for military purposes, and undoubtedly some refinements in techniques still remain classified. Infrared images are produced photographically from different altitudes. The differential heat radiation produced by a deer compared to the environmental background is recorded. In one 1968 test, a count of 98 deer was made (from the infrared scan) compared to 101 known to be on the two-square mile area. Although the method is promising, the equipment is expensive and problems develop when animals are shielded by leafy cover. Areas where animals have bedded recently show on the photograph and produce double images. Species of animals cannot be differentiated; sheep, deer, antelope, and cows would all appear as similar images on the infrared photograph.

The use of remote sensing or infrared photography has been widely adapted for gathering other types of information that might have value in biological research. Habitat patterns can easily be discerned. Ice cover and available water areas for waterfowl breeding can be evaluated periodically. Diseased compared to normal plants are easily separated. Differences in water temperatures can be vividly shown by use of this method. More and more of our water supplies must be used for coolant purposes as the demand for electric power increases. The construction of nuclear power plants as opposed to fossil fuel plants will also increase the use of water and the subsequent thermal effects in our aquatic environments. Forest fire detection is another important use of this method. A scanning device at 20,000 feet can detect a fire only one foot across on the ground.

Although there are problems to overcome in the employment of this particular new research tool, there are many potential uses for infrared photography.

BIOTELEMETRY

Perhaps one of the most useful and adaptable techniques available to the research biologist in recent years has been reliable and long-lived microtransmitters and receivers. Many researchers have devised unique harnesses for fastening these transmitters to various animals. They have gathered a large quanity of movement and behavioral data that could not be obtained in any other way. Transmitters vary in size, weight, and frequency as well as in strength of signal emitted. All are carefully selected to meet federal licensing requirements in terms of power output and signal frequency stability. Some frequencies are more desirable than others, depending on distances required, type of topography, and density of vegetation encountered in the field project area.

Studies utilizing transmitters have been conducted on a wide variety of bird species including quail, pheasant, turkey, swan, goose, gull, owl, pigeon, prairie chicken, eagle, and others. Mammal studies have included deer, woodchuck, skunk, marmot, mountain beaver, mink, rabbit, jackrabbit, raccoon, fox, squirrel, grizzly bear, black bear, and others. Some work is currently being done with snapping turtles and fish. Many biologists are now capable of assembling their own transmitters from component parts, but receivers are usually purchased. Receiving stations can be portable, either hand held or mounted on vehicles, or they can be fixed to tall towers for more intensive work in limited areas. Distances that can be monitored vary considerably depending on power output of the transmitter, quality of the receiver, type of terrain, type of vegetation, frequency of the signal, and height of the receiving antenna. Work in Yellowstone National Park on grizzly bears demonstrated that under certain conditions signals could be picked up as much as 40 miles away.

The design and construction of transmitters must be related to the type of animal to be instrumented. Transmitters have been built that weigh less than an ounce for use on small birds. Others weighing several pounds have been used on large mammals such as deer. Transmitter pulse and frequency can be varied to produce the best possible results related to the type of terrain and vegetation in the area where the animal is to be studied. Battery life can be adjusted according to signal output. Some developments are underway to devise methods whereby the transmitter can be turned on by remote signals and used only when necessary. Solar powered transmitters and special lithium batteries have been developed to extend transmitter life up to five years or more. Programmable automatic scanning and tracking receivers can be used to follow up to 40 transmitters on different frequencies.

One of the most important problems to be considered in using biotelemetry data is the subsequent method of data analysis. Great quantities of information are rapidly accumulated and must be mathematically analyzed for meaningful results. Some radio-tracking systems are automated and are capable of producing a fixed location for an instrumented animal once every few minutes for 24 hours a day. Methods for subsampling this data or reducing it to usable form must be developed for each specific project. The accuracy of each telemetry system must also be determined. A few degrees of error in direction at the receiver could mean a considerable error in location if the animal were five miles away. The assumption has been made that most animals do not alter their normal behavior patterns as a result of being harnessed with a transmitter. This is perhaps true, but for each species or individual studied this should be a consideration.

Many sophisticated systems have been developed for transmission of physiological information about the animal as well as its location. Temperatures on the body surface and internal temperatures can be determined with specially built transmitters that alter their pulse rate as the animal's temperature increases or decreases. In one study of mortality of jackrabbits, the animal was known to be dead when the signals dropped to a night temperature that was lower than the body temperature of the rabbit. This method has potential for studying the exact causes of mortality. Heart rate and blood pressure can also be determined from free-ranging animals that have been instrumented. One highly evolved instrument package for studying primates even included a radio-controlled injection syringe to immobilize the animal whenever the investigator desired. The future will undoubtedly bring even more refinements and unusual applications of biotelemetry in wildlife studies.

CONCLUSION

New tools for wildlife research are not limited by physical equipment, but more by the lack of imagination on the part of the research biologists. In many instances this has resulted from past training, which in many instances is narrowly restricted, and to the constant demand on their time for producing quick research to answer immediate practical problems. In some instances research biologists are stationed in remote areas where communication with scientists in other disciplines is not possible. Time and funds are not provided for them to attend conferences, short courses, or demonstrations so that the learning process might continue following their formal education. Wildlife administrators and supervisors must encourage the adoption of new methods and techniques, or at least respond positively to suggestions from research biologists.

Investments in training usually will enhance the productivity of research sections or divisions. The expenditure of funds for the purchase of sophisticated equipment may need to be justified to the public by researchers, managers, and administrators alike. If results from wildlife research programs are to be evaluated and accepted by scientists and engineers from other disciplines, a constant improvement in research techniques is necessary. Wildlife research biologists have demonstrated an amazing ability for producing significant research results under the adverse conditions of meager budgets, poor laboratory facilities, little technical assistance, and low salaries. How much more could be accomplished with moral and financial support from wildlife administration and the public?

SELECTED REFERENCES

Biotelemetry

There are numerous reports that have been prepared by the American Institute of Biological Sciences, Bioinstrumentation Advisory Council. They are available from the American Institute of Biological Sciences, 3900 Wisconsin Ave., N.W., Washington, D.C. 20016. A few of them are listed here:

FCC license application for biotelemetry. 1968.
Biotelemetry equipment sources directory. July 1967.
Current books in bioinstrumentation. May 1967.
Batteries for biotelemetry and other applications. February 1967.
A study of power and frequency requirements in biotelemetry. January 1966.

Other papers reporting research results using biotelemetry can be found in the Journal of Wildlife Management for the past five years.

Patton, D. R., et al. 1968. A transmitter for tracking wildlife. U.S. For. Res. Note RM 114. 4 pp.

Schladweiler, J. L. and I. J. Ball. 1968. Telemetry bibliography emphasizing studies of wild animals under natural conditions. Bell Mus. of Nat. Hist., Tech. Rep. No. 15. Univ. of Minnesota, Minneapolis. 31 pp.

Radiation

Corliss, W. R. 1964. Neutron activation analysis. U.S. Atomic Energy Comm., Oak Ridge, Tennessee. 23 pp.

Klement, A. W., Jr. and V. Schultz. 1962. Terrestrial and freshwater radio-ecology: a selected bibliography. USAEC. Div. Biol. and Med. TID 3910. Washington, D.C. 79 pp. An additional set of supplements are available of this same publication through at least Supp. 7 for 1971.

Mellinger, P. J. and V. Schultz. 1975. Ionizing radiation and wild birds: a review. Critical Reviews in Environmental Control. 5(3): 397-421.

McCormick, J. A. 1958. Radioisotopes in animal physiology. USAEC. TID 3515. Oak Ridge, Tennessee. 118 pp.

National Symposium on Radioecology: Four such symposia have been held since 1961. These large volumes are available from the USAEC and respective publishers:
1st 1961—Fort Collins, Colo. Reinhold Pub. Corp. N.Y.
2nd 1967—Ann Arbor, Mich. USAEC Conf-670503
3rd 1972—Oak Ridge, Tenn. USAEC Conf-710501-P1
4th 1976—Corvallis, Ore. Dowden, Hutchinson and Ross, Stroudsburg, Pa.

Overman, R. T. and H. M. Clark. 1960. Radioisotope techniques. McGraw-Hill Book Co., New York. 476 pp.

Peterle, T. J. 1966. The use of isotopes to study pesticide translocation in natural environments. J. Appl. Ecol. Vol. 3 Suppl., pp. 181-191.

Schultz, V. 1963. Radionuclides and ionizing radiation in ornithology. A selected bibliography on wild and domestic birds. USAEC. Div. of Biol. and Med. TID 17762. Oak Ridge, Tennessee. 27 pp.

————. 1969. Ecological techniques utilizing radionuclides and ionizing radiation: a selected bibliography. USAEC Rpt. RLO 2213-1, 252 pp. 1972 RLO 2213-1 (Suppl 1), 129 pp; 1975 RLO 2213 (Suppl 2), 67 pp.

———— and F. W. Whicker. 1974. Radiation ecology. Critical Reviews in Environmental Control. 4(4): 423-464.

Pollutants-Pesticides

Coulston, F. and F. Forte, eds. 1975. Pesticides. G. Thieme Pub., Stuttgart. 880 pp.

Getty, S. M., D. E. Rickert, A. L. Trapp and W. B. Buck. 1977. Polybrominated biphenyl (PBB) toxicosis: an environmental accident. Critical Reviews in Environmental Control. 7(4): 309-323.

Gould, R. F., ed. 1972. Fate of organic pesticides in the aquatic environment. Advances in Chemistry Series. Amer. Chem. Soc., Washington, D.C. 280 pp.

Haque, R. and V. Freed, eds. 1975. Environmental dynamics of pesticides. Plenum Press, New York. 387 pp.

Livingston, R. J. 1977. Review of the current literature concerning the acute and chronic effects of pesticides on aquatic organisms. Critical Reviews in Environmental Control. 7(4): 325-351.

Miller, M. W. and G. G. Berg, eds. 1969. Chemical fallout. C. C. Thomas Pub., Springfield, Illinois. 531 pp.

Peakall, D. B. 1975. PCB's and their environmental effects. Critical Reviews in Environmental Control. 5(4): 469-508.

Report of the Secretary's (HEW) Commission on Pesticides and their relationship to environmental health. 1969. U.S. Govt. Supt. Docu., Washington, D.C. 20402.

Stickel, Lucille F. 1968. Organochlorine pesticides in the environment. Spec. Sci. Rep. Wildl. No. 119. U.S. Dept. Interior, U.S. Fish and Wildlife Service. 32 pp.

Remote Sensing

Brown, W. W. 1978. Wetland mapping in New Jersey and New York. Photo. Eng. Remote Sensing. 44(3): 303-314.

Croon, G. W., et al. 1968. Infrared scanning techniques for big game censusing. J. Wildl. Manage. 32(4): 751-759.

Doyle, F. J. 1978. The next decade of satellite remote sensing. Photo. Eng. Remote Sensing. 44(2): 155-164.

Leonard, R. M. and E. B. Fish. 1974. An aerial photographic technique for censusing lesser sandhill cranes. Wildl. Soc. Bull. 2(4): 191-195.

McGinnis, D. F., Jr. and S. R. Schneider. 1978. Monitoring river ice break-up from space. Photo. Eng. Remote Sensing. 44(1): 57-68.

Odenyo, V. A. O. and D. E. Petry. 1977. Land-use mapping by machine processing of LANDSAT-1 data. Photo. Eng. Remote Sensing. 43(4): 515-524.

Weaver, K. F. 1969. Remote sensing: new eyes to see the world. National Geographic. 135(1): 46-73.

Dan Delany

penny Edwards

232

FISHERIES
MANAGEMENT

FISHERY MANAGEMENT PRINCIPLES

W. Harry Everhart

DEFINITION

Fishery management is the utilization of all man's knowledge to produce optimum yields measured in the pleasures of sport fishing or in tons of commercial fishery products. Two basic principles of fishery management are emphasized by our definition. First is the reference to *all man's knowledge* and second is the intended use of *optimum* rather than *maximum* yield.

SPECIAL CHALLENGES

Best management of our fishery resources demands fishery scientists with broad enough backgrounds to appreciate what other professions and professionals can offer. Fishery management is interdisciplinary. We cannot be expert in all things, but we can know enough to appreciate when we need help, and we can get it from the statistician, the chemist, the engineer, the physicist, and the economist.

Fishery scientists are not cast from the same mold. Rigid educational backgrounds for fishery scientists are impossible and impractical. The continually increasing mass of scientific data makes it more and more likely that future fishery problems will be solved by teams of specialists. Water quality specialists, for example, need firm backgrounds and experience in chemical analysis to help decide which water areas are suitable for fish and even which kinds of fish will do best.

Keeping up-to-date on all the new advances in our own and other professions is a special challenge to fishery scientists and to their employers. Fishery workers must avail themselves of periodic refresher courses. Continuing education must be accepted as a routine natural resource agency responsibility. Unless we all use knowledge available for solving resource problems we are not doing the best job.

Fishery problems are more complicated because the people we serve demand optimum yields rather than maximum yields. We work not only to channel as much energy as possible into producing fishery products, but to channel it in harmony with people's preferences. Sport fishermen who want trout are not satisfied with suckers. The best use of a water area may be a large population of small fish. But, sport fishermen call these small fish "stunted." A fact of life is that sport fishermen want to catch trophy-sized fish although they are biologically uneconomical and wasteful. In commercial fisheries, consumers demand certain species and accept others reluctantly or not at all. The same individual who will not eat hake because the ventral fins are "feeler-like" can somehow swallow a raw oyster. The basic principle of

Everhart, W. Harry. Head, Department of Natural Resources, Cornell University, Ithaca, New York

fishery management is the production of an optimum yield acceptable to the people—this yield may not be maximum.

Natural resources management, fisheries included, must be based on the interactions of the inhabitants and the habitat. Today this is frequently referred to as the ecosystem—as if it were something new. Ultimately, whatever you call it, we must consider all living organisms and the universe as a total ecosystem complex. Considering only what one does in a few miles of trout stream, or in one small pond, or in a small coastal bay, is missing the big picture.

There are no set formulas, no handbooks, and no set rules to follow in making the numerous decisions fishery management demands. This applies equally whether it be in the writing of an international fishery treaty or in deciding what size fish to stock in the local sportsmen club's favorite trout stream. Fishery scientists, as do all natural resource managers, live in a demanding world where decisions are colored gray. Definite blacks and whites are the exception.

LIMITING FACTORS

Limiting factors provide a complicated system of physical and biological checks and balances. Some marine fishes are capable of producing as many as a million eggs per female. What are the limiting factors that control so awesome a reproductive potential? Competition for food, decrease in growth rate, delayed maturity, and decreased egg production may all interact to prevent an explosion or excess of a particular species. Other limiting factors involve critical stages of life history, extremes of the range where survival conditions may be marginal, salinity of the water, oxygen, temperature, space, competition, predation, diseases and parasites, and the total productivity of the water area. Success of a fishery management program can easily depend on the recognition and proper priority listing of limiting factors.

Consider the example of a fish population that must have clean water and gravel to deposit and hatch the eggs. In addition, a year-long nursery stage will require a nursery area with rubble bottom for protection and for producing aquatic insects for food. A high dam with a long impoundment, which will flood out the spawning and nursery area, is proposed for power generation. An artificial spawning channel could be built and the fish would spawn there. However, the spawning channel cannot provide enough nursery area so this becomes the limiting factor. Someone suggests eliminating these two critical stages by simply introducing catchable trout to the impoundment. A limiting factor now could be inadequate fish cultural facilities or finances necessary to provide a large number of fish. Finally, provided that the other limiting factors have been resolved, the fishery manager may find the nature of the reservoir or its final productivity a limiting factor for the fish population. Understanding the numerous variables that influence living organisms and the likely interaction of these variables makes it easier to understand and support the biologists' crusade for long-term research projects.

Pollution can be a limiting factor. Dramatic fish kills, offensive odors, coloring of water, suspended solids or precipitates, and changed taste are obvious results. More dangerous are the pollutants that work at sublethal concentrations. No large fish kills result but rather the growth of the fish is retarded; eggs are not viable or the sperm are not able to fertilize them; the fish may simply not have enough energy to make the necessary spawning run or prepare a proper nest. Sublethal pollution is hard to detect and hard to prove.

POPULATION MANAGEMENT

The more adept we become in recognizing population and subpopulation differences, the more efficient will be our management. We are continually altering our habitat, and it is important to find fish populations that can adapt to various conditions and special needs. Two distinct populations of kokanee salmon have been reported from Oregon. Population A spawns from mid-September until 10 November. Population B spawns from 6 December until mid-January. Population A will choose either streams or shoreline for spawning, but Population B spawns on the shoreline. Population characteristics can be used to take advantage of water temperature differences and available aquatic environments.

Although all dogs belong to the same species, various breeds have been developed for specific uses in specific situations. Similarly all rainbow trout belong to the same species, but we cannot expect a hatchery-reared trout to be equally successful in large and small lakes, in large and small rivers, and in waters of various chemical and physical characteristics.

Working below the species and subspecies level requires refined and special population identification methods. Fish behavior is an excellent way to recognize populations. It may be the time a fish spawns, its movements, migration routes, courtship, or even its cover-seeking behavior that lets us identify it. The great variation in scales and fin rays is used by biologists to separate populations. Age composition of a population or periodic abundance and scarcity may serve as an indication of population separations. Blood types are helpful. Even the presence or absence of specific diseases and parasites can be used to separate fish populations.

HATCHERY-REARED FISH

Cold-water fish dominate fish culture, but a much broader understanding of the hatchery role is necessary. Warm-water fish, commercial rearing of other species besides catfish and trout, and the role of privately owned and state and federal hatcheries are some of the major considerations.

The 1974 national task force for public fish hatchery policy makes thirty-one recommendations including, "That the states assume full management and financial responsibility for stocking the inland public waters within their respective boundaries except for special situations which justify assistance from federal or local government or from private utilities or other appropriate sources." The other thirty recommendations are important, and a copy of the report should be available to public and private groups interested in fishery management.

Catchable trout stocking programs are here to stay, but the principle of providing fishing in this manner must be refined. More economical methods of production, distribution, and harvest are needed. Crowded fishing conditions and the effects of stocking programs on natural populations are problems to be resolved.

Other animal husbandries have provided us with animals tailored directly to our needs, and there is no reason to doubt that fish culture can do the same with fish. Geneticists can help in breeding new strains of sport and commercial fish better able to survive in a rapidly changing environment.

New fish culture methods have been suggested, but implementation is slow. Fish have been reared in commercial silos providing an economy of space and water. Catfish are being reared in wire baskets for efficiency in feeding and handling. Recirculation of water supplies could result in less dependence on natural water supplies, standardized water supply, sterilization, and a standard fish product. Fish nutritionists have made considerable progress with dry diets, but much research and development are necessary to give us better fish.

HABITAT ALTERATIONS

We make drastic alterations in the habitat, some good and some bad. Fishery managers have developed many techniques to improve fish habitat. Some are:

1. Large, artificial fishing reefs in the offshore waters of the oceans and freshwater lakes, constructed of everything from boulders and automobile bodies to specially cast concrete, provide hiding places and additional food that attracts the fish

2. Spawning channels to replace vital spawning areas destroyed or no longer accessible

3. Fish toxicants to destroy undesirable fish populations and restore the balance in favor of the game fish and the fishermen

4. Weed control

5. Fertilization and artificial enrichment

6. Various in-stream devices to make pools, provide cover, increase water velocity, and wash out silt

7. Aeration and recirculation of lakes and reservoirs promises the possibility of tailoring temperatures and fisheries to fit the needs of fishermen and other recreationists

Finally, fishery workers must develop an understanding of what motivates people and do a better job of understanding the public generally. We must, for example, recognize the difference between a public that expresses awareness of a problem and a public that also appreciates and takes action to solve a problem. Pollution is all around us. Every individual can see it, smell it, taste it, feel it, and hear it. A mountain of information describing all kinds of horrible fates for our habitat, and for us, has not frightened us into any real pollution abatement. Translation of natural resource management findings for public appreciation and positive action must become a way of life for all natural resource managers.

SELECTED REFERENCES

Bardach, J. E., J. H. Ryther, and W. O. McLarney. 1972. Agriculture. The farming and husbandry of freshwater and marine organisms. Wiley Interscience, New York. 868 pp.

Calhoun, A. et al. 1974. Report of the national task force for public fish hatchery policy. Task Force Rept., U.S. Fish and Wildlife Service. 295 pp.

Everhart, W. H., A. W. Eipper, and W. D. Youngs. 1975. Principles of fishery science. Cornell University Press, Ithaca, New York. 288 pp.

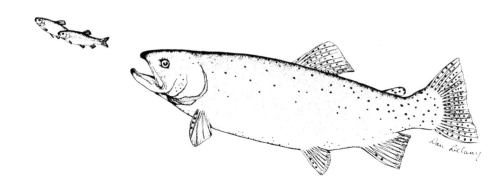

CHARACTERISTICS
OF FISHERIES

Robert T. Lackey

In 1975 nearly 54 million Americans over the age of nine fished. The amount of money spent on fishing (boats, motors, fishing tackle, camping gear, motels, food, entrance fees, and field clothing) was estimated to be in excess of $15 billion. Fishing opportunities are clearly a major attraction for tourists in many communities.

In commercial fisheries, demand for fish used as food for man and domestic animals is growing rapidly. This increase in demand for fisheries products has made the oceans, estuaries, and fresh waters important sources of animal protein.

Fisheries science is the profession concerned with effective management of aquatic *renewable* natural resources, the oceans, seas, estuaries, streams, rivers, ponds, lakes, and reservoirs.

A fishery is an aquatic, renewable natural resource system composed of three interacting components: aquatic habitat; aquatic biota; and human use of the aquatic biota. Aquatic habitat is the physical component of a fishery and includes such factors as lake, ocean, or stream water quality, soil characteristics, and bottom shape and contour. Aquatic biota, the second component, is represented by the animals and plants in a fishery. The biotic component ranges from microscopic plankton to bottom dwelling animals, higher plants, and, of course, all kinds of fish. The third component of a fishery, human use, deals with man's use of the biota, usually fish (although fishing for food or sport includes harvest of salmon, trout, crabs, catfish, frogs, shrimp, clams, oysters, bass, kelp, sponges, whales, and other forms of aquatic biota). Man's effects on aquatic biota may also be caused by industrial, agricultural, and domestic water use for waste chemical disposal, irrigation, or drinking.

The two fisheries components, aquatic habitat and aquatic biota, taken together are simply an *aquatic ecosystem.* Aquatic ecology—the study of the relationships between animals, plants, and their environment—is a very complex field. By adding a third component, human use, the discipline becomes even more complex—the status of all areas of renewable natural resources management.

Fisheries resources can be arbitrarily classified as to habitat: (1) estuaries at the mouths of streams and rivers; (2) coastal waters over continental shelves; (3) offshore waters above continental slopes and deep ocean basins; (4) flowing fresh water; and (5) standing fresh water.

An estuary is the aquatic environment where fresh water meets salt water (i.e., a stream or river emptying into the ocean). Estuaries have both marine

Lackey, Robert T. Leader, Water Resources Analysis Group, U.S. Fish and Wildlife Service, Harpers Ferry, West Virginia.

and freshwater characteristics. Coastal waters are those relatively shallow, inshore areas over continental shelves. A continental shelf is the ocean floor formed by underwater extensions of the continents, starting from land and extending outward to depths less than 200 meters. Offshore waters are the deep areas above the continental slopes and deep ocean basins. Continental slopes (200 to 3,000 meters deep) are sea floors that extend beyond the continental shelves at an average descent of approximately four degrees to the deep ocean basins (3,000 to 6,000 meters deep). Continental slopes make up the largest part (over 70 percent) of the earth's water cover.

Flowing fresh waters are the streams and rivers that vary in size from the smallest mountain trickle to the mouth of the Mississippi River. Standing freshwater fisheries resources are the ponds, lakes, and reservoirs. The separation between ponds and lakes is arbitrary. Reservoirs are by definition man-made.

Most of the worldwide marine harvest (70 million metric tons) is from coastal and offshore waters. The catch consists mostly of finfish and is taken mainly for commercial purposes. Recreational fishing (particularly in the United States and Canada) plays a more important role in fresh water, coastal, and estuarine areas. Crustaceans and molluscs are important resources along coastal areas and estuaries. In addition, estuaries are important spawning and nursery areas for maintenance of many coastal and some offshore fish populations.

Fresh water recreational fishing is extremely popular in North America. In 1975, nearly 40 million anglers fished warm-water streams, ponds, lakes and reservoirs in the United States. Over 18 million anglers fished in cold-water resources. Over 6 million Americans fished for sea-run fish. Marine recreational fishing, in contrast, was pursued by over 15 million anglers.

Many problems confront a fisheries scientist attempting to effectively manage a fishery. Suppose, for example, that a manager, employed by a state fish and wildlife agency, is responsible for managing a large reservoir, a mountain lake, or a coastal area. He routinely faces a number of problems and constraints in carrying out his assignment:

1. *Inadequate information upon which to base management recommendations and decisions*
As is true in all areas of renewable natural resource management, there is rarely enough information available to comfortably make management recommendations and decisions. Often a fisheries scientist must recommend positions and policies with relatively little available ecological or sociological data. The scientist may face situations such as: What will be the impact of channeling a stream on the aquatic ecosystem? How will this channelization affect public recreational opportunities? How does society collectively feel about the trade-offs in such decisions?

2. *Conflicting desires within the general public*
Lakes, reservoirs, rivers, streams, ponds, estuaries, and oceans may be used by anglers, boaters, bird-watchers, water skiers, farmers (irrigation), industrial interests (electrical generation, manufacturing), cities and towns (drinking water), and many other segments of society. Many of these uses cause severe conflicts. For example, use of reservoir water for agricultural irrigation often precludes quality fishing opportunities because of excessive lake drawdown. No one likes to drag a boat over extensive mud flats, but fewer people yet want to pay more for food.

3. *Conflicting desires within the fishing public*
Fishermen themselves rarely agree as to what fishing should produce. Should a particular resource, for example, be managed for trophy trout or "fryers"; for hatchery or native trout; for "catch and release" or consumptive use? These are some of the real and routine conflicts that face any fisheries manager in assessing what the public wants from a fishing experience.

4. *Largely uncontrollable nature of aquatic environments*
Managers are often faced with the frustrating reality that they can only partially control or influence aquatic environments. The number and kinds of habitat changes possible in a reservoir, lake, river, or ocean environment are few. Certainly the gross degradation of aquatic ecosystems by pollution can often be eliminated, but excessive runoff resulting from widespread land-use practices (i.e., urban, agricultural, etc.) is much more difficult to control. Alteration of aquatic habitat for increased fish production is possible in most fisheries, but it is most applicable in streams and ponds.

5. *Natural variation in animal and plant populations*
All populations undergo a certain amount of natural fluctuation. Crappie, for example, may be very common in a lake during one year and rare the next. Many of these population variations are poorly understood and take place at unpredictable intervals.

6. *Dynamic aspects of biotic populations*
All animal and plant populations under natural conditions are in a state of change even though the populations may appear to be stable. The total weight of fish, or other animals or plants, may be roughly the same year after year; however, the rate of death, birth, predation, growth, or harvest may be drastically different.

SUMMARY

Fisheries are complex, interacting systems. Fisheries management is carried out in a world of uncertainty, conflicting desires of various segments of the public, and dynamic aquatic ecosystems. The importance of fisheries resources is immense, and management is an essential component in wisely using these resources.

SELECTED REFERENCES

Bennett, George W. 1971. Management of lakes and ponds. 2nd ed. Van Nostrand Reinholdt Co., New York. 375 pp.

Benson, Norman G. 1970. A century of fisheries in North America. American Fisheries Soc. Spec. Publ. No. 7. 330 pp.

Everhart, W. Harry, Alfred W. Eipper, and William D. Youngs. 1975. Principles of fishery science. Cornell Univ. Press, Ithaca, New York. 288 pp.

Rounsefell, George A. 1975. Ecology, utilization, and management of marine fisheries. C. V. Mosby Co., St. Louis. 516 pp.

Royce, William F. 1972. Introductory to the fishery sciences. Academic Press, New York. 351 pp.

U.S. Fish and Wildlife Service. 1977. 1975 national survey of hunting, fishing, and wildlife-associated reaction. Dept. Interior. 91 pp., appendices.

STREAM HABITAT MANAGEMENT

Ray J. White

GENERAL OVERVIEW

Proper habitat is essential to maintain an abundance of stream-dwelling game fish, such as trout, salmon, smallmouth bass, and channel catfish. Inadequate habitat is a major and widespread reason for unsatisfactory fishing.

Stream habitat management is basically the manipulation of channel shape and materials to make the stream a better place for one or more kinds of fish, a place in which they can become more plentiful. Physical living conditions, including the structural effects of aquatic and riparian (stream side) vegetation and sometimes water temperature, are dealt with in this class of environmental management but not attempts to improve chemical or purely nutritional conditions.

The goal of stream habitat management is usually to provide increased opportunity for sport fishing of high quality. (Improving habitat for endangered species of fish could be another goal.) As high quality angling entails not only seeking and catching fish, but doing so in pleasant surroundings, management should be done with careful consideration for the natural beauty of the land and water. An artificial appearance should be avoided.

The greatest need and potential for game fish habitat improvement is generally in small streams that have moderate to high fertility but lack protective depth and in-stream cover. While creeks only one to ten meters wide and less than knee deep may look insignificant to many people, these small waters can, especially if properly altered, produce more game fish per unit of surface area than large rivers do. Small stream habitat is in many ways more fragile yet more easily managed.

Broad categories of stream habitat management are:

Habitat protection — preventing deterioration and decrease, especially that caused by humans or livestock

Habitat restoration — undoing human abuses or other damage

Habitat enhancement — creating more habitat than would naturally occur

Habitat maintenance — keeping up restorations or enhancements that are especially needed where habitat has been created beyond the natural capacity of the ecosystem to support it

"No management is best management" can, in some instances, be a worthy adage. Pure protection from problems associated with water diversion, channelization, mining, forestry, highways, agriculture, industry, and urban development may be the soundest conservation. In restoration and enhancement, restraint is important. There are cases where channel restructuring has

White, Ray J. Associate Professor and Extension Specialist, Department of Fisheries and Wildlife, Michigan State University, East Lansing

241

been overdone with wasteful and sometimes unsightly results. Where restoration is needed, it will often suffice to let nature alone do the repair, although the human hand is clearly needed to undo such human-caused damage as dam or road-building blockage of fish migrations. Culverts and other fish passes are a specialized habitat restoration topic.

In other cases, letting nature take its course, unaided and unguided, may be unsatisfactorily slow or may yield results contrary to objectives. For example, the natural development, called plant succession, from a meadow of high grasses and sedges on the banks of a small stream to a forest canopy over the stream destroys low stream-bank plants by shading. Not only is vegetational hiding cover lost, but the stream erodes a wider, shallower channel, one inhospitable to larger fish. It is often possible to arrest plant succession at the stage most productive for game fish.

While management usually focuses on channel banks, bed, currents, and riparian vegetation, attention must be given to broader land and water managements, such as those that retard soil erosion into streams or those that stabilize stream-flow discharge, the amount of water flowing in the channel. Maintaining adequate discharge is crucial to fish habitat. Adjusting the chemical content of water to make it physiologically more favorable for fish is a form of habitat management, usually involving pollution abatement.

Not classed as habitat management are such practices as raising water fertility, directly feeding a stream's fish, and eliminating the kinds of fish that compete with or prey on desired fish. While these are environmental manipulations (and ones with grave risks to stream ecosystems), they involve food supply and food web relationships primarily, not considered habitat. However, improved habitat for food organisms can be derived from altering the habitat for fish.

Also outside the realm of habitat management are the building of access roads, parking areas, picnic facilities, and guide signs. These may be part of an overall recreational development, but they do nothing for fish habitat and can be detrimental if constructed improperly or overdone. Habitat management can suffer when funds are siphoned off for such nonhabitat amenities.

We no longer apply the term "stream improvement" to stream habitat management because that phrase is so often used by waterway engineers in connection with drainage, channel straightening, "snag" removal, damming, and other practices that destroy fish habitat. In fact, a major subfield of habitat management is the undoing or mitigation of harm done in engineered watercourses.

HISTORY

Major North American programs of fish habitat manipulation began in the 1930s. The main impetus was a depression-time need to create jobs. Too much of the work was done with an inadequate understanding of fish, streams, or angling needs. Over 40 years later, cases of habitat ruined, scenery blemished, and effort wasted are still evident.

Another surge of stream habitat alteration followed World War II. Under public pressure, conservation agencies again forged ahead, in many cases hastily and without biologic insight. In the 1950s, however, methods of inventorying fish abundance by electrofishing came into use. This, combined with "creel census" measurement of anglers' catch, made it possible to gauge how well the fish and fisheries were doing before and after habitat management.

By the 1960s several studies of trout population responses to habitat management had been done. Substantial increases in trout abundance followed creation of greater channel depth and more shelter. Recommendations were made for eliminating useless or damaging methods, for further developing beneficial practices, and for better selecting streams worthy of management.

Such advances, together with improved construction techniques, have put habitat management on a much firmer footing than 20 years ago. Recent research on stream fish ecology and management has branched out from measuring gross population responses into studying microhabitat selection by individual fish and into the relation of habitat to the social behavior of fish. This research data enables finer tuning of habitat work.

Most stream habitat management has been done to benefit trout and salmon fisheries, and this article draws primarily from such work. Surely much of the information will pertain also to habitat management for small-mouth bass, channel catfish, and other fishes, but details of methodology remain to be developed for them.

PHYSICAL AND BIOLOGICAL PRINCIPLES

The habitat manager should thoroughly understand stream ecosystems, especially the interaction of stream flow and channel form, the ecology of stream and riparian plants, and the life histories and ecologies of the fishes and other fauna.

Improved living conditions increase fish abundance through better survival, body growth, and reproduction. For these processes to produce a thriving population, it is not sufficient that living conditions be merely tolerable, they must be favorable, and management aimed at creating *optimal* conditions (the best within the favorable range) stands to be most effective.

The trout population's basic requirements can be outlined as:

Structural Habitat Requirements	Nonstructural Habitat Requirements	Nonhabitat Requirements
Living space	Favorable water temperatures	Food
Concealment from enemies (cover)	Favorable chemical concentrations (dissolved minerals and gases)	Presence of others of own kind
Shelter from current		
Migration routes (for some kinds of trout)		
Gravel beds for spawning		

To the degree that any of these is unfavorable, fish abundance will be reduced. All are interconnected, some more directly than others.

The channel characteristics that most directly affect fish are water depth, current speed, bed materials, and concealment cover. Obviously, a fish cannot exist where water depth is less than its body depth—a fact sometimes ignored in water withdrawal compromises.

Diversity of water depths and velocity patterns is important. Many small fish, including the young of larger kinds, depend on shallow, slow water; others prefer shallow, fast riffles. Large fish use deeper areas, some inhabiting swift pools or runs and others living in slow pools.

A variety of streambed materials provides spawning habitat for various fish, as well as habitat for a diversity of food organisms. Roughness or smoothness of the streambed affects current speed.

Few game fish would last long in any stream without places to conceal themselves from predators. During daylight, game fish seldom venture into areas that lack in-stream cover within a few seconds' dash. A shortage of in-stream cover is common, especially of large cover for large fish. The emphasis of habitat management will often logically be on creating more cover.

Water depth alone may afford concealment from aerial predators, but not from underwater enemies. Visual barriers can be beneficial in deep water. Overhead and lateral cover is essential if small creeks and even some parts of large rivers are to support useful populations of game fish. Common forms of natural in-stream cover are rock ledges, boulders, logs, aquatic plants, and undercut banks with grass, brush, and root wads.

Trout prefer submerged cover, close to the streambed. The distance between overhead cover and the bed should just exceed the body depth of the fish for which it is designed. The darker the space beneath cover, the more attractive it is for trout in daytime. Large coverts close to the bed create darker hiding places.

Besides overhead cover, vertical surfaces at or near the streambed and parallel to the current are important. Trout like to press up against lateral surfaces such as logs and stream banks when resting or frightened.

Trout prefer coverts with slow current beneath but with fast currents nearby. This conserves body energy while providing the best food supply, as fast currents carry more drifting organisms per unit time.

The habitat requirements of stream fish seem to be most reliably met by the channel features that occur abundantly in *meandering* streams rather than in straight or braided channels. Stream fish must have evolved most of their adaptations in meandering channels, as that flow pattern prevails in nature. All flowing fluids tend to take regularly winding courses with the special bending (sine-generated curve) that is called meandering. Most streams clearly exhibit meandering, and all, given enough time, will carve it. While parts of streams deviate markedly from the regularity of meandering, these are now understood to be temporary aberrations, which it is the tendency of normal stream erosion to overcome. Deformations by fallen logs and rocks, by meander "gooseneck" breakthroughs, and by large-scale shifts of earth occur suddenly, while erosional carving is slower in restoring regular curvature.

Fish habitat is often improved when we speed resumption of full meandering. Moreover, greater sinuosity means greater length of stream to serve as fish habitat.

Natural channel dimensions (width, depth, radius of curvature, etc.) vary from stream to stream and from one section to another in the same stream, depending largely on the magnitude of discharge, especially that during high water of bank full or greater. On the other hand, the *proportions* of channel width to curvature and to the wavelength of meandering are remarkably constant for all streams, regardless of size. Manipulations such as channel straightening, which force radical changes in these proportional relationships, are likely to cause physical and/or biological catastrophe.

Streams undulate vertically in synchrony with their horizontal meandering. An example is the pool-riffle-pool sequence of many streams. Pools tend to occur at the outsides of bends (also elsewhere, owing to obstructions) and riffles form at the "crossover" or inflection areas between bends where direction of curvature changes. The depth of meander-bend pools and the accumulations of logs and other debris that the veering current causes create cover for large fish. Riffles have essential functions, such as serving as the spawning beds for salmon or trout.

DESIGNING AND IMPLEMENTING MANAGEMENT

Habitat management needs to be tailored to the individual situation in each section of stream. While certain management principles, as well as biological and physical processes, are common to all streams, each part of each stream still has its own special characteristics, needs, and potentials.

The following steps in identifying and solving habitat management problems resemble those in any other biological management, such as in medicine or agriculture:

1. *Have a clearly-stated goal.* This involves program philosophy, purpose, and direction.

2. *Examine.* Obtain data on the stream, its fish, and the fishery during

all seasons of the year. The habitat quality index (HQI) method of Binns and Eiserman (1979) is useful.

3. *Diagnose*. Analyze the data, characterize the situation, and determine what the limiting factors are. (The conclusion may be that there are no important problems. If so, stop here!)

4. *Set objectives*. Determine which limiting factors should be overcome in view of the program goal and budget.

5. *Prescribe*. Select managements for achieving the objectives.

6. *Plan*. Lay out a sequence and schedule for management.

7. *Organize*. Finalize the budget and arrange for materials, equipment, and labor.

8. *Treat*. Carry out the managements.

9. *Evaluate*. Determine if the project was worthwhile and if similar work could be done better in the future.

10. *Maintain*. Periodically inspect and keep up.

Goal, examination, and diagnosis are all too often ignored. Plunging blindly into the technique-application end of management without going through the preliminaries results in waste and even habitat destruction.

Care should be taken in all phases of design and management to respect the uniqueness of the stream and the angling traditions associated with it. Rare and endangered species of plants and animals should receive special consideration.

STAFFING

A professional fishery management ecologist should carry out phases one through six (above) in cooperation with a habitat manager experienced in field-work methods and equipment. The habitat manager would be responsible for execution of the managements and for later maintenance, the ecologist for post-management evaluation.

Trained employees tend to be more efficient and dependable than volunteer labor. However, working with stream habitat stimulates resource awareness among youth and conservation groups, and this may justify the larger amount of supervisory guidance and quality control needed.

MANAGEMENT OBJECTIVES AND METHODS

Providing More Living Space and Concealment

Preserving natural cover, such as undercut banks, low brush, and grass at the water's edge, as well as boulders, pools, and aquatic plants, is fundamental. Maintaining the meandering, pool-riffle form is essential.

Structures to deepen the channel and provide shelter can speed the recovery of damaged streams or enhance the carrying capacity of naturally deficient ones (Fig. 1). The current deflector device does this well in gently sloping or moderately steep streams (White and Brynildson 1967). Deflectors arranged in an alternating pattern accentuate or reestablish meanders and are best when they incorporate cover such as overhangs or spaces between jumbled rock. Similarly, revetments of the outer, current-swept banks at bends should have ledges or be made of loosely piled rock (rip-rap), which furnish shelter. Such bank covers can be tied in with deflectors or used alone. In alluvial streams, deflectors and revetments can guide the current to create beneficial channel.

Low dams can be used in steep streams, but cause unfavorable damming in low gradient situations. Dams should be placed so as to impound as little as possible, while creating a plunge pool below the overspill.

The greater the highwater forces that occur in a stream, the sturdier any channel restructurings will have to be. Large rocks seem to be the only durable material of natural appearance for use in streams that are large or

Fig. 1. Upstream view on a small, sandy creek, narrowed and deepened by a long structure of rock and sod on post-and-plank foundation. Trout hide under an overhang along its edge. Downstream part forms gradual deflector which slightly accentuates a meander curve. Original stream width shown by base of alder (right) and tree (left). Courtesy of R. J. White)

steep. Boulders of several meters diameter can be effectively used where smaller rocks would be washed away. Using a few revetments of large rock in key locations to "train" lengthy sections of braided rivers into single meandering channels that are narrower and deeper is a method of promise in large, steep waters. Blasting to form pools in bedrock has been a feasible method for facilitating anadromous migration in some streams.

Structures that directly oppose the current collect debris and unfavorably dam or deflect the stream (Fig. 2). Building devices low (less than 30 cm above base-flow) helps avoid flood damage. On the other hand, revetments must be much higher to be effective, but they usually become hidden by plants. Walls of sheet piling or rock-filled wire net gabions provide little cover and look artificial.

Such massive channel restructurings as deflectors, revetments, and low dams cost $10,000 to $30,000 per kilometer to install, plus several hundred

Fig. 2. "V-dams." Note that high water has been directed against the bank, causing widening of the channel through erosion. (Courtesy of Wisconsin Dept. of Natural Resources)

dollars per kilometer per year for upkeep. A far less expensive alternative—for use only in streams with penetrable bed material—is the half-log covert (Hunt 1977). This is a simple submerged shelter formed by a log sawed lengthwise, aligned parallel to the current, resting on low spacer blocks, and staked to the bed by iron rods. Other low-cost in-stream shelter devices include brush cuttings wired to stakes, boulders dispersed on the bed, and logs, stumps, or whole trees cabled to outer banks at meander bends.

Vegetational management may be an economical way of providing cover while also narrowing and deepening streams. Low, channel-edge plants not only furnish many hiding niches, but trap drifting silt, forming new, tough, root-thatched bank material. Along small streams, these beneficial plants can be promoted by judicious removal (or prevention) of trees and brush that would shade them out and by the reduction of grazing. Tree and brush removal is not needed along streams so wide as to prevent a forest or brush canopy.

Improving Reproductive Habitat

The improvement of spawning and/or nursery habitat should not be attempted unless lack of such habitat is definitely determined to be the population's limiting factor, and a potential for enhancement is shown. Streams often have a surplus of young fish, since each female produces many eggs, and a few successful spawnings can provide plenty of offspring—while the survival bottleneck is lack of cover for them as they grow larger. In trout streams with excellent spawning habitat and cover, the amount of livable space allows only two to five percent of each year's hatched young to survive the first nine months of life. Even with far less spawning habitat, about the same number of survivors would result.

Where a stream really lacks enough spawning habitat to supply the number of fish at any stage that space, cover, and food can accommodate, improvement of existing gravel beds is preferable to bringing in new gravel. Such improvement is often a side effect of restructuring channel form and cover. Where too little gravel exists, hauling in gravel to build riffles may be done, but amounts needed often make costs unbearable. Artificial riffles must be placed at points in the channel where it is natural for riffles to occur. Otherwise, they will be washed away. If current is too slow, the riffles become clogged with silt.

A "riffle sifter" machine, developed to flush silt from gravel in large salmon rivers, increased fry production fourfold at first, but the effects did not last long enough to offset costs. Artificial spawning channels with flow-control sluices are productive of Pacific salmon fry but do not appear suitable for trout.

Improving Water Temperature

Thermal problems include not only excessive warmth in spring and summer but also coldness in winter. If water temperature becomes intolerable for a desired kind of fish at any time, resident populations cannot exist, although migratory stocks may use the stream. In many streams where temperatures are tolerable for them the year around, fish may grow and survive poorly because temperature remains outside the *favorable* range much of the summer and winter.

Streams can be cooled by removing dams or by increasing water supplies, either from groundwater sources or from impoundments, providing, in the latter case, that flow is drawn from a thermally suitable layer of the water column. Where dams were not built for release of cool bottom water, simple "Olszewski" tubes can be installed for this (Pechlaner 1975).

Thermal improvement has probably been a side benefit of habitat management that narrowed channels, but less so than once thought. In some areas, managers may remove brush to warm streams for better fish growth.

Improving Stream-flow Discharge

Eliminating extremely high and low flows, especially the latter, can be of far-reaching benefit. Augmenting discharge during low-flow periods (enhancing base flow, the discharge at time of no runoff) not only creates more depth and space for fish, but also makes in-stream cover available that would have been above water, improves spawning beds, may improve temperatures, and can increase food production.

Maintaining discharge is one of the most pressing habitat issues in areas where water is withdrawn for irrigation, electrical generation, or other uses (Orsborn and Allman 1976). It has been amply demonstrated that less base flow means fewer fish. Stability of discharge is a major criterion of trout habitat. Agriculture, forestry, and other land uses may be adjusted to minimize flooding or to augment base flow.

Any system that promotes precipitation soak-in rather than surface runoff increases groundwater and hence, increases spring flow. Impoundments may be built and/or regulated to stabilize flow. Small, flow-maintenance impoundments in the Sierra Nevada Mountains are an example.

Beavers and Stream Habitat Management

The beaver influences fish habitat as a manipulator of channel form, current speed, water temperature, sedimentation, and riparian vegetation. The deep, quiet water of beaver ponds can benefit local trout populations in small mountain streams where living space would otherwise be scarce and the water perhaps too cold even in summer.

Beaver ponds can be very detrimental to trout in lowland streams. Their dams reduce water velocity throughout great lengths of stream, and the resultant silt deposition ruins spawning beds and within a few years reduces water depth to uselessness. Widespread ponding destroys riparian plants and excessively warms (or, in winter, cools) downstream areas. Beaver dams sometimes block necessary fish migrations.

Beaver can be promoted in areas where they benefit fish habitat. Where damaging, trapping can be used to eliminate them, the dams removed, and the channel habitat restored.

MAINTAINING WHAT HAS BEEN IMPROVED

Upkeep is essential if improvements are to last. The complete length of managed channels should be inspected several times a year, certainly after spring runoff and other flooding. Check spawning areas for impoundment and obstacles just before spawning starts.

Controlling stream-side vegetation is a key part of maintenance along streams where excess shading and blockage by trees or brush would ruin channel improvements. Livestock fences require frequent attention.

WHAT HAVE THE RESULTS BEEN?

Stream habitat management has traditionally been most successful in small, gently-sloping trout brooks, having rather stable flow, gravelly beds, and moderate to high fertility. Special methods for steep, rocky streams subject to severe floods also yield benefit. There have been over a dozen several-year, pre-/post-treatment studies of trout population response to habitat management. All showed increases in abundance (White 1975 and later studies).

Intensive use of deflectors and artificial bank covers to narrow and deepen alluvial spring creeks in Wisconsin has consistently resulted in more fish and greater angling catch. Total weight of wild trout per unit area is commonly doubled or tripled, despite a great increase in angler use and harvest. The greatest increases are in the number of large trout, a situation of high interest to anglers.

Fig. 3. Grazing along stream bank muddies water and destroys overhangs and vegetation that provide hiding cover for fish. (Courtesy of Arthur R. Ensign, Wisconsin Dept. of Natural Resources)

Placing single half-logs at about six-meter intervals throughout lengthy stream sections where cover was scarce has caused 25-centimeter (10-inch) and larger wild brown trout populations to increase by as much as 11 fold— from a three-year pretreatment average of 40/mile to 450/mile three years later (Hunt 1977).

Removing streamside trees and brush to allow channel improvement by low bank vegetation has achieved significant increases in trout abundance (Hunt 1977). Spectacular results (Figs. 3 & 4) have been obtained by fencing livestock away from badly grazed streams and letting riparian plants restore the channel as proper trout habitat (White 1975).

It should be emphasized again that the methods so effective in gentle lowland alluvial creeks do not generally work in steep, rocky streams. How-

Fig. 4. Instream habitat management on a gravelly brown trout stream in central Wisconsin. Bank fencing keeps livestock away from cover plants and from deflector (right) and bank cover (left). (Courtesy of Arthur R. Ensign, Wisconsin Dept. of Natural Resources)

ever, the special methods for those streams significantly improve trout populations.

Trout habitat management that is well designed and properly applied, even where this involves the most expensive types of stream restructuring, can be expected to have its costs more than repaid by more fish and larger fish in the stream and by increased opportunity for sportfishing of high quality.

LITERATURE CITED

Binns, N. A., and F. M. Eiserman. 1979. Quantification of fluvial trout habitat in Wyoming. Trans. Am. Fish. Soc. 108 pp.

Hunt, R. L. 1977. In-stream enhancement of trout habitat. Pages 19-27 *in* Ken Hashagen, ed. National symposium on wild trout management. California Trout, Inc., San Francisco. 69 pp.

Orsborn, J. F., and C. H. Allman, eds. 1976. In-stream flow needs. Proceeding of a symposium at Boise, Idaho. Am. Fish. Soc. Bethesda, Maryland. Vol. I: 551 pp.; Vol. II: 657 pp.

Pechlaner, R. 1975. Eutrophication and restoration of lakes receiving nutrients from diffuse sources only. Verh. Internat. Verein. Limnol. 19: 1272-1278.

White, R. J. 1975. In-stream management for wild trout. Pages 48-58 *in* W. King, ed. Wild trout management. Trout Unlimited, Denver. (Table 1 of the paper, summarizing all long-term evaluations of trout habitat management to that date, was omitted in printing but is available from author.) 103 pp.

————, and O. M. Brynildson. 1967. Guidelines for management of trout stream habitat in Wisconsin. Wis. Dept. Nat. Res. Tech. Bull. 39. 65 pp. (Out of print.)

SELECTED REFERENCES

Hunt, R. L. 1976. A long-term evaluation of trout habitat development and its relation to improving management-related research. Trans. Am. Fish. Soc. 105(3): 361-364.

Marzolf, G. R. 1978. The potential effects of clearing and snagging on stream ecosystems. National Stream Alteration Team, Off. Biol. Serv., U.S. Fish and Wildl. Serv., Washington, D.C. 39 pp.

Leopold, L. B., and W. B. Langbein. 1966. River meanders. Sci. Am. 214: 60-70.

White, R. J. 1973. Stream channel suitability for coldwater fish. Proc. 28th Ann. Mtng. Soil Conserv. Soc. Am., 61-79.

Wyoming Game and Fish Commission. 1978. Special fish habitat issue. Wyoming Wildlife 42(11). 43 pp.

MANAGEMENT OF WARMWATER PONDS AND RESERVOIRS

There seems to be no really accurate accounting of the surface area of water in farm ponds and large multipurpose reservoirs in the United States, but estimates exceed five million hectares. Various species of fish either have been stocked or have found their own way into these waters. Over 54 million anglers in the United States would like these artificial impoundments as well as natural lakes and streams to produce the best possible fishing. That is an awesome challenge to fishery managers, and it requires considerable people management as well as fish management.

The relatively small size of farm ponds makes them simpler to manage. However, do not be misled into thinking that smaller is necessarily better. Farm ponds of less than 0.1 hectare (0.25 acre) will be disappointing to most people because too few fish will be produced. On the other extreme the costs of stocking and managing a farm pond of four hectares (10 acres) often exceed what most owners are willing to spend. The Soil Conservation Service has many years of experience in the construction of farm ponds, and certainly their capable people should be contacted for help in planning and design. A private contractor will be needed for actual construction.

Whether or not the bass-bluegill combination popularized by Swingle (1950) has worked well in your state, the concepts of pond balance that Swingle developed through his work with this combination are important to the success of the pond. Swingle never meant to imply that a balanced pond was in some type of homeostasis as some people have interpreted; rather, he conceived balance simply as a relationship between predator fish and prey fish that resulted in succeeding annual crops of harvestable fish. A gross measure of this relationship is known as an F/C ratio, where F equals the weight of forage fishes and C equals the weight of carnivorous fishes. These weights are usually taken from several seine hauls in the pond. Although there have been exceptions, ratios of 3:1 to 6:1 have been most successful in producing annual crops of harvestable fish. Values below three indicate too little forage for good growth of carnivores, and values over six indicate overcrowded forage resulting in stunting of forage species and sometimes inhibition of carnivore reproduction.

Swingle further partitioned the forage and carnivores into what he called a Y/C ratio where Y equals the weight of individuals in the F group that are small enough to be eaten by the average adult C, and C is again the weight of all carnivorous fishes. The desirable range is from 1:1 to 3:1. This ratio is obviously difficult to determine. However, it is important to realize that in order to manage for C species (largemouth bass), consideration must be given to the forage available (Y).

Flickinger, Stephen A.   Associate Professor, Department of Fishery and Wildlife Biology, Colorado State University, Fort Collins

A third ratio of Swingle's, and perhaps the most important to his concept of balance, is the A_T value, or total availability value. This is the percentage of a fish population that is of harvestable size; it is derived by dividing the weight of harvestable sized fish by the total weight of all fish. The desirable range of A_T values is 60 to 85 percent.

Balance is affected by the number of fish stocked, vegetation, water temperatures, growing season, water level fluctuation, and most significantly, by man's harvest. First of all, no harvest should occur until the carnivorous species (most likely largemouth bass) has spawned the first time. Then somewhere around 10 to 25 kilograms of bass can be harvested *if spread out* over a six to twelve month period. Obviously (but often neglected) from the F/C ratio, for every kilogram of carnivore removed three to six kilograms of forage should be removed to maintain the desirable ratio.

Ponds that are way out of balance should be drained or poisoned and started again. Lesser cases of imbalance can sometimes be corrected with severe drawdowns to concentrate predators and prey, partial poisonings to reduce prey, and corrective stockings to augment whichever species is waning. Of course, the cause for the imbalance should be removed if possible so that imbalance does not occur again.

The combination of largemouth bass and bluegill is the most popular for warm water farm ponds. However, as prey, bluegill are not particularly vulnerable. More vulnerable forage are green sunfish, golden shiner, fathead minnow, black bullhead, tadpoles, and crayfish. In fact, these six forage species are so vulnerable that without some protection (vegetation, rocks, etc.) they are eliminated by predation. Farm ponds managed primarily for bass may be better off with one or more vulnerable forage species instead of bluegill. Additional forage species would have to be stocked every two or three years.

A combination of largemouth bass and hybrid sunfish may be a desirable combination for farm ponds. Various sunfish hybrids are mostly one sex. This restricts population growth. Hybrid vigor, plus restricted population size, promotes rapid growth of the progeny. Crosses of the bluegill male x green sunfish female and the bluegill male x redear sunfish female result in 97 percent males, and the cross of redear sunfish male x bluegill female results in 100 percent males. Although the redear sunfish male x green sunfish female cross results in only 70 percent males, the hybrid progeny show rapid growth, averaging one-half kilogram in the third year and one kilogram in the fifth year.

There are two drawbacks to use of bass-hybrid sunfish combinations in farm ponds. First, there must be no sunfish present other than the two parent species stocked. Furthermore, there must be no mistakes in sexing the fish to be stocked. Presence of both sexes of either species used in the hybrid cross will result in normal progeny and negate the value of hybrids. Second, the system must be rejuvenated about every five years because by then only a few large bass and large hybrid sunfish will remain.

Because of problems with "balanced" populations of bass and sunfish, experiments with bass alone have been tried. Surprisingly, total pounds of bass by themselves have been as large or even larger than standing crops of bass in combination with other species. Few lunker bass occur, though, when bass are alone. When stocking bass only, stock several year classes so that a dominant year class does not develop. Stunting will result if all bass are approximately the same size.

Perhaps the largemouth bass has been overrated as a predator. Walleye, northern pike, gar, and bowfin are more efficient predators, but more research is needed before recommendations can be made on the use of these predators in farm pond management. Channel catfish provide a bonus in farm ponds. They detract little from the standing crops of other species and contribute to the harvestable crop. Unfortunately, successful reproduction of channel catfish is unlikely in farm ponds. If adult largemouth bass are present, stocked channel catfish should be at least 150 millimeters long to be too large to be eaten.

Large reservoirs have long been thought too large and under too rigid operation by the builder to be managed beyond initial stocking. At least three significant management programs are being used on large reservoirs, giving hope that other types of management might also be possible. Proper timing of water level fluctuations can actually help fish populations, and fishery biologists have worked out schedules with quite a few reservoir owners. Seeding exposed shorelines with fast growing vegetation (sorghum, millet, etc.) adds to the value of water level fluctuations.

Another area of success in reservoir management has been the addition of cover similar to artificial reefs in the ocean. Tires, scrap from saw mills, Christmas trees, pipes, and cement blocks are the more common items that have been used. The main intent has been fish attraction so that fishermen could more easily locate fish, but enhanced reproduction and increased productivity (in the immediate vicinity) have been additional benefits. To a certain extent volunteer help can be utilized in this management effort.

The third significant area of reservoir management involves the use of subimpoundments for rearing fish that would have limited or no spawning success in the reservoir itself. Ideally a dam is built across one or more coves while the entire reservoir is under construction. The subimpoundments can be filled with runoff or with water from the reservoir (either pumped or from rising level). Broodstock from the reservoir or young fish from a hatchery are stocked into the subimpoundment. When the young fish are a suitable size, the water and fish are drained from the subimpoundment into the reservoir itself.

Just as in farm ponds man's harvest from reservoirs cannot proceed unchecked. Closed seasons, creel limits, size limits, and quotas are potential ways to limit harvest. Closed seasons are typically during the winter and early spring when few fishermen would want to go anyway. Also, the fish not caught then due to closure would quickly be caught by summer fishermen. Closed seasons during spawning have appeal to some people, but high recruitment is more dependent on other factors than it is on a large number of spawns. Creel limits would seem to reduce harvest. However, most fishermen do not catch a limit, and a surprisingly large number of fishermen do not catch any fish. Therefore, limits would have to be much smaller than they are now, and it is not known whether harvest would be reduced or just redistributed (maybe the people with zero fish would start having one fish).

In the past, size limits were on a statewide basis for ease of enforcing, but they probably did as much harm as good. Ignoring enforcement and thinking only about the effects on fish, size limits can be a powerful management tool. With a moment's thought it is obvious that a large enough size limit would eliminate harvest. With recognition of that fact, it is easy to accept that a well chosen size limit based on growth and recruitment *for a particular body of water* could eliminate overharvest. At present, size limits being tried on largemouth bass, walleye, and northern pike seem to be increasing standing crops to levels beyond what the forage can support. With refinement size limits will be one of the most useful management regulations devised.

An equally effective regulation is the quota. Again each body of water would have to be looked at, but once the harvestable surplus was determined, fishing would be allowed until the quota had been harvested; then fishing would be closed. The main drawback to quotas is the expense of determining allowable harvest and recording the harvest. Large reservoirs with many access points would need many creel census clerks. Also, a public relations program likely would be necessary if the results on one Missouri reservoir are typical. For several years the quota on largemouth bass has been reached in no more than five days and as few as three days!

Due to high construction costs and concern for alteration of the environment, there will probably be no major increase in the amount of water in artificial impoundments. Therefore, in the future more intensive management will be necessary to provide good fishing opportunities for the millions of anglers in the United States.

LITERATURE CITED

Swingle, H. S. 1950. Relationships and dynamics of balanced and unbalanced fish populations. Agric. Exp. Stat. Ala. Polytech. Inst. Bull. No. 274. 74 pp.

Bennett, G. W. 1970. Management of lakes and ponds. Van Nostrand Reinhold Co., New York. 375 pp.

Clepper, H., ed. 1975. Black bass biology and management. Sport Fishing Institute, Washington, D.C. 534 pp.

Funk, J. L., ed. 1972. Symposium on overharvest and management of largemouth bass in small impoundments. North Central Div., Amer. Fish. Soc. Spec. Publ. No. 3. 116 pp.

FISH PONDS— CONSTRUCTION AND MANAGEMENT

L. Dean Marriage and Verne E. Davison

A pond that provides good fishing is profitable and pleasant. Any pond intended primarily for fishing may also provide related outdoor recreation benefits such as boating, swimming, picnicking, water for wildlife, and landscape beautification.

Most ponds will produce some fishing, but produce more if they are built and managed well. Fish production is influenced substantially by (1) water temperatures, (2) the oxygen content of water, (3) control of waterweeds, (4) the kinds of fish stocked or present, and (5) the amount of food produced or fed. Extreme acidity, alkalinity, or muddiness may limit or prevent fish production.

CONSTRUCTION

Construction follows selection of a suitable site for impounding a reliable amount of good water. Any experienced technician can determine the suitability of soil for holding water and building the dam. He also will suggest designs, depths, and size of ponds for the selected site. Ponds less than one surface acre generally will not support enough fish, without supplemental feeding, to furnish much food or sport.

The pond specifications include: (1) width, height, and slopes of the dam; (2) location and size of a spillway; (3) size and placement of a drainpipe (with or without trickle tube and bottom-water overflow attachments); (4) removal of trees and brush; (5) elimination of troublesome shallow-water areas; (6) smoothing the bottom properly; and (7) landscaping the immediate area in an attractive manner.

MANAGEMENT

Management of a new fish pond begins with stocking one or more kinds of fish that are well-adapted to the water temperatures. Trout species, for example, are suitable for ponds in which surface temperatures seldom, or only briefly, exceed 70 degrees Fahrenheit (21 degrees centigrade) on the hottest days of summer. Bass, bluegills, and catfish are suitable for warmer ponds in which the water will exceed 70 degrees Fahrenheit regularly for periods of four months or more during the summer. Since different kinds of fish have different requirements, management must be adapted to the species desired. This is the ultimate key to success.

Marriage, L. Dean. Biologist, West Technical Service Center, Soil Conservation Service, Portland, Oregon

Davison, Verne E. Regional Biologist (retired), Soil Conservation Service, Jackson, Mississippi

Stocking

The number of fish to stock in a pond is related to (1) its surface area, (2) the level of food production or supplemental feeding, and (3) the size of fish desired. The surface area determines the amount of sunlight that will be available for the photosynthetic process that grows natural foods for the fish, and it is a common denominator for expressing total carrying capacity and predictable annual yields for various intensities of management. Carrying capacity is the total number of pounds of fish that a one-acre pond will support at one time. Yield is usually expressed as the number of pounds of fish per surface-acre that can be caught annually by fishing or other harvest procedures.

Fish Production

The direct relationship between food supply and fish production is generally recognized by fish culturists, but it is frequently overlooked or poorly understood by pond owners and fishermen. Building a dam, impounding water, and stocking with fingerling fish does not assure satisfactory fish production, good fishing, and economical use of fishing waters. Three or more intensity levels of food supply must be considered for management of a fish pond.

Food supplies in the aquatic environment begin with microscopic algae (phytoplankton), followed by zooplankton (microscopic animal life), which provides the principal food of fingerling-size fish. The basic production of phytoplankton is a function of the water's fertility. Nitrogen (N), phosphate (P_2O_5), and potash (K_2) are the chief elements that control the level of a pond's natural food supply. Almost all natural waters have insufficient fertility to grow bumper crops of fish. So, fertility management is highly important.

The natural level of production is relatively constant in each pond but may vary among ponds. Commonly the range is from 100 to over 200 pounds of fish per surface-acre, from which 25 to more than 75 pounds may be caught annually by fishing. Such low yields usually are not profitable for the operation nor satisfactory for the fisherman. These unfertilized waters usually are "clear" and permit heavy growths of rooted submersed waterweeds.

To produce enough food to support 400 or more pounds of fish per surface-acre, microscopic algae should be sufficiently numerous to reduce the water's clearness so that a white object held 12 to 18 inches beneath the surface cannot be seen. When this condition exists, sunlight cannot reach deeper than the visibility of the white object, and submersed waterweeds cannot germinate or grow. Unless a new fish pond is fertilized to this level of fertility, no dependable rate of stocking fish is possible, nor will the level of harvest usually be considered satisfactory.

The annual cost of fertilizer supplement is $25 to $50 per surface-acre. Annual yield of fish should be 150 to 200 pounds per acre by fishing, and submersed waterweeds are controlled in the bargain. In determining rates of fertilization, a pond owner should consult qualified local fishery biologists, because situations sometimes occur in which too much fertility may result in a fish kill from oxygen deficiency during periods when photosynthesis has ceased.

Highest fish yields, and most efficient and profitable use of pond waters, are obtained by supplemental feeding of commercial fish feeds. A one-acre pond will support and yield 1,000 pounds or more of trout, catfish, carp, bait minnows, or tilapia annually. Bass, bluegills, and crappie have not responded similarly to feeding, although recent experiments indicate some breakthrough may be forthcoming. The number and pounds of fish caught per hour or per fishing trip are increased substantially, and fishing can be "good to excellent." Furthermore, fed fish are in excellent condition and of delightful flavor. The "fed pond" maintains itself against submersed waterweeds, as the fish manures supply adequate nutritive elements for the growth of microscopic algae.

Waterweeds

Waterweeds can cause serious problems in fish ponds. They interfere with fishing, and use up the pond's fertility without adequately producing food for the fish. As waterweeds die and decay annually, they create low oxygen conditions for the fish, and often give fish an unpleasant flavor. No section of the United States and Canada is free of waterweed problems. Therefore, prevention and control of rooted submersed weeds, surface weeds, marsh plants, and filamentous algae are management problems— beginning with design and construction of a pond.

Deepening the pond edges to two or four feet, filling in shallow marshy areas, and diking off the shallow water at the inlet reduces areas for marsh-plant growth. Waterweeds that normally grow in two to eight feet of water can be prevented by shading the bottom from the sun's rays. Muddy ponds do not grow such weeds; however, they produce little food for fish and will suddenly fill with weeds when the cause of muddiness is controlled.

Chemical herbicides are capable of killing all kinds of waterweeds. Chemical control, however, is expensive and temporary, as applications must be repeated once or more every year. Furthermore, chemical herbicides do not materially increase the pounds of fish that a pond will produce, and some may result in accumulation of toxic materials in the flesh of the fish. Before using a chemical in fish ponds (or to treat fish diseases or parasites), be sure it has been cleared by the Environmental Protection Agency and the Food and Drug Administration for such use. Some states also have additional controls. Follow label instructions carefully.

Pond fertilization is the most successful, productive, and profitable way to control waterweeds in water two to eight feet deep in warm-water ponds.

(Courtesy of USDA Soil Conservation Service)

Moderately to highly fertile water grows millions of microscopic algae plants that shade the pond bottom from sunlight. Where submersed waterweeds are already present, fertilizers applied in winter will kill them. This process grows winter-annual filamentous algae that envelop and shade the plants until both weeds and filamentous algae die. A new fish pond should be fertilized before waterweeds become established. In either case, the waterweeds will establish themselves again during the spring and summer growing seasons unless sufficient fertility is maintained to grow the desired microscopic algae. The technique for fertilizing trout ponds (cold-water) for waterweed control is in the experimental stage and is not recommended.

Temperature and Oxygen Control

Water temperatures can be manipulated favorably during the warmer months of the year in temperate climates by routing the pond overflow. Cooler bottom waters or warmer top waters can be discharged as desired. Bottom water routing tends to warm surface waters and prevent lethal accumulations of hydrogen sulfide and excessive carbon dioxide. During the colder fall, winter, and spring months, however, pond waters maintain equal temperatures at top and bottom (except when ice cover exists). Nevertheless, bottom water overflow devices provide useful means of fish pond management at critical seasons of the year.

Oxygen, an essential element for fish life, is plentiful in ponds during most of the seasons. Some of the oxygen is dissolved from the air-water interface, but the greater part results from photosynthesis in green plants. However, oxygen deficiency sometimes occurs, resulting from (1) bacterial action that consumes decaying organic matter, such as dying waterweeds, peat, or fallen tree leaves, or (2) chemical conversion of such organic matter to hydrogen sulfide or carbon dioxide. Waterweed control, by microscopic algae (fertilization management), helps avoid oxygen depletion and chemical conversions. During photosynthesis, microscopic algae use carbon dioxide, a waste product of metabolism. Production of oxygen by green plants during photosynthesis ceases, of course, during any periods of darkness (including heavy snow cover), but the life processes of most living organisms continue to use oxygen during these periods of darkness.

Pond construction designs, that once specified water depths of 10 to 18 feet to avoid oxygen problems, have been replaced by the more dependable means of waterweed prevention, bottom water overflow routings, and water oxygenation by pumps or agitators that arch low-oxygen water through the air.

Harvest

Fishing is the pleasant recreational way to harvest the annual crop of fish. It is also an effective means of managing the fish population. Fishing removes a profitable crop that is ripe for the taking and stimulates a steady and healthy growth of the remaining fish.

Fishing should begin when the fish have reached about 75 percent of the pond's total carrying capacity. When fishing is delayed beyond this point, the growth rate declines sharply and will not accelerate until fish are removed. As each pound of fish is removed, a pound of growth is quickly replaced in the remaining fish population. If none is removed, no growth occurs after the carrying capacity is reached, resulting in a static condition between food supply and the fish.

Thus, a pond that provides good fishing and produces the most pounds of fish per acre per day repays effective management skill and investments.

SUMMARY

Construction and management of a satisfying fish pond includes:

1. Selecting a good site
2. A reliable water supply
3. Engineering design and construction that make management practices efficient and productive
4. Deciding the management level to be attained—low (natural conditions only), moderate (increasing nutrients by fertilizer supplements), or high (supplemental feeding of commercial fish feeds)
5. Selecting the fish species best adapted to the pond's seasonal temperatures
6. Selecting the desired number and size of fish to be stocked
7. Harvesting the annual fish crop to provide the most recreation and economic return from the investment and management

Information on pond construction and their management related to local conditions can usually be obtained from the offices of county extension agents, the Soil Conservation Service, or state wildlife conservation agencies.

SUGGESTED REFERENCES

Davison, V. E. 1953. Homemade fishing. Outdoor Publications, Ithaca, New York 14850. 205 pp.

Dillon, O. W., Jr. and V. E. Davison. 1971. Warm-water ponds. USDA Farmers Bull. 2250. 14 pp. *

Eipper, A. W. and H. A. Regier. 1962. Fish management in New York farm ponds. New York State Coll. of Agr. Cornell Ext. Bull. 1089. 40 pp.

Grizzel, R. A., Jr., O. W. Dillon and E. G. Sullivan. 1975. Catfish farming. USDA Farmers Bull. 2260. 22 pp. *

Scheffer, P. M. and L. D. Marriage. 1969. Trout farming. USDA Soil Conserv. Ser. Leafl. 552. 8 pp. *

U.S. Dept. of Agriculture. 1973. Building a pond. USDA Farmers Bull. 2256. 14 pp. *

———. 1971. Ponds for water supply and recreation. USDA Agr. Handbook No. 387. 55 pp. *

*Supt. of Documents, U.S. Govt. Printing Office, Washington, D.C. 20402 (often available free at local Soil Conservation Service and county agent offices).

TROUT
HATCHERIES
Robert Macklin and Larry E. Harris

Trout culture began over 200 years ago when Stephen Ludwig Jacobi began trout production in Germany in 1741. The State of Massachusetts established the first government owned hatchery in the United States in 1869. Since then, the role of fish hatcheries in management has been controversial. Once considered a tool of politicians, hatcheries were held in low esteem by many biologists who cited instances where the wrong species were planted in wrong places under wrong conditions. These scientists tried to sound the warning that planting fish was often not the answer to poor fishing. Caught in the middle of this controversy was the fish culturist. Exposed to the opposing arguments of scientists and politicians, he continued to raise fish, knowing that those that were properly used would improve sport fishing, and with the hope that those that were improperly used would at least do no harm.

Finally there emerged a new scientific discipline—fishery management—with biologists trained in chemistry, physics, biology, ecology, ichthyology, limnology, and population dynamics. The new fishery scientists possessed the ability to test and evaluate methods for managing the fishery. As the results of this testing became apparent, a new understanding of the role of hatcheries in fishery management began to emerge. Consequently, hatcheries assumed greater obligations and responsibilities while gaining the respect of fishery managers.

Unprecedented fishing pressure on the nation's trout streams since the late 1940's has led to extensive production expansion in national and state fish hatcheries. As an indication of the level of effort by the federal and state governments, in 1971 the federal government operated 95 hatcheries and funded another 15 that were operated by the states, while hatcheries controlled by the state governments numbered about 500. To get a picture of the total United States effort in fish culture, we must add more than 2,000 private growers to the above list. During 1973 the state and federal hatcheries produced approximately 214 million coldwater trout, weighing over 22 million pounds. Over 128 million of these fish were planted as fry. Nearly 78% of the total coldwater fish produced were rainbow trout. Brown, brook, cutthroat and lake trout, and kokanee and coho salmon comprised the other 22%. The state and federal hatcheries also produced roughly 100 million warm water fish. Over 90% of these fish were stocked as fingerlings. Data obtained in 1975 indicate a total production of 27 million pounds by private growers.

Macklin, Robert (deceased). Former Fish Hatchery Coordinator, California Fish and Game Department, Sacramento.

Harris, Larry E.   Fisheries Researcher, Colorado Division of Wildlife, Research Center, Fort Collins

Of this volume, about 20 million pounds were probably processed and 7 million pounds were marketed through fee fishout ponds.

Thus, it is apparent that fish hatcheries, with over 100 years behind them, are now producing fish to meet the needs of the American public. But, by the year 2000, trout production is expected to more than double. Hopefully, with years of experience behind them and newly developed technology, hatcheries will be able to keep pace with the needs of our society.

STOCKING PROGRAMS

Trout fingerlings (1 to 3 inches long) are stocked mainly in wilderness lakes and coldwater reservoirs. Many lakes provide ideal growing conditions for trout, but little or no opportunity for spawning. Regular stocking with small fingerlings provides fishing in many lakes where otherwise there would be none. Remarkably good fishing can be provided in large coldwater reservoirs when they are new. When first filled, these reservoirs are at the peak of their fertility and there are few large fish to prey on the fingerlings. These favorable factors often result in accelerated growth of fish. A few years later it may be necessary to supplement fingerling plants with larger fish.

Fingerlings are stocked in streams which have been damaged by forest fires, siltation, or pollution. However, in general, it is economically infeasible to stock fingerlings in streams because return to the angler is so small.

Good fishing can be supplied in some lakes by planting subcatchable-sized trout in the fall or late summer and letting them grow to catchable size when the season opens the following spring. These fish can be used in lakes which provide unusually good growth and survival conditions. Unfortunately, there is only a limited number of these lakes.

Depletion of roadside trout waters by heavy sustained fishing has brought about catchable-sized trout stocking. These waters require frequent, usually weekly, plants to maintain satisfactory fishing. In some areas, lakes and streams will support trout for only part of the year. Catchable planting during this period provides fishing in these waters. Perhaps the most significant feature of a catchable trout water, and one which is commonly overlooked, is that anglers catch from it many times the natural crop of fish each year.

Catchable-sized trout planting has stirred up more controversy than any other fish hatchery issue. Most people have come to associate catchable trout with recreation rather than natural resource management. Basically, one section of the angling public sees the program as an opportunity to catch a trout and a tangible reward for their license fee. A smaller group, which tends to identify itself as "the real sportsmen," is primarily interested in traditional trout angling. These people dislike the program and resent the cost which they feel could be better spent on other management programs. Nevertheless, it is safe to assume that whenever a trout stream or lake becomes readily accessible, heavy sustained fishing will result in depletion of the wild trout population. Public pressure will then develop for catchable-sized trout planting.

Return to the angler is the final measure of the success of a trout production and stocking program. Planting quality fish originating from carefully selected parents, reared in a good environment, and fed a well-balanced diet, is a necessary measure to ensure survival after planting. Another measure which is often ignored is selecting the proper strain of trout for the water planted. Failure to consider this factor may cause the failure of a fishery.

Fingerling rainbow trout from wild stock may surpass survival of most domestic strains. Research has indicated that Kamloops trout fingerlings from wild parents survive significantly better in California lakes than other strains of domestic rainbow trout, although they were much more expensive to raise.

Returns from catchable-sized domestic brown trout planted in lakes will be lower initially than from rainbow trout. However, they will continue to be caught over a three-year period. Most of the rainbow will be caught the first week or so. On the other hand, some strains of brown trout planted in lakes are so difficult to catch that returns are negligible. In most cases, brown trout of any strain do not perform well when planted as catchables in streams.

In summary, the nature of the water determines size and strain of fish stocked. Habitat conditions are especially important for fingerling and sub-catchable-sized trout. Catchable-sized trout supply fishing in heavily fished waters in which smaller fish could not begin to maintain fishing.

WATER SUPPLY

The most important single physical factor affecting trout hatchery success is the water supply. Ideally, the water should be clear with a year-round temperature range between 50 and 58 F. It should be slightly alkaline, free of undesirable gases, yet contain a plentiful supply of dissolved oxygen for the fish to breathe. Springs and wells most nearly approach these standards. They ordinarily have the advantages of moderate and uniform temperatures and absence of diseases and pollution. Tree-lined streams, lakes, and reservoirs, in some cases, make suitable water supplies. The hatchery should be built below the source to provide gravity flow through the hatchery.

Since there are few ideal water supplies, measures can usually be taken to correct many water supply problems. However, each measure adds to the capital and operating cost until eventually the expenses may become prohibitive.

Spring water supplies still available for hatchery use are rare. More and more, hatcheries are being supplied with well water. Pumping costs are an obvious disadvantage. Nevertheless, a large production hatchery with a supply of good well water is more economical than one with an unsatisfactory gravity water supply.

Recent developments in water treatment have made possible large-scale fish production on recirculated water (Fig. 1). The major mechanisms involved in water reconditioning for fish propagation are the removal of ammonia, solids and carbon dioxide and the addition of oxygen into water (aeration). The three methods most commonly used to achieve these objectives are: biological, mechanical, and chemical. Of these, biological filtration is the most practical for use in aquaculture. Mechanical filters require more care and labor and, so far, are less efficient in removing the polluting substances. Chemical reclamation of water is unsuitable because the chemicals used are toxic to most aquatic organisms. As little as 5% fresh water is all that is required to maintain a recirculating production hatchery. The fresh water is filtered and sterilized by exposing it to ultra-violet ray lamps. The reconditioning system reduces the amount of fresh water needed to the point that filtration, sterilization, heating, and cooling may become feasible.

HATCHERY DESIGN

The primary objective of a hatchery is to raise quality fish at the lowest possible cost. This requires mass production, which demands facilities to handle large numbers of fish at a time, yet flexible enough to separate small fish from large. A hatchery should be compact and provide a smooth flow of fish through the hatchery from the time eggs are received until the fish are planted. Methods and criteria for a modern, high-production hatchery follow.

Hatchery building needs include a combination shop, garage, warehouse, ice storage, public restroom, and office building, and a small, separate incubator building. Fish food storage areas should be located near the hatchery ponds where they will be convenient for the hatchery feed truck as well as the vendor's delivery truck.

The working area should be paved with asphalt or concrete to keep maintenance at a minimum. Landscaping should avoid lawns and concentrate

Fig. 1. Bio-filter used in removing toxic metabolites from recirculated water. (Courtesy of L. E. Harris)

on ground cover that does not need to be mowed frequently. Automatic sprinklers should be provided.

Giveaway pamphlets describing the operation should be avoided. People take them and usually drop them on the grounds where they must be cleaned up later. Instead, consider a tape recording system wired to appropriate signboards that may be activated by the viewer.

CARE AND FEEDING

After spawning, trout eggs are measured and placed in vertical incubators until they hatch and the fry are ready to swim. Egg and fry containers fit into water receiver trays. These fiberglass tray units are contained in aluminum-framed cabinets. Tray units slide in and out to provide access to the eggs (Fig. 2). Some hatchery superintendents prefer to place the eggs into hatchery troughs immediately after they are eyed. More eggs may be

263

maintained per incubator when they are removed after eyeing, and not allowed to hatch in the incubator tray.

The trout fry are kept in hatchery troughs when they start to swim. The standard hatchery aluminum trough is 16 ft. long, 16 in. wide, and 7½ in. deep, with a gradient of 1 in. in 16 ft., and when operated with a 5-in. outlet plug contains about 64 gal. of water. The length of time which fish can be kept in the fry troughs will depend upon available space and water supply. It is essential to keep the fry under controlled conditions in the tanks until they are all started on feed and osification is complete.

When transferred outside, the fish are generally placed in ponds or rectangular raceways composed of earth or concrete. A common rectangle raceway is about 80 ft. long, 8 ft. wide, with an average depth of 2.5 ft. From the upper to the lower end, the bottom has a slope of 1 in. in each 10 ft. of length. Ponds are classified as rearing ponds and circular ponds. A rearing pond is defined as an irregularly shaped body of water, large or small, sometimes found in its natural state. The circular pond is actually a circular raceway sloping down to an outlet drain at the center. Size and shape vary, depending on the needs of the hatchery and the contour of the land.

Fig. 2. Incubator tray loaded with fish eggs. (Courtesy of R. Macklin)

Overcrowding should be avoided. The number and weight of fish that can be raised in a raceway will vary with water temperature and amount of water flow. Overcrowding is indicated by the fish swimming near the surface, frayed fins, and slow growth rate.

Young fish should always be kept apart, and preferably in water above the older fish because they are more susceptible to disease. Fish do not all grow at the same rate, so it is necessary to grade them by size from time to time.

Young trout begin to feed after the yolk sac has been absorbed. This is one of the most critical stages of growth. Neglect at this point can result in serious losses or reduced growth throughout their hatchery existence. It is of the utmost importance that food be available throughout the day. As the fish grow, feeding frequency is reduced. Catchable size fish are fed only two or three times daily.

Most fish culturists use a completely balanced dry fish food which is a formulated compound high in protein and fat, that can be fed to rainbow trout of all ages and sizes. It comes in the form of fine crumble, which are fed to fry, and different grades of pellets, suitable for growing trout of larger size.

Feeding charts and computer programs are available and should be used as a guide, but consideration must be given to conditions. All sizes of fish require more feed at higher water temperatures and the amount will vary with the oxygen content of the water.

The raceways should be kept reasonably clean. Weekly cleaning is usually enough. Filamentous algae growth on the pond walls is not harmful. Often all that is required is to lower the water depth which increases the velocity, and the action of the fish will move light material downstream and out of the raceway.

EQUIPMENT

Hatchery fish production costs are divided among labor, fish feed, equipment, operating costs, and overhead. Labor is now nearly 50 percent of the total cost in an efficient, well-run hatchery. A little carelessness or failure to properly utilize mechanical equipment results in even higher labor costs. A well-designed hatchery provides an opportunity for maximum mechanization. Recently developed equipment, properly used, will slash labor costs in a raceway-type hatchery.

Mechanical fish feed dispensers and feeders are widely used. They are timed to turn on automatically, feed at fixed intervals during the day, and shut off automatically in the evening.

The most satisfactory feeder for large fingerlings and larger fish in raceway ponds is a blower mounted on a three-wheel scooter or a pickup truck (Fig. 3)

Fig. 3. Blower feeder mounted on a three-wheel scooter. Notice bulk feed bins behind the scooter. (Courtesy of R. Macklin)

A mechanical crowder and grader has been developed to handle fish in concrete ponds (Fig. 4).

An open-volute centrifugal pump is used to load the fish into fish planting trucks. On the way to the truck, the fish and water pass over a grating. The water and small fish fall through this grating and return to the raceway. The larger fish slide down a chute into the planting tank. Loading with a conveyor has also been used with success (Fig. 5).

During the next few years further significant advances in hatchery design and equipment can be expected. Feeding systems will be more highly automated. Water supplies will be sterilized to eliminate waterborne diseases. Indications are that as soon as the initial cost is lowered slightly, sterilization systems will be considered indispensable. Hatchery record systems must be computerized for better economy.

Fig. 4. Mechanical crowder and fish grader. When lowered into the water and moved toward one end of the raceway, larger fish are separated for planting while small fish escape back through one-half-inch space between bars. (Courtesy of R. Macklin)

SELECTIVE BREEDING

Broodstock are the heart of a hatchery system. They are the hatchery resource as the wild trout population is the management resource. The success of any crop of trout depends on the quality of the eggs from which the fry were hatched.

Selective breeding has achieved spectacular increases in the rate of growth, number of eggs per female, and egg size. However, breeding and management of a species requires dedicated effort.

Many traits may be inherited. Most of these traits are also affected by environment. For instance, no matter how much potential a fish has for fast growth, it will not be realized if it is raised under crowded conditions or does not receive enough food.

The more traits that are selected, the slower the progress will be for any one trait. The value of each trait should be carefully weighed when planning the program.

Inbreeding intensifies undesirable characteristics as well as desirable ones. Care should be taken to avoid brother-sister matings. These matings result in loss of vigor in the offspring.

DISEASE

Improvement of fish and egg transportation methods has made it possible to ship them long distances. Unfortunately, it has led to more rapid spread of fish diseases, some more deadly than encountered before. Some can and do cause 100 percent mortality. Once established in a wild population, they threaten the wild fish population and the water can become useless as a hatchery water supply. Even the spread of less serious diseases through the transfer of eggs and fish among hatcheries can disrupt production

Fig. 5. Loading fish from raceways to planting truck with the aid of a mechanical conveyor. (Courtesy of R. Macklin)

schedules and cost thousands of dollars. So much is at stake that planting or transfer of diseased fish or eggs can no longer be risked.

CONCLUSION

A properly managed and controlled fish hatchery program is a strong fishery management tool. Mismanaged or uncontrolled, it can destroy fishery management.

State and federal trout hatcheries operating on a nominal license fee cannot supply unlimited fishing, nor were they intended to. They can provide a buffer between the wild trout population and excessive fishing pressure and give the average angler an opportunity to catch fish. Present state and federal trout hatcheries are strained to meet demands within present budget limitations.

Fish production can and should be self-supporting. For example, the California Trout Policy states, in part:

"The annual cost of the trout hatchery program, not including fingerlings, shall not exceed the stamp revenue from trout anglers. . . . The number of trout anglers shall be estimated at half of all angling licenses, an approximation that has held for 20 years. If the proportion changes, appropriate adjustment will be made."

Since the policy was established in 1960, the sale of trout stamps has paid for fingerling production as well as other trout production. Such a policy is flexible enough to provide for population increase.

Metropolitan areas are beginning to demand more trout for their urban waters than state and federal hatcheries can afford to supply. Yet these waters can supply a great deal of angling recreation. State agencies can continue to struggle to supply fishing to these waters under traditional financing or turn to fee fishing. In fee fishing, participants pay daily fees to offset costs of providing facilities and stocking trout. Such a program succeeded at Murray Lake in San Diego, California. This 150-acre reservoir originally provided about 7,000 man-days of fair angling annually—all that the natural crop

267

would support. Two years after fee fishing was initiated, attendance increased to 50,000 man-days, even though the season had been cut two-thirds. The catch jumped from 7,000 to 50,000 pounds of fish. This operation has paid its own way. The success of Murray Lake was not an isolated case. Two other southern California reservoirs and four state-operated fishing parks in Missouri have been equally successful.

Urban trout fishing is recreation much as golf and swimming. Hence, license revenues are not an appropriate source of funds. They were established as use fees to regulate the harvest of wild fish and to provide revenues for protecting and improving natural fisheries. Catchable trout planting stretches this concept; urban trout planting shatters it.

Daily fee fishing offers a method of financing recreational fishing in urban areas where there is little opportunity under present procedures. These waters could be operated by municipal agencies which could purchase fish from private operators. Fishing opportunity would be limited only by room and public willingness to pay the cost.

SELECTED REFERENCES

Brown, E. E. 1977. World fish farming: Cultivation and economics. Avi Publishing Co., Inc., Westport, Connecticut. 397 pp.

Bureau of Sport Fisheries and Wildlife. 1968. National survey of needs for hatchery fish. Resources Publ. 63. 71 pp.

———. N.D. Sport fishing U.S.A. 464 pp.

Leitritz, E. 1976. Trout and salmon culture. Calif. Dept. Fish and Game Bull. 164. 197 pp.

FISH DISEASES

Stanislas F. Snieszko, Glenn L. Hoffman, and Phillip E. McAllister

Fish have a variety of diseases caused by parasites, viruses, and abnormal growths. These conditions are of interest to fish culturists and pathologists and also to resource administrators, public health officials, resort operators, and sport and commercial fishermen. Increasing numbers of people rely on the physical well-being of our vast North American fisheries resources.

The latest count of hatcheries in the United States shows about 100 national fish hatcheries, 500 state operations, and 1,200 commercial production units. Very few hatcheries have been fortunate enough to escape some disease problem, and in recent years an increase in the number of disease outbreaks has occurred. We are experiencing new diseases introduced from other continents. "Whirling disease," a crippling and sometimes fatal disease of trout and salmon, was not discovered in the United States until the late 1950s.

It would be difficult to estimate the financial loss and the millions of fish lost each year from diseases in hatcheries and in wild fish.

PARASITIC DISEASES

Over 1,000 species of parasites are found in or on North American freshwater fishes. Some are extremely harmful, even causing death, and some produce no detectable damage. The environment, as well as the condition of the fish, often has an effect on the parasite, so that in one situation it may cause no harm, but under other circumstances it may be very dangerous. Unfavorable conditions existing in hatcheries or small ponds are conducive to the production and spread of a large population of parasites. The result is usually damage to the fish.

Obviously, it is impossible to enumerate all fish parasites here or to elaborate on individual parasite species. References on this subject are listed at the end of this chapter for those who desire more detail. Some of the important parasites are:

Snieszko, Stanislas F. Retired. Employed part time as Senior Scientist of the U.S. Fish and Wildlife Service, Kearneysville, West Virginia

Hoffman, Glenn L. Parasitologist, Fish and Wildlife Service, Stuttgart, Arkansas

McAllister, Philip E. Research Virologist, National Fish Health Research Laboratory, Kearneysville, West Virginia

Algae

One alga (*Chlorella*) has been found as a serious parasite on the gills and internal organs of small fish. The other parasite is a filamentous green alga (*Cladophora*) and has been found growing on the gill covers of brood fish.

Fungi

A water mold, or fungus, known as *Saprolegnia*, is the most common fungus infection in fish. This, along with several related forms, is often found on injured fish. Other fungi may infect dead fish eggs, enclose adjacent healthy ones, and kill them.

Another important fungus, *Ichthyophonus*, occurs in most tissues of marine as well as freshwater species. It may become very damaging.

Protozoa

All major groups of one-celled (usually microscopic) animals have representatives as fish parasites. Only the most dangerous ones are mentioned here:

1. "Velvet disease" (*Oodinium*) is a serious problem of marine aquarium fishes.

2. Trypanoplasma (*Cryptobia*) is a protozoan found in the blood and visceral cavity of salmonids of western North America.

3. Ichthyoboda (*Costia*) is found on the outside of fish in the so-called "blue-slime" disease. It may cause high death loss in crowded hatchery waters.

4. Hexamita (*Octomitus*) is an intestinal fish parasite that may cause serious mortality in trout.

5. "Ich" (*Ichthyophthirus* spp.) is one of the most dangerous of fish parasites. It burrows beneath the skin of freshwater fish and often kills them. Fish farmers have suffered heavy fish losses from this parasite.

6. *Chilodonella* often causes serious disease in cultured fish.

7. *Trichodina* and relatives attack trout, bass, and other fish and have caused heavy mortalities in hatcheries.

8. "Whirling disease," caused by *Myxosoma cerebralis*, is a protozoan that invades the cartilage of trout. It requires a longer time than some diseases to mature and become noticeable, so it has been gradually spread from Europe to the eastern United States and on westward. Authorities believe this serious disease can be controlled. Three-quarters of a million fish were destroyed and the entire facilities disinfected at the Lahontan National Fish Hatchery (Nevada) during early 1970 after this disease was discovered in that installation's cutthroat trout population. Fortunately, the range of this disease has not been extended in the United States in the past decade.

Trematodes (Flat Worms)

This is a large group of parasitic flat worms, often called flukes.

1. *Gyrodactylus* is the most notable and dangerous parasitic worm in North America. It has "hooks" that are used as grasping organs. If numerous enough on the gills and skin of freshwater fish, great damage and even death of the host occur.

2. The "blood fluke" (*Sanguinicola*) is very damaging to fish. Damage occurs when the larvae hatch and burrow out of the gills.

3. Metacercarial trematodes. These are larval flukes in fish and usually occur as small to rather large cysts.

Tapeworms and Roundworms

Fish may have adult tapeworms in the intestine or larval forms in the body organs or muscles. Intermediate hosts are usually copepods (Crustaceans) or fish. The intestinal forms generally do little damage except for

270

Bothriocephalus gowkongensis of cyprinids. The larval forms, particularly the bass tapeworm and *Diphyllobothrium sebago* of salmonids, are often very damaging.

Parasitic roundworms are often present in large numbers, both as adults and larvae. Some thorny-headed forms thrust their thorned heads into tissues of the intestine, producing great damage. Small fish, particularly bait minnows and ornamentals, may be killed by large numbers of *Eustrongylides* larvae in the body cavity.

Leeches

Leeches can be damaging if present in large numbers and may transmit other diseases to fish through wounds. They are also vectors of the blood flagellates, *Trypanoplasma* and *Trypanosoma*.

Fish-Lice

Parasitic copepods sometimes are worm-like in appearance. The anchor parasite *Lernaea cyprinacea* is the most dangerous one. It has a large forked head that is anchored in the tissue of the fish. The wound often becomes infected with bacteria, fungi, or algae. Large numbers of this parasite will kill fish. Gill and fin "lice" (*Salmincola*) of trout may be damaging, particularly in heavy infestations.

Bacteria

There are many diseases of fish caused by bacteria that affect feral and cultured fish. Bacterial diseases are common in cultured fish and are considered as the main obstacle in the further intensification of freshwater and marine aquaculture. Considerable progress is being made in control of these diseases by immunization.

1. Furunculosis, caused by *Aeromonas salmonicida*, is a very serious disease of salmonids in fresh water and in mariculture.

2. Bacterial hemorrhagic septicemia or motile Aeromonas septicemia is a disease of worldwide distribution; it affects mainly freshwater fish. It is caused by *Aeromonas hydrophila* (*A. punctata*).

3. Pseudomonas septicemia is caused by *Pseudomonas fluorescens*. It affects mostly fresh and warm-water fish. Outbreaks usually occur in fish under conditions of stress.

4. Vibriosis is mainly a disease of cultured marine fish, but occurs also in open waters. It is caused by *Vibrio anguillarum* and is very similar to furunculosis and is often called saltwater furunculosis.

5. Enteric redmouth disease, which originally was limited to the northwestern intermountain area, is now present all over North America and some foreign countries. It is caused by *Yersinia ruckeri* (name recently given). It is a disease of freshwater salmonids, frequently characterized by eroded mouth area, and is very destructive in fish hatcheries.

6. Edwardsiella septicemia is caused by an enteric bacterium *Edwardsiella tarda*. It is a disease of cultured fresh- and warm-water fishes in North America and in Asia.

7. Myxobacterioses are diseases of freshwater and marine fishes in cold and warm water. They are common all over the world, are usually divided into columnaris disease, cold-water disease, saltwater myxobacteriosis, and gill disease, and are very destructive to cultured fish. Some strains are virulent, but others apparently are causing a disease in fish that are exposed to considerable stress.

8. Pasteurellosis is mainly a septicemic disease of warm-water fish in marine and estuarine environments. It is caused by *Pasteurella piscicida* and led to a great epizootic in 1963 among white perch and striped bass in the

271

Chesapeake Bay. It is common and destructive in marine aquaculture in Japan.

9. Bacterial kidney disease is one of the most important diseases of cultured salmonid fish in North America. It is a relatively slow progressing disease, characterized by granulomatous lesions in visceral organs and sometimes in the dermis. Infected fish seldom, if ever, recover.

10. Mycobacteriosis (fish tuberculosis) is a disease of freshwater and marine feral and cultured fish. It is a rare disease of salmonids, unless exposed to infected food, somewhat more frequent in cyprinids, fairly frequent in feral tropical marine fish, and a problem disease in ornamental and aquarium fish. These bacteria are also pathogenic to humans who become infected from ornamental fishes or even from swimming pools.

VIRUSES

A number of virus and virus-like agents have been recognized in cultured and feral fish, principally in association with disease (McAllister 1978).

Those virus diseases that are considered serious are:

1. Infectious pancreatic necrosis (IPN) is a disease that affects young trout and salmon and has been reported worldwide.

2. Infectious hematopoietic necrosis (IHN) affects young salmonids and occurs principally in the Pacific Northwest region of North America. The designation IHN is now used for two diseases formerly considered distinct from IHN, Oregon sockeye virus disease and Sacramento River chinook virus disease.

3. Channel catfish virus (CCV) disease occurs only in the Americas, principally in the southeastern and southwestern United States. The disease is limited primarily to channel catfish less than four months of age.

4. *Herpesvirus salmonis* disease affects young rainbow trout. The disease has occurred at only one location in the United States; a similar disease occurs in Japan.

5. Golden shiner virus (GSV) disease occurs in southeastern and midwestern regions of the United States.

6. Viral hemorrhagic septicemia (VHS) is a disease that affects primarily rainbow trout. Fish of all ages are susceptible to VHS. The disease has been reported only in Europe. Federal regulations have been assigned to prevent its introduction into the United States.

7. Spring viremia of carp (SVC) occurs in most countries of eastern and western Europe. Carp of all ages are susceptible to spring viremia. Federal regulations have been assigned to prevent introduction of SVC into the United States.

8. Pike fry rhabdovirus (PFR) disease occurs in at least four countries in western Europe. Federal regulations have been assigned to prevent the introduction of the disease into the United States.

These diseases may cause high levels of mortality and are spread by infected fish releasing virus into the environment. Fish that survive an infection may harbor the virus for life and subsequently infect future generations. Certain control measures may be used to minimize the potential for an outbreak of a disease of viral origin: (1) eggs or offspring should originate from fish certified as specific pathogen free, (2) a vigorous egg and hatchery disinfection program should be maintained, (3) the hatchery water supply should be protected and free of all fish, and (4) environmental and management factors that promote physiological stress should be obviated. In the future, viral diseases may be controlled by immunization.

CONTROL OF FISH DISEASES

Treatment

Fungi, protozoa, and trematodes can often be controlled with chemical baths. "Ich" is the most difficult, because the parasite burrows under the skin and cannot be reached with chemicals. Flatworms are best controlled by reducing the snail population with molluscicides or other means. Tapeworms may be removed from the intestines of fish with certain chemicals. Chemicals are also used to kill larval stages of fish lice (copepods).

Bacterial fish diseases can be treated with several external disinfectants, sulfonamides, antibiotics, and nitrofurans. Efforts are being made to obtain clearance required by the Food and Drug Administration for use of disease treatment chemicals. This procedure takes time and is costly, but is necessary for adequate protection.

Once serious outbreaks of diseases occur in hatcheries, it may be necessary to (1) destroy all fish and (2) disinfect all facilities.

Prevention

It is better to avoid fish diseases than to control an outbreak. Infected fish, or their eggs, should not be shipped to places where the disease does not exist. Important also is protection of fishes from stress caused by crowding, water pollution, or rough handling.

Immunization against bacterial fish diseases is possible, but not yet practical due to the need to handle fish for injection of antigens and their slow production of antibodies. Mass immersion of trout in salt water followed by mass immersion in water containing killed *Vibrio* or enteric red mouth bacteria has given favorable results. Another possibility for controlling disease is the development of disease-resistant strains of fish.

State, federal, and private industry are working to provide closer inspection programs similar to the system used by the livestock industry and coordinated by the U.S. Department of Agriculture.

The following means of controlling fish diseases are being proposed by authorities:

1. Authorizing legislation to establish a national fish disease control program
2. Expanded fish disease research and chemical registration
3. Improved diagnostic and fish inspection services
4. Better use of control knowledge we now possess
5. Cooperative efforts by all segments of the fisheries industry

LITERATURE CITED

McAllister, P. E. 1978. Viruses and virus infections of fish. *In* H. Fraenkel-Conrat and R. R. Wagner, eds. Comprehensive virology, Vol. 14. Plenum Press, New York (in press).

SELECTED REFERENCES

Amalcher, E. 1970. Textbook of fish diseases (translated and updated by D. A. Conroy and R. L. Herman). T.F.H. Publications, Inc., Neptune City, New Jersey. 302 pp.

Bullock, G. L., D. A. Conroy, and S. F. Snieszko. 1971. Bacterial diseases of fishes, Book 2A in Diseases of fishes edited by S. F. Snieszko and H. R. Axelrod. T.F.H. Publications, Neptune City, New Jersey. 151 pp.

van Dujin, C. 1973. Diseases of fishes. 3rd ed. Charles Thomas, publisher. Springfield, Illinois. 372 pp.

Fish Health Section, American Fisheries Society, editors. 1975. Suggested procedures for the detection and identification of certain infectious diseases of fishes. Fish and Wildlife Service, U.S. Dept. of the Interior, Washington, D.C. (not paginated). Revised edition in press.

Hoffman, G. L. 1967. Parasites of North American freshwater fishes. Univ. Calif. Press, Berkeley. 486 pp.

———— and F. P. Meyer. 1974. Parasites of freshwater fishes: a review of their control and treatment. T.F.H. Publications, Inc., Neptune City, New Jersey. 224 pp.

Kabata, Z. 1970. Crustacea as enemies of fishes. *In* S. F. Snieszko and H. R. Axelrod, eds. Book 1 of Diseases of fishes. T.F.H. Publications, Neptune City, New Jersey. 171 pp.

Lucky, Z. 1971. (Eng. transl. 1977, G. Hoffman, ed.). Methods for the diagnosis of fish diseases. Avail. as TT 75-58005, NTIS, U.S. Dept. Commerce, Springfield, Virginia 22161.

Ribelin, W. E., and G. Migaki, eds. 1975. Symposium in fish pathology. Univ. of Wisc. Press, Madison. 1,004 pp.

Roberts, R. F., and C. J. Shephard. 1974. Handbook of trout and salmon diseases. Fishing News (Books) Ltd., West Byfleet, Surrey, England. 168 pp.

Schubert, G. 1974. Cure and recognize aquarium fish diseases. T.F.H. Publications, Inc., Ltd., Neptune City, New Jersey. 128 pp.

Sindermann, C. J. 1977. Diseases diagnosis and control in North American marine aquaculture. Dev. Aquaculture Fish. Sci. No. 6. Elsevier Sci. Pub. Co., Amsterdam. 329 pp.

Wedemeyer, G. A., F. P. Meyer, and L. Smith. 1976. Environmental stress and fish diseases (Diseases of fishes, Book 5, ed. Snieszko and Axelrod). T.F.H. Publications Co., Neptune, New Jersey. 192 pp. New Jersey 07753. 192 pp.

Ralph Oberg

INDEX